The Yummy Mummy's

Family Handbook

Liz Fraser

HARPER

Harper
An imprint of HarperCollins*Publishers*
77–85 Fulham Palace Road,
Hammersmith, London W6 8JB

www.harpercollins.co.uk

This paperback edition 2008
1

First published in Great Britain by
Harper Collins 2007

A catalogue record for this book is
available from the British Library

Author photograph by Sven Arnstein

ISBN 978 000 726 273 1

Set in Monotype Plantin by Rowlands Phototypesetting Ltd
Bury St Edmunds, Suffolk

Printed and bound in Great Britain by
Clays Ltd, St Ives plc

Mixed Sources
Product group from well-managed
forests and other controlled sources
www.fsc.org Cert no. SW-COC-1806
© 1996 Forest Stewardship Council

FSC is a non-profit international organisation established to promote the
responsible management of the world's forests. Products carrying the FSC
label are independently certified to assure consumers that they come
from forests that are managed to meet the social, economic and
ecological needs of present and future generations.

Find out more about HarperCollins and the environment at
www.harpercollins.co.uk/green

Having left Cambridge armed with ▓▓▓▓▓▓▓▓▓▓▓, Fraser worked in TV, prese▓▓▓▓▓▓▓▓▓▓▓▓s *Holiday* and Channel 4's *The Virtual Body*. ▓▓▓ ▓▓▓▓n of her second child, she gave up work to become a full-time mother. Six months later, in desperate need of adult conversation and a creative outlet, she returned to work part-time. She is now a freelance writer and lives in Cambridge, in a house that is not quite as tidy as she'd like, with her husband and three children. Liz Fraser is also the author of the *Sunday Times* bestseller, *The Yummy Mummy's Survival Guide*.

Visit www.AuthorTracker.co.uk for exclusive updates on Liz Fraser.

By the same author

The Yummy Mummy's Survival Guide

For Emily, Phoebe and Charlie. xxx

Contents

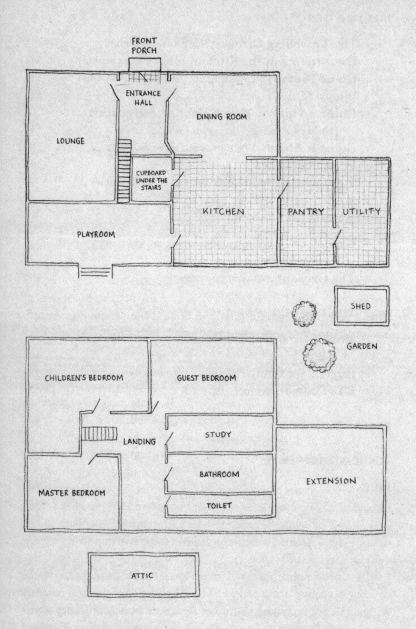

PART ONE

Bricks and Mortar

Laying the Foundations: An introduction

Families, eh? What a nightmare: it's all kids, marriages, oversized cars, arguments, stressful holidays, affairs, the school run, snotty noses, admin, tantrums and break-ups – who the hell would ever want to go through *that*?!

Well, funnily enough rather a lot of us take a stab at Family Life, and despite what you may have heard in the press about divorce rates rocketing, all men being bastards and children being less desirable than global warming and shell suits, families are having something of a revival. Hurrah!

After decades of monumental fuck-ups caused by wanting to Have It All, leaving a legacy of rich divorce lawyers and psychotherapists, it seems that an increasing number of people are thinking there may be more to life than high-powered careers, flat-screen TVs, mind-blowing sex and holidays in Barbados. Not much more, obviously, but a little, and perhaps something worth putting a good deal of effort into.

It is almost impossible to define a family these days, as any sense of what's 'normal' vanished years ago. I had a conversation recently with a friend who talked about her daughter's ex-stepmother's girlfriend. I got there in the end, but it was pretty confusing. Families now come in all shapes and sizes: there are married parents, step-parents, step-children, cohabiting parents, gay couples with kids, small families, gigantic families, happy families, miserable families, and families you really wouldn't want to get stuck next to on a campsite. My own set-up of being married with three kids is probably far from the norm these days, but it works (mostly) for us.

Whatever the actual bricks and mortar of a family, and however you go about living in it, two things seem pretty clear: firstly, married (or effectively married) people are generally happier, healthier and more contented than those who aren't; and secondly, children brought up in stable family homes grow into happier, healthier and more contented adults. And thus the cycle continues.

But keeping it all hanging together – through the years of child-rearing, career changes, financial wobbles and the inevitable middle-age spread – is really hard, and I am yet to meet a single married person with kids who doesn't occasionally want to buy a one-way ticket to Rio and live it up a little! Happily these feelings of frustration, boredom and an interest in sexy beachwear usually pass quite quickly and we all get back to making packed lunches and putting away fifty pairs of socks before we get as far as finding our passports.

My theory as to why we find family life so challenging, even though generations before us stuck together like limpets, is that we are not trained or encouraged to commit to anything. Our lives are geared towards *change*, and fast change at that: we can return goods to shops should we decide blue isn't really our colour, throw things away if we don't like them any more, choose between a hundred television channels and swap electricity suppliers in one phone call. Nothing is 'forever' and choice is everywhere: if we don't like it, we move on and get something better . . . until we don't like that any more either. Our attention spans now compare with those of goldfish, and our children's are even shorter. In short, we are addicted to convenience, speed and choice.

Commitment? Hell, no!

When it comes to material things, all of this choice and ability to jump ship is rather good: if I want to get a better microwave, why shouldn't I trade the old one in? If I buy a shirt for my husband that turns out to be a size too small because he's been eating all the pies again, what's the harm in swapping it for a bigger one? None. But family life cannot operate under these terms and conditions. It requires a completely different way of thinking: you are not *owed* anything – you all owe it to each other to be there, to help, to support, and to put the bins out on a Monday.

This book won't, I'm sorry to say, tell you how to reach the Nirvana of a perfect family life, because it doesn't exist. It won't bring you beautiful, well-mannered children, a fulfilling job, a perfectly risen sponge or a man who pays you compliments while remaining faithful for the next fifty years.

What it will do is take you on a journey through a family home, and, room by room, tackle some of the most common issues that face many families on a daily basis. Through my own (mixed) experiences of raising three kids and living with one man for thirteen years I will share my survival tactics for making it to the next wedding anniversary (see, there is an incentive to hang in there . . .) and there are handy hints and tips from some of my friends who have done the Family Thing too. There are some topics that I have omitted, such as going through a divorce, coping with teenagers or dealing with step-families, because I haven't been there and got the T-shirt yet. Give me a few more years, though . . .

Hopefully you will laugh, learn and be reassured a lot along the way, as I attempt to convince you that nobody does it perfectly, we all have our family troubles, and that with a little humour, patience, hope and plenty of good chocolate, you will get through the bad bits and thoroughly enjoy all the rest.

And so, ticket for the guided tour in hand, I invite you to make your way towards the start and prepare for some fun. See you on the next page . . .

Clash of the Tartans: Bringing two Families together

One day you marry a guy, and you become husband and wife. Or you don't marry the guy, but live with him long enough to know every hair on his stubbly chin, every album he's ever owned and when it's best not to tell him that he's making a pig's ear of some DIY. So far so as-it-should-be: you like him, he likes you, and life is rosy.

But then you go and spoil it all by saying something stupid like, 'Why do you always have tea before breakfast? We never did that in my family – we always had tea *with* breakfast, which is much better.' Aaargh! Why did you say *that*? Why should he care two hoots when your family – that's *your* family, not his – takes their tea, or that you think your way is better?

Well, he shouldn't, of course, and probably doesn't, but the point is that *you do*. Or, at least, you might not care all that much about the tea thing, but about a great many other small but habitual, ritual or comforting things that your family always did as you grew up, and that you think you'd rather like to carry on doing now, thanks very much, so let's stop this ridiculous tea-all-over-the-bedclothes lark and get up!

Bringing two families together is always bound to throw up this kind of dispute, and many far more serious ones. Everything from what time you get up on a Sunday morning to what you have for lunch (Sunday roast or beans on toast), how much telly you watch, where you go for Christmas, how to do DIY, whether women with kids should have a job and what kind of school you send your little angels to, is in some way influenced by your own family upbringing.

Christmas is a classic situation for conflict:

Christmas Day 2003

I want to go home. I feel like an alien here: nothing is as it was at Christmas when I was a child and it doesn't feel Christmassy to me at all. I want to be with my mum and dad right now, not with someone else's family. I know they're my family now too, but it's not the same at all. I feel I have to ask at every turn, in case

I do something which isn't traditional here, and it's really getting to me now.

Even in the most welcoming, adaptable, easy-going family there is bound to be some friction and even the occasional explosion, so it's best to be prepared:

☆ **Don't assume your way is right.** Many people fall into the trap of always assuming that if their way works, or has been handed down through even one generation, it is the Right Way, and everyone else is sadly misguided or stupid. Avoid wearing this arrogant, highly unflattering hat by keeping your eyes open for new and possibly better ways of living.

☆ **Do some detective work.** It's much easier to spot any potential clashes if you have studied your partner's background and rituals carefully. If no woman in his entire family has ever had a job, and has started child-bearing within six months of her wedding, then you might be foolish to assume he thinks any other way. It's unlikely that you've settled down with somebody who has wildly different views on life from your own, but it's often the little things that grate as badly. Learning about his family's traditions and habits will make it much easier to understand when he starts doing things that annoy you, like leaving the dishcloth wet after he's used it. Grrr!

☆ **Spot the problem before it becomes one.** (This is illogical, I know, but you know what I mean.) It's much better to talk about anything you find annoying or impossible as soon as you spot it. Once things have been left to take a hold they are very hard to stamp out. Separating whites from coloureds in the washing machine was a case in point in our house: I managed to get this unthinkable practice wiped out within the space of two spin cycles.

☆ **Compromise.** If you are both really set in your ways it can be very difficult to come to any kind of agreement and the only way forward is compromise. Do things his way one weekend and your way the next. Alternate festive traditions every year.

Let him have the final say in naming one child, and you the next. And so on. What you may find is that, very slowly, you let go of some of your habits, which you thought you couldn't live without, as you find that you actually can.

☆ **Keep it friendly.** The clash of two families coming together can be, if not bloody, then certainly quite messy. Somebody is bound to get hurt if you let things get too personal and critical. Be sensitive; remember that you are two people coming together from different backgrounds, philosophies and ways of hanging the washing – and something's gotta give. You can't expect your egos to remain bruise-free but you can avoid any major injuries to your relationship by joining ranks and staying on good terms. Maybe your habit of leaving the cucumber end uncovered could be one you leave behind . . .?

☆ **Stick to your guns.** There is more about this in the Guest Bedroom (see page 316), where we meet the in-laws and your Mum and Dad, but it's worth noting here that the two of you should never, ever do things in your new family because of pressure from your respective parents. Listen to them, consider their advice, but do what the two of you feel is right *for you*. It may hurt them, offend them or just baffle them, but it's *your* life, and you do with it what you like. Home education it is, then . . .

House Structure: Establishing the family hierarchy

Once upon a slightly more miserable and unfair time, families had a very clear hierarchical structure: men up in the penthouse, women in the middle (usually the kitchen) and kids either up a chimney or in the gutter. There were some half-landings reserved for elders, whether male or female, but apart from that it was very simple: everyone knew their place and it worked.

'Yes,' you say, 'but unless you fell into the "elder" or "man" camps, it was also shite.' Indeed it was, and that's why most of us are glad that the structure of most families today is less 'four-storey townhouse', and more 'one up, one down'. Parents still hold most of the authority upstairs, while the kids play downstairs, and family meetings are regularly held on the landing for everyone to have their say. So far, so much more democratic.

What is slightly problematic, I think, is that some families have taken this improvement a step too far and have adopted a bungalow layout with everyone on a level with everyone else. There is no hierarchy, no authority and no control. In the same way that bungalows are unnatural (where are the stairs, woman, the *stairs*??), confusing and unattractive, so Bungalow Families are built on shaky ground, and should be denied planning permission.

Don't get me wrong – I'm all for equality, human rights, democracy and Saturday sweets. Of course children have the right to have their say in family matters as much as any adults do. The problem lies in allowing everyone to have their way, which obliterates any sense of authority or control, leading to Family Anarchy. The success of the TV series *Supernanny* was dependent on this collapse in hierarchy: family after family where the kids run riot, the parents have no control over them whatsoever, and they resort to violence, abuse and much head-shaking. *Where did we go wrong? Why have we been lumped with a child from Hell?* I wonder . . .

When you start to build your family, you both have to agree on what structure it will have: either vertical, where you guys basically make all the decisions, have the final say and can withhold pocket money if necessary; or horizontal, where you and your little darlings are on an equal level and all family decisions are made jointly. Here are some things to bear in mind if you are struggling between Dictatorship and Anarchy:

☆ **Social responsibility.** The way you bring your kids up will greatly influence how they behave outside the home. Some people don't seem to mind if their kids are unruly, rude, arrogant and uncontrollable and live quite happily in their bungalows. If you feel it might be better to instil some sense of respect, authority and having to do as one is told occasionally, then perhaps you'll need to take more control by adding a second floor. 'I know you want crisps, darling, but I'm your mother and I say "no" because you had them yesterday. End of discussion!'

☆ **Welcome to the Real World.** If kids never hear the words, 'Well, sometimes life sucks, so you're going to have to do as I say this time, I'm afraid', then they are in for a rude shock one day when they come across a teacher, policeman or employer. Best to get this Life Lesson learned early, and teach them that we all have to do as we're told sometimes, however unfair, unjust or inconvenient it may be.

☆ **Having their say.** Children who feel they have no sense of power or control over their lives at all can become very aggressive or depressed and may even grow into evil dictators who threaten to take over the world. It's vital that kids are allowed to have their say on matters that affect them. It's important to listen, but not necessary to agree: so long as you explain why then they get a sense of having had a good shot at it. Anyway, they know when they are well wide of the mark – they're not stupid!

☆ **Family meetings.** This might seem a bit 'organised' but I know families who have weekly gatherings to go through who's not happy about what, how to improve the situation and whose turn it is to clean out the hamster cage. Quite a few disagreements are resolved this way, without anyone feeling downtrodden. This is Bungalow living in a sensible way: there is still some authority because Mum and Dad have to agree to what is being proposed, but everyone has an open mic every week to speak out.

☆ **Authority works.** If you decide to go for something a little more high-rise and authoritative, don't feel you're a cold-hearted relic of the Victorian age: many families are now realising that establishing a clear hierarchy within a family works very well, doesn't lead to screwed-up kids and makes life a lot more pleasant both within the home and outside it. If you lay down simple rules from day one and follow them, you should avoid ever living with tearaway tots.

Nobody wants to see children being silenced or bossed about by their parents, but there is something positive to be said for children understanding that their parents are superior to them and for there to be mutual respect and parental control. This isn't child abuse; it's sensible family management.

Once you have got over the initial nerves, planning permission and design of your Family Home, you can get on with the fun job of building the thing and living in it. As with all construction, things will go wrong – you'll go over budget, there will be delays and you'll end up with something not quite as you drew up in the plans, but which you'll come to love just as much anyway.

And so, my brave companions, let us take our key in trembling hand and open the front door.

(Bugger, I dropped it. Hold on a sec . . . aha: here we are! In you come . . .)

PART TWO

The Front Porch

The F Word: Becoming a family

Welcome, welcome! Come in off the noisy, dirty street and let me take your coat. This, my friend, is where we begin our tour of the chaotic, thriving, occasionally hellish but more often colourful and very jolly place called the Family Home. Please don't mind the mess – this is a *real* family home, not an interiors feature, and I have quite deliberately left it in its natural, somewhat cluttered, finger-marked state so that you can get a sense of what really goes on in here.

If you have any doubts about whether the family *thing* is for you, then stride forth with me into the madness and mayhem and let me try to convince you that family life isn't quite as unattractive or unmanageable as it may occasionally appear.

If you've already been raising your own family for years and have come to terms with the fact that you are no longer free to fly off to Mexico on a whim, are somehow expected to have all the answers to Life's Big Questions, and will never bathe in peace again, then you can skip straight through to the Entrance Hall and take a seat for a while. Feel free to nose around while you wait – nothing is behind closed doors in this house. Just mind the loose cable by the door. I've been meaning to fix it for months, but you know how it is . . .

For everyone else, let's pause here in the Front Porch for a moment, and consider what a shock it can be to become A Family.

What constitutes a 'family' differs between cultures, but where I, and probably you, live it means a group of people connected either by marriage or by birth. Yes, the lady next door may be very lovely, and by way of thanks for looking after your kids on a regular basis be awarded 'Honorary Auntie' status, but she's not, strictly speaking, Family. Kind neighbours aside, the reach of the branches of a family tree is almost limitless – indeed, I've read somewhere very clever and reasonably trustworthy that we are all related to one another somehow, if you look back far enough, which presumably means we are all also incestuous and inbred. Great.

For the purposes of this book a 'family' consists of you, your partner and all of your respective parents, siblings and children. Great Aunts are allowed in too, because they are usually very sweet and doddery and need as much family as they can get, as do any grandparents you still have. But that's about it. All the cousins, second cousins, nieces, nephews, godparents, Almost Uncles, and so on, are excess baggage as far as we are concerned. They are all very much a part of the family, of course, and dutifully turn up for Christmas or if there's a big family party going on with lashings of free booze, but to deal with the ins and outs of all of them here would be to cause this book to break your coffee table with its enormous weight.

Sticking with the tree analogy for a moment – it kind of works if you try hard enough – then just as big trees make little trees, so families go on to create new families. The idea of breaking free and starting your own New Family can be very daunting and take years to get used to, so don't worry if you sometimes feel you've taken a leap too far from the trunk and want back in: it's normal. It's been ten years since I started my own New Family and I still feel utterly unqualified sometimes and expect somebody to knock on the door at any moment to take me 'home' again.

Here's how it happens: you spend the first major part of your life dangling happily somewhere towards the topmost branches of your family tree, waving in the breeze, getting a little older and hopefully wiser with the passing seasons and trying not to fall off due to excess cider drinking. Then, one wonderful, sunny day you rub against the leaves of a nearby tree, and – whoosh! The course of your life changes forever: you fall hopelessly in lust with a particularly handsome, sexy, clever piece of foliage and decide to spend the rest of your days with him, all going well and assuming no pert, tempting little variegated or evergreen ones get in the way and wreck everything. And so, you jump! Into the exciting world of cohabitation you go.

Things go pretty well for a while – lust turns to love, you blow along with the wind, travel together, work your way up the career ladder a bit and rent a tiny flat that almost puts you on the breadline but leaves just enough spare cash for Ikea tea-lights and the occasional curry. And then, just when you thought things were ticking along very nicely, thank you, you arrive at an unforeseen crossroads, and find yourselves having to decide where to go next without so much as a map or a compass.

To Have, or Have Not?

For most couples there comes a time, after they have investigated and familiarised themselves with every nook and cranny, fiddled with all the knobs and dials and got to level twenty, when they ask themselves, or each other, if they are very brave: 'Where now, Captain?' Should they take a left turn into Spousedom, or run for the hills and shack up with the Next Bloke to Come Along?

Well, it's a hard decision, and one which can become so agonising that it splits strong couples apart, because one or the other of them isn't brave enough to take the plunge. I am a great believer in the personal benefits and social importance of marriage and I hang around reasonably happily married people most of the time. Over much wine and cheesy nibbles we gathered together the following bits of advice for anyone not sure of which way to go:

☆ **Don't wait for the Perfect Man and the Perfect Moment.** If you do, you will be waiting forever. No man is one hundred per cent perfect, and neither are you, so work out if you can live with his faults and love him despite any mistakes he may make on the way. Of course things may change, but you have to go on what you see before you now.

☆ **Is he your best friend?** People always say you should marry your best friend, and they are right. Don't marry the most beautiful, rich or sexy man: marry the guy you can't live without – whom you trust and who makes you laugh, feel completely at peace with yourself and who you would always choose to be with in a crisis.

☆ **Are you, as a couple, greater than the sum of your parts?** If you always become a stronger, nicer and happier person when you are with this guy, then you could be onto a good thing.

☆ **Don't focus on potential failure.** Yes, lots of marriages fall apart, but to approach yours with a 'how long will it last' attitude is to pave the way for failure. This is why prenups are such a distasteful idea. Decide to make it work 'come what may' and you stand a much better chance. (If you are the proud owner of a shitload of cash, then prenups are possibly worth considering, but as you are probably not quite in the £200 million bracket let's push on . . .)

☆ **Are you equals?** A marriage requires absolute equality and respect for it to be a happy one. This doesn't mean having the same level of job, doing equal amounts of childcare and house-work or being as good at something as your partner is, but that neither one of you feels or acts superior or more important than the other.

☆ **Do some research.** It's best not to jump into something as big as marriage without checking a few things out first, as it's a little late once the ink has dried. Using your expert female intuition, and some cunning questioning, see if you can find out:

1. **What he expects of a wife.** Someone to be there when he gets home, with a smile, a four-course dinner, and a gin and tonic for Monsieur? Or has he grasped the concept that women might like to have, like, you know, a job or something as well as hoovering and plumping up the cushions?
2. **When, or if, he imagines you will have kids.** If you are thinking of 'some time in your thirties, once your career has reached a certain level', but he had something more along the 'as soon as we've consummated our marriage' in mind, then there will be big trouble ahead.

☆ **Is there complete trust and respect?** If there is, then you can both criticise and laugh at yourselves, and at each other, without getting upset. Yes, even jokes about your bum being huge should be well within limits.

☆ **Very Important Questions:** Will he take the bins out without moaning about it? Can you live with his inability to put wet towels in the laundry basket? Will he look after the kids when you need some extra time to work or to have a break, without feeling emasculated or hard done by? Does he think your work is an unnecessary distraction from your more important roles of cooking, cleaning and making yourself look *real pretty*? Will you wash the bath after him? Will he after you? And so on. If you don't ask yourself the questions, and get answers you are happy with, you are taking a leap into the unknown and the fall is usually rather messy, and expensive.

The 'kids' issue is *massive*, by the way, and not even talking about when or whether you might have children before deciding to marry someone is a bit like chopping your left arm off before you've thought whether you might like to be a concert pianist or not. You don't need to scare him off with persistent baby talk or spending Saturday afternoons in Baby Gap, but if you can't even raise the subject then what does that say about your relationship?

Ah, it's hard to find the Right Man, but, contrary to what you may have heard, not all men are bastards. Some are absolutely bloody fantastic, and do believe in equal rights, sharing the remote control and opening the window after they've made a bit of a smell. Seek, and ye shall find him.

Popping the question: On your knees, ladies!

Once you've decided to take the road towards Married Life then somebody is going to have to pop the question.

But who, and how? In a moment of 'anything men can do I can do better' madness, fuelled by a growing fear of losing the man I wanted to grow old with and a large streak of impatience, I decided to don some Woman-Trousers and ask him to marry me.

It was a terrifying experience, and I sometimes wonder how I managed it without forgetting what it was I wanted to say, backing out in favour of chewing my right leg off or just throwing up right in front of him through nerves. (Never a good move, that.) But, hideous and frightening as it may be, popping the question is actually no more than just that: asking a question. Why, oh *why*, do so many relationships have to be relegated to the 'It's, like, *totally over*' pile because a woman waits for her man to ask?

We have mouths, don't we? And brains? And guts? SO ASK!! Seriously, if you love him to bits and want to marry the guy then just ask him. He can always say no, but if you take courage from the tips below you should avoid having to tear your hair out or go undercover for a year:

☆ **Don't over-rehearse.** 'Will you marry me' is hard enough to say without laughing or crying, but too much practice can give a genuine request more of a daytime soap opera feel to it, and he'll either laugh or cry, so that's both of you in a state. Seize the moment, and go for it.

☆ **Say it slowly.** Nervous words are always likely to come out in a bit of a rush, and sound more like 'William Harry, me?' or 'Will your marrow mean?' Neither is likely to get the response you are after.

☆ **If he says 'No'** you have to find a dignified way of leaving the room which makes it look as though you are perfectly happy with the outcome, and were expecting it anyway – a kind of elegant 'Am I bovvered?' This is one good reason not to propose on a nine-hour flight. If you can also leave an air of 'You are a complete shit and have just screwed up the rest of my life', then so much the better. Then you can cry for a month and put on two stone due to excessive comfort-eating.

With all of this reassurance under your belt and your journey into Family Life begun, it's time to enter the Family Home itself. No more hanging out in the draughty front porch – we're ready to get into that entrance hall, muddy the carpet and have a good look around. You might not like all that you see, but there's a stiff drink at the end for those who survive the trip. Onward!

PART THREE

The Entrance Hall

You are now in a room of great activity: shoes coming off, coats going on, bags being thrown on the floor and keys being lost. This part of the house is where family life really kicks off: from deciding to start a family of your own, to finding out how this new lifestyle suits you both, and then dealing with some of the social and administrative sides of your lively gathering. There really is no backing out now.

When Two Become Three

Despite living together in married bliss (ahem!) for a number of years, one day you may both feel that there is something *missing* – something that would take your relationship to the next level and give you more to talk about again, other than what you did at work, what's on the telly or whose turn it is to do the washing. So you decide to have a baby.

And there it is: the enormous, irreversible leap from Coupledom to Family Life. The minute you fix your roots by producing little pooing, vomiting, tantrum-throwing branches of your own, you shed your neat 'Just-the-two-of-us' way of life and get to wear a grubby, slightly squashed but very cosy 'family' hat instead.

Nobody ever tells you this – because it's assumed you will be overcome with wonder at your new arrival and will spend six months floating on fluffy pink clouds of Family Joy – but suddenly having your very own family can be terrifying. There you were, eating take-aways, having sex in the kitchen, worrying whether you should invest your birthday money in an almost-affordable work of modern art or blow it all on a dirty weekend in Bath, and having marathon *Lost*-watching sessions accompanied by too many bottles of wine, when suddenly – Holy Shit! – you have a family. A real, live family complete with enormous won't-go-away-if-I-close-my-eyes-and-think-of-something-else responsibilities, and financial constraints, and a baby, and a husband-who-is-also-a father, and a family car, and … can't breathe, must get out … what's happened to me? HELP!

Debbie, married six years, mother of Arthur, four, and Mary, eighteen months:

I have found the loss of independence since becoming a family very hard to adjust to. I love what I have more than anything in the world, but I do miss the life I had before sometimes, and wish I could be free again to muck about, travel and meet new people. I didn't expect to feel this way, but it's a compromise I'm happy to make.

OK, here's some help:

☆ **Relax. This is a completely normal reaction** to being made to grow up overnight, from overgrown child – albeit a child with an overdraft, a job and an impressive CD collection – into responsible parent. It can take years to wear the family badge with ease, so give it time, don't run out of the door as soon as the panic sets in, and try to remember that what you have is a Good Thing. The sensation that you may have bitten off more than you can chew and are now choking on all the baby rice and family-size *everything* often doesn't happen the moment your offspring squeezes itself into the delivery room, but creeps up on you over a number of months or years. Remember that you would be very unusual if you felt any of this transition phase was easy-peasy, and congratulate yourself on your healthy levels of uncertainty. Top marks so far.

☆ **Ease yourself in.** If it all feels a bit too much too fast then give yourself a break and go back to something more familiar for a day or two. Go home to your parents for a weekend, go for a day out all by yourself or hang out with some good friends (who don't have kids). You'll soon remember that your whole life hasn't changed after all, and you'll be pining for the rest of your family before you know it.

☆ **Get ready to make mistakes.** Like most works of art your family almost certainly won't end up quite as you intended, but hopefully you will avoid making any irreversible gaffs that even Tipp-Ex can't cover up. For everything else there is usually a way to smooth things over, and a secret credit-card-busting handbag obsession or even the hideous smudge of an infidelity can add something positive to the canvas if it ultimately brings you closer together.

☆ **Beg, borrow, or steal.** The work you produce will be influenced to some degree by other struggling families you observe as you stumble along Family Lane. This is good – all the best artists nick stuff from people they admire, whether consciously or not. If you observe another family dealing with toddler tantrums better than you, then watch what they do and steal their technique. If you don't seem to be coping with your work/life/soaks in the bath balance and know someone who seems to have it all under control, then ask how they do it. You'll probably discover it's all a front and they are struggling just as much as you are, but even that can be enough to cheer yourself up.

☆ **Talk.** Not to your Mum, your friend or your cat. Talk to your partner – the person who is going through this weird transition with you, and tell him if you're feeling apprehensive, lost or plain shit-scared about things. If he's half the man he should be for you to have started a family with him, he won't burn all your books, tear up your store cards or eat all your chocolate. He'll help you, support you and give you a shoulder massage. He's probably feeling exactly the same way anyway, but didn't want to say so in case you thought he was getting cold feet already. Talking sorts it all out.

Best in Show: Keeping up appearances in public

If everybody in the world let on what was really going on in their heads, what mood they were in or how their family lives were running, it would be carnage out there. There would be tears, fights, rampant sex and hysteria on every street corner. Luckily, natural selection has ensured that those people who are completely honest about things when they are out in the public arena have long since died out, because nobody wanted to sleep with anyone who moaned about their medical problems, mother-in-law or hefty workload, and we have now evolved into a species of finely tuned fakers.

'Oh, yes, we had a marvellous holiday – the kids were happy, the place we rented was perfect and we all feel really rejuvenated' is fake-talk for, 'That was a fucking nightmare. The kids drove us nuts, there were rats in the kitchen and I'm completely bloody exhausted. We're never going away again.'

My favourite one is the 'Hi, how are you?', 'Oh I'm fine – you?', 'Fine!' exchange that takes place a thousand times a day between people who are not fine at all, who haven't had sex for three months and who want to send their kids away to a boarding school. It's hilarious. We all wander about, putting on a united, happy family front when the reality is rarely anything approaching such harmony or bliss.

Of course, a certain amount of fakery is essential for life to be bearable: if you ask somebody how they are, you're only ever expecting a 'fine thanks' if you're honest. You don't *really* want to know how they are at all, and if they tell you then you'll think they are a bit weird and avoid them for a week. But it's the *level* of this fakery that can become a problem, if we start to believe what we see and hear. Don't and remember the following:

☆ **Everybody feels they are failing** at being a family sometimes. Some are just better at hiding it than others.

☆ **Be vigilant**, and never convince yourself that other families are doing a much better job than you. They are probably just as exasperated, exhausted and extremely bored as you are occasionally.

☆ **Open up.** Sometimes, being honest and telling somebody that you are in fact *not* all that well, and that things on the home front are pretty rough at the moment, results in a torrent of similar confessions and tales from your relieved listener. Opening up about your problems means people are much happier to be honest with you, and you'll soon realise that you are not surrounded by picture-perfect families at all!

☆ **Beat it with a smile.** Putting on a happy exterior might sound superficial, but often if you stand tall, smile and try to be cheerful, some of your problems will melt away, and after a few hours you might well feel a lot better. No, it might not last after you get home, but just having a few hours away from your troubles can make what follows a lot easier to bear.

Etiquette: Here comes a family – run!

Families have got themselves a bad name. They have come to represent all that is loud, rude, inconsiderate, stressful and unpleasant, and I can see why. There they are in every café, car park, restaurant, cinema and shopping centre shouting at each other, arguing, looking as bored and miserable as it's possible to be, spoiling or neglecting their kids, making a mess, a noise and a pretty ugly spectacle of themselves.

Obese families, rude families, families on the verge of a nervous breakdown and even entire families wearing – wait for it – *hoodies*! Lord, what's the world coming to? Just look at them all, messing up our tidy, leafy towns and villages with their horrible *Family-ness*. Bring on the family-sized ASBOs, that's what I say. Lock 'em all up and throw away the key!

I am exaggerating just a teeny-weeny bit here, as you may have cleverly guessed, but you get my drift. Families are not quite the respected and valued pillars of society they once, perhaps, were. Seeing a family of four struggle over to the check-in desk, sticky lollipops and electronic toys in hand, can be enough to make the most tolerant, hard-of-hearing and child-friendly person cancel her holiday plans and head home again.

Well, it needn't be this way, and with some simple old-fashioned examples of social etiquette and manners we might be able to give families an image overhaul, and put them back in vogue.

☆ **Consideration of others.** This is probably the most important thing families can do when they step out of the front door. At this point you are no longer in the seclusion of your home, but sharing the space with other people: people who might not like kids putting their feet on chairs, leaving wrappers on park benches or picking their nose; who don't want to hear your private disagreements aired in loud voices over a latte and a muffin; who keep themselves to themselves and would appreciate it if you would do the same. If more families considered their impact on others they would be doing us all a huge favour.

☆ **Basic manners.** Once upon a time people held doors open to let others through; they said thank you when somebody did the same to them; they closed their mouth while eating, didn't interrupt, never shouted in public and sent birthday cards that arrived on time. There are tons more, which your Granny probably taught your Mum and your Mum taught you, but now you're too busy and we all know it's a lot easier to fire off a text than walk to the post office and send a letter. This is a shame: if even *some* of these basic manners were re-introduced and taught to our kids, things would be a lot more pleasant out there. See page 248 for more on manners.

☆ **Bring something for kids to do.** This applies to cafés, restaurants, aeroplanes and anywhere else where kids might get bored and start to be a nuisance. Nobody normal expects kids to behave perfectly and remain silent all the time, of course, but letting them rip up paper napkins, scratch tables with cutlery, kick the back of other people's chairs or throw their unwanted carrots under the table is unacceptable. If you are going to take a child into a child-unfriendly place, always bring a book or a notepad and pencils and try to keep the little darlings happily occupied.

☆ **Leave.** If everything fails, including the notepad and pencils mentioned above, and you start to disturb other people in the room, then leave before you do any more damage to the already dented and scratched reputation of families everywhere. Why should two people have their Sunday morning coffee ruined by a bunch of noisy, drink-spilling, bickering members of a family?

☆ **Do a good turn.** Help old people across the road, offer to do some shopping for a neighbour who can't get out easily, write to grandparents just to say "hi", or bake some biscuits for the lady next door who's had a hip operation. In our self-obsessed lives we quickly forget other people, and this teaches our kids to be selfish too. Anyone for a flapjack?

This is a very small list and there are hundreds more examples, including not farting in lifts, and not spending twenty minutes in a public loo checking out your eyebrows in the mirror when there's a queue outside. I'm not suggesting we all behave like little prissy, nineteenth-century society gals, but a modicum of decent behaviour wouldn't go amiss.

The Family Uniform

One of the things I have found it hard to get used to, since morphing from young, child-free babe (or something . . .!) into my role as 'mother and member of a family with kids', is having to wear the Family Uniform. What exactly this uniform consists of varies enormously according to where you live, what kind of friends you have and what your daily life entails. If you work it is likely to be much as it was before, because you'll be in work, not 'family', attire during the day. But when you don't you'll find yourself in full family swing, and this, for most busy, playground-frequenting mums, means dressing down.

I live in jeans or casual trousers, trainers or flats, some kind of pretty but unfussy top and any jumper or jacket I can lay my hands on that doesn't clash with the bottom half. I also come moulded to my bicycle, which has two child seats and a large wicker basket on the front. My hair is rarely anything other than swept back into a child-friendly but unsexy ponytail and my make-up consists of moisturiser and some blusher. In short, it really is as unglamorous as you can get.

As somebody who wears clothes to both reflect and dictate my mood, and devours several fashion magazines every month – despite the fact that I cannot afford to buy any of the stuff inside them! – this is something of a problem for me. Wearing the required Family Uniform day in, day out means I can almost never get away from 'Mumsy, family me' and become the stylish me I know must be lurking *somewhere* under all the stained tops and out-of-date jeans (if I look hard enough . . .). But wear it I must, not only because I would otherwise stick out like a sore, overdressed thumb on the school run, but also because I would break my ankles trying to chase my son around the playground in high heels.

Wherever you live, whatever the 'norm', it's almost certain that you will conform in some way, and this can become restrictive and boring after a while. So . . .

☆ **Dress up on top.** If pushing a pram or chasing children around the park restricts your bottom half to flat shoes and sensible trousers then try to keep the top half pretty, and use accessories like jewellery or scarves to add colour, individuality and style.
☆ **Dare to wear.** Not all mothers live in tracksuit bottoms all day, thank goodness. I occasionally stray into the very daring world of skirts and pretty shoes, but when I do I'm generally asked what the special occasion is. If I reply that I just fancied wearing

something nice for a change, my effort is generally welcomed, not laughed at (at least, not to my face . . .).

☆ **Vary your look.** It's far too easy to slip into wearing almost exactly the same thing every day. Try to avoid this monotony by forcing yourself into a different look every other day: jeans, then a long skirt, then something sporty, then some smart trousers, and then start all over again. Your kids will appreciate this too, as will your husband!

☆ **Having a job helps.** One huge advantage of having a job is that you can be somebody else for at least a few hours a week. Whether you go to work in suits and heels or just something a little smarter than usual, it gives you the chance to legitimately dress up, or at least dress *differently* for a while. Many of my friends find this to be a lifesaver.

Don't Mind the Mess: Simple ways of making it *look* tidy

The entrance hall is the first real room people see in your home, and it's where they form their first impression of what sort of person you are, how you live and whether it will be safe to have a cup of tea without giving the rim a quick wipe first.

A quick glance around my hall today leaves any visitor in no doubt at all as to my life and personality: a pram (currently with a sleeping baby in it), a plastic fireman's axe, a trumpet made of a plastic milk bottle and a cardboard box, sunglasses lying on top of a pile of wet children's socks and trousers after a puddle-splashing session this morning, a pile of half-opened mail, a sticker book, five coats hanging off the banister, three pairs of shoes at the bottom of the stairs (despite there being a virtually empty shoe rack three feet away), a selection of toys, hair bands and bits of my jewellery waiting to be taken upstairs, and three sweet wrappers. It is, without wanting to do myself down too much, an absolute disgrace, and it screams: *slightly hectic working mother of three who knows how she wants her house to look* (the entire *Elle Deco* back catalogue visible in the lounge is a dead giveaway) *but is fighting a losing battle on account of her own and her family's inherent slobbishness and inability to put anything away where it lives, ever.* There it is – my family exposed in one room.

The good news for anyone like me is that with some clever tricks and new habits, an entrance hall can be transformed from something that looks like a car-boot sale, to a space belying you as a balanced, well-behaved, orderly family. I don't suggest for a minute that you stick to this at all times – who wants to always be orderly and well-behaved? – but I have learned the following from my years of pretending to have it all under control:

☆ **Clear the decks.** Get rid of any surface where things can be 'put'. Until very recently we had a hall table. This looked like a jumble-sale stall most of the time, as every member of my family dumped whatever they couldn't be bothered to put away on it. Keys, water bottles, apple cores, hats, hand cream, you name it. Now we have no hall table – and no mess, because everything gets put away immediately or hidden . . .

☆ **Create hiding places.** These are not for you to hide in when people come inside and realise what a slob you are, but so you can easily hide all the mess. Put curtains or cupboard doors in front of lower shelves to disguise all the toy boxes; find furniture that doubles as storage, such as benches or window seats; and store all the children's stuff in big, beautiful baskets or chests. When all that bright plastic is piled into a gorgeous container it looks much better!

☆ **Coordinate and conceal.** Even the ugliest collection of odds and ends can look reasonably smart if it is well-housed. Matching pretty boxes, baskets or other containers create an air of unity and organisation, which conceals the fact that all is chaotic. Keys, gloves and the rest of the usual entrance-hall para-phernalia can be thrown into coordinated storage places and suddenly all looks neat again.

☆ **Habits.** Nobody can help you out here except yourself. Get out of the routine of chucking your coat on the table as soon as you get in and leaving your shoes beside the shoe rack. Relearn new, tidy habits through lots of practice and you will eventually find that the place looks after itself. Now, if you can just get the other family members to do the same . . .

You've Got Mail: Dealing with the family admin

What is it about being a small group of people who live quite peacefully and law-abidingly together that makes so many organisations, institutions and double-glazing companies send you so much mail? Every week the contents of our paper recycling box represent the wood from a small sapling at the very least, and possibly even that of a small tree, and half of it is unopened.

Bank statements, bills, reminders (for me, usually), credit-card offers, child-benefit forms, inland-revenue notices, school letters, magazine subscriptions (oops, me again), party invitations . . . the list of things to deal with can become overwhelming, even for the most efficient paper-pushers in a household. And that's to say nothing of the mess all of this paper creates.

There are only two outcomes of being flung into a sea of paper-work: you sink, or you float. Assuming that floating is the preferred option, avoiding as it does any tut-tutting from your in-laws and a visit from the bailiffs, then systems need to be put in place to help you swim. These do not involve pushing forms under the carpet, moving unopened envelopes from one table to another, or assuming the other person will deal with it. Instead, you need a family in-tray and a clear idea of who deals with what.

☆ **Deal with as much mail as you can the moment you get to it.** At least half of it will go immediately into the recycling box, and this will make the job look less daunting.

☆ **Sort the rest into urgent and non-urgent.** Leave all urgent things in the middle of your work space in the kitchen so you can't do anything until you've paid that bill or RSVPed that invitation.

☆ **Get a nice container for all non-urgent incoming mail.** Ours is a pretty, metal hanging basket, and it's very narrow so it fills up quickly. As soon as it looks even full-ish we know it's time to go through it. This means nothing is ever more than a week old when we come to deal with it, which is usually fine – it's non-urgent, see?

☆ **Know who pays which bills.** In impressively forward-thinking fashion, my husband pays all the household bills and credit cards. Actually, we only have one credit card, but he still checks the bill and pays it every month. This is so embarrassingly old-fashioned that I cringe as I think of it, but it saves me so much hassle that I am prepared to live with the scolding from ghosts of feminists past. Anyway, I deal with everything else, like baby-sitters, all school correspondence, sorting out school holidays and half-terms, making sure my children get to see a dentist more than twice before they are teenagers, and tons more. This set-up works for us, and it means we avoid most 'What do you mean, "Have I cancelled the direct debit for the gas"? I didn't even know we had one' arguments. Sometimes old-fashioned rocks.

☆ **Destroy the evidence.** Never throw away any documents that have your bank details or address clearly visible on them. This goes for recycling too. Either get a small shredder for such material or make sure you rip it up into teeny-weeny pieces before throwing it away. Those identity fraudsters are not ashamed to go through your bin.

☆ **Be honest.** This applies to every chapter of this book, of course: honesty is the bedrock of all relationships, along with firm abs and a man who knows his wife is always right (it's best you know right from the start that I'm joking when I say things like this, otherwise the next 400 pages won't go down well at all). Not owning up to the girly lunch and spending spree you enjoyed last month will not only cause trouble when it crops up on the statement, but it will also result in understandably wavering trust on his part. If you love each other there's nothing you need to hide, or feel so bad about that he won't forgive you. Honesty, trust and forgiveness – it's quite simple, and it works.

Family Notice Board: Weddings, funerals and other family gatherings

If there's one thing guaranteed to create some kind of family ripple, wave or tsunami it's a family gathering. It's hard enough just getting along with those in your immediate family, without throwing grannies, aunts, in-laws and lots of alcohol into the mix as well, but it's occasionally required that the whole gaggle of you get together to celebrate somebody's birth, death, marriage or whatever.

Enough has been written about such gatherings to fill the hole in the ozone layer, because there is just so much potential for a good story. A bust-up, a reunion, a love affair, a drunken argument, grannies getting sloshed, uncles flirting, mothers weeping – oh, it's all there when a family gets together, so you had better be prepared for some fireworks.

Weddings

I've been to a silly number of weddings in the last ten years, and they have all fallen into two categories: those that allow children, and those that don't. There is rarely any in-between category, unless the bride and groom are prepared to fight it out with those relatives or friends whose kids have been singled out and banned from attending. 'No, it's not because they are evil, noisy, smelly little bastards, but because there isn't enough room in the chapel' will never work.

Having kids at a wedding can be lovely: it brings a special kind of 'Ah, this is what it's all about' joy to the occasion, and there are always moments of mirth when a three-month-old burps loudly, or a toddler is heard asking why the bride's mother is wearing such a disgusting hat. But it can also be a pain in the neck. Nobody wants the 'I do' they've been rehearsing for three months to be drowned out by screaming, their table decorations to be used as ammunition between rival cousins, or the dance floor to turn into a Wiggles concert.

☆ **Never dispute what's on the invitation.** If it says no kids, that's it.

☆ **Never, ever ask if your child can be a bridesmaid, pageboy, flower girl thingy, etc.** It's unbelievably rude, and someone will only get hurt.

☆ **Take some sweets for the service** that don't come in noisy wrappers. Oh, and a small book, and an extra dummy if your baby uses them.

☆ **Sit by the aisle** to facilitate a hasty exit. Near the front is fine, so they can see, but an aisle seat is essential.

☆ **Leave immediately** if your children start to make noise.

☆ **Don't get there too early.** They will be bored before the bride arrives.

☆ **Don't get wrecked at the reception.** You still have to be able to look after your kids, even if Jane and Tom *did* just get hitched. *Hic!*

☆ **Try to find a hotel with a babysitting service** near the reception. Then you can really let your hair down without worrying about them (much).

☆ **Agree who is taking the kids home** before you get there. It is usually me, because I fall asleep at 10 p.m. and am happy to go to bed. My husband likes to be the last man propping up the bar at 3 a.m. More fun, yes, but he looks like shit the next day – hah!

Funerals

Parents often debate whether children should come to funerals, and indeed whether they should know about death at all until they are well beyond the tooth-fairy stage. How much this becomes an issue for your children obviously depends on how many grandparents and other elderly relatives they have, and lose, as they grow up. Our kids had young parents and so were lucky enough to have four of their great-grandparents still alive until recently. This number has now dwindled to leave only one, very youthful great-grandmother, with the result that they have already been to a number of funerals. We have always been very open and honest about death, preferring to tell it straight rather than making up any 'going to sleep for a long time/going to heaven' type of stories, but it's a personal choice. Here are some death-related tips worth knowing:

☆ **Know how much your child can understand.** We felt ours could handle the whole Death thing, so we told them. They have never had a problem with it. If you think yours isn't ready (but remember they are often a lot more matter-of-fact and ready to accept the weirdest of notions than we are) then you'll have to find some way of explaining it gently, or of keeping schtum.

☆ **Don't tell lies.** Kids are so smart it makes us 'intelligent' adults look several sandwiches short of a decent picnic. If you say you're just off to a family party and then everyone sits there dressed in black and sobbing for an hour, they might smell a rat, and never trust you again. Tell them it's a funeral, tell them people might be crying, including you, and explain why. Not to do so is to insult their intelligence and to set them up for a nasty shock.

☆ **Show your emotions.** I think it's very important for our children to see us crying, whether out of happiness, sadness, despair or anger. If we hide our emotions from our kids they won't have a clue how to handle their own, and they will have a very peculiar impression of what being an adult entails. I sat next to my six-year-old at my grandfather's funeral recently, and cried uncontrollably because they played the *Lacrimosa* from Mozart's Requiem – enough to send me into the deepest pit of sorrow for several hours, even if I'm in a good mood. She held my hand, comforted me and was amazingly grown-up and sensitive about the whole thing. I asked her afterwards if she had minded seeing me like that and she just said: 'No, of course not. I cry sometimes, so why can't you?' What a girl.

☆ **Ask if they'd like to come to the funeral.** When we asked my daughter about it she said: 'I think it's important for us to come too. I mean, he was in our family too, not just in yours, and we should all go and say goodbye.' Really, they blow me away sometimes.

☆ **Ask the nearest relatives what children should wear.** All black can be inappropriately sombre for children, so I always customise a normal outfit for a funeral. I make tiny black velvet drawstring bags for a handkerchief and some essential 'keep 'em quiet' sweets, tie black ribbons in the girls' hair and around their waist, and make sure they all have black shoes. This way they look very smart, respectful and funereal without going over the top. On one occasion my son wore some grey trousers and a shirt and waistcoat that I borrowed from a friend, and looked lovely. If black is expected, though, then you should go along with that. Ask, and you'll not go wrong.

☆ **Take it easy.** With emotions so high, it's possible for things to be said that really shouldn't be. If you can try to keep all other family ructions out of the equation for the day, it'll be a lot easier for everyone.

While we're on the cheery subject of death, it's a very, very good idea to **have a will made up** once you become a family and actually deal with the issues of who would look after the kids, who you would leave what to, and suchlike. It's something most people don't want to think about, are superstitious about, or just can't be bothered to do, but the amount of heartache, work and confusion that is caused by two people dying and leaving no will is pretty huge, and that's not fair on anyone. If you want to find out how to go about it, then go online and search under 'making a will', and you'll find hundreds of websites offering advice and information. Alternatively, speak to somebody who has done it and ask them for their top tips.

Family parties

Birthdays, wedding anniversaries, christenings – there's always a reason to have a family party, and always a possibility that something will go wrong if you have kids in tow. Children have this knack of going ever so slightly over the top, and turning an enjoyable occasion into something almost as fun as having your fingernails pulled out by George Clooney – what *could* be so much fun somehow turns into a living hell. As the parents, it's your unfortunate duty to spot when this is about to happen, and make swift moves to diffuse an imminent explosion.

☆ **Don't bring your troubles to a party.** Bring a bottle, of course, but don't bring your bottled-up issues. Having a husband-and-wife spat at Great Uncle George's eightieth is unforgivable. If you must, then avoid each other for the duration, and have the row when you get home. Ditto for disagreements you are having with your kids: save it for another time.

☆ **Don't tell your children about the party until you're about to go there.** If they have three weeks to get excited, they will be so wound up by the time it comes you'll be scraping them off the ceiling. And that's before they're plied with chocolates, fizzy drinks and those wretched orange crisps. Some degree of anticipation is fun, but more than a day or two is asking for trouble.

☆ **Bring something for kids to do.** Just a few books or small toys can save the day. Having something for your kids to do while you natter away for hours about boring adult stuff can mean the difference between staying all day and leaving as soon as the speeches are over.

☆ **Be prepared to take the kids out for a while.** Children can get rather excited at parties, and this is almost always followed by mild hysteria and large amounts of noise, and possible damage to valuable pieces of china. If there's a park nearby you are saved, but otherwise just a quick walk around the block really helps to calm them down.

☆ **Time out.** If it all gets too much for you, then find a quiet corner to get some peace and recharge, before you face the mob again. I always have to do this at large gatherings, and taking a moment to be alone with your children or to help in the kitchen can be just the ticket.

Christmas

I used to love Christmas: just me, my brother, my mum and dad, and my grandparents. A few presents, some nice food, crackers, staying up late, leaving a mince pie and some brandy for Father Christmas, stockings and huge amounts of excitement. It was simple, it was fun and it was a close family occasion.

These days I have to confess that I have come to loathe the very idea of Christmas. Not for any religious reasons, or because there's never anything I really want any more, but because of the whole hoopla attached to the event. The run-up to Christmas starts in mid-August now, with shops putting up baubles and magazines running features about Christmas wrapping ideas or places to visit over the festive holidays while the scent of Ambre Solaire is still in the air.

Then there is the sheer *volume* of presents kids get nowadays, brought on by the fact that they have more friends and relatives than they can shake a candy stick at, who give not one, not two, but at least three things each, most of which cost well over £20 and none of which the children need! At school they give teachers presents, they give each other presents, they give the school pets presents, and we, the overwhelmed parents, can feel under quite a lot of pressure to dig deep and give, give and give some more.

Top this off with the unnecessary but inevitable stress associated with cooking a Christmas dinner, plus all the meals, snacks, nibbles and alcohol apparently required to keep everyone happy, a huge number of relatives, high emotions and utter bollocks on telly, and you have a recipe for some kind of explosion. I find Christmas to be a very trying experience all round, and I know I'm not alone because some of my friends have told me they feel the same way since having kids.

Here are some ways of making it more enjoyable for the whole family:

☆ **Where to have it.** If both of your parents are still alive, and still talking to you, there is always the awkward question of whose parents you spend Christmas with. Our solution is to take turns, which is very diplomatic, and it's what most of our friends do. Alternatively, spend Christmas with one lot and New Year with the other. Either way, parents can get very hurt if you seem to be avoiding coming to them for such an important occasion, and you do need to use some tact here. Your mum's roast turkey may well be dry and tasteless, but it's only for one day, so buck up and eat up.

☆ **Have it at your place.** In all the worry about which grand-parents you will descend on, it's easy to overlook the possibility of just you and your kids staying in your own home and starting a tradition there. It can feel a little quiet compared with the hoards of family members usually present at this time, but it can be a lot less stressful – and a lot cheaper because you won't feel obliged to buy stocking fillers for all fifty of your in-laws or bring a couple of bottles of sherry for great-granny, so bear this in mind if you are a bit strapped for cash one year.

☆ **Too many cooks can spoil the Christmas dinner.** If you spend Christmas with your parents or in-laws, chances are that Christmas dinner will be taken care of by them. My advice: offer to help as much as possible, do exactly as you are told and don't even *think* about doing it your own way. *You* may prefer roast potatoes to be irregular, but if the head chef says 'perfect one-inch cubes' then perfect one-inch cubes it is. You can have your irregular ones next week, at home.

☆ **Get some breathing space.** It can get very claustrophobic in an overheated house, with overheated people telling overheated stories, so make sure you get outside as often as you can, to clear the fug and refresh yourself. This is essential for kids as well, who can go completely nuts with all the excitement, chocolate and over-zealous relatives. Allow them to let off some steam outside, even if there's a blizzard out there, and they'll be ready for the next round of 'cover Uncle Julian in cushions and jump on him' before long.

☆ **Chip in.** Christmas is a very expensive time of year, even if you take all the presents out of the equation: just feeding all of those relatives can cost enough to build the extension you need, and the alcohol bill can be prohibitive. You must, must make sure you all chip in, whether it's cooking a meal or two, providing some drink or keeping the snack and nibbles supplies coming. Ask whoever is hosting the event what you can do to contribute – some people want to handle all the food or wine themselves, and you might be treading on toes.

☆ **Limit the presents.** We tried this last year, and it almost worked (some people, like me, were a bit naughty and exceeded their limit, because there was something irresistible they just *had* to give the kids). Try limiting every family member to giving only one present, which can't cost more than a tenner. Not one present per person, but one in total, and do a lucky dip to decide who gives to whom. Bags not my father-in-law *again*! For kids this is almost impossible – there are so many fantastic toys, books and games to give them – but if you can even set yourselves a 'no more than three presents per child' limit you will find that it's less of a distasteful consumerism orgy, and more of an exciting, happy time with some lovely gifts being exchanged and appreciated.

☆ **Wait for the sales.** We started doing this about three years ago and I'm very glad we did: my husband and I give each other one very small, cheap present on Christmas Day, and then something bigger for each other, or for the house, when the January sales start. This works for our kids too, and we now give our kids a couple of small presents each on the day (which always rises to about twenty by the time the rest of the family has thrown theirs under the tree too) and let them choose a couple more things they would really like when they go down to half-price two days later. This saves us a fortune, and it makes the number of presents they receive on Christmas Day more reasonable.

☆ **Combining traditions.** I have found this to be a bit of a problem, because my family does Christmas so differently to my husband's. I prefer some of their ways, but not others, and I sometimes feel that I'm not having a 'proper' Christmas, as I remember it, at all. I also feel uncomfortable about some of their traditions being passed onto my kids, because I'd like them to do it 'our' way. We get over these hurdles by following the rituals wherever we spend Christmas, and this variety year on year seems to be enough to give us both a little of the childhood we remember, and to expose our kids to different ways of celebrating the occasion. (But I still think my way is better, of course!)

☆ **Start your own traditions.** The lovely thing about starting your own family is that you can start up some new traditions. Presents before breakfast, one present every hour, eating Christmas dinner in your new Christmas underpants and socks, going for a long walk afterwards, or whatever it is. Why stick to what you've always known, and maybe don't even like? It's your family, so stay at home for a change and do it your way!

It's a real shame that Christmas has become such an endurance test for so many families, but you don't have to be sucked into the distasteful world of commercial excess and lavish gift-giving. Stick to your principles, cut down on everything, and enjoy a relaxing family holiday all together. Because behind the presents, television marathons, brandy butter, party poppers, nuts, mince pies, carol singing and hangovers, whatever your religious beliefs or family hang-ups, this is an opportunity for you all to be *together* – and that happens far too little in most families. Season's greetings to you all . . .

While we're here, we should probably take a peek at what lurks in the space under the stairs. Some pretty grimy things, I suspect, but those are always fun to uncover . . .

PART FOUR

The Cupboard Under The Stairs

Before Harry Potter moved in and complicated matters, the space under most people's staircases was one of two things: it was either a downstairs toilet – you know the ones, where your knees hit the wall opposite when you sit on the loo and the 'basin' is actually a triangular teacup attached to the wall with dolls' house taps above it, guaranteed to splash water all over your crotch however careful you are – or a hideous mess. Mine is the latter. Under my stairs lurks everything from the under-used hoover and ironing board to several mismatched tennis rackets, climbing boots, a pram raincover, a torch, several tennis balls, random gloves and broken pairs of sunglasses and about two hundred spiders. It is where we throw all those bits and pieces we have no idea what to do with, or don't want to have to deal with. There are, of course, houses where this place has been transformed into a stunning feature, with built-in shelving, subtle lighting and hidden storage space for colour-coordinated shoes. But that's not my experience, and probably not yours.

For the purposes of this book, the cupboard under the stairs will house all those family issues you would rather not deal with. It's the place where skeletons lurk, waiting to come out and disrupt the harmony, along with arguments waiting to happen, bits of unfinished business needing completion, and enough worries to fill a mansion house, let alone the two square metres we've got to play with. As with anywhere that gathers dust and festers slowly into an unhygienic, disorganised, arachnid-infested disaster zone, we must occasionally take a deep breath – it's pretty airless and smelly – arm ourselves with a torch and a broom, and face what lies within. It's scary, it will result in a few shrieks, but maybe also contains some happy discoveries, and it will almost certainly make you feel better by the end of it.

Skeletons: Leave 'em in or get 'em out?

Every relationship brings some skeletons with it. These remains of loves, lives and issues past can cohabit with the meatier members of a household quite happily for years. Others clank and creak about the place, causing unrest, upset and scaring the bejeebies out of us every so often as they threaten to expose themselves.

Most skeletons in relationships between married people represent past loves. Men we once kissed, relationships we had but have never talked about (because he's your husband's best mate, for example) or sexual experiences we'd rather not share. Others involve all sorts of dishonesties from those little white lies we all tell ('The shoes were seventy-five per cent off – what a bargain!' *What a liar more like . . .*) to the occasional whoppers ('I'll have to stay at the office really late tonight to prepare for a meeting tomorrow . . .' *Hmmm. Funny sort of office, that, where they serve half-price cocktails and where all your friends happen to 'work' too.*)

Whatever your particular bony friends represent, you have two choices. Option one is to reveal their true identity and own up to the Christmas party kiss, the fact that the new chandelier in the hall wasn't really a birthday present from your mum and you forked out nearly a grand for it, or that you were once caught shoplifting in Selfridges because you were temporarily out of your mind with PMT and a caffeine rush and just *had* to have those egg cups. Option two is to leave them where they are, as a sentimental reminder of your former life, because you like having secrets or because you want to avoid the biggest row you have ever had, which may result in permanent scarring.

Here's some advice to help you decide:

☆ **Is the rattling disturbing you?** If the presence of a particularly large skeleton makes you anxious, guilty or both, then you should speak up. This kind of stressed state of mind can only breed more unrest, and it's much better to rid yourself of all the worry and angst, and be done with it. If he can't handle the fact that it's in your *past*, and therefore isn't a threat, then this is a sign of more serious mistrust and insecurity on his part, which needs addressing.

☆ **Ask a friend first.** Everybody should have a friend whom they can ask very difficult or embarrassing questions. She, or he, might not be able to advise you much, but at least you can see how someone else reacts to your news. If they stare at you open-mouthed and then don't call for two months, it's best to close the cupboard door and keep your mouth shut. If they laugh or don't seem very fazed at all (or own up to something much worse), you are probably good to go for it and confess.

☆ **Do you like secrets?** Some people actively enjoy having secrets from their partners. It makes them feel they still have a life outside coupledom and it adds a small amount of exciting risk. For these types, sharing a home with a few naughty skeletons isn't a big deal at all, and they can enjoy their new life without the risk of upsetting their partner when they spill the beans about the time they kissed Lucinda in the locker room when they were fifteen. Shame, because he'd probably enjoy that one . . .

Little White Lies

When is a lie not really a lie, but a slight rearrangement of the facts, an embellishment of the truth or a carefully edited version of events? What if telling the truth, the whole truth and nothing but the truth would cause more hurt and upset than telling a little, tiny fib?

Well, as with all relationships, whether with a friend, a daughter, a mother or a husband, there are times when not quite telling it exactly as it happened seems like an attractive option. I have often fibbed to my kids that the swimming pool is closed for lessons or that the telly is broken when what I *really* meant was: 'I don't want to take you swimming because I waxed my bikini line yesterday and it's gone a bit red', or 'The telly is all mine tonight because I want to watch *Gosford Park* again to stop me thinking about the three litres of water I'm retaining in my thighs!' I don't worry about this kind of little white lie (LWL). Telling the truth would require hours of explaining myself and apologising, and my life is so crammed with doing things for them that I just have to say NO! and put my own interests first every so often to avoid going insane. Anyway, it's not in the same league as telling them, oh, I don't know, that I won an Olympic gold medal at swimming or I *invented* television, is it? It's just a convenient, harmless, occasionally convenient untruth.

With husbands, LWLs are more serious, and should be used with caution. The very nature of your relationship means that you should be able to say everything – *everything* – to each other without any fear that you will be sent to the doghouse for a week, or that he will bear a grudge.

☆ **This is all to do with trust.** If you don't trust one another 500 per cent and *know* you will be forgiven the occasional misguided handbag-buying session or catastrophic poker night, then you really are going to have a lot of work on your hands to keep this relationship going for very long.

☆ **LWLs erode this trust.** Perhaps only a very little bit, but it's the tiny cracks that always lead to serious splits. Keep things open and honest, and you should have a much stronger partnership to work with.

☆ **Confront it.** If you feel uncertain about something he's told you, or feel uneasy or suspicious about something, for goodness' sake don't keep it to yourself. I have had a few paranoid moments like this, when I've found mobile phone numbers in his trouser pocket as I empty them before a wash, or if he says he'll be home by 11.30 and is still out at 4 a.m. when I get up to go to the loo. In the wee hours (is *that* why they're called that?) everything can seem a bit bleak and I convince myself that he's in the arms of a childless, nymphomaniac sex-kitten. When I ask, there is always an embarrassingly logical, provable explanation, and I have to eat humble pie for a day. But I'm always glad I asked, and he's always happy that I did – and to tell me I'm a silly girl who should know better.

☆ **Beware of habit-forming.** One problem with telling the odd porky is that it can become a habit, and before you know it you have become completely used to bullshitting your way out of many a tight spot, and you lose sight of what's true and what isn't. This is a very slippery slope towards almost certain disaster in the marriage department. Keep a check on yourself, and if you think you are falling into bad habits then get a grip and try to mend your ways.

I see a pattern emerging here . . . Spending money on little treats for themselves or the home is the main reason the mothers I asked told lies to their partners. If that's as bad as it gets, then I think they can all sleep soundly, but it does say a lot about their relationships: they feel guilty for spending money frivolously, or on themselves. There's a whole PhD in *there*! Happily, not everyone feels they are so answerable to their other halves and can enjoy some guilt-free treats:

How open and honest you decide to be depends on what kind of relationship you have. Some can take a lot more deception and secrecy than others. But from what I can tell, the cleaner that the cupboard under your stairs is, the better for the long haul. Time to grab a duster, perhaps?

To Clean or not to Clean?

Having a cleaner is a luxury. I don't care who you are, what your background, income or size of your pad is, but being able to have somebody else wash your toilet, scrub your bathroom and polish your mirrors is a huge luxury.

A few years ago I decided to spoil myself rotten and get a cleaner, and it really turned my life around. I had a baby at the time, and two older children, and instead of spending every minute that the baby was sleeping either washing the floor or hoovering under the sofa, I could use that hour to do some different, satisfying brain work like writing (to earn just enough to pay the cleaner!) or sorting out the photo albums, or even to have a rest, and I'd feel ready to play again when the baby woke up.

But there are also disadvantages of having a cleaner. One, it costs money, obviously, and you have to be sure that this is money you are happy to spend on that, rather than something for the kids or a treat for yourself. Two, it means you are not only letting a stranger into your home but also letting her (it's usually her, as far as I can tell) see what lurks behind the bathroom bin, on top of the picture rails and under the toilet seat. It's all very embarrassing, but necessary if you are to have a clean house once again.

Here are some considerations and tips for deciding whether to get a cleaner:

☆ **Can you afford it?** How much a cleaner charges varies enormously. I know of people who pay £5 an hour – a bit mean, I feel – and some who shell out £50 a week for more general cleaning and housework. The only question you have to ask is: Is paying a cleaner something I can easily afford or is the financial strain outweighing any benefit I might be getting from the extra time and relaxation it buys me? Only you can tell, but do be honest with yourself – remember, it is a luxury, not a given.

☆ **Are you both happy with the idea?** My mother spent twenty years working up to asking my dad if she could have a cleaner, and a further ten years asking him why not. This enraged me – if she wants a cleaner, and can afford it, then let her have one!

Alas, it's not so simple in all marriages, and your partner may not be entirely happy with you spending the family money on a lady who gives the house a quick dusting every week. Talk about it, and see if you can work out who is being more unreasonable. If you still can't agree, give it a try for a month or two, and then review the situation. If you can have sex a lot more often than usual during this period, showing just how beneficial the cleaner can be, you should be on to a winner.

☆ **How often should the cleaner come?** The best way is to leave it flexible. Most cleaners come weekly, but I've found that I sometimes don't need it that often, because we are away, or I've done some cleaning myself. We're not so dirty and untidy that I need her *more* than once a week, I'm happy to say!

☆ **How proud are you?** Here's what I do: the evening before my cleaner comes I spend about an hour tidying up, putting away the washing and sometimes even giving the bath and kitchen sink a quick wash. *Before* my cleaner comes! A good friend recently admitted that she does the same thing, and for both of us it's a question of pride. I know I pay my cleaner to clean my dirt, but I don't want her to see how messy and grubby it has become since the last time she came. She'd think we were a family of pigs! This is very common, so don't feel silly if you give your house a quick once-over before she comes – it shows you have some pride left after all. Just don't spend hours or it defeats the object.

☆ **Trust.** You have to trust your cleaner one hundred per cent as she may well have access to your house keys, which means access to everything inside as well. If you find the change you dropped down the back of the sofa neatly put to one side, you are probably quite safe.

☆ **Tough talk.** Becoming friendly with your cleaner is essential, because you want her to like your home and so clean it as well as she can, not chip the paint on the skirting board with the hoover nozzle or try on your jewellery while you're out. But you also need to maintain some kind of distance, because at the end of the day you are her employer, not her best mate, and you may need to have the occasional quiet word if standards are starting to slip, as they might do over time. It's a fine balance, but you need to be able to tell her when she's not cleaning behind the taps properly or never empties the upstairs bins any more, without blushing or feeling rotten about it. If you're on good terms she won't mind being told this at all – it's better to say so than spend money and still have a dirty house!

☆ **In or out?** I am usually in when my cleaner comes, because I work from home and she comes on one of my 'work' days. This has its benefits: I know that she does the full two hours, she can let me know when we're running low on products and we can have a friendly chat before and afterwards. If you're always out when your cleaner comes it's hard to tell just how much time you are getting for your money, and it also means you have to trust her with a key to get in.

☆ **Doing it yourself.** I sometimes give my cleaner a rest for a few months, if the cash isn't flowing quite as it might, or if I just fancy doing it myself for a while. Housework is fantastic exercise (I work up a huge sweat and ache for days after a big three-hour cleaning session) and I do all the bits that she misses. It's also a great way to do a lot of sorting out, because you'll come across all sorts of odds and ends that needing fixing, organising or throwing out as you whiz about the place with the polish. Finally, doing it yourself means you save a lot of money, so you can treat your family to something special after a few weeks – drinks are on me!

☆ **Keeping it quiet.** Not everybody feels comfortable with the idea of having a cleaner. I still find it quite embarrassing – it's like having staff or something, and I feel like a posh lady of the manor when I say I have one. This is mainly because I live in a very un-showy area where being down-to-earth is admired and giving yourself airs and graces is detested – which is how I like it. But if you want a cleaner, or feel you need one, then go for it. Don't be ashamed or feel you're being pathetic by not doing all the housework yourself: you'll probably find everyone else either has one already or follows suit very soon, when they see how relaxed you are in your gleaming home!

Bluffer's guide

If you are having friends round and your house needs a quick tidy up or clean, then here are some one-minute wonders to fool the keenest eyes:

☆ **Clear surfaces.** It doesn't mater where you hide the junk, but clear, tidy sideboards, shelves, coffee tables and tables give an immediate sensation of cleanliness and order. Find a cupboard and chuck it all in, then sort it out properly when the visitors have gone. Similarly a pile of dishes drying on the draining board looks messy, so quickly put it away and give the draining board a wipe to make it gleam: ta da! – a clean kitchen.

☆ **Middle of the floor.** Don't bother about the corners and edges, just whiz the hoover over the central bit and you'll have what looks like a clean house in minutes.

☆ **Smell.** Light a candle for a few minutes or make some fresh coffee before they come, or open some windows and doors to let some fresh air in – you don't notice how stuffy a house becomes when you're in it, but an incomer will.

☆ **Fresh flowers.** You don't need to spend money buying a gorgeous bouquet: just some pretty branches or blooms from your garden will do to make the place look fresh and loved. Try to do this regularly even when you don't have visitors – you deserve it too!

Meter Beaters: Reducing the household bills

Running a family is an expensive business. So expensive, in fact, that many people decide not to have a family at all, because they don't think they can afford it. This is extremely sad – unless, of course, they are mean, ugly, child-hating bastards who would rather spend their pennies on spa-breaks and a wine cellar, thus making the rest of us jealous.

There are two facts about the average amount of money families in the developed world spend every month of which I am certain: one, it is colossal; and two, it doesn't need to be.

If you need confirmation of either of these facts and have nothing better to do on a Saturday morning then pop down to your local Big Supermarket and take a look at the trolleys being pushed by puffing, panting, frowning parents towards the extra-large parking spaces reserved for those unsexy, environmentally catastrophic family cars. You will notice that these trolleys are piled far higher than can be deemed even remotely safe or elegant, with plastic bags literally bursting at the seams with *stuff*. Food, drink, clothing, electrical goods, garden tools, hoover bags, hair accessories, cleaning products, DVDs and nappies all fight for space before being loaded into the aforementioned Family Transportation Vehicles and ultimately consumed by starving and needy family members back at home.

And that's just the supermarket. It's a similar story in toyshops, clothing shops, DIY stores and – my personal favourite – interiors shops. Just look at all the *stuff* people are buying to keep every member of the family happy! It's shocking, fairly sickening and it makes one wonder just how people survived before they were able to buy themselves into £30,000 worth of credit-card debt. Poor them.

No: poor, stupid us. We have somehow convinced ourselves that *not* having everything we desire is tantamount to failure and that a family without a newly fitted kitchen, a fridge full of fresh pasta and organic prawns, three holidays a year, enough clothes and toys to fill several large warehouses, a designer sofa, two flat-screen televisions and hot water on demand is a family that is letting things slip.

There are, of course, two schools of thought on running your finances. The first is to say 'I am going to spend less than I earn, and save the rest for a rainy day, or for a time when I am buying something frivolous and pretty that will make up for the fact that my boobs are getting so saggy.' This is the school I attend, and it is rather dull and safe, but it means I know there's something in the bank should I need it. When I get paid less, I spend less. If I hit a particularly cash-rich phase, I spend a little more. Usually on shoes.

The second way of looking after your money is to say 'You only live once, and what I want I shall have. When I die, somebody else can pay off the debt.' Credit was invented for people who think this way, and the almost £1 trillion worth of debt in this country seems to indicate that there are quite a lot of them. On the face of it, it's a wonderful way to live: 'What the lady wants, the lady shall have' has always been a dream of mine.

But there are obvious drawbacks. Being in debt is very expensive. Credit-card companies don't just lend you the money, after all – they want it back with a little sweetener, in the form of interest. That holiday didn't cost you £1,000, more like £1,200 and a lot of worry. Living beyond your means is risky, and any kind of risk brings with it the biggest wrinkle-producer after a week in Majorca: stress. However much fun people may seem to be having, spending all that non-existent money on designer kids' clothes and new sofas, they are living under quite a lot of stress, and this can become so bad that families crack under the strain and no amount of Botox can fix the furrows.

Of course families are expensive, but they needn't be cripplingly so. There are simple ways of reducing the monthly bills that don't require you to move into a yurt and wear shirts made of old bits of sacking cloth. Try some of these and you should have some pennies left over for treats for all the family. Just not too many, mind . . .

☆ **Go Green.** There is a full list of all the Green things your household could, and probably should, be doing on page 403, and most of them not only help to save the planet but can also save your wallet from being permanently empty as well.
☆ **Spend cash.** Few people carry much, if any, cash any more, but if you want to cut down on family spending then try only paying in cash for a month. You'll be amazed at the number of things you don't buy because you haven't got the dosh to hand, or

because handing over all those notes hurts too much, and which you never miss at all.

☆ **Compare prices.** This applies everywhere, of course (why pay £4.99 for a T-shirt which is only £1.99 down the road if it's going to get wrecked within a month anyway?), but especially to your utility bills. Oh, it's so boring and dreary, but if you can be bothered to do a little research you might find you're spending much more than you need be. And that extra cash means treats for you all, Mrs Economical. Try www.moneysupermarket.com or www.pricerunner.co.uk.

☆ **Use leftovers.** Leftovers have an element of suspense and surprise that eludes the boring 'Here's something I have prepared from start to finish' dishes: you never know what you will find hiding in there, and with a little imagination you can rustle up something truly unique – and free! Leftovers are also essential for late-night hunger pangs: cold curry, straight out of the box, is to die for at midnight. Put larger quantities of leftovers straight in the freezer, so it doesn't go off if you forget about it – as you invariably will.

☆ **Shop late.** Supermarkets are always desperate to get rid of stock that is about to go off, and you can pick up some real bargains in the evenings. As most manufacturers err on the side of super-caution when it comes to best-before dates, even something that is *best* before today is still pretty damned good most of the time. I sometimes go at this time if I've been stuck in the house with kids all day, and just fancy getting out for half an hour. Be warned, though: doing this regularly is bound to lead to some kind of late-night-shopping crush on that gorgeous student who comes in every Thursday to buy more coffee and cheese. Go home, fast.

☆ **Check the label.** Compare prices per unit as well as actual packet prices: often you are paying more per unit for, say, nappies, than another make, because it's not clearly marked. They like to catch us out.

☆ **Tantric shopping.** I do this with most of my purchases over a tenner. If I see something I desperately want (usually because

Kate Moss has worn something similar or because *InStyle* says it's this season's 'must buy'), I'll look, yearn, and walk away. If it's still there when I look a second time, maybe a few days later, I salivate for a while, and maybe even try it on, but I leave wanting more again. Finally, when I can stand it no longer, I'll check one last time, and if it's still there in my size, it was meant to be: I reach straight for the G-spot in my wallet, and leave with a big smile on my face. This kind of delay tactic can save you a fortune, as the joy of buying often lasts no longer than a day, after which we'd rather we hadn't spent the money. Giving it a day or two to be sure avoids all those 'Damn, why did I buy *that*?' irritations.

☆ **Buy in bulk.** There are precious few positive things to be said about the big, out-of-town supermarkets, but if you are trying to economise then they can help. Buying larger sizes, economy packs, buy-one-get-one-free and other 'the more you get, the more you save' promotions do make a big difference to your monthly bills. Buy local for fresh items such as meats, fish and vegetables if you can and for occasional top-ups, but for the big monthly shop a big super-duper-market is cheaper.

☆ **Going cheap!** As you cannot fail to have noticed, vintage is the biggest style must-have so far this millennium. What this means in non-fashion circles – i.e. for you and me – is that anything old, cheap and utterly bargainous is hot, hot, hot! This is the only trend I have ever been way ahead of: I've been buying clothes, toys and furniture at car-boot sales, jumble sales, second-hand stalls and flea markets for years, but not because I am stylish – merely because it's cheap. Why spend £80 on a child's bicycle when you can pick up a perfectly good one for under a tenner? Start thinking like this and you'll be rolling in it.

☆ **Grande skinny overdraft.** The explosion of the coffee culture in the UK over the last ten years has, on one level, had a positive effect on many people, who now take ten minutes out of their hectic day to sit, read the paper, meet friends, or just think and watch the world go by. Ahhh. On most other levels – the terrifying amount of caffeine we consume, the enormous wastage as gallons of milk and piles of cups and packets of sweetener are thrown away etc. – it isn't quite so wonderful. And on our wallets it can be catastrophic: even if you buy only four coffees a week, which is far less than many people do, that's almost £350 per year on coffee! Throw in a few muffins and pastries and you are well on the way to drinking away a weekend break and a new school PE kit.

☆ **Look after the pennies.** It shouldn't be surprising that many filthy rich people use second-class stamps, get their shoes mended rather than buying new ones, and know where to buy the cheapest pint of milk. Being penny-wise is a habit that can be hard to adopt, but once you're there, and can see that the pounds really *do* look after themselves, you will be grateful for the new outlook. They didn't get rich by frittering it away on clothes and take-aways, did they?

☆ **Sell your unwanted items.** Good old eBay. Once upon a time selling things you no longer wanted – or never really wanted in the first place – was a nightmare and required enormous amounts of time, dedication and disappointment. Nowadays you can sell almost anything you could ever imagine, in whatever used, worn, tattered or stretched form it comes in, with less effort than it takes to put it all in bags and drive to the local charity shop or rubbish dump. Somebody out there wants it, and all you have to do is put it online, sit back and wait for the 'Congratulations!' notice to appear. That's one empty cupboard and £20 for the lady in the corner.

☆ **Eat in.** Eating out is a luxury. It is not something you are entitled to, or need to do in order to get through a week, but a real indulgence. It is also very addictive –what's not to like about having somebody else cook and wash up for you? – but sadly, in this country at least, it is also prohibitively expensive. Eating for two is bad enough, but bring your kids along for a couple of plates of food they won't eat, and drink they will spill everywhere, and you are talking about at least £50 for a fairly stressful evening, and that's without the service charge. Unless you are really raking it in then eat at home as often as possible.

☆ **Forget take-aways.** When I say 'eat at home' I don't mean 'but still get somebody else to cook for you'. Take-aways are only marginally less expensive than eating in a restaurant, and they are often less healthy than anything you could cook at home for a fraction of the price. Of course it's fun to do every now and then, but if you are watching the pennies – and the waistline – then more than once a month is asking for trouble.

☆ **Economy brain.** People who manage not to fritter away all their money do so because their brains are hardwired to economising. It's very annoying for the rest of us, who can't walk past Zara without a strong, invisible force pulling us towards the door, but if you can start to think just a little bit sensibly about money you will soon find yourself buying three-for-twos without even realising it, and the family kitty will get heavier again.

☆ **Be a voucher vulture.** Some of my friends are so good at this that they haven't paid for a family holiday, trip to the cinema or meal out for years. Store reward points can be exchanged for everything from a meal to a trip to Legoland, and if you can be bothered to read all the options and save up then you can really win. Loyalty cards are also great for getting things for free, whether it's a cup of coffee, a haircut or a DVD rental. Keep a lookout for such cards and start collecting!

Your back must be aching by now, so come on out of this tiny little cupboard and let us head somewhere much more exciting, noisy and spacious . . .

PART FIVE

The Utility Room

I always suspected that I was a little peculiar, but now I am quite sure, at night, I sometimes dream of utility rooms. A place I can put all the noisy kitchen appliances and shut the door on their whirring, humming, spinning and clanking. Alas, *I* can only dream of such luxury, but hopefully you are more fortunate and don't have to share your evening meal with a washing machine and seven loads of ironing still waiting to be done.

Here we shall look at family chores, who does them, and how to cut down on the elbow grease.

My Not-So-Beautiful Launderette

Living in a family is a dirty affair. It's grimy, sweaty, muddy, stained and smelly. Of course, living alone is often not the cleanest existence either – how many bachelor pads have clean tea towels or a scrubbed toilet floor? – but a family dwelling produces more filth than seems possible or manageable at times.

If somebody had told me, before I embarked on this 'getting married and having kids' journey, that I would require a degree in cleaning techniques and that a considerable portion of my waking life would be taken up with my head in a laundry basket, I might have reconsidered. It's not that I have an especially mucky or careless family: talking to many friends, I know that they live with the same level of spillages, stains and general gunk as I do, and none of us would consider ourselves unusually wild or unruly.

Children are, of course, the primary culprits. It is very, *very* usual for me to have to change my three-year-old within an hour of getting him dressed, because half of his porridge is down his front, he found some chalk and smeared it into his shirt, or he sat on a wet cloth in the bathroom. If they do make it beyond 9 a.m. without a change of clothes, it is almost inconceivable that any of my kids will come home from school in any garments fit for a second day's wearing: paint, sand, felt-tip, somebody else's lunch and several unidentifiable and quite unsettling marks will be found on everything from their tights to their hair like a sticky, smelly snapshot of their day.

Generalising wildly, men aren't much better. Watching most men eat, I wonder why somebody hasn't produced designer Man Bibs – like overgrown toddlers they drop, spill and splat their food, seemingly oblivious to the fact that other people manage this task without such trouble. Then there's sweat – Man Sweat – which means no shirt can be worn more than once, if it even makes it beyond midday before becoming unacceptably whiffy. Socks reek of overripe blue cheese and gym kits morph into a stinking, sweaty heap, having often resided in an airtight bag for more than a week.

Women – actually, let's say mothers, as most childless women keep themselves reasonably clean as far as I can tell – bring their fair share of dirt and household cleaning into the equation: most of my clothes end up splattered with some child-related gunk by the end of the day, my shoes are worn out by all the dashing about and need regular cleaning and re-heeling, and I almost never take my shoes off when I come into the house, either because I get straight into unpacking the shopping and cooking for my starving children, or because I am more than likely to be going outside again very soon to play football in the garden or take the newly-fed children to some extracurricular activity or other. This means my house is often littered with bits of grass, twigs and mud.

Yes, living in a busy, modern family brings with it a large amount of mess and dirt, and if you don't adopt some strategies for dealing with it, you could soon drown in your own dirty laundry. Luckily for you, I have picked up some tips along the way, which I pass on here to ease the strain and free up some 'me' time for you, in between spin-cycles.

☆ **Ironing. Don't**, unless it's absolutely essential – for example, white shirts, or clothes for an important meeting or party. I have vivid memories of my mother sweating over the ironing board on a Sunday evening, making piles of crease-free handkerchiefs, underwear and pillow cases, while we all sat there watching telly. It always seemed very unfair – she was mostly ironing my dad's shirts – and enormously pointless to me, and still does. Most clothes look fine after a good shake and a dry on a hanger, and if you fold them as you take them off the washing line, rather than chucking them in a laundry basket, you will save yourself eighty per cent of your ironing. Do what's required and leave the rest – life's too short to iron pants.

☆ **Delegate.** I really don't mind cleaning up after other people. If I did, I'd have run away years ago. Neither do I mind ironing other people's shirts, putting away their underwear or mending the holes in tights. But I expect some help from the other members of my household, which I think is only right and fair. I don't want my kids to think that Mummy = Servant, or my husband to take me for granted. In today's family, asking your man to empty the dishwasher or your kids to make their beds and tidy their rooms shouldn't be met with shock.

☆ **A stitch in time.** Lots of jobs are much easier, or even negated, if you get in there straight away. Soak stains immediately in water (blood stains should only ever be soaked in *cold* water), rinse pots and frying pans as soon as you've finished using them, shower the bath down as soon the water has run out, and so on.

By doing things like this you'll halve the amount of scrubbing you need to do.

☆ **Have one laundry basket for the entire family.** I've stayed with people whose children have their own laundry baskets and where each member of the family decides for themselves when to put on a load of washing. The consequence is that dirty clothes can lurk for weeks at the bottom of laundry baskets, and the washing machine is put on half-full almost every day. This is so wasteful in terms of water, electricity and washing powder that poor Planet Earth has her work cut out to stay operational. A communal place for the dirties means everyone gets clean clothes when they need them, and the machine is only used when there's enough to fill it.

☆ **Shoes off!** My mother is obsessive about this, having been brought up in a Communist country where everyone was allowed exactly the same amount of living space (usually almost enough to swing a very small cat if you kept your arms bent and moved most of the furniture out) and the inside of each apartment was considered filthy if it had the tiniest grain of dust in it. I now understand how sensible this obsession is: taking shoes off the second you enter a house, and preferably just outside it, keeps most of the dirt out and means you have a lot less housework to do. I will try!

☆ **Little and often.** Don't wait until the cleaning and tidying jobs mount up: you will feel horrible in the mess, and worse as you trudge through the list of things to do. Always take something back upstairs as you go, and keep putting things away as you wander about the house, and you'll find that there is much less to tidy and clean at the end of the day. I know it's obvious, but it's amazing what a big difference it makes if you can get into the habit of it.

☆ **Linen cupboard.** Keep this as clearly labelled and organised as possible. Nobody likes such boring jobs as making the beds or putting out clean towels, but you can make it easier on yourself: separate doubles, singles, towels and sheets, and attach pretty labels for each one to their appropriate place on the shelf. There's something very pleasing about opening an airing cupboard (or laundry room, should you have such a posh thing) to find it full of beautifully folded, clearly labelled laundry. I *must* get out more!

Sharing the Load: How about some help around here?!

June 2006, 8 p.m.

Sometimes I honestly believe that I am the only person in this house who is even vaguely aware of their surroundings. I swear, if I didn't continuously go around like a neurotic hen, picking up, putting away, wiping, sweeping, adjusting, mending and improving this place, we would still live in a hideous, smelly dump of a place with 1970s carpets, embossed wallpaper and carpet in the kitchen! The worst thing is that I am made to feel that all of this house-improvement is solely for my own benefit, and that nobody else really minds living in a shit-hole. This is so unfair. Surely all my effort is making life for all of us more pleasant, and probably increasing the value of the house at the same time? A little appreciation and HELP really wouldn't go amiss.

It's astounding to me that, at the beginning of the twenty-first century, when we can fly to Mars, communicate with the other side of the world almost instantaneously, watch crap on over a hundred television channels and buy jeans to fit every imaginable shape of man, woman or child, the workload required to run a family home is still utterly unequally divided between the members of the family. On the home front, it's as though we haven't progressed since the Dark Ages – bar the better-fitting clothes, of course – and it's something that brings out the raving feminist in me, even when my husband is being especially helpful.

Let me give you some examples from my dear, honest, worn-out friends.

Suzie, photographer, mother of three and wife for eight years:

I do ninety per cent of the housework and homemaker stuff. When I didn't work I didn't mind – it made sense. But I now have a part-time job AND the kids to manage, and I still do all the shopping, cooking, cleaning and school stuff. I sometimes wonder if I'm being taken for granted, or if I'm just being a wimp.

Julie, data analyst, mother of four and wife for twelve years:

I wish I'd set out some different rules at the start, but I just did it the way my parents did: I do all the housework and my husband does all the admin. I know he's doing his bit but I do feel I do a lot more than him, because the housework never, ever stops. If I say so he just says I'm being over-sensitive and that I don't really have to do so much – but I do!

Julia, community nurse, mother of two and wife for six years:

David does nothing to help around the house. He gets home very late from work most nights and at the weekend he likes to spend time with the children or play golf. The problem is, I work too, and I'd like to spend time with the kids or do some exercise as well. But somebody has to cook the food and clean the house, and it's always me. I don't want to nag so I get on with it – I don't want arguments.

And now a few words from some brave, honest men:

John, software developer, father of two, married for five years:

I work long hours so I can't really cook because the kids are fed when I get home. And I love cooking too! I don't do much housework because it's often taken care of while I'm at work, but I think I could do more at the weekend, like go to Tesco or do some washing.

Peter, scientist, father of three, married ten years:

I hate housework. I work so hard all week that I need to relax and unwind when I leave the lab. Anyway, I don't mind if the house isn't perfectly clean – it's my wife who likes it that way, not me.

Ed, musician, father of one, married three years:

I've never heard Annie complain that she does too much housework, but come to think of it, she does a lot. But I think it makes her happy to have things the way she wants them. She can always ask if she wants me to do more – I don't mind helping out.

Interesting. The women all feel they are doing the lion's share, despite having jobs outside the home as well, but they either say nothing to avoid rows, or feel their words fall on deaf ears. The men know they are doing less, but don't seem to want to offer their services, and some even seem to think that we *like* doing all of the work. Perish the thought that they should deprive us of the sweeping, trolley-heaving and underpants-sorting we so adore!

Come on now, ladies: can we please show some respect to all our foremothers who worked so hard to give us more freedom of choice, and be brave enough to ask, pretty, pretty please, that we be treated as equals – not better, or more gently or patronisingly – but as equals with the people who share our home? Would it not be just slightly intelligent if the adult members of a family shared the workload equally between them, and if the kids chipped in a little bit too?

Yes, it would. A whole fucking lot more intelligent than it is at the moment, where by far the majority of working women still do the most housework. (The statistics are there if you don't believe me – just go and look.)

The 'Why do I do everything?!' question is one I ask frequently, usually at a high volume, with a child on one hip, a basket of laundry in my arms and a car insurance document between my teeth. Happily, there are ways of reducing the number of times you have to ask this:

☆ **Speak up!** Make your dissatisfaction known, not in an aggressive way, but by simply stating the facts and saying you want things to change. He probably hasn't stopped to think how the clean clothes arrive in his wardrobe, why there are always clean mugs in the cupboard, or beers in the fridge. They just magically appear. Well, make him aware of who the magic housework fairy is and tell him you want to divide these tasks up a bit – or the fairy isn't going to be very happy any more . . .

☆ **If you work** you have a watertight case for sharing the housework. When I had no job (other than looking after my kids and house) I did almost all of the housework and I didn't mind at all – I was at home, he was at work, so it made sense. It *was* my job. But as soon as I started working again we had to share the load differently, and it took a little while to adjust to. If you and your partner both work, then it is completely unacceptable that it's assumed you will do most of the childcare and housework. You *have* to talk about it and find a way that works for you, or you will become too resentful and angry to be any fun any more.

☆ **Leave it to rot.** I don't recommend this strategy at all, as I've seen it tried a few times and it was always a disaster. If you adopt a 'Fine, well I'll just stop doing it and we'll see how well that goes, shall we?' approach, here's what will happen: your house will resemble a squat within a month, you will spend all the money you could have spent on a much-needed cleaner in the local take-away because there will be no food left in your cupboards, and your partner will think it's fantastic. He won't notice all the dirt and mess, and he'll wonder what all the fuss was about. You, on the other hand, will go mad living in such squalor. Much better to carry on keeping your house as you like it, but working on the 'It's completely disrespectful to expect me to do it all' line. And he'll get no sex *at all* until something changes . . .

Competitive Exhaustion

I come from a family where this condition is rife, and I really, *really* hate it. Everyone sets out to out-exhaust everyone else, citing all the tasks they've had to do, how little sleep they've had, how stressed they are, how ill they are, and how their life is just so much harder and more exhausting than anyone else's! It's nothing more than a big, childish quest for sympathy, attention and cuddles, and it doesn't work: it just pisses everybody off.

If you feel yourselves slipping into such a scenario, then learn from someone who has lived with it for years, and try to make changes as soon as possible:

☆ **Identify why it's happening.** Whether it's you or your partner, try to think of why there is such need to explain how much work is being done or how much you/they are suffering. It's almost certainly due to feeling down, lacking attention or being in some way jealous of each other's life. Silly, I know, but very common.

☆ **Stop it.** This kind of behaviour is very hard to stop once you get into the habit, so stop as soon as you feel it coming on. If it's been going on for a while, then you'll have to get help with it, so get the whole family involved: ask your partner or children to point out when someone is starting out on a 'my life is so hard' rant, and have a chat about what's the matter instead. Often someone just needs a bit of love and some help with some chores, and they feel much better.

☆ **Listen to yourself.** Nobody can sound anything other than pathetic, miserable, attention-seeking or self-obsessed when listing all the things they've done, saying how tired they are or moaning about the amount of work they still have to do. If you can hear how awful you sound, you might snap out of it.

☆ **You are part of a team.** Families are a bit like teams, and the whole point is to work together to support and encourage one another. Banging on about how hard you have it immediately causes a rift in the team, usually resulting in bad words in the dressing room and studded, muddy boots being thrown. Don't. You have to work together and *not compete against one another*.

Cook, Cleaner, Nanny, Whore: How many jobs can a woman have?

Jerry Hall's mother may have been right. She is often quoted as having said that to keep a man happy you must be a maid in the living room, a cook in the kitchen and a whore in the bedroom. To which her razor-sharp (and presumably not short of a bob or two) daughter replied that she'd hire the other two and take care of the bedroom bit. Well said, lady.

These days Granny Hall would have to add another few jobs to the CV to keep her man, if not happy, then certainly as he might like: maid, yes; cook, yes; whore, yes please; but also nanny, diary organiser, interior designer, decorator, money-earner, accountant, doctor, counsellor and seamstress, to name but a few. In other words, the world's best PA.

The number of things a lady feels she is required to do these days to qualify for a Gold Star is enough to tire us out just by thinking about it – which is probably why so many of us are exhausted half the time. But if we stop for a moment, and ask ourselves a few fundamental questions, we soon see that the situation isn't quite so daunting or depressing after all:

1. **Do we have to be all of these things?** Clearly the answer here is 'no'. We do not have to be perfect in every aspect of our lives, and to try to be so is ridiculous and self-destructive. Something's gotta give, baby.
2. **Who are you doing it for?** If you can honestly say that you are trying to be the best wife/mother/cook/cleaner/decorator etc. because it makes *you* happy, then hats off to you, but maybe you need to lower your expectations a little. Even the most talented, hardworking woman in the world can't do it all. If you are doing it to please your partner, then you have some very serious thinking and talking to do: if he doesn't love you without all the trimmings, then he doesn't love you at all. He loves the life you give him, not you.
3. **What does it say about us?** The more we take on, the more successful and accomplished we are as women – no? Well, no, I don't think so. It's great to be *able* to do so many things, and to multi-task 24/7, but I don't think it makes us any more complete or admirable. If anything it shows us to be more needy of praise and desperate to impress than ever, and this always smacks of insecurity.

So what's a modern family girl to do? Keep slogging away, cooking sumptuous meals, hosting dinner parties, performing breathtaking sexual acts every night, redesigning and decorating her stunning living room, raising her kids perfectly while wearing gorgeous clothes to complement her perfect skin, perfect figure, perfect home and perfect bloody life??! NO. She is far too intelligent to give herself away like this – to become a slave to what others might say about her. If you feel that you are wearing too many hats at once and are in danger of taking someone's eye out with one of them, then the following should help:

☆ **Put the blinkers on.** Who are you trying to impress? Your friends? Your husband? Your parents? Who are these people who you think will judge you according to whether your cushions match your curtains or your freshly baked scones rise as well as your salary. It doesn't matter what anyone else thinks – you do as much as feels sensible and stop if it gets too much.

☆ **Get real.** As soon as you can rid yourself of the feeling of trying to impress someone, you can get on with the more important business of spending time with your family and enjoying yourself a little. This is what life is really about, not worrying whether your DVD collection is arranged alphabetically or by genre. Nobody cares!

☆ **Be honest with yourself.** I know that many of the jobs I do, from cook to nanny to gardener, I do because I *like* them. I like decorating my home, organising the kitchen, keeping on top of the school admin and making sure the children's clothes are labelled. If I moaned about it I would be unforgivably hypocritical, because I would complain more if the jobs were done badly by someone else. Sometimes it's much easier to do it myself, and do it well. Many of my friends also admit that while they often complain about having too much work to do, they actually quite like getting so much done themselves. That's fine – just be honest with yourself, and know whether you are doing it for you or for everyone else.

☆ **Cut down.** It's amazing how much you can ease off on the Perfect Wife thing and still have a happy, clean, fed and satisfied family. Sure, some people might admire you for being good at a million jobs, but much more impressive is to be *able* to do them all but to only do the ones that are most important for you and your family, and stick to making those work. So take the test – see how much you can cut down on without your entire family coming apart at the seams. I think you'll find it's quite a lot – so put that iron down!

☆ **What example does it set your kids?** I was brought up in a family where my dad had the 'main' job and did all the Man stuff, like tax returns, mending the car and reading the paper at the weekends, while my Mum had a part-time job and did everything required to keep us all alive. Without her we wouldn't have had anything to eat, wear or wash with. Honestly. We kind of joke about it now – 'Ha, ha – Dad can't even boil an egg! And he doesn't know where the washing powder lives, even after thirty years! Ha ha!' – but really it's pathetic and I grew up believing this was how marriages had to be. My husband thought I was really weird when I assumed he couldn't cook, clean or shop and it took him years to get me out of that old-fashioned mindset. He deeply regrets this transition, of course – now I expect him to pull his weight equally around the house – sucker!

You know you are fantastic, he knows you are fantastic and your kids will always think you are fantastic because you are their mum. Working yourself into an early grave through excess polishing, baking, tidying and weeding won't make them love you any more.

All of this housework has made me hungry. Let's leave all the cleaning products behind and head towards the kitchen, stopping off along the way to check out what we've got to choose from . . .

PART SIX

The Pantry

Oh, this is a treat – going into the pantry. My own house doesn't have a pantry (you will have gathered by now that my own house is really rather small!) and neither do the majority of homes today: they were either never built in the first place or they have long since been knocked through into the new, open-plan kitchen-living areas or converted to utility rooms or back porches. But *this* house has a pantry because it means we can separate all the food buying and storage from the cooking and eating. *So* cunning.

The Weekly Shop: Easing the strain

Anyone who has ever shopped with children in tow will know what a hideous, exhausting, depressing, frustrating and miserable experience it can be. What makes it even worse is that shopping is supposed to be enjoyable – a treat, even. To have this self-indulgent, therapeutic, and leisurely pastime ruined by a toddler who refuses to sit in a buggy until you buy him a *Bob the Builder* magazine, asks for a chocolate bar every thirty seconds and manages to clear the bottom shelf of the family planning aisle in Boots with his left shoe, leaving you struggling to put back as many packets of condoms and jars of Vaseline as you can before the whole of your street walks past, is enough to drive the most level-headed mother slightly mad.

☆ **Shop while they sleep.** This mainly applies to very young children who still have a nap in the day. I know there are a million and one other things you could be doing while you have this period of quiet, but when you watch babies screaming in buggies, toddlers pulling clothes off rails and mothers becoming exasperated at the checkout you realise why shopping with a sleeping beauty in the buggy is a good deal more sensible. Little kids *hate* shopping and you really can't be surprised when yours kicks up a huge fuss while you are in the changing room and you are forced to chase him across the accessories department wearing a grey bra and fraying knickers. Take him to the park instead, and keep the shopping for when he crashes out afterwards.

☆ **Shop quickly.** If a sleep is out of the question and you have to bring your little darling along, then for heaven's sake do it fast. This is not a time for window-shopping, browsing the sale rails or buying your entire autumn wardrobe. Just go in, get what you need, and get out FAST.

☆ **Leave plenty of time.** Now then, having said all that about speed, there are occasions where you can turn a quick shopping trip into a half-day expedition, provided you leave yourself *lots* of extra time for child-orientated delays. These include nappy changes, walking at a snail's pace to examine every stick, cigarette end and elastic band, going up and down the escalator five times, chasing some pigeons, falling over and crying several times and stopping to chat to lots of friendly old ladies who want to say 'Ahhh, aren't you a clever boy!' If you are in no rush this can all be a lot of fun, because rather than getting in the way of what you are trying to do, all of this slowness *is* the activity itself.

☆ **Promise a treat.** Some people would call this bribery but I prefer to see it as necessary motivation and positive reinforcement. You *have* to stick to your word, though, or you are a dishonest, mean woman and deserve never to be trusted again. If she's been good, get her that box of raisins or there'll be hell to pay.

☆ **Have a snack to hand.** There's an old Chinese proverb that goes: 'Child who snacks on something in buggy is happy; child who has nothing is pain in the arse.' Or something like that. It shouldn't be a doughnut or a chocolate bar ('Child who eats lots of fatty food becomes obese' . . . but that's for another chapter) and I usually rely on breadsticks, grapes and raisins to keep mine happy while I whiz around the aisles. Always have fresh supplies in your huge bag.

☆ **Do something for them.** Of course, there are many times when kids just have to come along while you go to the shops because you have chores to do and they have nowhere else to go. If you build enough child-centred activities into your itinerary (e.g. going to the library between Boots and Sainsbury's, feeding the ducks before going to the bank, etc.) it makes it more bearable for both of you.

☆ **Involve your child.** It's amazing how few parents ask their kids to help out while they shop. Even simple tasks like getting a basket or putting some carrots in a bag can make a child really happy and proud of his achievements. Sure it takes ages and he gets all the shitty carrots which you have to put back, but so what? At least you are doing something *together*, rather than him sitting there, disconnected from your frenzied activities above his head.

☆ **Go with a friend.** This can go either way: either your kids keep each other amused and happy while you mums have a great time shopping and chatting and showing the world how wonderfully behaved your kids are, *or* the little blighters see this as an opportunity for some devilish schemes and naughtiness, resulting in both of them getting lost or crashing into a huge display of suncreams in Superdrug. If you shop with a friend it is vital not to get carried away with your idle gossip and moaning about your partners and to remember that you still have your kids to keep an eye on. Hang on – where's the little tyke gone . . . ?

☆ **Make up games.** In a moment of sheer Motherhood Madness I made up a 'Tesco Quiz' a few years ago when I had to take all three of my kids shopping with me, and it was fantastic. I just spent about ten minutes thinking up all kinds of questions for all age groups: e.g. How much are cucumbers? If I bought three, how much change would I get from £5? What is to the left of Marmite? How heavy is the biggest box of cornflakes? And so on. It was sickeningly worthy of me, but it made the whole trip enjoyable and stress-free. I saved the quiz on the computer and can easily update it any time I like. OK, I never have, but I could if I wanted to!

The key thing to remember when shopping with children is that, in general, they don't enjoy it as much as you do and it's not something they should be made to do more than is necessary. Those embarrassing checkout tantrums happen because kids are bored to death, feel ignored and want some attention. Amazingly, lying on the floor kicking and screaming seems to get your attention very quickly. Ooh, they are clever.

Not In My House: Banning certain foods and drinks

Every family I know has its Not In My House list. For my vegetarian friends this obviously consists of meat, fish, and any dairy if they are being extra vigilant, and for others its Sunny Delight, beef, Ribena, reconstituted cheese, Cheerios, chocolate (eek – not spending much time *there*!) or whatever else they deem to be Out of Bounds.

There are many reasons why you might want to add something to your Not In My House list, and here are just a few you might encounter:

☆ **Allergies.** Obviously. If anyone in your household is allergic or intolerant to certain foods then it's an absolute must to keep the contents of your larder under strict supervision and to make sure everybody sticks to the rules.

☆ **Good Health.** When you are trying desperately to keep your family healthy and 'crap-free', this is where all the 'no sugared cereals, no chocolate, no sweets, no fizzy drinks, no processed foods, no additives, no salt . . .' and so on comes in. The more you can think like this, the easier it will be to avoid obesity, rotten teeth or scurvy. It is possible to go overboard, however. A house with *no* bad things in it at all is in danger of becoming a house of No Fun, and that's not where you want your kids to grow up, is it? Remove even seventy per cent of the junk and you are already doing a fantastic job – what harm is the odd processed, sticky cheese string going to do?

☆ **You are on a diet.** This is a tricky one. If you are trying to shed a few pounds of unwanted, post-holiday love handles and you find that living in a house full of choc-chip cookies and Sugar Pops makes this less than easy, then banning anything with more than 20 calories and 0.1 grams of fat might seem like a good idea. It isn't. It will just make you crave any food that actually *tastes* like something, and make the rest of your family grouchy and hungry too. Kids – and husbands, in my experience – need to eat a lot, and clearing the cupboards of all the potentially fat-making stuff is not an option for a family. It is possible to compromise, however, and there's nothing wrong with giving the whole family a month off sugary cereals and choc-chip cookies but keeping the occasional bowl of nachos. It might be the start of a new, healthier lifestyle for you all.

☆ **Keeping up with the very healthy Joneses.** This is more of an issue in some areas than in others. Where I live the level of inter-family comparison isn't as bad as I know it to be elsewhere (West London being one example, where *everything* is fresh, wild, organic and bloody expensive, as far as I can tell). But just from what I hear when my kids go to a friend's house for tea I know who has fishfingers on a regular basis and who is more likely to have home-made organic falafel and freshly baked pitta bread. Consequently, when I have other children round to my house for tea I make a concerted effort to cook something much prettier and healthier than I normally would for my kids alone.

Yes it's pathetic, and it means I am just faking it and begging for brownie points, but I share this so that you know the phenomenon of Competitive Healthiness exists, and you don't panic when everyone else seems to eat better food than your family does. They do – but only when it shows.

Cathy, mother of Jonathan, eight, and Millie, four:
I used to buy lots more processed and frozen food than I do now – going to other people's houses and seeing what they fed their kids made me think I should be a bit healthier, and I was embarrassed if I had sudden visitors for tea and they said they weren't allowed to eat such-and-such. Now we have frozen meals once a month, and I have also stopped buying fizzy drinks. I just hadn't realised how much junk we consumed until I noticed what other kids said when they came to ours for dinner!

Given the massive effect food has on your family's health, this heaps a large portion of responsibility onto your already aching shoulders. Don't be swayed by anyone else's bad habits or Pringles tendencies: if you don't want them in your house, you keep them out! For all you know you'll start a trend: 2007, the year the chicken nugget died.

Storing It All: Tips for keeping food fresh and organised

Filling your pantry with food is easy; knowing what to do with it once you've moved it from shop to bag to house is another matter.

We are constantly bombarded with information about food: what's in it, where it was made, who made it, how it is packaged, how it made its way to the shop, how we should cook it, how long we should keep it and even how we should eat the damned stuff! Leave us alone – it's just grub and we're hungry! The result is that we look at it suspiciously, wondering what evils lie beneath the packaging, and whether we shouldn't just chuck it away and go for some beans on toast instead (again).

By following some very basic guidelines and using your own head to work out what works and what doesn't you will save yourself a lot of money, waste a lot less food and have to go shopping a lot less often – hurrah! Below are some suggestions; add your own to this list and pick up tips wherever you go:

☆ **Perfect food.** The fashion for consuming 'perfect' food, where anything short of 'regulation' is rejected in favour of something more perfect, uniform, unnatural and characterless seems to be on its way out. There is now a movement towards going back to eating food just as nature intended it, marks, bumps, knobbles and all. This is great news. If kids get used to you saying 'Uugh!' every time you see a tiny brown bit on a banana they will do the same. Cut it off, eat the rest, show them that food doesn't need to be perfect in order to be healthy and delicious and stop being so fussy!

☆ **Best before . . .** I'm going to be a little careful here, as I don't want anyone to get food poisoning, but manufacturers are very keen to avoid being sued by customers who get stomach problems that might possibly be the result of eating slightly mouldy or less-than-absolutely-fresh food. Consequently they put 'Best Before' dates on their packaging that always err massively on the side of caution. Use your brain and nose, consider whether you think the hummus really *is* off, or whether it still has another day or two in it, and make up your own mind.

☆ **It's just a bit of mould!** Some mould is bad for you, and is best not consumed. But a tiny bit of blue on the side of some cheese, or a piece of slightly 'off' melon will almost certainly not kill you; in fact, it's probably good for you, as our digestive system needs some mouldy action every now and again to stay alert. It's not quite the same as drinking a Yakult, but it's not going to do you any harm. Throwing food away the minute it goes beyond picture-perfect is wasteful and stupid.

☆ **Plastic fantastic – not.** Any fresh fruit or veg that is packaged in a plastic bag should be taken out as soon as you get home: it can't 'breathe' in there and will go off very fast. Transfer to bowls, paper bags or storage boxes and you should get an extra day or two out of them.

☆ **Rotten apples.** The people who package supermarket fruit or veg, like cherry tomatoes, nectarines and so on, into those plastic boxes have the nasty habit of sticking a rotten one right in the middle. My theory is that this is to make the whole lot go off faster so that you have to come back and buy more. If you buy fruit like this then take it all out when you get home and check for rogues – take them out asap or it'll spread like wildfire.

☆ **Wet or dry?** Biscuits should be stored in an airtight container in a cupboard – not in the breadbin. Bread and cakes are slightly moist and this spreads to the biscuits and makes them soft and yucky.

☆ **Open tins.** When you open a tin, don't leave the leftovers in it. Decant them into a clean container – something to do with the metal oxidising and it being bad for you ... anyway, it's not pleasant so don't do it.

☆ **Fridge or not?** Fruit should never be eaten straight out of the fridge: it needs to warm up a little to be really tasty. Ripe tomatoes, strawberries, melon and so on can be *stored* in a fridge if you want to keep them for longer, but take them out twenty minutes before you want to eat them. Vegetables also store longer in a fridge.

☆ **Ripen at home.** Most supermarket fruit is unripe. Let's not even go into the madness of all of this, but if you must buy your fruit there then you'll need some ripening techniques: bananas really do ripen faster in a brown paper bag, and avocados can be speeded up by putting them in there with the bananas. Store unripe soft fruit like melons, mangoes and peaches in front of a window and turn every day until ripe. Leave vine tomatoes on their vines until you eat them – I'm sure it makes them taste better.

☆ **Keep things separate.** Get a simple, safe fridge-storage system in place: yoghurts, butter, cheese etc. at the top, cooked meats and leftovers in the middle, and raw meat at the bottom. You don't want raw meat juices dripping onto your cheese . . .

☆ **Box it in.** Chucking food in a fridge willy-nilly is much quicker at the time, but it causes chaos later on. Get some containers for different foodstuffs and you'll find it much easier to get to what you want: a box for cheeses, one for cooked meats, another for condiments and so on.

☆ **Start at the front.** Put all the food you have just bought at the back and shuffle the older stuff forward. That way you avoid the Granny Situation of finding tins and biscuits at the back of the cupboard, which went off in 1978.

☆ **Buzz off!** In the summer, fruit flies and ants can become a real nuisance, making the smartest of kitchens look like a bug-infested jungle. Keep fruit covered with pretty cloths, cover your compost pot at all times and empty it regularly.

OK, that'll do for now – it's a good start and you will find your own clever techniques as you go along. I'm getting really peckish now, so let's take some supplies and go into the room where we can actually start to prepare some of it. Might just need a biscuit to keep me going . . .

PART SEVEN

The Kitchen

The Heart of the Home . . .

. . . and here we are in the kitchen – ah, the kitchen!

I'm going to get all traditional and Olde Worlde on you in this room, because I shall assume (deep breath, Liz, and prepare for considerable Female Wrath and Loathing) that the kitchen is a room where the Lady in your house spends more time, and has greater influence and control, than the Gentleman. I know, I know, it's going against everything that women burned their shapeless bras and cut their long tresses off for all those years ago (and a great many more serious sacrifices, I do realise) but, despite all the great advances in sexual equality, bra design and hair products, in every household I can think of, it's the adult with the female genitals who is at home more, cooks more and considers the kitchen Hers.

Please don't get all huffy – I'm not making the rules here, and there are obviously exceptions where the Man of the house wears the apron and likes to pretend he's Gordon Ramsay for the evening. However, for most of us – having won the unquestionable right to work down a coal mine if we should so desire – perhaps we should now try to embrace our relationship with the kitchen: it usually has groovy electrical appliances, pedal bins, tea- and coffee-making facilities, a radio, and *all the food* (hurrah!!). It's also the room where the family congregates, celebrates, debates and argues most. Thanks to the trend of smashing walls down to create huge, open-plan kitchen/entertaining rooms and the arrival of some breath-takingly stylish kitchen units, worktops and appliances, this room is returning to its original place at the Heart of the Home. And about bloody time too.

So if we stop and think about it for a moment, we soon realise it's the best room to be in, as it acts like a kind of Family Mission Control, with us at the helm. Doesn't seem so bad now, does it?

. . . And the Unofficial Front Line

As we all know, kitchens can be troublesome places, and there are two main reasons for this crossfire: firstly because, despite it being what you consider as *your own* space, because you work there more than anyone else, it is necessarily a *shared* space for the entire family to use and make a mess of. This is akin to allowing babies, toddlers, moody teenagers and pre-menstrual mothers to all hang out in somebody's office just because it happens to have biscuits in it. It's a recipe for disaster, and someone will probably lose a limb before the day is out.

The second reason for the somewhat volatile nature of the kitchen is because most of what happens in there centres around *food* – who buys it, prepares it, cooks it, eats it and clears up after it. Whatever your own relationship with food, there is little doubt that it is the source of an enormous amount of stress, and we'll come to this confusing subject in a little while.

For now, we are dealing with the problem of *intrusion*. You want the kitchen organised and maintained *just so*, because you are in there three hours a day and feel it should be your own space with everything where you want it to be: condiments above the toaster, tea and coffee near the kettle, utensils near the sink and pots stacked in the big cupboard in the corner. Perfect. Everything is going well, until He decides to help, by moving the condiments next to the oven, the utensils to a new drawer next to the fridge, and hanging the pots from a special rack thing. Aaargh! Now you can't find anything, the Marmite has melted and you have banged your head five times on a large frying pan dangling above the sink. Cheers, mate.

The most distressing thing about this kind of Kitchen Conflict is that it leads to the most petty and unwinnable arguments, where each of you knows you are partly right and partly being an arse. You can't exactly turn around and say, 'Look, will you just fuck off and leave my kitchen alone – it was just fine before and now you've messed it all up', firstly because he was only trying to help, and secondly because by saying 'my kitchen' you commit yourself to being perfectly happy to cook and wash-up for the rest of your lives together. Oh dear.

Similarly *he* can't turn to you and say, 'Jesus, I was just trying to help – I can't do anything right, can I? *Fine* – have it all your way but don't expect me to do anything in here again', firstly because he knows he will sound like a moody seven-year-old, which is not a turn-on for most women, and secondly because he will absolve all his power in the kitchen forever, thus rendering his late-night bacon sarnies and beer shelf in the fridge Out of Bounds.

Throw children into the mix, with their woefully bad sandwich-making technique, inability to drink from a cup without pouring half of it onto the table and penchant for leaving the cheese unwrapped so that it dries into a brick within hours, and you have a kitchen that no longer bears any resemblance to the one you so carefully planned and maintained before everyone else trashed it.

So how can a group of people come to share such a communal space harmoniously? Well, it's certainly a tall order, which even Jamie Oliver would struggle with, but let's have a go:

☆ **Don't beat about the Aga.** Make sure everyone knows how you feel about the kitchen (whether that means you like it, hate it, begrudge it or relish it in there) and ask them to appreciate this. Assuming it's your domain, or treating it as their own playground, will both lead to rows and smashed plates.
☆ **Share the load.** Make it understood that the kitchen is a *shared*

space, which means everyone has to chip in and keep it tidy and useable. It's not 'Mummy's job' to put the dishes away and scrub the dried grease off the roasting tin. Mummy has cooked it, so you help to clean up afterwards, mate.

☆ **Open your eyes and ears.** As much as we hate to admit it, just occasionally somebody clever will come along and suggest a much better way of doing something, which we thought we were already doing just perfectly, thank you. When it's something kitchen-related it's twice as hard to swallow the large, dry lump of pride blocking your oesophagus, because – if you spend more time in the kitchen than the person making the helpful suggestion does – it means they have just scored a point in *your* territory. It's as though you, having only popped into his place of work once or twice because he left his glasses at home or forgot to wear any shoes, coolly suggested a far simpler and more efficient way for him to do whatever it is he does there for hours on a daily basis. Cheeky minx. Try to listen to any suggestions, and be happy to learn from a fresh pair of eyes. You can always lie and say you were just about to do that, as it happens.

Cooking with Mother (. . . and Father . . .)

Cooking alone can be very satisfying and therapeutic: the radio is on, everything is relatively under control, your kids are otherwise occupied pulling each other's hair out upstairs or trying on all your make-up, and a warm 'Nigella' glow softly envelops you for a few minutes. Aaaaah.

Then you burn the chicken, there's a blood-curdling scream from upstairs followed by one of your offspring entering the smoke-filled room clutching a handful of hair, with black mascara all over his cheeks, and all is back to normal again.

If this kind of solo cooking is the only way your family's meals are ever prepared then not only can it become quite lonely for the chef, but it also means that your children never get to see, feel and learn anything about food at all. This is a shame on a scale way beyond that of Sienna Miller chopping all her hair off or Opal

Fruits suddenly being called Starburst. Teaching kids how food *works*, what it is, where it comes from and how it turns from packets of this and that into a finished meal, albeit a slightly burned or tasteless one, is an absolutely *crucial* part of their education that will stay with them forever.

Asking a class of eight-year-olds where honey comes from and getting the answer 'From Tesco's, Miss' or being met with blank stares when requesting the simplest recipe for a cake is hardly something we should be proud of as a nation. I realise that few of us have much time to spend watching our kids hacking carrots into huge, irregular chunks with a blunt knife or sloshing milk and flour all over the hob in an attempt at junior béchamel sauce. But how many of even the busiest parents can honestly say they couldn't cook *one* meal a week, from start to finish, with their children?

Sarah, mother of Louisa, five, and Robert, two:
When the children help to cook their dinner they always eat much more of it – probably because of all the effort that went into it, but I think it's also because they like the idea of trying what they have made. They are proud of it, and I know they will be able to cook healthily for themselves one day.

Cooking with my mother is something I remember very well and she passed on all of her recipes, techniques and clever tricks to me. I then discarded the bad bits (putting cottage cheese in a lasagne) and kept the good stuff (cleaning up as I go, keeping one chopping board for onions only, etc.) and I shall pass these edited highlights onto my kids.

Even if children aren't actually *doing* anything, just being with you in the kitchen and watching what you do can rub off a lot: I learned how to knead dough by watching my granny squish hers to death with her scarily strong hands; and my mum's well-trained sense of 'Oh, that must be *roughly* four ounces of flour? Just chuck it in and see what happens' is invaluable. Perfect scones and no fuss.

Nurturing an affinity and a familiarity with food is essential for children to have a positive relationship with it for the rest of their lives. It also teaches them essential lessons in how to cook healthily for themselves, and to be aware of what goes into their meals. But it takes time and you will have to be prepared to get a little floury along the way. The following tips should help:

☆ **Don't rush.** If you are pre-menstrual, the dishwasher man is due any minute and your two-year-old is getting tired and fractious, then it's really not the best time to suggest a communal cook-a-thon. Cooking with kids means Things Will Go Wrong, and you need loads of time to spare and a good sense of humour. Snapping at them when the egg so inevitably ends up dripping into the cutlery drawer will put them off for life. 'Never mind – you're doing really well' is much more what they want to hear, even if that's bollocks and you all know it.

☆ **Get the kit.** If it entices your mini Raymond Blancs into the kitchen, then get some gorgeous children's aprons, chef hats, mini mixing bowls, wooden spoons, chopping boards and biscuit cutters.

☆ **Let them invent their own.** *I* know it will taste disgusting, *you* know it will be a waste of ingredients and *they* know you will hate it, but letting them add bits of this and dashes of that is a great way to get them excited about cooking. If it's something like soup or a fruit cake it doesn't really matter what they chuck in so long as it's edible.

☆ **Get them to clear up.** Every chef worth his or her Michelin star knows that the cooking is only half the job, and that it's the cleaning up afterwards and storing the leftovers that really separates the good eggs from the lazy yolk. When your children see how much work goes into putting everything back as it was, they might try to get some of the batter into the pan next time, instead of all over the hob.

☆ **And dinner is *served*!** Again, the patience of a saint is required here, but children *love* serving up the slop they have cooked, and staring to see if anyone likes it. Best to pretend you do, but not enough that they will ever make it again.

What's for Dinner?

This is a question that every mother is asked every few days, and often every few hours as her kids get older, and one to which she has to come up with a suitable answer. 'Suitable', in this case, means an answer that won't generate any of the following: a long, weighty *sighhhh*; the word 'Yuk!'; or a face screwed up and disgusted as though you just said 'Pig shit and fried toenail clippings again, darling'.

Much better is to be able to say something that makes them appear to be pleased you bothered to go shopping and prepare the meal. When I go to all this trouble for them (and it *is* for them – when I'm on my own I am quite happy to eat the same dish for four days on the trot or live on toast and Marmite if it means I don't have to cook) and I am met with anything other than gratitude and pleasure, I want to throw my apron at the nearest ungrateful member of my family and shout: 'Well if you hate what I'm cooking so much, then *YOU* come up with something better! Your ten minutes start now – I'm off to read the paper!'

Given that this kind of storm-out would result in my children dying of scurvy, my husband turning into a ton of lard and all our money going to the local curry house, I generally just tell them to go away and come back when it's ready.

Which brings us to *what* you can rustle up in the frantic ten minutes between getting in from swimming lessons and having your starving family raid the biscuit tin. This is where some clever preparation and a Top Five Quick Family Meals list can save your bacon, so to speak. But hang on – what's that I see below? Well, if it isn't a Top Five Quick Family Meals list! Hope they like it . . .

1. **Pasta and something.** Pasta is a very safe bet, and you can chuck almost anything on it to create what I would class as a meal. Some 'and something' options could include the very simple pesto and grated cheese, the more exciting fried bacon, tomatoes and mushrooms, and even the extremely daring tuna and sweet corn (wow!). None of the above should take more than ten minutes, even if you fry a couple of onions and make a salad to go with it.

2. **Baked potatoes.** Again, hardly a culinary delicacy, but with a little effort you can stray away from the baked beans and grated cheese served from a Jacket Potato Van near you and venture into the magical worlds of chilli, or bacon and blue cheese, or grilled vegetables. Open your fridge and let your imagination run wild.

3. **Pizza.** If you have the time, or you want to turn it into a fun cooking/bonding session with your kids at the weekend, then make the pizza bases yourself and freeze them. If you don't have enough time, or, as ninety per cent of us honest mothers will admit, cannot be bothered, then buy pizza bases and add the toppings yourself. Don't pay more for the ones with tomato and cheese on already – it only takes two minutes to spread it on yourself, it means the cheese hasn't become indented in the dough, and it's all fresher. Decorating pizzas is one of the best ways to involve your kids with cooking, and we always put on a thick layer of frozen peas and sweet corn, so I know they are getting their vitamin C too. Chuck on bits of ham or sliced salami, tuna, chicken, any vegetables – just about anything really – and then cover with a good layer of grated cheese to keep it all together. It'll taste great and look pretty, which helps.

4. **Stir fry.** If any meal was designed for busy families who want to eat well, then this is it. Stir fry means quick, healthy and no tricky cooking techniques: just slice up any vegetables you find lying around your fridge or vegetable store (anything from trusted carrots and peas to broccoli, bean sprouts, peppers and courgettes will do) and fry then for about four minutes in a very hot wok with some oil. Chuck in some thinly sliced meat if you

want to (chicken is a favourite in our house, but beef is also great. Fish can fall apart somewhat), add soy sauce for great flavour and colour, and it's move over Ken Hom.

5. **Fish.** Don't panic. This isn't difficult or time-consuming fish. Fish is one of the healthiest things you can eat, and for children it's just Wonder Food, but it comes with a certain amount of fear, from the 'Ooooh, no. I couldn't manage *that*' to just not having a clue which fish is which. If bones are an issue then just get a fillet, or practise pulling the skeleton off in one rather fancy move once it's cooked. For the simplest, quickest fish meal (just don't tell any celebrity chefs, who will only scoff at such simplicity) just put a whole mackerel or trout or some salmon fillets in the microwave for three or four minutes under a cover, turn them over and do it again while you finish the veg and some couscous, shout at your kids to wash their hands and come down, and pour yourself another glass of Sauvignon Blanc. By the time you've asked them three more times and put some cutlery on the table you are serving a healthy, colourful, delicious meal for the whole family. Have a go, see how easy it is, and start buying the real things instead of expensive oily fish pills. *Bon appétit!*

I am aware that this list borders on the Offensive to My Intelligence, and I am starting to feel Gordon Ramsay breathing fury and contempt down my neck. But I stick with it, knowing that a great many people still cannot think of anything to make for dinner, feel that cooking is an unfathomable challenge and an ordeal, and go to the chippy three nights a week to break up the microwave-meal monotony. Jamie Oliver has done wonders in making healthy cooking seem more manageable, but most people still cling to their three or four 'safe' dishes. If these dishes are quick, fresh and healthy then that's absolutely fine.

Practise, Practise. It does get easier . . .

How confident you are when the time comes to rustle up something to feed your hungry brood depends entirely on how much time you have spent cracking eggs, peeling potatoes and playing with the electric whisk. No, not in *that* way . . .

I remember sharing a flat in college where we took it in turns to cook a big communal meal at the weekends. Apart from separating those who could cook while drunk from those who couldn't, what really showed up was who had had some previous cooking experience at home and who hadn't. Those who had were able to rustle up something edible and tasty out of the typical student ingredients on offer with no trouble at all. Those who hadn't were terrified of the chopping, peeling, stirring and frying and ended up serving something that even slightly-the-worse-for-wear students couldn't swallow.

If you didn't have much practice as a child, don't worry – there is plenty of time to catch up, and the more you get your hands dirty and stop being afraid to try new combinations and techniques, the easier it will be for you, and the more you will pass on to your kids.

Granny knew best: Cheap, healthy cooking tips

It is possible that your granny *didn't* know best, and fed your dad on a well-balanced diet of fat, salt and sugar. In my own case this was partly true, but only because of the countries concerned: the Czech national dish is dumplings and fatty sausages washed down with strong beer, and Scotland is famous for having the highest level of heart disease in the world thanks to a diet of all things fatty and sweet, sweet, sweet. Oh, and whiskey.

But let's pretend that the granny in this house did know best, and was one of many who could cope in times of financial hardship, half-empty shelves and rationing and still manage to feed her family of twelve a healthy meal for less than a fiver (in today's money) a day. *How?* Well, once you've had plenty of the practice recommended above, and no longer eye your steamer with suspicion or fear the frying pan, you will be able to do at least some of the actual cooking. But the question remains: what, and how?

Here are some top tips that should keep everyone in your household, and your bank balance, in tip-top condition:

☆ **Make soups.** If every ten-year-old were taught how to make a good soup, and then actually made and ate the stuff, there would be half the level of obesity and bad health we see in this country today. I'm not certain about this, of course, but there's no doubt that soup is the king of cheap, healthy meals; and it's so easy to make! Level One: just get a load of vegetables (carrots, potatoes, parsnips, leeks, etc.), chop them up small, fry them in butter and oil until they go a bit glazy and soft, pour on a couple of pints of boiling stock (which you can make from a cube if haven't got round to Level Two yet, where you make it yourself), bring it to the boil and leave it for half an hour or so. Ta da – soup is served! Level Three involves the heady task of adding things like noodles (steady on . . .) or bits of meat left over from dinner yesterday. Soup costs almost nothing to make and one big pot with some hunks of bread is enough to feed a whole family very well. At about 20p per serving with almost no fat or salt compared with £5 from a chippy with the lard-levels set at max, I'd say we're onto a bit of a winner here.

☆ **Use leftovers.** Made too much pasta last night? Don't worry; keep what's left, and tonight you can heat it up and chuck on some beaten egg and milk until it turns into scrambled pasta. Or add it to that soup you made at the weekend. Or cover it with some cheese and tuna and bake it into a tuna-cheese melt. Leftover meat is perfect for pies, risottos, or just having cold with some bread or potato salad, and leftover veg is never a problem: I eat it for lunch, or, if it's not very appetising-looking, I whiz it up with some tomatoes to make a kind of vegetable coulis thing to pour on top of pasta or couscous. Leftovers are the queen of cheap, healthy meals. Use them.

☆ **Don't add salt.** There is tons of hidden salt in lots of the food we eat, from bread to baked beans. Eating too much salt can cause high blood pressure, so keep to low-salt foods and don't add any more yourself.

☆ **Remove excess fat.** Skinning chicken is quite gross really, but if you can bear it, it will greatly reduce the amount of fat your family eats.

☆ **Grill, don't fry.** If you own a deep-fat fryer, then either get rid of it pronto or put it at the very back of your 'kitchen implements I never use' cupboard, along with the fondue set and the toasted-sandwich maker, and just talk fondly about it from time to time. I have never, ever understood why people take beautiful healthy food and then throw it into gallons of hot fat. It's criminal! If you grill, roast or lightly stir-fry your meat and vegetables instead of condemning them to Death by Fat then your family's arteries and hearts will thank you for it.

☆ **Stop murdering the vegetables.** There is a belief in this country that all vegetables, especially carrots and cabbage, are evil and bad, and need to be severely punished for being so . . . well, just so *vegetably*. This punishment can range from ten minutes to a whopping twenty in a pot of boiling water, until the poor things are drained of all vitamins, minerals, taste and texture, and resemble little more than wet papier mâché. Please can we all stop this brutality, and realise that vegetables are our saviours and should be treated with the utmost respect. Three or four minutes is ample time to soften most veg up enough to call it cooked rather than raw, and anything approaching ten is cruelty.

☆ **Buy local.** Buying local, fresh food is one way to reduce environ-mental damage (no flights or plastic packaging involved here) and cuts out the amount of pesticides or other chemicals your family may be unwittingly ingesting. I know it's lovely to have blueberries on your porridge every day – but this is the middle of January and they were in season six months ago! Buying local is good for the local economy too, which is an added bonus.

☆ **Keep things in proportion.** There is some debate about the 'best' ratios of protein to carbohydrate to vegetables you should put on a plate. It really depends on the amount of exercise each person is doing and how much they are growing: active kids need lots of healthy carbs to give them energy; sedentary adults need less. If you always make sure there is lots of fresh veg and some protein on each plate you won't go too far wrong.

☆ **Hey – go easy on the lard!** Every time you add butter to your family's food, be it on a jacket potato, melted on top of peas or in the kids' packed lunch, ask yourself: could I use a little less? Am I using the right kind of fat? Using olive or light spreads is much healthier than dolloping on blobs of unsaturated fat. That was OK in 1970, but we are a little wiser now to the importance of low fat and 'good' fats and oils.

☆ **What they don't have, they won't miss.** If you only ever drink water, your whole family will get used to only drinking water, and there will be no fights about juices, squashes and so on: you don't drink them. Period. It's the same with all 'bad' foods: if you never have them, nobody knows they're missing anything and they just get used to eating well. Of course they'll come across them at some stage outside the home, and having them as a treat is fine, but if the habit at *home* is for healthy stuff then that's what's 'the norm'.

TOP TIP: Smoothies. *We've all tried serving less-than-perfect fruit to our kids, only to be met with looks of disgust and shrieks of horror. One technique is to insist they eat it and learn that this is what fruit is supposed to look like. The other is to chuck it in a blender with some ice cubes or milk and serve up a fruit smoothie deluxe. They don't know what's in it, you've wasted nothing and your kids think you're Mary Poppins – success!*

Hopefully some of this has convinced you that you are not alone in finding the kitchen to be somewhat fraught at times, that there are things you can do to make it a happier place and that you will be able to cook something resembling a decent meal without too much fuss. With this newfound confidence and culinary nous let's move through into the dining room, and tuck in.

PART EIGHT

The Dining Room

Most houses have what estate agents would call a 'dining room', and what you or I would probably call a God-awful mess. The very word 'dining' implies an activity long-since abandoned in favour of snacking, grazing, picking and shovelling, and most of this ingesting occurs either in the kitchen, on a sofa or in a supermarket queue when we can't wait any longer. But with a little luck and some determination, we can revert that lost room full of children's toys, *AA* manuals and un-ironed shirts back into something used for dining. In the meantime . . .

Feeding time at the Zoo: The importance of family mealtimes

Once upon a time (a time that is very hard to pinpoint precisely but which occurred somewhere between the invention of tables and chairs and the emergence of the sixty-hour working week) many families in England ate their meals together: breakfast, lunch and dinner. Together.

And these days? Well, it's a brow-wrinklingly sad and shocking fact that an estimated twenty per cent of families in this country eat together once a week or less. *Once a week?* That's so awful and depressing that it makes you want to bang your head against the microwave before reaching for the frozen peas and feeling like an idiot with a swollen forehead. By looking at the way most people I know live and work, I assume that the other eighty per cent of families, while managing slightly more than the unimpressive 'once a week', are probably not eating together more than ten times per week or so, which is still lamentably seldom.

Of course, we all live insanely busy, stressful lives, and to propose that everyone should be home from work by six o'clock every evening to sit together around a large table, laughing merrily and devouring a delicious pot roast, is as ridiculous as suggesting we all stop worrying about our weight or remember to go to bed before our eyes go dry and we fall asleep in front of *Green Wing*. It just ain't gonna happen. What *can* happen is that we make much more of an effort to sit down as often as possible for meals as a family, and that we try to make it enjoyable. Yes, you were pissed off this morning because somebody put their muddy trainers on top of your new white bag, which is now marked and ruined, but now is not the time to bring it up.

OK – how exactly is this supposed to happen, when neither of us gets in from work or after-school clubs until 7 p.m., I work shifts and often leave before the kids are even up, and breakfast, if it happens, is whatever anyone can find and make edible during the mad rush to get out of the door to school and work, huh?

It's a good point, and probably applies to thousands of families up and down the country, but there are ways of eating more meals together, if you are prepared to make some changes and forgo the odd cappuccino and muffin in Costa in favour of Rice Crispies and chaos at home.

☆ **Find the time.** It's there. I promise you, if you really, *really* look, you will find the time to eat together more often. See p. 159 for ways of doing this.

☆ **Make changes.** If you have looked properly, and I mean *properly*, which includes your twenty-minute make-up sessions, his frequent after-work drinks, and your children's mind-bendingly slow getting-out-of-bed procedure, and you *still* cannot find any wasted time that could be allotted to the 'eating a meal together' section of the day, then you need to make serious changes. Maybe he needs to go to work earlier to come home for dinner with you all. Maybe you need to get your kids up ten minutes earlier to have the time for breakfast together. Maybe you need to be happy to wait until 7.30 p.m. to have dinner as a family. Something will have to give, or move, or change.

☆ **Weekend wonders.** If you are lucky enough not to have to work at the weekend, then being able to eat together at least six times a week shouldn't be beyond you. If you are unlucky enough to be working on the weekend, then see if there isn't something you could do about this.

☆ **Sunday lunch.** Making Sunday lunch (or Saturday, if that's the only day that works for your family) a ritual event where you all eat together in an unrushed way, while talking and laughing, can have a very positive effect on the whole family. Try it for a couple of weeks and see if it can become a habit.

☆ **Prioritise.** Most of the above points involve prioritisation. If, for you, being a family and putting in the work required to keep this chaotic unit together is worth a lot, then you will have to lower the priority of, say, meeting your friends for a drink three nights a week, or going for a run at breakfast-time. Nobody would suggest you need to forgo *every* evening out or early-morning jog, but sometimes it's worth a quick, 'Do I really *need* to do that, or could I be at home now with my family, and do it some other time?'

☆ **Enjoy mealtimes.** When I say eating together as a family, I mean 'in a fun, noisy, relaxed, laughter-filled way', not like a scene out of a pre-war boarding school. Think Dolmio adverts and you're on the right lines. Mealtimes should be fun, not frightening.

Bums on Seats: Table manners and other essentials

I am a huge stickler for manners. This is almost certainly the result of both of my parents carrying the Stickler for Manners gene, which showed itself by them making me say my pleases, and thank yous and, horror of horrors, insisting I *make eye contact* when greeting guests. The older I get the more of a stickler I am becoming: I am now almost obsessive about instilling some decent manners in my own flock of hooligans, and the dining room is one of my favourite haunts in this quest.

I'm not sure if manners really do maketh man – I am rather of the opinion that it's possessing a penis and having the ability to reside in a house for ten years and still not know where the whisks live that separates us from them – but they certainly help *a lot*. They also maketh children and women, by the way, and there's no better place to start establishing some civilised behaviour than at a table.

It is for this reason that there is a hand-written poster on the wall beside our kitchen table, bearing the following Rules:

Rules
1. Be polite.
2. When Mummy calls you go to the toilet, wash your hands and come down.
3. Sit up straight, but sit down at the table.
4. Don't spit or stick your tongue out.
5. Do not sing, hum or whistle.
6. Don't talk with your mouth full.
8. Say thank you to Mummy or Daddy before you start.
9. Do not get down from the table unless you have asked Mummy or Daddy and they have said 'yes'.
10. No elbows on the table.
11. Never say 'Yuk!'
12. No shouting.
13. No sitting on the high stools at the table.
14. Don't wave your hands about in the air.
15. Don't distract one another.
16. Don't get other people into trouble.
17. No sitting on the table.
18. No taking food off other people's plates and no putting

food on other people's plates (unless you are Mummy or Daddy).

19. No sitting on anything except the bench or chairs.
20. Don't spit your food out.

Careful readers will notice that No. 7 is missing. I'm not sure whether this is because my kids can't count properly, or whether they are so very, very clever that they have deliberately left a gap into which any clause required to win an argument can be inserted. I rather suspect the latter, and am constantly on my guard for any 'It doesn't say we can't hide peas in our belly buttons' type of cheek.

All of these rules have been created because whatever they refer to was either done or not done so many times that either my husband or I couldn't stand it any more. They are still frequently broken, but we can always refer to the list and threaten Bed with No Stories, which pulls everyone back into line. There have been minor attempts at revolt (No. 5 doesn't say you can't Kazoo at the table; No. 14 doesn't say you can't wave your hand about in front of your siblings' faces, and so on), but in general it has really worked a treat.

Do as I Say, Not as I Do. A busy mother's mantra

I am totally guilty of this in the Dining Room area, and I am not embarrassed or ashamed to admit it at all. This is because I know for a fact that every normal parent I have ever met is as guilty as I am, and has a whole host of naughty eating habits that they would tell their own kids off for. Yes, I do Bad Things.

Like what? Oh, how much time have you got? Like picking at food while I'm cooking it, thus ruining my appetite. Like eating far too fast and not chewing properly. Like often eating bits with my fingers because it's much more fun. Like talking with my mouth full, reaching across the table to get things, getting down from the table every thirty seconds to fetch something, and starting to clear the plates away before everyone has finished.

But before you chastise me for being a complete pig at the table, I have a perfectly good explanation, which any reasonably faulty, human, honest mother will identify with. Family mealtimes are almost always very hectic: there are a dozen things to be getting on with the moment they are finished, and sitting up straight, eating slowly, asking if your moody three-year-old could kindly pass the salt while ignoring the dramatic spillage that has occurred down the other end of the table is nearly impossible. Instead, we get it all over as quickly as we can, before tidying up after the event.

There are two schools of thought on this one: the first, that parents should always set a good example and to eat badly in front of children and then expect them to eat properly definitely classes as Bad Parenting. The second, that the life of a parent is tiring, stressful, relentless and thankless enough without ruling out finger-licking and eating straight out of the fridge for good measure. Here are some tips that might help:

- ☆ **Practise what you preach** at the dinner table as often as possible, but don't feel you have to be perfect all the time: occasionally talking with your mouth stuffed full of half-chewed pasta is absolutely fine and only shows you're human.
- ☆ **The all-seeing eye.** Most children observe a million times more than you might think by the way they loaf about looking bored. Beware the little eyes watching as you sneak in a square of chocolate ten minutes before dinner: they see you, and won't understand the mystifying rules of PMT. Try to be more subtle and you'll have less to explain later.
- ☆ **Chill out.** The list of 'Rules' above was written with a good deal of humour by the whole family (except Charlie, who was about one at the time and just wanted to smear mashed banana in his hair). Nobody is expected to stick to it all the time, and some rules are mainly there for laughs. Our kids know that, and I don't think they feel as though they are being brought up in a Victorian orphanage. If family mealtimes are an ordeal then something is seriously wrong – food is to be enjoyed, not endured, so do remember to laugh occasionally when your son

knocks his entire plate of food onto his sister's lap. It is *quite* funny, if you think about it.

Why Isn't Mummy Eating?

Fact 1: Many ladies have complicated issues with body image and food.
Fact 2: All mothers are ladies. (At least, they once *were* ladies, but are now exhausted, stretched and irritable forms of such beings, hence all the shouting and unladylike behaviour in the checkout queue. Be kind to them.)

Using basic logic, we can deduce from the above two facts that many mothers have issues with body image and food. There, I've said it, and by the sound reasoning above you can hopefully see that it's true.

The result of this is that in every city, street and household in the land, lots and lots of ladies are trying to change their body shape, either to make it thinner, curvier, firmer, or just 'more like that gorgeous actress I saw in that film last night.' It's really rather sad, when you think about it, that so much energy, money and time is wasted on a few rolls of subcutaneous fat, when there's the planet to save and people unintentionally starving all over the place, but there it is: women obsessing about muffin tops and bingo wings are everywhere.

Every mother I know has been on one weird and wonderful food programme or another at some point in her post-childbirth life, because the body she once inhabited has been replaced by something two dress-sizes larger and covered in a saggy outer shell of loose skin. This is fine if you live alone, or perhaps with a cat or a cactus collection, but when you are eating together as a family, any peculiar eating habits come sharply under the spotlight, because everyone can see what you are, or aren't, eating. Most children need *a lot* of food to keep them going through all their tree-climbing, growing, brain-using and sibling-bashing, so 'family food' needs to be wholesome, healthy and full of energy. When you are trying to shift a pound or two, or are about to go to a Legs,

Bums and Tums class at the gym, sitting down to a two-course, filling meal isn't really what you want to do. So you don't.

This is where the '*Why isn't Mummy eating?*' question arises, and it's a very tricky one to field. Do you say: 'Well, darling, it's because when Mummy sits in the bath and looks at her enormous wobbly thighs and her Michelin Man tummy, she feels like a beached whale and wants to drown herself', or do you plump for something more heartfelt, like: 'Because I'm fat! Fat! Fat! *Fat!* Now eat your dinner!'

All joking aside for a moment, the way you handle your own food fads and body issues is *critical* when you have kids, because the last thing you want to do is introduce the body issue before they discover it for themselves in the school changing room. What I do, if I'm just having vegetables while everyone else is tucking into the accompanying shepherds pie followed by bread pudding, is to be very logical and casual about it, and move the conversation on. Explanations that work include:

☆ I tasted a lot as I cooked, so I'm not very hungry any more.
☆ I had a very big lunch so I just want a small dinner. (Liar!)
☆ I've been sitting at my desk all day but you've been running about for hours and are growing like a sunflower, so you need much more than me!
☆ I'm going to meet a friend for dinner later. (Double liar!)

There are lots of other things you can say, which may also be true by the way, and my kids always accept any of these perfectly rational explanations very happily. I have the double problem that my husband is six foot five and can eat more food than anyone I've ever met without gaining an ounce, so there is a stark difference between what he consumes and what I do. This often leads to, 'But Daddy isn't growing either, and he eats lots'. This is easily explained by my replying, 'Yes, but Daddy's about three times bigger than me, and if I ate that much I would explode!' Lots of laughter and satisfaction all round, and we move on.

Yuk! I'm Not Eating That! Dealing with fussy eaters

If parents could pick and choose the characteristics of their children (and if you are reading this any time after about the year 2020 then they probably can, so please forgive my antiquated musings) then Fussy Eater would lie somewhere near Bad Sleeper and Tantrum Thrower. Fussy Eaters are a nightmare, but almost every family has at least one and it can affect the way the entire family eats.

Before I go into how to a) prevent this from developing, and b) solve it once it's set in, I should probably define my terms. By 'Fussy Eater' I do *not* mean a child who doesn't like broccoli. That's just ninety-nine per cent of children out there, and it's nothing to worry about. Neither do I mean a child who hates every breakfast cereal you offer except for *Sugar-Crunchy-Lard-Pops*™. This child is very smart, and knows how to piss you off. He actually rather likes healthy Bran Flakes, but knows that refusing them makes you cross, so continues with his game.

No, a true Fussy Eater won't eat at least fifty per cent of the food you offer him if it's not *exactly* as he likes it.

Let's take bread as a simple example. Surely he'll eat one slice of a humble loaf of bread? Well, white's OK, but not brown. Oh no, wait: *some* brown breads are OK, but not if they have those little *seed* thingies in them, and definitely *no crusts*. Righty-ho. Next up, vegetables. Peas: yes. Carrots: yes, but only if they are raw and cut into sticks. Slices are disgusting and will be hidden under a potato skin. Potatoes: baked, yes (but not the skin); boiled, never; roasted, yes (if cut into triangles, not slices). Broccoli: didn't you read what it says above? NO broccoli. Courgettes: eeeuugh! Are you trying to *poison* him? If he can't pronounce it, he certainly won't be eating it.

And so on. *That's* a Fussy Eater. As you can imagine, living with one of these is tantamount to being in purgatory, because every time you think you've cracked what it is he does and doesn't like, the blighter will change his mind and go off peas for the season. *Oooh, you little . . .*

So, how can you avoid finding yourself in such an unpleasant situation? Well, there are two methods – prevention and cure – and I strongly recommend the former. I know I said above that some kids are just *born* Fussy Eaters, and I stand by that having seen my second baby spit out anything with tomato in it from the age of four months unless it was precisely the same temperature as slightly-too-cold tea, but there is a lot you can do to stop this tendency from taking hold and giving you an ulcer:

☆ **Serve a large variety of foods** from an early age. Kids who only ever eat sausages, peas and potatoes will find it very hard to move onto such delights as curry, pâté and bean sprouts later on. Keeping their palette stimulated and their diet very varied makes them much more adventurous in the food department.

☆ **Think about why your child is refusing the food.** Is it because something in it tastes bad to her or she is allergic to it, or is she just testing the limits of your patience? If you think she *really* doesn't like it – and not everybody likes the same tastes – then leave it out of her diet for a while and find an alternative. Then try re-introducing it a few weeks later when the aversion may have passed. If she is just mucking about (e.g. the slices versus sticks example above, or eating only certain *kinds* of yoghurt) then I have found that using a 'don't be ridiculous, it's that or nothing' approach can work, because they eventually get hungry and eat anything they can.

☆ **Give an incentive.** The old 'Mmmm, it's *really yummy*!' trick doesn't work on any smart kid beyond the age of about three months. If a child thinks it's disgusting, then it's disgusting however much you smile as you eat it and rub your tummy with glee. If, however, you tell your F.E. that David Beckham loves drinking milk, then that could be the clincher.

☆ **Persist, persist, persist.** If my kids have started refusing certain foods that they liked perfectly well before and therefore just seem to be making fuss about, I carry on serving it every day for a while. After a week or two they realise Mummy isn't going to budge on this one, and get on with eating it again.

☆ **Rising to it: don't.** The less you react, the less successful their mission to irritate you or make a point is turning out, and the faster they will stop. If you pretend that it's neither here nor there whether they eat their potatoes, they will often finish them while you're not looking.

☆ **Talk about it.** If none of this is working, then have a chat about why they don't like so many foods. It could be something completely different, like being worried in case they drop spaghetti or peas down their front, or that the seeds in bread hurt their teeth (in which case a trip to the dentist is in order) or something they've read or heard somewhere else.

☆ **Serve smaller portions.** There's no point putting a mountain of mashed potato in front of a child who you know hates the stuff. Giving just a few spoonfuls is much better, as they are more likely to manage that amount and feel happy. Once you've cracked such a small helping you can start to increase it gradually.

☆ **Get them to suggest something else.** I don't mean this as a 'Well, *you* come up with something better then!' retort, but sometimes children can suggest all sorts of alternatives you hadn't thought of:

Gaby, mother of Liam, four:

Liam refused to eat peas or carrots for almost a year. I thought I had tried everything and was getting so desperate for him to eat easy-to-cook vegetables. He then suggested mashing the whole lot together and putting cheese on top, and he loves it! It looks disgusting, but I don't care if he eats it.

☆ **Pick 'n' mix.** This kind of meal often fools the most stubborn eaters into consuming rather a lot. Put lots of different foods on plates and in small bowls, and let them help themselves. Anything from grated cheese, cherry tomatoes, corn on the cob, chicken drumsticks, cups with breadsticks in, little bowls of pasta or couscous will do. Your kitchen will look like a Harvester, but that's the appeal for children: it looks more interesting and is more fun to eat than a meal handed to them on a plate.

☆ **Fry me a rainbow.** Actually, don't fry me anything, but grill or roast me a rainbow and I'll be happy. If their dinner has lots of (natural) colour in it, kids find it much more appealing, and it's healthier too. Yellow sweet corn, red tomatoes, green broccoli, orange peppers – try anything that looks vibrant and you might find yourself serving them seconds.

The Food Wars

There is a deeply rooted instinct in all parents, and I think possibly more so in mothers because we can breastfeed, to want to feed our children. Whether they are particularly hungry or not, whether they are clearly well-nourished or even overfed, we want them to eat: to nurture them, make them grow stronger and healthier and become better able to fend for themselves when they finally leave us alone to enjoy some uninterrupted gardening and jazz music. Or whatever we will do when we are bored, middle-aged and undersexed.

Children know this. They know it from birth, and, because they are cleverer than a very sly fox, they also know that this gives them a colossal amount of power over us. We want them to eat, so by refusing to eat they are causing us much anguish and pain.

Mothers are constantly telling other mothers how well their babies eat, how fast they are growing and how they physically cannot produce enough milk to satisfy the needs of their calcium-guzzling balls of baby-fat. This continues throughout the early years, and on into school, where the tallest, strongest-looking children are consistently praised for being so tall and strong-looking. You rarely hear, 'Hello darling – my, you're looking so pasty and small today', do you?

Children who refuse food are often doing no more than playing a power game with you, and going into battle with large helpings of filling food will almost certainly backfire. Much better to try and think of why this stand-off has occurred in the first place. (Are you still giving him enough attention? Is there some bullying happening at nursery or school? Does he really, *really* want the Power Ranger you have said no to?) Chances are if you play it cool and don't make a big issue out of it, he will soon tire of trying to annoy you, and start eating normally.

Small but perfectly formed

Not all children like eating. This sounds ridiculous to a grown woman who would happily eat two tubs of Häagen-Dazs and an entire Sunday roast for breakfast, and is regularly on some kind of fat-busting, bikini-wearing, stomach-shrinking diet or other, but it's true. There are kids out there for whom eating is less interesting than visiting Byzantine churches on Saturday afternoons when they could be at a friend's house playing Cover Me in Blankets and Jump on Me.

I have one of these kids. She has always been totally uninterested in food, could go for a whole day on nothing more than a few Shreddies and will almost never ask for something to eat. At the age of six she is still quite small and has a tiny frame with not an ounce of fat on her. But she does eat. She eats well, and regularly, and I have absolutely no worries about her at all. She just needs reminding that it's time for more fuel, and then she realises she's starving and eats like a horse. She is how she is, and forcing her to eat more than she wants or drawing attention to the issue would be a terrible idea that might result in big problems.

So if you have a child who doesn't seem to eat as much as you might think they need, or is not at all interested in food, don't worry. So long as they are getting some of all the food groups, still have three healthy meals a day and are roughly within the normal size range for kids their age, you probably just have a small one. If you have any concerns go to your doctor.

Eat your greens! How to get their daily five portions down the hatch

Unless you have been living in Outer Mongolia for the last two years, or watch no telly, read no newspapers and never eavesdrop in cafés, you will know that we are all supposed to be eating at least five potions of fruit or vegetables every day, according to the People Who Know. If we don't, and live on lattes and cigarettes instead, we will shrivel up, get scurvy, look really ugly after the age of forty and die young, so it's advice worth following. This advice goes for children too, although obviously three mummy-sized potions is equivalent to five kiddy ones, so don't worry if they're not quite fulfilling their quota. Scurvy is some way off yet if they're eating any at all.

This is nothing very new, in fact: children have been told to 'Eat Your Greens!' for decades, and today's young mange-tout munchers have it luckier than their predecessors, because the range and quality of fresh fruit and veg is really fabulous. No longer are bendy carrots and Granny Smiths the only options: these days a child can also refuse to eat bean sprouts, shiitake mushrooms, mangoes and passion fruit.

But however fresh, crunchy, tasty or ripe the food on offer, the age-old question of how to get kids to eat this stuff remains. Here are some ideas we have tried and have found to work:

☆ **Breakfast bounty.** Kids are often most hungry in the morning, having had nothing to eat for about twelve hours. Putting a large plate of colourful, delicious ripe fruit in front of them, *before* they get their hands on the horrid sugary cereal, is a great way to get them to eat almost all of their five portions in one go. After a few months, starting the day with fresh fruit becomes one of the best habits they will ever learn, which might just stick for life.

☆ **At dinner time, serve the vegetables first.** This is similar to the 'if they are hungry they will eat anything' theory above. Serving the vegetables on their own, as a starter, can really help with veggie-phobes. There's nothing else to eat yet, and veg can often look prettier served alone on a plate, which might help. If they know that the sooner the little green things are gone the sooner the chicken and noodles will arrive, the shovelling will begin and you can relax, knowing some vitamins have passed their lips today.

☆ **You choose.** This one worked a treat for all our children: we would give them a couple of pounds in the local market, or in the supermarket, and let them choose and buy their own vegetables. The joy of being able to spend money themselves and of examining all the weird colours, shapes and smells seemed to make all the difference: they ate sweet potato, pomegranate, runner beans and cucumbers with no fuss at all.

☆ **Let them prepare it.** Children almost always eat food they have made themselves much more readily than the stuff you plonk in front of them, so encourage all the peeling, chopping and presenting, and you will have your kids eating their greens and fruit more happily than you would have believed.

Dinner Time: But when?

One problem with eating as a family is that it requires you to all eat together, and this rather implies that you all have to be hungry at exactly the same time. If, like most people I know, you don't have exactly the same hunger patterns, amounts of exercise or metabolism as everyone else in your household, this can prove somewhat inconvenient.

To decide on a 'correct' time to eat meals is to force some people to eat when they are just not ready to, but it's something we all do. Typically this works out as breakfast at about 7.30 a.m., lunch at 1 p.m. and dinner with the kids at 5 or 6 p.m. and with partners who come home late at about 8 p.m. For mothers this is particularly tricky in the evening, because we are often feeding our kids at a different time from ourselves, but when we are actually quite hungry, and the temptation to pick at their dinner is almost impossible to resist:

You are almost certainly nodding vigorously at this point, thinking, 'Yes! I feel exactly the same way almost every evening!' And so do I, and most people I know. It's just one of those 'fitting every-body's lives into one day' problems that comes from living in a family, but there are ways of combating it without turning into a double-decker bus:

☆ **Eat when you are hungry.** Of the thousands of diets and 'eating plans' ever devised, the only ones that anyone ever says actually *work* in the long run are the ones where you eat when, and only when, you are hungry. If you're not ready for a meal, then don't feel you need to eat at that time. See if you can delay it by half an hour, or just feed the others and have some later.

☆ **Find your own pattern.** Everybody has a different eating pattern that suits them. I am about two hours before most people (I like lunch at 11.30 and dinner at 5.30), so I now eat this way and it fits in brilliantly with my kids, who also seem to be hungry around then. Of course we vary this occasionally when we are going to friends' houses or waiting for Daddy to come home, but in general it suits us well and we're sticking to it.

☆ **Be open about it.** Discussing this subject with your partner is really important. It's completely unreasonable for him to pressure you into eating dinner with him later than you'd like, just because he is home late, or for you to feel you must eat a big breakfast just because everyone else is. Say if you would rather eat with the kids, but still sit with him and have a drink and a chat while he eats his later on, and he should understand.

☆ **Do whatever it takes.** For some of us, self-control and reasoning just don't always work. If you are someone who simply cannot leave a plate of your children's food alone without picking something off it, then you'll need to find ways of not doing so in order to really enjoy your meal properly when it comes. Some of my friends resort to drastic measures, which quite surprised me:

Dawn, mother of Isabel, six, and Louis, three:
I eat chewing gum while I feed my kids so that I don't want to taste any of theirs.

Sue, mother of Robert, eight, Ben, five, and Bethany, two:
I do the washing up while they eat and squirt washing-up liquid over the bits they leave so that I don't finish them off. It's impossible not to eat it all otherwise.

If you simply cannot resist, then you might need to come up with something similar. It would be better not to waste so much food, of course, but we all know how hard it can be sometimes not to spoil our appetites with leftover fishfingers!

Bottoms Up! Alcohol and other delights . . .
We have a very peculiar attitude towards alcohol in this country. Before the age of ten it's often hidden away, out of sight – a slightly mythical substance that parents enjoy together after hours (or before hours during times of stress). The result is that when kids

finally reach the age of being able to get their grubby hands on some booze – usually around the age of twelve or so if they know the right people at school – they go completely mad over the stuff.

How you decide to discuss and use alcohol in your home is, of course, up to you. But the friends I have whose parents didn't make alcohol out to be something naughty or secretive were pretty sensible around it as teenagers and are now happy to let their own kids see them enjoying a glass with dinner.

We adopt this strategy at home too, and our kids regularly see us sitting down to a meal with a beer or a glass of wine, and don't seem that interested at all. If they want to taste we let them have a sip, and they almost always hate it. As babies they all loved to dip a finger in some wine and suck it, but this alcoholic phase seems to have passed now, thank goodness.

The best advice is probably something really dull, like: don't make alcohol out to be something special or prohibited, because this immediately makes it exciting and desirable; and don't drink a lot when your kids are around because a drunken parent is not pretty under any circumstances. Discourage your kids from smoking by telling them that it stinks, it kills you, it costs more money than they'll ever have and you can't run about or climb trees properly when your lungs are full of tar. They're free to do it when they're old enough, of course, if they want to be penniless, wheezing, stinking – and half dead. So far, no interest.

You Are *How* You Eat: Stop shovelling; start enjoying

Enjoying food and the act of eating – the smell, taste, texture, sensation of chewing, salivating and swallowing, savouring and appreciating – is something cultivated from birth. Sadly, eating on the move, grabbing a muffin for breakfast as we dash to work, chomping on characterless, loveless ready-meals in front of the telly and drinking to get as pissed as possible is how many of us eat and drink these days, and it does nothing to encourage healthy relationships with what we consume. Being relentlessly told by the media that food is the Devil's work because it makes us fat (like those wobbly people in *Heat*), but that not eating enough makes you anorexic (like those skeletons in *Heat*); that eating the wrong stuff makes us ill, but eating the right stuff can make us glow with health, get loads of sex and have a stylish living room, makes the whole subject of food and eating nothing more than a huge, calculated operation. Where's the fun in *that*?

The '*You Are What You Eat*' mentality really hasn't helped at all: I am *who* I am, *how* I think and *what* I choose to do for myself and for others, not what I eat. What we eat can make us more or less healthy, but that's about it. *Enjoying* what we eat can almost certainly make us happier, and worrying about what we're eating will make us miserable and stressed. Perhaps '*You Are HOW You Eat*' would be a better way to think.

Here are some suggestions:

☆ **Scares. Who cares?** With all the food and health scares thrown at us with alarming regularity, it's very hard not to pass some alarm on to our children. In the last few years alone we have had scares about eggs, salmon, prepared salads, beef and poultry, confusion over carbohydrates, bottled water and vitamin supplements, and excitement over oily fish, so-called superfoods and local organic produce. Try not to let your kids overhear any of these (usually unsubstantiated) fears and carry on feeding them a balanced, healthy diet.

☆ **Take the science out.** Food is becoming nothing more than a list of scientific facts and figures for kids. As young as five they learn about how much and what kinds of food they should be eating, and I've seen many a young girl passing on the pudding in favour of an apple because they are worried that they haven't had their 'five portions'. This is madness. They don't need to know all of this: they need to understand the link between healthy food and regular exercise and general health. That'll do for now.

☆ **Eat what you like.** Everyone's tastes and needs are different. If you force-feed your family with stuff they neither like nor want, you will make food into a real problem. Of course they need to get enough, and to eat a balanced diet, but try to offer a choice (let them serve themselves, or offer two or three types of veg, for example) and it will become more enjoyable for them.

☆ **Eat slowly.** Most of us don't. We shovel our food down the hatch as fast as we can, because we're always rushing to the next thing, be it the school run, a piano lesson or something on telly. Eating slowly is not only physically good for you (it makes food easier to digest and reduces that Noughties obsession: bloating), but it's also psychologically beneficial, as it means you are enjoying and savouring every mouthful, and getting pleasure from your food. It usually makes you eat less as well, if that's something you're keen on.

☆ **Never qualify people by their size or weight.** My mother does this *constantly*, and it made me see food as a huge threat because it could make me fat (and therefore, the implication was, bad, lazy, stupid and worthless). A person should be seen as either nice or not nice, not fat, thin or any other shape.

That's Entertainment: Reducing dinner-party stress . . .

September 2006

Gave a lovely dinner party last night – eight of us, lots of great conversation and laughs and too much wine . . . I just did some tapas and salads and got a massive basket of warm bread and some cold meats and cheeses, and managed to spend the whole evening in the dining room without getting up once – perfect. Have a bit of a hangover, though. . !

The dining room is not just where you and your noisy rabble eat, but also the place where any friends you may have picked up along the way occasionally sit to taste some of your less haphazard meals and to be 'entertained' by you. Oh dear: entertaining guests! What is it about these words that makes otherwise rational, intelligent people tremble, cook things they have never even heard of, try to tease napkins into exotic orchid shapes and apply far too much make-up? Why the big fuss?

The fact is that what constitutes 'entertaining' has changed a lot in recent years, thanks to an explosion of 'perfect home' magazines and television programmes that try to convince us that we can all look, cook and entertain like society princesses, and the bar has now been raised to impossible levels. It's no longer acceptable to open a bottle of plonk and serve up an overdone casserole. These days, nothing short of cordon bleu food with perfectly coordinating tableware, music and wines will do, along with a generous portion of stress, a new dress that doesn't quite fit or suit you, and frantic tidying and cleaning beforehand. What was once an enjoyable social activity is now a military operation taking days to prepare and weeks to recover from.

This is just ridiculous: entertaining should be *fun* for you and your guests, not exhausting and nerve-wracking. It's also a very important part of family life, as it's your friends who help to keep you sane, cheer you up and break up the breakfast, school, work, bath, bed, sleep routine. Seeing them outside of the school run or office means you can actually get to know *them*, as opposed to the frazzled 'parent' them, and that makes a friendship much stronger.

Luckily there are some very simple ways of cutting down the stress and ensuring that you don't have a heart attack before the main course . . .

☆ **What's the point?** Entertaining guests is easy if you remember one thing: the whole point is for all of you to have a good time, not to prove what a master chef, comedienne, hostess or wine-buff you are – all of these things are lovely additions to the evening, but basically all anyone who comes round for dinner wants is tasty food, some relaxed conversation and company, and not to have to clear up afterwards. That's it.

☆ **Keep it simple.** Bearing the above in mind, you can save your-self a lot of time and unnecessary effort by keeping things very simple: cook something easy that you have cooked many times before; don't worry about how clean your house is; wear something comfortable and relaxed; and just enjoy yourself.

Your guests will have a much better time than if you are fussing about with the CD player or trying to light hundreds of floating candles.

☆ **But not too simple!** I went to a BBQ recently where all we were offered to eat was burgers, white bread rolls (still in the packet) and some iceberg lettuce (also still in the bag). Nobody expects The Ivy, but *some* effort is appreciated!

☆ **Practice makes almost perfect.** When you have kids, jobs and shelves that need putting up, it's easy to put entertaining at the very bottom of your 'To Do' list. Don't. The less you do it, the more daunting it will become, and this becomes a vicious circle. Similarly, the more you entertain, the easier and more enjoyable it becomes, so pick up the phone and set a date before you develop the social skills of a hermit.

☆ **Prepare beforehand.** Things have a nasty way of going very wrong when you are flustered: if your guests are due in twenty minutes and you haven't had a shower, laid out any nibbles or decided what you're having for pudding yet, you are heading for Entertainment Catastrophe. Serve something you can prepare almost entirely the night before, or during the day (e.g. lasagne), or which can be thrown together at the last minute (e.g. pasta, a simple sauce you've prepared already and fresh basil), and leave yourself the last hour for getting ready, having a glass of wine and just finishing it off. *Et voilà*: one (apparently) very relaxed, competent hostess.

☆ **Get out of the kitchen.** When you finally do get people round for dinner, don't spend the entire evening in the kitchen! I've been to dinner parties like this, and I am always left wondering why they invited us at all, and didn't just open a restaurant instead. Your guests want to see *you*, not your food, so get yourself to the table and stay there as much as possible.

☆ **Check dietary requirements.** Serving up a succulent leg of lamb only to find that three of your guests are vegetarians is a bad start to the meal. Avoid this monumental error by checking beforehand and either making something especially for them, or having a vegetarian dish for everyone. Don't do what my mother used to, which was to say, 'Well, if they must be bloody vegetarians they can have some baked beans!'

☆ **Help yourselves.** I absolutely hate having my dinner handed to me on a plate. I like to serve myself, take what I fancy and not have to leave fifty per cent of the food on the plate, as this is very rude and embarrassing. It's very sociable and communal to let people help themselves, have seconds and generally relax as if they were at home. Try to make something where people have some choice of what, and how much, they have.

☆ **Timing.** This is a real problem when you have kids: if they are going to be present it means the evening will be quite hectic, noisy and not-at-all relaxed, but if they don't come it means the evening can't kick off until 8 p.m. at the earliest because they have to be put to bed or settled down with the babysitter. This means staying up and drinking until well after eleven, which makes the next two days unbearably tiring as kids have the mean habit of not realising Mummy was up late, and they still get up at 6 a.m.! It's a tricky one, but see if you can be honest with your friends and ask if they would like to come for a meal but not stay too late. They are often very pleased you suggested it, as they didn't want to stay up all night either, but did want to come and see you.

☆ **Be spontaneous.** The best way to reduce the fuss surrounding entertaining is not to plan too far ahead. Call your friend up and say, 'Hey, do you guys fancy coming round for a bite tomorrow night, or even tonight? At such short notice it's often easy to say yes and come. You just make much more of what you were going to have anyway and you all have a fun evening without any build-up or panic at all.

☆ **Pretend you are Italian.** Lashings of food, wine, laughter, kids, noise, and fun. Forget the perfectly sliced carrots, the stiff upper lip and the polite conversation: these guys know how to do it properly and we could all learn a thing or two from them. Now *that's* what I call entertainment!

After such a sumptuous feast we are more than ready to put our feet up and digest, in the comfort of the living room. The fire's on, so come and have a nice sit down.

PART NINE

The Living Room or Lounge

Well, which is it?

You are now entering one of the biggest and most important rooms in the house. Biggest, because it has to fit the sofa, a huge telly, a coffee table and a million books and magazines, and most important because it contains the aforementioned large, squishy item of furniture on which you can park your wobbly bottom. This is where you all relax, chill out, and stop rushing about like crazed ants. Some people call this chill-out zone a living room, others refer to it as a lounge, and which term is most appropriate depends on what you do – or intend to do – in there.

Where I grew up, it was called a lounge, which is odd because I rarely remember actually doing any 'lounging' in there. More likely I was bashing away at the poor piano for hours on end, dancing badly to *The Sound of Music* or watching something intellectually stimulating on the television, when really I wanted to slob out with some popcorn in front of *Grease*.

In our house now, I have made it my mission to do as much lounging about in this largish room as I possibly can, without having to be surgically removed from the sofa. Everything is arranged with such lack of activity in mind, from the position of the furniture to the contents of the bookshelves. Lying at forty-five degrees, clutching a glass of wine and having your feet tickled while watching a film or pretending to read last Sunday's paper is what I call proper lounging. No noise; no stress; no clutter; no kids.

And there it is: no kids. Of course they can come in as much as they like during the day, and there is a big toy basket in the corner as well as all of their videos and DVDs and some children's books. But it is basically a place for us to come and sit down, relax, read and be calm once the kids have gone to bed.

Sometimes, usually after I have come within eye-range of an interiors magazine showing vast loft apartments or light, airy Scandinavian dwellings, I am overcome by a desire to have a living room instead: a large, open-plan set-up where we all cook, eat, play, entertain, relax and watch telly together – while looking gorgeous, happy and not-at-all stressed out and irritable all the time, of course. A 'living' room.

But then I remember how wonderful it is to have separate rooms, to be able to walk away from the clutter and family-related chaos, and to escape. That, for me, is essential to my survival in our family, and what suits you may be quite different. Whatever our chosen roles for this room:

☆ **Decide which it is, and stick to it.** Whichever of the above options you choose, making sure that everybody in the family is clear and sticks to it is key, as it removes any overlap, confusion or 'Get that bloody tricycle out of this room *immediately*!' outbursts.

☆ **Kids in, or kids out?** An entirely personal choice, and there is no right answer. I sometimes feel I should ease off a bit and make the lounge more of a general 'everybody can hang out here' zone, but frankly that would lead to yet *another* room being invaded by small plastic objects, Playmobil pirate ships and pens with no lids. As most of the other rooms house lots of that, I don't feel too mean in trying to keep my evening sanctuary relatively child-free. There are still smudges from small hands and feet on the sofas, and small trains under it, but it takes less than five minutes to put everything back to right at the end of the day and . . . relax.

☆ **His or hers.** Aha – a tricky one. Like the main bedroom, this is a shared space, which means you both have the opportunity to 'make it yours'. If your taste in home furnishings, artwork and lighting match, then you are in luck. If, however, he likes black gloss on the walls, metal furniture and leather flooring, while you favour something a little more 'Laura Ashley meets *Sex and the City*' then there may be trouble ahead. If you are really lucky, like me, you marry somebody whose interest in interior design is zilch, because it gives you carte blanche to do whatever you like in there. Either way you really have to make sure each of you are happy with the décor and furnishing, because this is meant to be a place you can both relax and feel very comfortable in.

☆ **Mix and Match.** If you really can't agree on one unified style that you both like, then try doing what friends of mine have done: their lounge is an amazing mix of styles reflecting both his love of motorbikes and heavy rock (two vast motorbike tyres have been transformed into a unique coffee table and an electric guitar stands in the corner) and her passion for antiques and all things feminine (there's a gorgeous old French chandelier, white sofas and lacy cushions). What could have been a terrible clash has turned out to be an eclectic success, by using key pieces and keeping the bulk of it quite neutral and simple. He feels at home, she feels at home – all is well in the Robinson household because of clever compromise.

PG Tips: Should they *really* be watching that?

This week brought a classic example of this recurrent and increasingly frequent dilemma to our house. My daughter, who is eight, wants to watch *Pirates of the Caribbean – Dead Man's Chest*, because lots of the kids in her class have seen it and, understandably, she wants to 'fit in'. I think it is completely unsuitable for a child of her age (so does the British Board of Film Classification apparently, as it has given the film a 12A certificate) and I don't want her to see it.

My husband agrees with me (good – he's learning) but has thrown away his brownie points and parked his bum firmly on the family fence by saying that he also thinks she *should* see it because of the 'fitting in' issue. My two-year-old says: 'Pirates are my favourite – I *love* them!' and my six-year-old thinks the people in her sister's class are stupid anyway. Great – all in agreement then.

The problem with this kind of situation is that no matter what we decide to do, somebody will be upset. Do I want to make my daughter miserable by forbidding her to see something she really wants to see? Should I make myself miserable by abandoning my beliefs and allowing her to see images of spurting blood, walking skeletons and horny pirates? Should I tell my son that pirates are actually not his favourite – he means 'pilots'?

The problem arises because much of what is supposedly aimed at children contains scenes and images that many parents would consider to be utterly unsuitable. Television has become louder, faster, more hysterical, more aggressive and much, much more sexy than it was thirty years ago. Forget *Jackanory* and *Take Heart* – now it's a minefield of fast-paced special effects, gritty dramas and shouting presenters who often seem to be dressing for the adult male audience rather than the more junior viewers.

There is also the problem of massive advertising and promotion of films and programmes. Barely a double-decker bus drives by without the latest must-see film being thrust into kids' view; shops overflow with every imaginable type of film-promoting merchandise before a new release; there are film trailers on television, competitions on cereal boxes, and much more. With so much exposure it's no wonder kids want to be a part of it – even if they have little idea of what 'it' is.

It's very hard to decide what is suitable and what isn't, but one thing is sure: this kind of stand-off is only going to get more frequent the older your children get, and you had better arm yourself with some successful methods of reaching a satisfactory solution:

☆ **Get it off.** If you don't want your kids to watch music videos with barely clad ladies wiggling their arses and fondling their breasts then don't have this channel available on your TV.

☆ **Do your research.** How can you decide what's suitable if you don't know what's out there? Watching children's television occasionally is a must for all parents, because it's the only way you can be sure of what they're seeing. Things move very fast in this industry, and what was considered new and edgy one year will be outdated and slow the next. What you thought was a gentle cartoon with a simple storyline and positive message may turn out to involve mum-zapping aliens armed with death-rays. You may also be pleasantly surprised to find there is a lot of great stuff available for kids to watch – it's just a case of sorting the wheat from the truly awful chaff.

☆ **Use videos and DVDs instead of television.** There are, of course, programmes on *CBeebies* or Five's *Milkshake* that are all aimed at young children, so you should be able to sit them down and be confident that they're watching something appropriate and vaguely educational. Alas not: I still only like a small percentage of the programmes they show, and on commercial channels these are interspaced by whine-inducing adverts, which usually prompt an hour of, 'Mum, *please* can we have that little plastic pony thing that has plastic hair you can brush, like that little girl in the advert who looks so happy to be brushing some plastic hair on her plastic pony thing? Please?' To be 100 per cent sure what your kids are watching, get some DVDs they like and you approve of, and you can relax. Favourites in our house for pre-schoolers include *Kipper*, *The Hoobs*, *Fimbles* and – oh God – *Bob the* sodding *Builder*; and for the older girls *The Worst Witch* is going down a treat at the moment.

☆ **Always know what they're watching and keep an ear out.** If you think they are watching *Noddy* and you hear sounds of gunfire and screaming coming from the lounge then it's just possible that some nimble fingers may have changed channels. Having a look in every five minutes or so is a good idea anyway –

it satisfies younger children that you are still there, and means you can keep an eye on what older children are watching without looking like a policeman. My kids quite like it when I come and watch with them for a few minutes, and always start pointing things out to me.

☆ **Read the label.** If a film has a 15 certificate, then not only should this make you think twice about showing it to your seven-year-old, but it also provides you with the perfect reason why you are forbidding it. Look – it says so here!

☆ **Watch it first.** If you are not sure how suitable a film will be, make sure you have seen it before letting your kids watch it. One person's slap on the back is another's violent blood-fest. You watch; you decide.

☆ **Watch it together.** Sometimes it's impossible to tell how a child will react to something. Mine have sat through *Harry Potter* quite happily, but cried and had nightmares for days after watching *The Jungle Book*. If you are not sure, watch it with them. Oh, OK – *Piglet's Big Movie* is probably fine, but even that throws in the odd teary moment or two towards the end, so being there for comfort is a good idea.

☆ **See 'The Making of' first.** This is a great tip I learned from a friend. Many DVDs come with extra footage showing how the film was made. If kids know that the hideous skeletons are actually CGI creations or that their hero wasn't really dangling off a 500-foot cliff but was in a warehouse in LA with a green screen behind him and twenty people in the room, it can make the more terrifying scenes a lot more manageable.

☆ **Forget 'everybody else'.** No two children react in exactly the same way to what they see and hear, and knowing how developed and sensitive your own child's emotions are is crucial before you let them loose in front of a film. Where one child whoops and shrieks with delight as yet another head is blown/cut/ripped off, another needs several years of therapy to get over the shock. Sadness is another emotion that some children find very hard to handle, and this can be 'happy' sadness (Piglet is reunited with Pooh after a death-defying fall into a Heffalump's hole) as well as bog-standard sadness (Piglet is mauled by a herd of Heffalumps and only his tail remains). This last one didn't happen, by the way, you're right. Ignore 'everyone' and concentrate on your own offspring's sensibilities.

☆ **Give your reasons.** Just saying 'no' is very unhelpful and may make your child hate you even more. If you tell him he can't watch something, at least have the decency to say why. It has lots of sex in it; or there is far too much violence, blood, death and so on. If he knows you are not just being a boring old fart, and are actually trying to help him in your own irritating, un-cool way, he might not mind quite so much. Maybe . . .

☆ **Set a time limit.** Sometimes suggesting you wait a month or two and then reconsider whether a film is suitable can ease the pain a little. Bear in mind that 'a month' sounds like 'after the next ice age' to a child, so prepare for much anguish, despair and pleading, but then stick to your guns anyway.

It's very hard to control what your children watch on television, because the pressure they can put you under is enormous. When you've just had a terrible day at work, or your baby has been up all night again and you want to crawl into a hole and stay there for a week, giving up and letting them watch whatever they like just to keep them quiet seems like a good option. Most often it's not. Films and programmes for kids are not what they used to be, and it really is worth being a little bit careful about what gets the green light.

Switch it off! The television wars . . .

When I was a child we had a television. It was very small, and too high up, and you had to walk over to it and press a large, clunky button to change between one of the three available channels. As ITV was as good as banned ('mindless, hysterical rubbish!') there was, in effect, a choice between two channels.

Most of the time the screen would show a little girl, holding a guitar and a teddy bear (I think), with a noughts-and-crosses board behind her, and there would be an irritating *beeeeeeeep* noise for added entertainment. Sometimes we were treated to bright, wide stripes instead, still accompanied by the *beeeeeeep*. Then, unannounced and as if by magic, all would go quiet and black, and a large, orange number '2' would slowly be drawn on the screen. (My memory is rather sketchy, so it could have been green or blue. Bear with me.) There followed fifteen minutes of sheer joy: *The Flumps, Pigeon Street, Bod, Mr Ben* . . . there they all were, dancing, singing and doing funny walks across the little box in the corner. All too soon it was over, the *beeeeeep* returned and I went back to climb trees, conduct scientific experiments in the kitchen and annoy my brother instead.

But it was wonderful: simple, entertaining and harmless. In other words, perfect for children. Today it's a very different story: not only are there over a hundred channels to choose between, but most of what is aired is violent, loud, aggressive, sexually explicit or plain stupid, and many households have televisions in the kitchen, bedroom and children's rooms as well. Programming never stops, there is no '*beeeeeeep* – go outside and play' restriction any more, and many kids watch several hours a day with no parental supervision at all. And then everybody is surprised when kids have behavioural and learning problems, can't read or write and become obese. Hmmm, whatever could be causing these problems? It must be one of Life's Big Mysteries . . . now, what were we watching?

All joking aside for one small moment, it's a bloody tragedy that kids watch as much telly as they do, and that so much of it simply fills their head with crap. And it's only getting worse: BabyFirstTV is a cable channel recently launched in America that broadcasts programmes round the clock aimed at children aged six months to two years, and it may have hit these shores by the time this book goes to print . . . If something isn't done soon, natural selection will come into play and favour those humans with bigger bottoms to withstand all the sitting, stronger thumbs for using the remote-control and bigger eyes to take in all the images. We owe it to our children's children to stop this trend, and ensure future generations still have small bottoms, regular thumbs and round eyes. But how?

Here are some methods that I and some of my friends use:

☆ **Take control.** We can, and do, try to blame everything from the hectic nature of modern life to hidden fats in food to the evils of advertising for making our kids aggressive, obese and unable to hold a thought for more than three seconds, but at the end of the day the buck stops with *us* – the parents – to ensure they don't watch too much telly. An hour a week in fifteen-minute chunks is ample for a pre-schooler, and this needn't increase to more than a couple of hours a week for those under the age of ten or so. Yes, there is a lot of good stuff on, and it's fine to let them watch a bit of that and have their chill-out time. But then switch the bloody thing off and send your kids outside to run around, play football, make a den out of your newly washed sheets, pour sand into the watering can or anything else they find to do. Anything – *anything* – to get them using their imagination and getting some exercise.

☆ **Only have one television in the house.** Putting a television in a child's bedroom is a *bad, bad, BAD* idea. At least watching on the family TV set means they are still almost a part of the family, but shutting themselves away to watch hours of goodness knows what means cutting themselves off from you and the family, and that can't be a good thing. It's also almost impossible to control what is watched that way. Having an extra kids' TV in the play-room can work, but it does mean that it's always in sight so they are more likely to want to watch it instead of playing. Having one TV in the lounge means it's much easier to separate 'TV Time' from playing, eating or just hanging out together.

☆ **Restrict times when your kids can watch the TV**. Now that we can all watch telly twenty-four hours a day we need to find ways to restrict this potential viewing. Having 'TV time' is one way to attempt this. In our house we have a strict 'No TV before School' policy – it's hard enough getting out of the house as it is, without spending time in front of the box as well, and it's nicer to be all together as a family before we go our separate ways for the day. It also means there are never any rows about it: it's not an option, so they don't even ask. My kids watch most of their TV at the weekend after they have been busy doing ballet, tennis or whatever, and need a rest before the next whatever it is. Weekends are also the only times they watch a film, as they don't have to get up early the next day for school and it feels like a special treat that way.

☆ **Don't use the TV as a replacement nanny.** At least, not too often: every mother I know, including my good self, sometimes lets her kids watch telly so that she can prepare their dinner in relative peace. That's fine. In fact, this is one of the best times for them to watch as you can't really play with them while you're peeling potatoes, and they can calm down before their meal. Using the telly as a way of getting rid of them so you can read *Grazia*, file your nails or chat to your best mate is not fine: it's called being neglectful.

☆ **Switch it off!** Sometimes you just have to. They will hate it, but press that red button you must, before suggesting something more interesting, active or imaginative for them to be doing.

Setting the boundaries for television watching is something I find very hard, because it feels horribly hypocritical: if I'm really honest, I could spend most of my waking life watching films. It's my favourite, favourite thing, and I suspect it's the same story for my kids. It's made worse by the fact that I watch about three films every week on average, plus quite a lot of the news, the occasional documentary that has managed not to be ruined by deep, breathy voiceover, and quite a lot of comedy. Oh, and some complete shit as well, but that's essential if I'm to feel human at all. All in all, it's about ten times what my children watch, so telling them to go out and play when they've just watched ten minutes of *The Hoobs* seems unfair.

And maybe it is, but you know what? Life *is* unfair! Of course they can watch more as they get older, but for now, while they are young, less *is* more. Go on – outside with you, and play!

On the Couch: When counselling can help

Some of you will already have decided that this chapter is not for you. Counselling? You? Talk to some beardy weirdo about your first sexual experiences and why you find it hard to turn left at traffic lights? I don't think so.

Well, maybe you *don't* think so, but maybe also, if you stopped to consider the possible pros, you might decide it's not always such a ridiculous idea after all.

The problem with the word 'counselling' is the images many of us associate with it: it's for really screwed-up people who can't cope with everyday life, who are in the middle of a nervous breakdown, who were made to eat curly kale as a child or whose paranoia would make Woody Allen look unnaturally self-assured. This image may have been reasonably accurate many years ago, but now it's not considered strange, freaky or American to visit a counsellor for a huge range of conditions, from panic attacks to postnatal depression to simply needing to talk to somebody who isn't related to you.

I have had counselling of one kind or another several times during my adult life, and it has led me to conclude one thing: it is fantastically useful, and far, far more people should try it. Not forever, or even because they really need it, but just occasionally during periods when things seem a little trying; when life isn't as manageable, rosy or enjoyable as it could be.

Here are some things you may or may not have thought of, but perhaps you could bear them in mind next time a family issue concerns you:

☆ **All on the couch.** Counselling isn't reserved for adults on their own: there's family counselling, marriage counselling and child counselling, all of which can result in a huge improvement in life on the home front when things get fraught or stressful.

☆ **What's to lose?** If you are having problems in your marriage, or you are very concerned about the behaviour of one of your children, and you have tried as hard as you can to sort it out yourself to no avail, then it would be more sensible to seek professional help and advice rather than letting it get worse until it's possibly unfixable.

☆ **A session in time saves nine.** The earlier you can spot a problem and set about trying to put it right, the better. In your marriage this means being very aware of any niggles and disagreements, and making a mental note of them and how much they bother you. If you feel they are growing too big despite your efforts to talk about them and get over them, why not consider getting a neutral third party to wade through the 'I said, you said' and suggest ways to improve things before they get out of hand?

☆ **Kids.** With kids you need a similar level of observation, without becoming neurotic (all kids have weird traits and foul moods at various stages – it doesn't mean they have a 'problem'). Be aware of when your child might benefit from talking to somebody who isn't his Mum, Dad, brother, teacher or best friend; somebody who will never tell and never laugh at them. Several children I know would benefit enormously from this kind of 'therapy'.

☆ **Ignore everyone else.** I would say this, of course, but you should never feel that you are weak because you have counselling. It is those who refuse to even consider the idea who are really weak, because they can't cope with the fact that they may not be able to manage everything all by themselves. Nobody has a problem with going to a doctor if they have a persistent headache, so why not go to a psychologist if you have a persistent problem in your family? If you think it would help you or somebody in your family, then you go right ahead and get some help. For all you know half the inhabitants of your street are seeing a shrink, but nobody admits to it!

☆ **Family maintenance, not repair.** I know of couples that visit a marriage counsellor for a few months every year, just to keep things under review and working well. There are no problems in the marriage at all, and the idea is just to keep it that way. Sounds sensible to me.

So there you are. Don't knock counselling – it's usually the ones who do who end up needing it. Find a couch that feels comfortable and get talking. It's only words, but just getting them out can make the difference between the walls staying up or crashing down.

Space Rage: Sharing your chill-out zone

Assuming that this room, whatever you decide to call it, is used at some time or other for hanging out and relaxing, then you need to find some way that you can all do this together. When the children are very young this isn't a problem: they are in bed before you can even think about relaxing, and the only person you have to share the chill-out zone with is your partner.

Oh, well that's all right then – I only have to share my space with the biggest, heaviest, most-likely-to-fart-and-want-to-watch-football person in the house. How hard can that be? Well, very, if you do it for a long time.

The evidence for this 'stepping on toes and invading other people's space' is partly seen in a new kind of rage being reported in homes across the country: remote-control rage. This is exactly as it suggests: he wants *Cities at War*; you want *How to Have a Small Bottom and a Lovely House* (they're working on it, I'm sure).

This lack of personal space and an inability just to do what you want can spill into what you do together of an evening (go out, have friends round, watch a film, go to bed early for a three-hour shag-a-thon), and agreeing on what you want to do can become problematic after a number of years together. This can all lead to Space Rage, where you don't feel you have any say, space to breathe or time to be alone and undisturbed.

When the kids start staying up late enough to encroach on your relaxation time then Space Rage can really get interesting, with more mutually exclusive desires than you get in the average toddler group: *I want to watch telly*; *well I want to read the paper*; *but I have been waiting all day to listen to my new CD*; *that's not fair – I asked yesterday if I could listen to mine* . . . And so on and on and on. By this stage I have reached for a second glass of wine and some ear plugs and am heading for some peace upstairs.

There are ways of avoiding such Space Rage. They don't always work – that would be far too easy! – but they are worth a try, in a very diplomatic 'we all have to live together so let's all try to get along' kind of way. It's that or each man for himself, but that leads to a bloodbath, which we're hoping to avoid . . .

- ☆ **Vote on it.** If lots of you are all in the same room and can't agree on what to do/watch/listen to then put it to the family vote. If Daddy says he gets an extra vote for being the biggest, oldest or most hairy he is immediately disqualified and has no input whatsoever.
- ☆ **Take turns.** Monday night is Mummy's, Tuesday is Child A's, Wednesday is Daddy's, Thursday is Mummy's again (I know I've had a go, but I tidy the room the most, so I get two), Friday is Child B's, and so on. If there are no kids to consider then just alternate your evenings. I know this can all sound a bit silly, but if you *really* can't agree then you'll have to resort to such pettiness.
- ☆ **Make a watershed.** This is essential when your children start staying up a little later. You and your partner *need* some time alone to be a couple, instead of Mum and Dad, and kids need to understand this. We have an eight o'clock watershed at the moment, though this will gradually become later, I'm sure. After that time the living room is an adults-only area except on rare occasions such as when *Strictly Come Dancing* is on (a favourite with our little dancers), or if we have friends round with their kids too.
- ☆ **'Everybody needs a place to think.'** Too often, the value of being able to stop, be quiet and just *think* is hugely underestimated. It's all go, go, go, and not enough stop, stop, think. Everybody needs time to mull over, digest and ponder every so often, and the living room is usually the place where this happens as it's where you collapse at the end of the day. Communal pondering is also quite fun, in a 'we love each other enough to sit in a room

saying nothing for hours' kind of way. Who needs the telly, music or games of Jenga when you can just *chill* for an hour? Set aside one evening a week for such inactivity and ask anyone who needs to make a noise or 'do' anything to go elsewhere.

☆ **Get over it.** If you live in a family you have to get over the fact that you want your own space all of the time. It just ain't gonna happen like that any more. The more you hate your lack of personal space and choice, the more you resent the people who have taken it from you, and this negativity reverberates throughout the whole family. Accept it, make times when you have the living room to yourself, and learn to like it the way it is now. It's that or a single bedsit . . .

Sharing a space is tricky at the best of times, but living in a family can feel like permanent camping – you can't move for bumping into somebody, and getting your *own* space or doing what *you* want has to be planned around everyone else's wants and needs. You'll find a way, but don't worry if it seems a bit of a struggle – it's just family life, and it's a damned good one, even with all the glitches!

If all of this lounging has left you wanting to romp about a bit and have some fun, then let's make our way to the back of the house, and check out the playroom. There's a pram just to your left as you go in, and there's sometimes a baby sleeping in it, so mind how you go . . .

PART TEN

The Playroom

I hope you're ready for this – if you thought the kitchen was in a state, then this room will raise *both* your eyebrows. I do *try* and keep their toys organised, but it's like trying to keep water in a sieve: the mess just keeps on coming as fast as I can tidy it. Still, perhaps there should be a room like this in every house: where kids can be kids, and there are no grown-up 'tidy' rules to comply with. A real 'play' room.

I'm not assuming for a moment that you have a designated playroom, by the way – we don't, though I wish we did – but many people do, and the sections found in this room will deal with all things 'play' and activity related. Mind your feet, and let's take a look at some of the debris . . .

Do we really *need* all of these toys?

If your children's playroom looks like most of the ones I see regularly when collecting my children from their friends' houses, then the answer is almost certainly 'No'. Most resemble a Toys "R" Us catalogue, with shelves upon shelves of brightly coloured plastic, wooden, electrical, mechanical and truly amazing-looking toys and games, in various states of disuse and repair. Occasionally this vast collection is neatly ordered into boxes labelled 'Lego', 'Dressing up', 'Art' and so on, but more usually there is a 'post large explosion' feel to the place, and it's impossible to see more than two square feet of floor space for all the dolls, keyboards, paper, swords, miniature kitchen equipment and construction tools.

If you've never spent more than two minutes watching children play, then all of this will sound wonderful – such choice! So many things to play with! But no. Stay a while longer and watch what really happens in there: nine times out of ten, a toy is taken out, looked at and occasionally played with, and than abandoned in favour of Exciting and Expensive Toy Number Two. This is soon replaced by Expensive Toy Number Three, and so on, until the shelves are nearly empty and the floor looks likes a jumble sale. Almost nothing has actually been played with and the kids still manage to look bored and argue over who gets to play with what.

I have frequent 'Oh! What is the world coming to?' conversations with many of my mother and nanny friends, not all of whom are over fifty and remember the Good Old Days of hoop and stick and the occasional thrashing with a hard slipper, but young women for whom the words Tiny Tears and Rubik's Cube still mean something. There is a strong consensus that most kids these days have far too much but don't seem to get any *pleasure* out of most of it. Trying not to become too misty-eyed, we reflect on long afternoons playing happily with one doll and some hand-made clothes, or digging mud holes at the bottom of the garden before setting off on adventures into the Amazon rainforest with a knotted handkerchief full of bits of bread and biscuits nicked while Mum wasn't looking.

Today, give a ten-year-old girl one doll, a cardboard box and some old fabric and she will look at you as though you are trying to torture her. 'Is that *it*? What am I supposed to do with *that*?' is likely to be the reaction.

I'm not quite sure why kids have so many toys these days. Is it because there is so much more choice, so that owning one bouncy ball and some Plasticine no longer cuts it in the playground? Or perhaps it's just because we can afford them, thanks to many of today's parents having considerably more expendable cash than their parents did. Is it because credit is so darned easy to obtain and we have lost the Save for a Rainy Day ethic? Maybe there's more pressure to Keep Up with All the Little Joneses, who have the latest gadgets and computer games before we have even heard of them? I often wonder whether buying hundreds of toys for children is actually for *their* benefit at all, or rather because we want to show our friends that we have enough money but not enough sense.

Whatever the reason, the effects on children of such lavish – but fun – consumerism are clear: it makes them less able to concentrate because there's so much choice, less appreciative of what they have, and more dissatisfied. Well done us!

It is very hard to break this mould: short of emigrating to the Back of Beyond, you will have to accept that your kids will see things and want things, and very quickly equate obtaining these things with happiness. This false reasoning sticks for life (I still regularly convince myself that having those shoes/that coat/that matching stationery would make me feel better – and they would for about two hours until I realised I was now £40 poorer and really didn't need them after all!) and the longer we can prolong the onset the better. But how?

☆ **Just say NO.** Ooooh, this is the hardest one, because you know it's the right thing to say but you still break into a sweat when you remember how your Mum refused to buy you a Cabbage Patch Doll (like everyone else). You were a laughing stock for a term. Fear not: there will be tears, but if you explain why not (somewhat sadly I really do go through the whole 'I don't want to spoil you, you don't need it, and it's best you get used to not having everything you want', and I think they do understand, despite the moans) then most 'essential for my happiness and cool rating' items are forgotten about quite quickly.

☆ **Recycle toys.** By this I don't mean put them in those big black and blue bins most people have outside their front door, which are emptied noisily once a fortnight but help to save the planet. I just mean have a rotation system, where some toys are out and can be played with and others are packed away somewhere. After a month or so, swap them around, and what seemed soooo boring last season suddenly has an air of excitement and novelty. It takes some discipline and organisation, but if you can put your Anal Mother hat on you'll manage.

☆ **Join a toy library.** This applies mainly if you have pre-school children, as most of the stuff available would be scoffed at by 'cool' five-year-olds. You can find yourself working your way through a collection of excellent, if slightly broken and occasionally chewed, toys and games that would have cost you a fortune to buy, and which you give back just as they start to become old hat. Your house isn't cluttered and your children think you are the kindest mum the world because you give them new things every three weeks. Suckers! Call 0207 255 4600 for your nearest one.

☆ **Be ruthless.** Sometimes adopting a hard-nosed attitude to children's toys works wonders. Take anything they haven't played with for a year to a charity shop and throw away or recycle anything that is broken or has missing pieces. If you do it while your children aren't there you will save yourself a lot of arguing. 'But I love that ripped, slightly mouldy, never-played-with grubby thing. You can't get rid of that!' Oh yes you can, and you must if your kids aren't to drown in unnecessary junk. Family heirlooms and 'special toys' should be stored for the next generation, of course. There's having a clear-out, which is good, and selling your Dad's vintage Tonka Trucks for a quid or two, which should be a criminal offence.

☆ **Swap toys.** Swallow that pride and ask your friends if they would be up for lending you their Mechano for a week in return for a go with your kids' Space Hoppers or something. Most of the time they will be only too happy to get rid of it for a while and everyone's a winner.

'Mum, I'm *bored*!' Oh Help

Following directly on from the section above is this one. The words 'I'm bored' cause alarming reactions in most parents, ranging from blood-curdling rage and energetic arm-waving to despair and tears. This is not because we are uncaring, mean or hysterical beings, but because those two words are usually uttered by children who are surrounded by enough potential for fun, interest and activity to keep half the children of the world occupied for a year.

There are several common replies to the dreaded 'I'm bored':

1. That's ridiculous: how can you be bored? Go and find something to do!
2. When I was little I only had some pieces of coal and a rusty nail to play with and I was never bored. Go and find something to do!
3. Only boring people are bored. Go and find something to do!

This last one is particularly effective, because it's quite true in general, and I think kids sense this but don't want to acknowledge that it's *they* who are being boring, not their Awful Boring Life. The other retorts are usually given because Mummy or Daddy are busy doing some hideously uninteresting yet essential chore at the time, and they would give their right arm to be bored for ten minutes instead of making dinner, filling in an insurance claim or writing cheques for school trips and recorder lessons.

I happen to think that boredom is an essential childhood experience: it's during periods of not knowing what to do other than pick their scabs, chew on some snot or see if they can put their leg above their head without farting that children start to free their minds of all the daily routines and pressures, and the constant stream of information, questioning and activities. It is during times of so-called 'boredom' that, if left to work through it, children start to use something so neglected and underrated these days that many of them don't have much left any more: their imagination.

I have good evidence to support this stained armchair theory of child psychological development. Actually it's perhaps not what scientists would class as 'good evidence', but it's what I've got, and most scientists fudge their results anyway and we believe them, so here goes: When we go on holiday, we don't pack any toys. Instead, we bring some blank paper, pens, scissors, glue and Sellotape.

For the first day or two our guinea pigs are often restless, and the B-word crops up whenever we are not feeding them or buying them tourist tat. But after this initial period something magical happens: they start to play beautifully with the simple things they have to hand. They stop arguing over who has which irritating musical toy, stop looking as though all the woe, sadness and misery of the world had come to rest on their slumped shoulders, and enter a new world of creativity and imagination. Stones become little people and piles of leaves and grass their homes. Paper is fashioned into clothing, restaurant order sheets, aeroplanes, diaries, wobbly boats, fans and trumpets. They invent new games simply by lying on their backs and using various cracks on the ceiling as prompts. Most of what they come up with is beyond anything we boring, unimaginative adults could understand, and that's why it's so special. It's a kid thing.

So if you think your child is constantly bored because you haven't bought him enough toys to fill a toyshop, then rest your weary credit card and consider this: it's probably all this stuff that is making him restless and unsure of what to do next. Go back to basics and see what happens – if it's a disaster and the situation worsens then please accept my apologies. Perhaps my kids are just weird, and a visit to your nearest toy department is in order.

When Push comes to Shove

Once upon a time, children went to school, learned some stuff and became a little older. If they picked up something useful on their way into adulthood then it was three cheers all round and who's a clever boy then – here, have a job for life and a house you can afford (lucky bastard!).

These days, in what is generally accepted to be England's ever-expanding middle class (and also in the class above, but I don't think I know anyone in such high echelons of British society, so I have only dog-eared editions of *Tatler* in the dentist's waiting room to go on), growing up is a very different affair. Children are required to absorb knowledge like the kind of kitchen roll that allegedly soaks up about five litres of blue fluid in one sheet. They must become proficient not only in our national sports of Bad Cricket, Bad Tennis and Bad Rugby (sorry!) but also in music, art and languages, and succeed at all the things their parents failed at.

Children must have their progress monitored and tested with such frequency as to reduce even the most self-confident child to a gibbering wreck, and, when their time is up eighteen years after being signed up for the best school mortgages can buy, anything short of a Cambridge Music Scholarship, a gold medal in the National Junior Sporting Show-Offs Championship and the ability to write poetry in perfect French is a sign of delinquency and laziness. Worse still, it means the child's parents have been slacking, and that's the crux.

Pushy parents. Ugh. You know some, I know some – Hell, maybe one or both of us even *are* some. Pushy parents are not simply those who take their two-year-old to music and gymnastics classes, who spend every spare minute of an already crammed weekend ferrying their kids from ballet lesson to choir practice to drama club. Such dedication in itself is not what I class as Pushy, if the kids genuinely want to do all of this extra-curricular activity. (I know I did, and I'm glad I had the opportunity.) Such enthusiastic, Dedicated Parents only turn into Pushy Parents when they talk about it. Loudly. In front of you, and in such a way as to pretend that they're not really that fussed at all about whether Clemency passes her Grade Three tap-dancing tomorrow, or that Alfie's Saturday football practice clashes with his pottery, because it's OK – he can move pottery to immediately after his trombone lesson on a Tuesday evening. (You know Tuesday evening – the one where you lie on the sofa reading a good book and don't take your kids to any educational events whatsoever. Oh, bad, bad you.)

The difference between a Pushy Parent and a Dedicated one lies in motivation: if you do all of this for *your child*, because he loves football and playing it makes him as happy as a hippo in a bath of warm mud, then go! Stand on the sidelines on dark winter afternoons with other freezing, dedicated parents – it's your duty, and he'll thank you for it. But if *you* wanted to be a ballet dancer when you were a girl, or still wish you could tread the boards of the local theatre, then don't live out *your* fantasy through your child. Many are the little girls trussed up in tutus or driven to cold church halls to be a Girl in Market Scene for an afternoon, because Mummy wanted to do it. This is just mean and really quite juvenile, and she won't thank you for it.

Another dreadful but common reason for making children screech through that extra violin practice is to get them a place at their parents' desired school. There's nothing like a music scholarship to ease the financial strain and a few extra private maths classes should make that entrance exam a lot easier. Poor little things. (More about school on page 262).

As most of us never stop to consider, because we'd be a bit sad and geeky if we did, the word education comes from the Latin *educare*, meaning 'to lead out'. It's not the stuffing of information and skills *into* the kids that's important, although a certain amount of that is fairly useful of course, but the drawing out and developing of whatever is there already, be that musical ability, a gift for art and creativity, or a natural tendency to take things apart and put them back together again. Which leads us neatly on to . . .

Talent Spotting: Finding your own Picasso, Mozart or Shakespeare

You should know by now that I am not big on pushy parenting at all, so this is absolutely not about throwing your child into the nearest drama group, ballet class or modelling agency and hoping that they will be spotted by a talent scout and whisked away into the limelight. Rather, it is to point out that if we can take a step back as parents and observe what each one of our children enjoys doing, or seems *naturally* good at, we can help to nurture these talents without trying to force something upon them. This sounds very easy, but actually very few parents are any good at it, and they just can't resist the urge to encourage or praise something which their child, for whatever reason, has no aptitude for or interest in at all.

It is a big mistake to treat all of our children the same. Equally, yes, but not the same. I think the key to really excellent, sensitive parenting is to observe and listen to every child, notice what it is that makes each one tick and treat them accordingly. Some kids like activities that are very logical, with a clear purpose and outcome, such as puzzles, drawing something or reading. Others respond much better to inventing something out of random objects, thinking of unusual ways of solving puzzles or playing imagination games. The two ways of thinking are completely different, and neither is 'better' nor 'worse' than the other. They are just different and instinctive to each person.

Some kids do well at school because they like learning and repeating information, as required in most schools. Others hate school and do badly because their talents lie outside the classroom, dealing with people or being very freely creative. This is often a problem for them, as they can be labelled stupid, lazy or naughty, but actually it's just that they think in a different way, and need some other way of learning.

Here's an example from my own children. If I give them a piece of paper and some pencils and suggest they draw a house, one will look very worried for a while, as she wonders how to draw a house 'correctly', before setting about trying to draw the most symmetrical, picture-perfect house she can. She will then decide she hates it and screw the paper up. The other will have a fantastic time ripping up the sheet of paper and modelling all the bits into a wacky, wonky, completely unique 3D house, complete with a pencil sticking out of the top as a chimney, and will be very proud of it. This is a perfect example of how they think and act completely differently, and we have to find things that such unique characters can enjoy and learn from. It's a little difficult at times!

Every child has their own individual talent, and it is an observant, selfless and open-minded parent who can truly spot this, accept it, and put in the hours required to help it develop. If you can avoid thrusting your own wants and desires for your children onto them, and just watch and see what kind of learners and players they are, you will be able to encourage their natural talent, and this will make for a very happy, and possibly very successful, adult.

The talent is there – our job is to spot it and nurture it. Now, if I can just work out whether my three-year-old son is destroying my radio because he's a budding engineer or because he is a complete pain in the neck . . .

WWW Dot: Surfing the World Wide Worry

Just when parenting looks like it might be getting a little easier thanks to magnetic travel games and no-spill cups, something terrifying comes along that threatens to undermine the very core of family life and signal the end of innocence and decent conversation forever. Like the Internet. OK, this is perhaps overstating things a trifle, but using home computers and the Internet is so normal in almost every family now, that even saying 'home computers' makes me sound like an old woman who is still struggling with the switch to metric.

Obviously the Internet is an absolutely wonderful, almost incredible and fantastically useful thing, and it has made much of our lives easier: booking a holiday, checking store opening times, buying just about anything you care to mention or dream about are all just a few clicks away. For kids the possibilities for learning and information-gathering are also almost limitless: school projects these days look more like conference presentations than the scrappy folders we used to hand in, complete with gallons of Tipp-Ex and bits of badly photocopied pictures of Roman ruins we had spent hours tracking down in the local library, and which were now coming unstuck.

There are websites for children which are so well-designed, user-friendly, crammed with information and fun for them to use, that teachers must be quaking in their sturdy shoes. How can they possibly make their lessons even one-tenth as exciting, fun or up-to-date? Give it ten years and children will be learning about these strange things called 'teachers' in their Internet history lessons.

Yes, the Internet is fantastically useful and positive for children for the most part, so www.thankyou.com. But if ever a sword were double-edged, and very, very sharp, it's this one. The potential downsides of children using the Internet are so terrifying that you'll be on that computer surfing for 'Anti Anything Which Will Damage or Shock My Child' software before you've had time to read to the bottom of the next . . . Hey! Hang on – don't go away yet. I haven't even started.

The trouble all stems from the fact that the Internet Revolution, as journalists like to call it, happened so bloody fast. One year we were booking holidays in stuffy high-street travel agents, spending entire weekends trying to find somewhere that stocked a kitchen sink in the correct style to fit with the rest of the house, queuing endlessly for the library microfiche to find one sodding piece of information for an article we had to write, and failing to help our kids with their geography homework because we couldn't remember whether it was a *shaduf* or a *wadi* that Ethiopians use to draw water out of the ground. The next year it was click, click, click and the holiday was booked, sink bought, and the rest of the information found within an hour. Miraculous.

Unfortunately, though, this kind of high-speed change brings lots of equally speedy problems, and most of these troubles are caused because there are lots of sick bastards out there, and also because the English language is full to bursting with innuendo. Thus it happens that letting your child happily search for the origin of 'hot chocolate' will throw up images of hard-core, black lesbian sex, and something as innocent as 'I love horses' will neatly illustrate how abused Polish girls manage to copulate with their equine friends. All very disturbing to a young mind, and certainly nothing that you could go any way to explaining or eradicating. When it comes to naughty things, once seen or read is never forgotten.

So the Internet is both good and bad for children, but what can be done to leave the good and remove the bad? Well, quite a lot:

☆ **Don't let your child have Internet access in their room.** Most of my friends have a family computer that their children can use. If it's in a room where you are, so much the better; but if not, like for us, you'll just need to keep popping in every so often to check there's nothing dodgy going on.
☆ **Buy some software that can control and limit accessibility** to websites you would rather they didn't visit. A quick search on the, er, Internet will direct you to many. Oh the irony . . .
☆ **Establish clear rules and explain why they are in place.** I was shocked to find my daughter typing in her name, address and telephone number to sign up to some Funky Girls Club or other, when she hadn't asked and just assumed it would be OK as it was on a pretty-looking website I had let her use. When I explained the idea of people not always being who they say they are, she was pretty stunned and hasn't done it since.
☆ **Time out.** Setting a maximum computer time of half an hour is very sensible for kids up to the age of ten or so – it's enough for

their eyes to handle, and it's usually after this time that more adventurous surfing starts. Anyway, they should be outside getting covered in dirt or ruining your flowerbeds, not sitting in front of a screen.

'Can I go to Tom's house?' The joy, and hell, of 'playdates'

When children start school they acquire lots of clobber including book bags, PE kits, drink bottles, and, most importantly, friends. (If they haven't got any friends after a term or so, you might want to make some enquiries and see if your child smells bad or something.)

Assuming that they do acquire these nit-ridden accessories, then very soon a new after-school event will present itself, ensuring that you never have an afternoon to yourself until they leave the nest: playdates. Not only is this a most hideously naff term (you almost can't say it without coming over all 'Hey kids! Let's all be happy and have a playdate!') but it also means that either your house will be full of somebody else's little people, or kids will require collecting from somebody else's house just as you are in the middle of making dinner, it's pouring with rain and your toddler is having a tantrum. Oh joy.

Before you get sucked into the complicated world of Children's Social Calendars you will think playdates sound like a wonderful idea: two kids having a lovely play together outside the pressures of the playground – what could be better for them? And this is largely true: children play very differently when there are just two of them together, and much of the competitive nonsense that larger groups seem to generate evaporates, leaving them free to get on like a house on fire. (Which yours hopefully won't be, unlike my husband's friend's house after the two of them decided to build a small campfire under a bed during a playdate. They've grown out of it now, I think.)

Another advantage of having a friend round to play is that you don't have to do much to amuse them – they will take themselves as far away from you and your dull, adult, mummyish embarrassing-ness and you won't see them until it's time to feed them, or a parent (hopefully theirs) comes to take the friend home.

Sadly, one of the drawbacks is that, while holed-up in their No Adults Allowed den, they will almost invariably take out every toy you never knew you had bought, build a secret hide-out using duvets, sheets, clothes pegs and your best cashmere blanket, and cover themselves with face paints. When the time comes for little Isabella to go home it will take the best part of an hour to find her clothes, change her back into them from whatever strange attire she has adopted for the afternoon, put everything back where it lives and smile a sweet, 'Goodbye – come again soon!'

Having a friend to play brings the added complication of having to feed the beast. Just because you are familiar with the feeding rituals of one small *Homo sapiens* does not mean you are in any way prepared to feed its little friend. I've had children sit in front of what looks to me like perfectly lovely food, attractively presented and with the option of ketchup to drown out any unusual tastes, with a look of such disgust and fear of death-by-eating-off-an-unfamiliar-plate that I sometimes want to open their little mouths and cram the whole lot in. There! Eat, you ungrateful, rude, non-eating excuse for a person! Usually, I resist.

Overall, I love it when my kids have playdates, I really do, and I have learned some cunning techniques for ensuring they run smoothly and don't encroach too much into my already devastated personal breathing space:

☆ **Don't go crazy in the first two weeks.** You probably will, and I do every new school year, but it's best to pace yourself – and your kids – when it comes to socialising. Working through the entire class register within a fortnight will result in exhaustion and overkill all round, and you will be back to Annabel, Adam and Arthur by half-term. We try to stick to one or two per week, which leaves the other five or six for after-school clubs and just relaxing at home as a family.
☆ **Be clear before the school day starts whether there will be a playdate later or not.** From what I can glean, little girls are

much more proficient at organising their social calendars than boys: they arrange playdates in the cloakroom at 8.58 a.m. and spend the rest of the day plotting and developing elaborate games and adventures and working themselves up into a friendship frenzy. When they burst out of the school gates, red-faced with the anticipation of all the fun to come, and you say you're very sorry but you are taking them to your mum's for the afternoon and they should have asked you first, the tears and hatred will last for hours. Make it clear before school whether a play will be OK that afternoon or not, and, better still, arrange it with the relevant parents in advance.

☆ **Check friends' eating requirements.** When you've made bangers and mash and your small guest turns out to be a vegetarian, you will wish you had put in a call to the small guest's elders to check. Ditto for allergies, likes and strong dislikes. These days 'you'll eat what you're given' doesn't seem to apply to other people's children, however much you might like it to.

☆ **Make sure there is a clear pick-up time.** This especially applies if you have younger children – dragging them out at seven to collect their sibling from a friend's house throws their 'bath and bed by 7.30 p.m.' routine out of kilter, and it's the same when asking children to be collected from your house. It also means you can spend that half-hour getting everyone back as they were when they arrived and be ready when the doorbell rings.

☆ **Regular check-ups.** Playing with a friend seems to signal the green light for 'do anything you like, and ignore all the rules you usually adhere to perfectly well'. You know exactly the sort of naughty things that normally nice, sensible children get up to when they go to play at a friend's house, because you made a pig's ear out of all your friends' mums' make-up and fed chocolate éclairs to their guinea pig when you were a kid too. Your offspring are no different, so checking up on their progress every twenty minutes or so is a sensible precaution if you want to avoid similar disasters.

☆ **Thank you for having me.** Getting your kids to say this as they leave, and not look as though they are being asked to suffer enormous hardship, is a challenge, but one I think we should all take up. It sounds a little naff, but it's just common courtesy.

Choosing their Friends

In a word: don't. I defy any parent to honestly say they have never wished their child to either befriend or stop being friends with another child. Whether it's wanting them to hang out with the 'cool gang' because you never did, or wishing they would stop talking to the geeky one, or the aggressive one, or the plain weird one, it's a very open-minded parent who can completely take a step back and not mind who her children play with at all.

My advice? Keep it to yourself and use extreme caution and subtlety. Nothing will make a child hate you more than telling him you don't like his best friend – even if you clearly don't. It shows you in your worst, most judgemental and snobbish light, and it's not a pretty sight. Children's friendships often come and go with the weather anyway, and before you know it he'll be off with another little pal who seems much more your cup of tea. The important thing is that he's your *child*'s cup of tea, so keep your opinions to yourself and be happy they have any friends at all!

Play Nicely!

Oh, how many times do I hear this said by parents like myself, whose lucky, lucky children have more toys than two floors of Hamleys and yet stand there arguing over who had the shitty plastic boat or whatever, which nobody has ever wanted to play with until right now? Play nicely!

Playing nicely is less common the more children have. I have come to this rather mean conclusion having watched children in developing countries all over the world 'playing nicely' for hours with no more than a dry stick, some leaves and a healthy dose of imagination and generosity. On returning to the UK, I am always sickened by the tragically low level of sharing and patience exhibited by most kids I see, who have to have everything NOW!, where everything is MINE!, and whose idea of playing 'nicely' is letting somebody else have a turn for the minimum time it is possible to actually hold the toy and work out how it works, before having it snatched away again.

It's sad, and true in many cases, but there are ways of encouraging 'playing nicely' that don't involve confiscating things, inducing tears or working yourself up into something one step away from a heart attack.

☆ **Keep calm.** Getting cross when your kids won't share is a sure-fire way of making things worse and getting everyone in an aggressive mood. Just explain that if they don't share it will mean they are not very nice at all, and you will have to take the toy away, or just stop the play session altogether.

☆ **Start them young.** Children who regularly visit playgroups, nurseries or friends' houses learn from a very early age that not everything in the world belongs to them, and they have to share with others. This is especially important if you have an only child, who has less opportunity to learn about other kids nicking his stuff than children with siblings.

☆ **Distraction.** It's amazing how fast young children stop crying about things the moment they are distracted by something better. 'Look, Jack – a fire engine! Let's play with that . . .' Pull-along truck trauma over.

☆ **Persist.** It's far too easy to give in when your child is being possessive, especially because other mothers will often jump in to 'help' by giving the toy back to your mean child, thinking that will stem the tears. It will, but it teaches her nothing about having to share. Persistence is the only way to get the message across, and it only takes one incidence of weakness of will on your part for your child to think you will fold every time. Stand firm!

☆ **Blank it.** Remember that a child often makes a fuss just to get your attention. If you make it clear that this won't work, and that you won't give him cuddles or positive attention if he refuses to share with others, he might give up after a while and be generous more often.

Becky, mother of Robbie, five, and Charlotte, two:
When my children argue I can feel the life draining out of me. It makes me exhausted just to listen to it, and if I could stop it I know it would improve my quality of life enormously. I feel like a policeman, just breaking up fights all the time. I hope it'll pass as they get older.

Louisa, mother of Helene, six, Peter, four, and Alfie, two:
I was in a toddler group last week and Alfie bit another child. I was absolutely horrified, and so was the child's mother. He has started to do this more and more and it's really upsetting. He only does it in public, when he doesn't want to share with another child. I just take him away, but I want him to be able to play well with other children.

All kids squabble. A child who never squabbles over toys, choice of game, place to sit at the table or colour of plastic cup is more of a worry than one who does, I would say. It's immensely draining for parents, so if you can practise some ways of getting peace and harmony quickly and with minimum fuss, your life will be a lot easier. Remember, it will pass, like all difficult phases, so try to stick it out calmly for your own sanity, and wait for the clouds to lift.

Fear Factor: The cotton-wool effect

15 June

I am absolutely livid. I am so cross that I can hardly write. When I collected Phoebe from school today her tights were glued to an oozing, sticky graze on her knee. I asked why she didn't have a plaster on it and – get this – she said they weren't allowed to put a plaster on!! And then it turned out that they weren't allowed to apply antiseptic cream either without my permission, so she has been walking around all day with an infected cut on her leg and nobody has cleaned or dressed it. I am incensed! What the bloody hell is wrong with a world where teachers can't even perform basic first aid on a child, for fear that they sexually abuse her or infringe her civil liberties? It's utter bloody madness.

Something very strange happened towards the end of the last century as a result of increasing amounts of litigation and media over-excitement: we all became frightened of things. Frightened of certain foods, frightened of kids getting hurt, of mobile phone radiation, of bottled water, of medicines and, most worryingly, frightened of other people.

Suddenly there were paedophiles, child-abductors, murderous doctors, religious fanatics, hidden poisons and unusually holey pavements everywhere – we were lucky to be alive at all! As a result of all this fear, people, and the Government, took it upon themselves to wrap everybody up in as much cotton wool as possible, in the form of legislation and constant monitoring. Kids stopped being allowed to walk to the shops or to school alone, to climb trees, play with matches or drink hot drinks without being warned first. Now teachers aren't allowed to put kids on their knees to comfort them, check their hair for nits or make jokes about their funny sticking-out knees in case anyone's delicate sensibility should be hurt. It's pathetic.

And what are we left with? An entire generation of children who don't have any fun, adventure or ability to deal with the real world at all. Well done all of us – what a magnificent achievement!

This is a disaster, and unless we all stop this cotton-wool effect and let our kids experiment, take small risks, jump off that wall, hurt themselves a little and actually learn how the world really works, we will make them dangerously ill-prepared to look after themselves in any way at all.

I know it's hard if you are used to being there all the time to make sure they're OK, but you will honestly be doing them a lot more favours by letting go a little and allowing them to work things out for themselves. It's not negligence, it's child-rearing.

Playdough is for babies!: Finding things for them to do as they get older

When children are very young they like to play – they like building Lego towers, setting up train tracks, doing finger-painting and making sausages out of Playdough. They play hide and seek, peek-a-boo, dressing up and How Many Coins Can I Put in the DVD player? It's just playtime from morning till night, with the odd break for eating, sleeping and pooing.

But at some stage between coming out of nappies and going into school they tire of such simple games and toys, and don't want to 'play' any more. As part of the natural process of growing up and heading towards heavy metal and shapeless clothing, they move on to bigger things. Exactly when this happens is impossible to say, as all children are so different. One simple way of telling when your playtime – as you have come to know it – is up, is when you suggest a game your child has always really enjoyed and you are met with an incredulous stare and a cry of 'That's for babies!' Ah.

This moment came as a shock to me, as I had been quite happily trundling along trying to be a Good Parent, getting all the right toys for the right age and thinking I was doing a satisfactory job as we played for hours without getting bored. (Actually, I was generally quite bored, but you get used to it after a few years!)

But what next? Where were the instructions, the guide or the roadmap for what a child should do after she had grown out of everything she always liked doing perfectly well? After Lego, potato-printing and baking flapjacks – what next?

Well, that's just it: this is where the roadmap ends, and you have to start playing it by ear (literally – they'll soon tell you if your suggestions are babyish or *sooooo* boring). From now on keeping your child entertained, interested and happy is much less simple than opening a box of bricks and looking forward to half an hour of peace. However, the following should help you stay on target:

☆ **Don't worry.** If you find it hard when your child suddenly seems 'bored' or disinterested then try not to worry. Remember that this is a very common stage, and you'll suss it out within six months or so. Everyone goes through it, and you are not failing him – or yourself.

☆ **Move on.** It's tempting to try and fight the rapid progression from Toddler to Teenager by keeping all the old toys around and hoping this will stop time. It won't. It will lead to a frustrated child and miserable parents. Accept that things are changing and go with the flow. Yes, it's a bit scary when they start to become independent beings with their own thoughts, likes and talents you never knew they had – but it's also fantastic because this is what those early years were all about: preparing them for the changes to come.

☆ **Turn on, tune in, get the money out.** Sometimes all you have to do is listen to what your child says he really, really wants, and then shell out for it. This is definitely not recommended every time – a little thing called Spoiling comes into play if you do – but occasionally children can suggest a toy or game that they would love to have, and they then play with it for weeks. It can be an expensive gamble (we still have an unused Sylvanians set, which they 'really, really' wanted . . .) but sometimes it's the only way to go.

☆ **Get some advice.** If you're finding it hard to know what other children of your little darling's age like doing, playing with or fighting over then just talk to other parents. I came to a bit of an *impasse* recently during an 'I don't have anything to do!' phase in one of my kids. It seemed to me that she had *everything* to do, but just didn't want to do any of it. I asked a couple of friends what their daughters were up to in the play department, and it turned out that they were in a similar position to me. None of our kids were interested in 'things' any more, but in simply being and playing *together*, and what solved it was getting them together a couple of evenings a week: they stopped being bored and invented games happily for hours. It soon passed, and we moved on to Top Trump cards and sticker books – for a few weeks . . .!

☆ **Keep the old.** If you think your child has outgrown his old toys, try not to get rid of all of them. I've found that even after a break of a year, my kids sometimes come back to their old toys and play with them again – just in a different way this time. Obviously quite a lot of it will have to go, or your house will be overrun with plastic trains, doll-sized beds and pull-along cows, and local charity shops or friends with younger children will do well out of you. But hang on to some things, which can be used again by older children. Dolls' houses and any construction toys often get their second wind after a decent break.

☆ **Keep on your toes.** I think the main thing to keep in mind as your child grows up is never to be complacent or lazy about what they have to do in their 'downtime'. Something that fascinates them one day will bore them the next, and this continues into adulthood, as that unopened rowing machine in your garage illustrates neatly. Whatever age they are, you need to keep checking that they have enough to do, and are happy with what they have on offer. There are no rules, but part of the fun is discovering what tickles each child's fancy. Rollerblades and tennis rackets for one; china tea-sets and tiny beads for another. Whoever said parents were allowed a rest?

Don't Break it! Getting kids to look after their things

When I was a little girl, my mum used to describe me as her 'little bulldozer': 'If you ever want anything broken, spilled or lost, just give it to Elizabeth', she would joke. Except it wasn't funny, it was quite true. Plates were dropped, toys broken, drinks spilled and enough gloves to warm the hands of a sizeable army lost. If ever a hesitant 'Ooopsy . . .' was heard, it meant I had wrecked something again.

But there is a difference between children like I was, who are curious as to how things work, and have minds that jump and wander and tend to forget where things are just for a second – ooopsy . . . there goes my elbow knocking another glass of milk onto the floor – and those who have no respect for things and don't even try to look after them. In my case there was no sense of neglect or lack of care for my things; I really did appreciate what I had but I just had trouble keeping them in quite the same state as I found them, due to my somewhat clumsy, speedy nature. 'Ooopsy . . . I think I may have accidentally dropped the stylus onto your favourite LP *again*, Daddy . . .'

But there is a new kind of bulldozer on the scene today whose 'little accidents' are less the result of understandable childlike enthusiasm and heavy-handedness, and more due to a complete lack of care for anything. 'If something breaks, Mummy and Daddy will buy a new one, so who needs to look after it?' seems to be the new logic. Nice.

I am almost unable to write this chapter without sounding like an old lady who thinks children should be seen but not heard, but having talked to many of my friends – none of whom have blue rinses either – I know I am not alone in being fairly appalled by the lack of care that seems to have crept into many homes.

The simplest explanation is that many families have a lot more expendable cash than they did thirty years ago, so the 'Mummy can easily buy me a new one' idea is quite true in most cases. And Mummy or Daddy usually do. The result is that kids have never had to look after things as our parents – and to some extent we – did. I remember my mum darning socks, gluing pieces of dolls back together and spending many an evening sewing tiny clothes for those patched-together dolls to wear. These days most holey socks or broken dolls are thrown away, and if my kids want dolls' clothes, I just go and buy some.

As problems in families go, this carelessness isn't the worst one, unless money is a real problem. But if it signals the start of a generally sloppy, careless attitude to everything, which surely can't be good for any of us, then maybe we should at least *try* to do something about it:

☆ **Spell it out.** Strange, but humans are remarkably good at missing something very obvious unless somebody sits them down and says it very slowly and clearly. In bold, if you can manage it.

You – must – look – after – your – toys.

I – am – not – made – of – money – and – it – was – very – kind – of – me – to – buy – you – that – tricycle – so – stop – bashing – it – into – the – wall – before – it – breaks. Please.

Aha – he's stopped.

☆ **Make them pay.** As children get a little older and start to have pocket money you can play this game, which usually works. It's amazing how well they look after it if they have to buy it themselves.

'Oh please, Mummy – it's only £6.99.'

'If you want it, you pay for it – you've had lots of things recently, and you don't need it.'

'But it's £6.99! That's loads.'

'My point exactly.'

'Fine, I'll buy it, but nobody is allowed to touch it, and it'll live in a very safe place and I'll have it forever!'

Important lesson learned; your job done.

☆ **Make them wait.** This is my favourite one because it works so well for adults as well as kids. The best things definitely come to those who wait. If a child has to yearn for something, he is far more likely to enjoy it and make the most of it. In other words, to appreciate it and look after it. Success!

☆ **Show the way.** The best way of teaching a little respect and care is by showing some yourself. If you buy stuff for yourself all the time, chuck things out willy nilly, and don't look after what you've got, then I'm afraid you can't complain when your kids turn into spoilt, careless, wasteful, unappreciative little shits. (Or even just a little bit wasteful.) Show them how you hang up your coat properly so that it doesn't stretch; polish your shoes; leave your books neatly shelved rather than left bent open on the floor; and press buttons on your radio or remote control gently. If they see all of this kind of careful behaviour they might just adopt some by osmosis, rather than by you banging on at them all the time to 'Look after your things!!'

Well, folks, that's the whole of the downstairs covered. For those who are brave enough there are more rooms to be discovered upstairs, and these contain such delights as in-laws, pushy parents, the school run and – at last – sex! Off we go . . .

PART ELEVEN

The Landing

Before we go into any of the upstairs rooms and poke our heads into such personal spaces as the main bedroom or the family bathroom, let's catch our breath for a moment on the landing and address some general family worries that can strike at any time, and almost certainly will do more than once before you make it to the family crypt.

Whose Life is This Anyway? When you have a little wobble . . .

Even the most seasoned family member can have a wobble every so often. Wobbles can manifest themselves in many ways, but the most common seem to be a prolonged bad mood, inexplicable episodes of crying or a slightly panicky feeling of being trapped and unable to breathe freely.

If you have ever asked yourself what you are doing here, in this house, with this life that you never expected to happen so fast and so full-on, whether you will manage to stick it out through thick and thin, and if anyone would really notice if you were to run down the road very, very fast and not come back, then you need to take a break right here on the landing and read a few things.

First off, you are not alone at all. Creating a family and trying to make it work is the biggest challenge you could ever have undertaken. It's not like running a marathon or trying to knit non-stop for twenty-four hours, because, however embarrassing and defeatist this would be, you could, if you really wanted to, just stop, and nobody – apart from you – would care that much. With a family it doesn't work like that at all: once it's there *it's there*, in whatever constantly changing form it takes, and there's no going back – ever. Even if you do run away with somebody else or throw in your apron and decide to live alone in Antarctica for the rest of your life, your family is still there, and you will know it. Your children, your partner, your children's children, your house, your in-laws and any pets you may have accumulated with time will all be affected by your actions too.

Julia, mother of Katie, eight, Louis, five, and JJ, two:

I love the life I have, and I wouldn't change a thing, but I did find losing my independence very difficult to begin with, and I still get pangs every so often and wish for another life away from all of this family business. I wonder if I've made the right choice, and if I'm good enough for it. It never lasts long, but I'm still surprised that I haven't got completely used to being a family person, rather than just a single girl!

Given the enormity and permanence of being a founder member of a family, it's hardly surprising that it can feel overwhelming and frightening sometimes. I occasionally feel that I must have been mistaken for someone else, someone far more responsible and capable, and that I was just *playing* at being a mother/wife/home-maker for a while. I've done that now – can I go back to being just me? Er, no, Liz, sorry.

I think part of the reason the wobbles happen is that playing happy families *is* just like playing a game in a way – kind of an extremely elaborate, expensive, highly consequential dressing-up. It's when you realise that this 'game' now involves children, a mortgage, a family car, home insurance, five bicycles, nursery fees, ballet lessons and toy cars in every room that you want to scream: '*HELP!* I want to get off! I can't breathe! I'm still just a little girl who likes ice-cream and building rock pools. I'm not this person with the wifely smile wiping chocolate smears from a three-year-old's face – I don't know how to look after *myself*, let alone a child, a husband or a large house plant. Really, there has been a mistake – please let me go!!'

This is when an understanding friend, a gin and tonic and a very good cry can all help. Remember:

☆ **We are all many people:** little girls, moody teenagers, entrepreneurs, friends, wannabe rock stars, business women, daughters, mothers and wives, to name but a few. Living in a family means the last two are at the forefront, most of the time, and this can cause a degree of smothering for the other side of your character. Give your inner ten-year-old a voice occasionally, by climbing a tree with your kids, having a water fight or doing some painting, and you'll probably feel a lot better.

☆ **You are not a failure.** Talk to three good friends and ask if they have every felt anything similar. The one who says 'no way' is lying. Seriously, it's as normal as ingrown hairs to want a break from family life every so often. Not to have any needs or desires outside the family home would make you pretty dull.

☆ **Take a break.** If you really feel that you need to have a break from your commitment as matriarch, then try to arrange to go away with a friend for a few days, do something silly but fun, go and see a film by yourself or do anything else that makes you feel more you, and less everybody else's.

☆ **Don't do anything rash.** If you feel a wobble coming on, don't make for the nearest train station and buy a one-way ticket to

Paris. Paris is lovely and everything, but your family are here, and they need you. Be calm, have your wobble, and wait to get over it in a few days, or weeks at a push.

Will I Ever Know Exactly How To Do It?

No. Very sorry to disappoint anyone who thought their graduation into the world of Totally Competent Mother/Wife was imminent, but it's a trick – damn it! – and you can never pass with the full marks required. Just when you thought you had mastered it all, along comes a new illness, moody phase or marital tiff and you feel that you're back at Grade One yet again.

But why? How can it be that after years of looking after your children and living in your family, you still get presented with new problems to which you have no sensible answer? Why are you still trying to find your feet half of the time?

Well, my frazzled friend, it's because families change, *all the time*, and you may be doing very well one day, only to find that what worked that day is near-as-useless the next because your child has suddenly decided to move into a new, awkward phase or your husband has been asked to work extra hours for the next three months. The only thing you know well how to deal with is what has already been. Everything else is new, unknown and a challenge for you to overcome. Yes, it's hard work, and it can feel that you are climbing up a steep hill all the time, but it really does get a lot easier as the years go by, because your skills of adaptation, inventiveness and general coping develop and improve, and so any new situation is easier to deal with than it would have been a few years back. You might not be a Totally Competent Mother/Wife but you certainly will be a Competent Enough to Handle Most Situations one, and that's good enough for all the people I know.

Don't fret if you feel you ought to know it all by now and are still struggling or questioning things at every other turn: this is the way it is. It's not a failure on your part, or a lack of natural talent for doing the family thing. It's absolutely normal and to be expected – unlike the disaster waiting for you around the next blind corner . . . good luck with it!

Getting Out Of A Family Rut

Family life, as you have probably already gathered or experienced, can be very hectic, stressful and unpredictable. One day everything's hunky-dory, the kids aren't fighting, your husband listens to what you're saying and puts his socks *in* the washing basket, the washing dries without having to be re-hung indoors and you open the fridge to find edible food. The next day your two-year-old screams from the moment he wakes up, your husband goes back into deaf, untidy mode, and it pours with rain for the duration of the school run.

What's odd about something that is so variable is how horribly routine and boring it can become. Every day, despite being a fresh, unknown challenge, is almost exactly the same: get up, dress, dress everyone else, eat, feed everyone else, brush several sets of small teeth, badger kids to get ready for school, go to school, work/spend day with younger child, pick up kids, cook, feed the mob, homework, bath, stories, drink wine, bed, sleep. And tomorrow it starts all over again. Weekends can be a similar picture if your children have a number of extra curricular activities or birthday parties to go to, and by the end of the week you can be left wondering what you have achieved, other than surviving another week with all your kids and your marriage still intact.

This is very common among my friends, and all of us occasionally end up with the whole family getting stuck in a rut. We are like robots, operating on automatic, just going through the motions of being a family, but not really *enjoying* it, feeling anything or getting much pleasure from it. There is only one solution: you must get yourself and your family out of the rut and back onto the highway of life (if that's not overstating it a little.) Here are some 'self-help' tips, and if you can overcome the fact that I sound like an American lifestyle guru and try some of the suggestions, you might find things picking up on the home front very quickly:

☆ **Smile more.** (See, I said it was a bit naff, but don't pooh-pooh it before you've tried.) How many times have you seen families walking down the street or shopping together and really smiling, or even laughing together? Almost never, that's how many, and it's really tragic. When I do see a happy family having a laugh together it lifts my spirits and makes me put more of an effort into having fun with my own family. It can take a bit of work, especially if everyone else is scowling over their Bran Flakes or telling you that your bum looks big in your new skirt, but persist you must. Smile, make a joke of something you'd normally get pissed off about, play the fool, lark about and keep smiling – I can almost guarantee (note the cunning get-out word 'almost') that the rest of your family will smile with you.

☆ **Do something new.** When did you last go for a long bike-ride as a family? Or visited somewhere new and had Sunday lunch there? Or had a picnic breakfast down the bottom of the garden? The easiest way to get out of a rut is to do something completely new – it may turn out to be a disaster, but at least it wasn't the same old thing you usually do.

☆ **Make small changes.** This is a very simple psychological trick, and I've found it really works. As much of our lives involve retracing the same routes every day, we become numb to our surroundings after a while and get little positive mental stimulation. We cross the road at the same point, cycle the same route to the park, shop in the same shop and so on. Well, don't! Take a different route to work or into town; buy your groceries in a different supermarket for once; have a juice instead of your usual latte; get up ten minutes earlier and make pancakes for breakfast for the family, instead of serving the same cereals as usual, and so on. Just a few small changes can jolt your family out of its rut and give you all a spring in your step.

☆ **Play a different tune.** If you've ever caught yourself being in a bad mood for no discernable reason, and just being generally moody and grumpy when inside you don't *want* to be like that, but you can't help it because it's just how you've become over a number of trying weeks, then STOP. Nobody is going to get you out of your grump except you, and your mood is having a huge impact on the mood of the whole family. Go for a walk on your own, think about it, look at yourself in the mirror, look at photographs of happy people you admire or anything that makes you decide that enough is enough and you are going to be happier and take the whole family with you.

☆ **Have sex.** It's an old trick, but it rarely fails. When things are as dreary as they can get, and you feel nothing exciting or fun has happened in your life for months, then set the mood and indulge in some good old-fashioned sex. He's not exactly going to complain, is he, and it will almost certainly put a contented smile on your face. Hold that thought, and start the next day with a new resolve to put some 'Wow!' back into your family life.

There are, of course, other ways of breaking the monotony that can descend on a group of people living busy, repetitive lives together, and if you find any that work better for you then write them down and do them when you feel things grinding to a halt again. There's nothing wrong with you or your family – you've just become bored – so try to snap out of it and make some changes around the place.

But We Don't Have the Time!

This is a common complaint in many families: how can they do more things together as a family when they just don't have the time available? Dad goes off to work at 6 a.m. to catch the commuter train and doesn't get home until 8 p.m.; the kids are at school all day long and are too tired to do much after that, or they have after-school activities to go to and then have to get some sleep before the next long day; weekends are a jumble of sport classes, trips to Ikea and the supermarket, catching up on admin and sorting the garden out. Then it's back to Monday again and you've spent less than two hours together as a family all week. This is not enough, so what can you do?

Well, the first thing to remember, if any of this sounds even vaguely familiar, is that you are among millions of families in exactly the same boat. The second thing to remember is that you *can* find more in your week to be together. Not only that, but if you follow some of the advice below, you will.

☆ **Go out for breakfast.** Breakfast, in case you hadn't noticed yet, is the new lunch. Where business people, media darlings and pretty girls who have nothing better to do used to 'do lunch', now they 'do breakfast'. This is one of the only trends I have ever been way ahead of, as we have been doing this for years. Going out for dinner is often tricky for families as it's too late for kids to be out and about, lunch is impossible as everyone is at school or work, but breakfast is perfect: everyone is up, fresh-faced and hungry, and not many people are about so you're hardly disturbing anyone. If you start the day having a relaxed family meal then anything that work or life throws in to disrupt the rest of the day doesn't feel too bad: you've had some family time, so you're on to a winner already. Many cafés open at 7 a.m., and most people don't have to be rushing off to work that early. If they are, perhaps they should rethink their work hours . . .

☆ **Talk to the boss.** If your or your husband's working lives are making it impossible for you to be together as a family for dinner or breakfast more than twice a week you must – MUST! – have a word with the boss and see if you can change this. Perhaps you could go in an hour later twice a week, or come home earlier and work from home in the evening? Whatever it is, you *must* make more time to be a family. Otherwise you aren't being a family at all; rather a collection of people who share a home and pass each other in the hallway occasionally.

☆ **Consider a big change.** Commuting is disastrous for family life, as it means the commuter misses out on lots of time at home. It may seem impossible at first, but even discussing the idea of moving closer to work, or getting a new job closer to home, might bring up new possibilities neither of you have considered before.

☆ **Free up the weekend.** Again, weekends are at risk of being swallowed up by separate activities, chores or catching up with the extended family. Be strict, work out what can wait for another week, and get some time together to go for a walk, have lunch together or spend some time at home doing nothing but *being* together.

☆ **Lose the distractions.** Sometimes when we all go out to a café together, I deliberately don't take any newspapers or books so that we are forced to actually *talk* to each other. This is also an advantage of going out if you can, rather than always staying in the house. Yes, it's more expensive, but there are no distractions such as toys, the laundry, the phone or the television, and the only things you can do are be together and talk. It's bliss – try it.

Wave Theory: A lesson in family physics

In one of my infrequent Eureka! moments, I came up with a wave theory of family life. It's actually stolen from some simple physics I remember from school but isn't nearly as nerdy or complicated as this may suggest. If we concentrate on the 'wave' aspect, and pretend it's all about surfing or something, I think we should be fine.

Here's how it works. Every member of a family is like a wave. They have their Ups (a promotion, a new handbag, making friends with the new cool girl at school) and their Downs (frustration at work, new handbag stolen, new girl turns out to be a two-faced cow who draws on your books and steals your best friend). Just for example . . .

Now, as time moves along, all of these Ups and Downs keep coming and going, and you all go through periods of being happy, depressed, irritable or excited. This is life, and it would be dull without it. If you were living alone this would be easy – you would enjoy the peaks and get through the troughs like any normal person. But in a family your wave patterns are not isolated: they all interact and influence the others because living together means one person's mood strongly influences everyone else.

If I walk around like a black cloud all week, because I had a row with my mum on the phone or have developed a rash on my chin, chances are that some of this misery and gloom will rub off on my kids and my husband, and they all start feeling down. Which makes me feel even worse! If the children are being especially lovely and easy-going for some reason (usually because they want something, but hey – I don't care, so long as they're being especially lovely) we all feel happier for a while because we no longer feel as though we're being dragged through a pit of snakes and sharp nails by our underarm hair, just to get to the end of the day.

Just occasionally, something amazing happens that dramatically changes the entire dynamic and mood of a household: lots of peaks or lots of troughs coincide. If it's peaks you are on for the best fortnight you've had in years: everyone is brimming with joy and positive energy, the credit-card bill is low, you have sex every night like you did when you first met, your children play merrily together without a single squabble, Film Four runs a season of films all starring Joachim Phoenix and your toddler decides to potty-train himself overnight. Things really are UP, UP, UP.

Sadly, the reverse can also occur, when all of your troughs come crashing together, hurling every member of the family into a deep, seemingly inescapable pit of family disharmony. Your children fight all day long; you get your period; you suddenly find the way your husband drinks his tea brings you out in an irritable sweat; he has to work late every night, and you put on half a stone just by *looking* at the fridge.

It's simple physics, as I said, but unlike our boffin friends in the laboratory, we can wear heels while we're doing it. Here are some essential coastguard tips for living with Wave Theory:

☆ **Ride the waves.** The power of waves is enormous, and so it is with family ones. Trying to fight the natural flow of people's lives and moods is futile: you will just exhaust yourself, inhale lots of water and possibly drown. Best to get up on that surf-board and ride with it when it's good, and lay low for a while when things are bad.

☆ **Go with the flow.** Always remember when things are feeling unmanageable, negative, unpleasant and frictional, that you can snap out of it as quickly as you fell in. You won't know when it'll happen, but if you can bear with it, somebody's wave will start to rise sooner or later, and the knock-on effects can spread through all of you. Yes, it's tough when you're in a bad patch, but it almost always stops after a few weeks. Don't give up – weather it out.

☆ **Swim free.** Just occasionally, you can pull yourself out of a deep Atlantic low, and bring everyone else with you. It takes a lot of determination, and usually a piece of good luck, but you *can* turn a family's mood around if you keep at it, and don't give in to the general moodiness. Gloom breeds gloom, so try to be the one to shed a ray of sunshine, and see if it catches.

☆ **Throw in a life raft.** Sometimes family members can go for weeks just getting on each other's nerves, being irritable and snapping at each other for no real reason. This is common to every family I know, so if you find yourself in such a situation, please don't panic – it's called Family Life, and it's normal. Bringing the subject up directly, especially with your partner, but also with your kids when they get a little older, and talking through the way you are all behaving, and why you are all being so self-destructive and negative, can be the life raft needed to save you all from sinking. I've found that we usually either realise how silly we're being and end up laughing about it, or find the root of the problem and can then set about mending it. Either way, it clears the water and sets a course for better times ahead.

That really is enough of this water-related analogy – I need the loo now. The point is that you need to be very aware of how all of your moods affect the others in your family, and be prepared to weather some storms that seem to rise out of nowhere.

Now that we've overcome a few common worries you may have had about family life in general, and you have realised that you are not the only person on the planet who wonders what they are doing here or if they are up to the task, we are ready to proceed into some of the upstairs rooms. To your left is the children's bedroom (tidy, I hope); straight ahead is the bathroom and toilet; and just here, to the right, is the Master Bedroom. I'm game if you are . . .

PART TWELVE

The Master Bedroom

Love and Marriage . . .

All sentimentality and delicate wording aside, on the face of it marriage stinks as an idea: two human beings sharing their lives, home, holidays, bed, food, friends, body wash, space and TV remote control *every day* for as long as they both shall live? Move over!

Clearly there is a good deal more to it than that – I wouldn't have been married for ten years and counting if there weren't! – but here's the thing: at our most basic level (and most men are their most basic level half of the time, let's face it) humans are not biologically programmed to be monogamous. In order to survive, we have to reproduce, and the best way to make lots of little men and women is for the men to sow their seeds as often as possible. Doing this with one fair maiden is a good start, but the chances of producing some Super Offspring are greatly enhanced if he spreads himself about a bit in a big, hairy, primal, adulterous orgy of sperm-meets-egg.

I can already feel every man in the land leaping to kiss my cheeks as they read this, because I have all but given them the green light to go forth and do the dirty with Suzie from marketing this very day. Steady on, lads – and ladies – I'm not finished yet.

Times have changed and these days most people favour the Settling Down with One Person approach over the Shag Anything That Moves set-up practised by our ancestors and still kept alive by some dutiful government ministers and well-groomed media types.

Most, but not all. There is no acceptable 'norm', which I think is a very good thing. What suits one couple results in smashed crockery for another. Where some marriages survive perfectly well on a diet of 'The usual tonight, madam?' others like to mix things up a bit and work through the entire menu. Each to their own. What doesn't work is when spouses want different things, and this is where open lines of communication are key: if the cards are on the table, then you and the gym instructor can be too, if that was what was agreed. If it's not, then you can expect some hefty conversations to follow.

But what of marriage? Why bother getting married at all if there really is a basic human need to sleep around, and if you can live perfectly happily together without spending a fortune on rings, flowers and watching Auntie Betty get drunk at the reception? Well, it's a tricky one, but for me it boils down to something big, warm, cuddly and very difficult to define, which has to do with stability, commitment, and true, *true* love for another person. Love that changes with time, as you do as individuals; that forgives the pants on the floor and that overcomes any desire to stray. Commitment that stays true despite the arrival of husky French colleagues, disagreements over light-fittings and one of you stealing the duvet every night.

Of course, you can have all this commitment and stability without being married, but there is something in the public declaration of this love, the permanence of the union and the implied solidity of the relationship, which sets marriage apart from other long-term relationships. Marriage may well sound like a ridiculous idea in theory, but, when it works, it's the best thing there is – married people tend to live longer and be happier than those who aren't. It may not float everyone's boat, but I'll take love and marriage every time.

I Love You, I Love You Not, I Love You, I Love You Not: Falling in and out of love

When you live with somebody for twenty, thirty, forty or more years, it is highly unlikely that you will be unwaveringly in love with them for the entire period. Far more likely is that you both go through stages of loving each other, disliking each other, hating each other, being allergic to one another, and then come back round to loving each other again. This is normal, and nothing to be worried about at all.

During the lovey-dovey phases everything is just like the good bits of a romantic novel: you know you've made the right decision to marry this guy, you couldn't be happier, the sex is good, the house is filled with warm, purple light and you lose half a stone without thinking about it.

Then, quite suddenly, but often after a period of domestic boredom and two weeks of asking him to move his rusty old bike out of the garage so you can get your nice new one in there, BOOM! You fall out of love. He pisses you off. Everything about this man irritates you: his walk, smile, haircut, breathing, voice, smell – everything. You are, in fact, allergic to this person, and if he so much as *looks* as though he's going to come near you, you repel him with a glare so menacing that no man would dare to ignore it.

Over the course of my thirteen-year relationship with my (usually delightful) other half, I would say that I have fallen completely out of love with him about four times, usually for about a month or two each time. This pales into insignificance when compared with the number of times he must have fallen out of love with me – I imagine I must be somewhat tricky to live with, but I can do really good handstands if requested, so that seems to make up for it.

Falling out of love is very frightening the first time it happens. This usually occurs either several months before getting married, when you see your respective parents discussing wedding arrangements; just after the honeymoon, when you are entering the 'What the Fuck Have I Done?' phase common to all sensible people; or about a month after you have a baby. This last one is usually quite worrying, because for the first time since you met, you love somebody else just as much – and often even more – than you love each other. That this new love of your life shits itself every hour, can't even hold its own head up and has rendered your breasts out of bounds must come as a double blow to your poor, rejected partner, who feels he has been cast aside like a soiled nappy and is received with the same level of disgust and revulsion.

Any two people who spend as much time together as most couples do would go off each other occasionally. Feeling that you need a break, and just don't really want to be together much for a few days, is absolutely not a sign that your marriage is over at all. Thinking that it might be is ridiculous, and the divorce courts would be half-empty if more couples were to give it time, give themselves a bit more breathing space and accept that they just need to be individuals for a while, as opposed to a part of a couple.

Whatever the cause, there are some key things to remember when you feel you have fallen out of love:

☆ **Do not panic.** You are not doomed, but are simply going through a phase where things look a little bleak and confusing, and you don't feel very much in love for a while. If you treat this as anything other than a phase, and start to obsess about the problem and convince yourself that the Fat Lady really has sung, then it could be all over when it absolutely shouldn't be. Take a step back, see it for what it is, and wait for the love fairy to sprinkle magic dust on the pair of you again.

☆ **It will happen again.** Falling out of love can happen following a busy period at work; as a result of your children being in particularly challenging, difficult stages; when the bathroom tiles don't turn out to be quite the colour you had anticipated; when he forgets your birthday for the third year in a row; or for more reasons than I could possibly fit into one book. Just when you thought it was safe to be complacent again, expect it, and be prepared.

☆ **Why, oh why, oh why?** When it happens, try to identify what could have brought on this lovelessness and remember that it was probably a combination of many reasons involving both of you and usually some external factors such as in-laws, children and the national rail network. If you can identify the source, you can see why it isn't just your partner whom you find irritating, but several aspects of your domestic life, your life in general, or your mother-in-law in particular. That should make things a little better for a start.

☆ **Just because.** Sometimes you stop being in love for no discernable reason, and this is something you need to be particularly aware of. My personal theory (unless somebody cleverer has got there first) is that falling out of love is beneficial to a relationship. Not long-term lack of love, of course, but it's the Absence Makes the Heart Grow Fonder approach (damn it – maybe somebody *did* think of it first) where having periods of abstinence from kissing, cuddling, and general lovey-doveyness means when you *do* get all smoochy again it feels better then it did before and you appreciate it all the more. It's just a theory, but it's the one I'm sticking to.

☆ **Take action.** If you are not a 'sitting it out' type of person and like to take a sledgehammer to domestic 'situations', then coming straight out with it can work. I have sat my husband down and told him I was in an Out of Love phase several times and it was quite a successful move. He stopped asking me why I was so grumpy (there is rarely a rational reason – I just *am*!), which had been irritating me even more; we largely ignored each other for a few days, he spent a lot of time in the pub with his mates, and come Friday we were both gagging to be in love again – and were. All done until the next time.

So fear not. If you are never anything but hopelessly in love with one another for thirty years, then well done you. You are unique. If, like everybody else, you go through ups and downs then please remember that there is almost always an Up after a Down – you just need to work your way towards it, or wait for it to come, and communicating is, as ever, essential.

A Room of One's Own: The problems of sharing a bedroom

In this country, most couples share a bedroom, which contains all of their clothes, some personal items and a double bed. This room, known in estate-agent speak as the 'master bedroom' and by kids as 'Mummy and Daddy's room', is a *shared* space. It is neither His nor Hers, and, while it's a sensible-enough idea and works for millions of people up and down the country, I don't think it's necessarily the best arrangement. (I should mention at this point that it is *our* arrangement, and most of the time I really like it this way, but not always.) The reason most people share is for financial and conventional reasons: it's hard enough to buy *any* dwelling these days, and seeking out something with *two* master bedrooms is just being fanciful.

The problem with sharing a room is that you don't get the privacy, solitude and 'me' space that everybody needs. Sure, you can steal a corner of the dining room and call it your own by putting garlands of Habitat lights and all your favourite books and magazines in it, but having your own *bedroom* is infinitely more special. It means going to bed and reading for as long as you want without disturbing anyone, and getting a decent night's sleep (allowing for the many rude awakenings by children, of course) without somebody nicking the duvet or snoring. Having your own room also means you can decorate it in your own style, keep it as you would like it to be, and not find boxer shorts, pieces of old tissue or books about computer games lying about the place. Most of all, it means being able to say 'Your place or mine?' every night. Wouldn't that be nice?

In the real world, accepting that you will probably share a bedroom with your partner for ever and ever and *ever* is made easier by the following:

☆ **Put your own stamp on it.** Just because he's a motor-racing nut does *not* mean you have to go to sleep with ten back-issues of *F1* magazine on your bedside table and a giant poster of a Ferrari above your head. Nor should he have to be surrounded entirely by your clobber, so decorate most of the room in something you both like, and keep your zone as yours, and his zone as his. If you're *really* lucky, like me, he won't care at all and you can have the whole lot to yourself – whoopee!

☆ **If you want it a certain way, do it yourself.** If you really love having everything tidy in your room, and no clothes on the floor and your shoes all neatly arranged, but you live with a guy who likes to display every item of underwear he owns on the floor and believes that bedside tables should be covered with enough tissue, unread books and receipts to make dusting impossible, then rather than nag constantly you may have to just keep it clean yourself. It only takes a few minutes every day, and if it's that important to you then it's worth it.

☆ **Have separate wardrobes.** No matter *how* much you love somebody, sharing your beautiful clothes, shoes and bags with his equivalents is to give up your personal space just that little bit too much, even if he is a very well-dressed member of the male species (in which case, well done you! You bagged a snappy dresser, and they're rare). I don't care if you have to see me weeing, waxing my legs or squeezing my spots, but you will not, *NOT* invade my sacred, private wardrobe space!

☆ **Have your own bedtimes.** I used to stay up for hours, straining to keep my eyes open while waiting for my husband (then boyfriend) to stop reading or whatever and just *come to bed*. Looking back on this I realise how ridiculous it was. I now go to bed whenever I want to, which is usually at least an hour before he does, so I can have some time to be alone and get my full eight hours' kip. It's obviously important to go to bed at the same time sometimes, unless you only like having sex when you're asleep . . . a tad weird!

☆ **Get an eye-patch and ear-plugs.** There are times when you will both be in bed at the same time, and one of you wants to be awake while the other wants to sleep. This is not the six days out of seven when he wants sex and you want to sleep more than *anything*, but those other times when you want to read in bed and he wants to sleep, or he wakes up three hours before you need to because he's 'thinking about something', or one of you has a cold and snores like an old man. Investing in something to block all light and sound is essential for whoever needs those extra forty winks.

Who's in the Driving Seat?

Being in a marriage is much like driving a car down a long, bumpy track to an unspecified destination: you journey from place to place, milestone to milestone, chugging along and trying to mind the potholes (affairs); you sometimes revisit favourite picnic spots (where you first ripped each other's clothes off and went for it all night); you refuel every so often to keep the engine running (dirty weekends in the country); you argue over directions or who was in charge of packing the forgotten raincoats (daily life); and you occasionally feel like you're going round in circles (marital boredom). And just as with driving a car, *you cannot have two people at the wheel at the same time.* At least, you *can*, but it's quite dangerous and will lead to both of you fighting it out at the bottom of a ravine somewhere.

Every relationship between two people, whether lovers, friends, family members or colleagues, has its own allocation and division of power and responsibility. What works in one relationship doesn't work in another, and learning and sticking with what works for *both of you* will be what makes or breaks the journey. In some families it's the mother who runs the home single-handedly while Dad earns the cash. In others he makes all the domestic decisions while she holds the purse strings. Some friends always arrange get-togethers in the pub while others wait for the phone to ring and are happy to come along if asked. No way is more correct or workable than the other, if everyone understands how it works and is happy with it.

Here are some tips that have helped us and many of our friends:

☆ **Take it in turns at the wheel** and learn who handles the faster roads better and who should take over for the bendy bits. If you are the more sociable one and find inviting people for dinner easy and fun, then you do that. Don't expect him to if he's shy or works sixty hours a week and just wants to crash out in the evenings. If he is better at organising the social things, or paying the bills, or choosing what to put on your walls, then realise this and let him get on with it.

☆ **Talk, talk, talk about it.** If you don't like it, and feel that you would like to have more input in certain areas, then say so, and try to work out a way you can share some of this stuff. If you don't say anything, he probably thinks you are happy doing the weekly shop and organising all the holidays. He's not a mind-reader!

☆ **Learn what works for you.** Don't try to live in a way that just doesn't work for you two. Just because your friend Rachel has a partner who gave up work so she could be a full-time barrister does not mean that's what you want. In my own marriage we have fairly fluid and overlapping roles (we both cook, both share the school run and both work) but there is a pretty old-fashioned lean to it if I'm honest. I do most of the domestic stuff and daily admin, I work part-time and I spend more time with the children. He works every day, sorts out all the financial matters and sees the kids at the weekend. For us, this works brilliantly for one key reason: *we both like it*. I *like* this traditional role of homemaker and mother, and he *likes* having a wife who is there when he gets home but who also has her own career. If neither of us liked the way we divided our roles and time, then we would either have split up years ago, or something would have changed by now.

After many years of subtle attempts at role-reversal ('Frankly I don't care *what* we do this weekend, but *you* think of something!') I now realise that this set-up, despite putting most of the decision-making pressure on me, has huge advantages. Being in the driving seat, while also remembering the directions, stopping the kids from killing each other on the back seat and knowing which petrol stations sell decent coffee, is tiring, but do you know what? I, like most women I know, wouldn't have it any other way.

Of course, I complain that I'm doing it all, but I know that I would actually find too much help annoying: somebody else's plans would only get in the way of my own, which are carefully built around the school week, my ever-changing work arrangements and my time of the month. Anyway, isn't it a wife's *duty* to complain about things, especially if she's perfectly happy with them? Life would be far too simple otherwise.

My other half hit the marital nail on the head a few years ago after I spent an entire evening moaning that he never organised surprises for me. 'Liz,' he said calmly, which is one of his traits I both love and detest, 'you are *impossible* to arrange a surprise for: if I did, you would be so pissed off that I had just ruined whatever it was you had already planned that it would be a disaster.' He was right, and I realised that he knows me like nobody else does, and that's part of what I love about being in such a long-term partnership. You know each other inside out.

What's Yours Is Mine. Mostly ...

One of things I love about being married is that everything – *everything* – we own is shared. We have a joint bank account and our house, car and all our possessions belong equally to both of us. Hell, despite months of gestating, three agonising labours and so far eight years of going to toddler groups I am even kind enough to share the children! It does require a lot of trust to share absolutely everything you own with somebody, especially if this somebody has trouble doing two things at once and thinks reflexology involves a doctor tapping your knees with a small hammer, but the idea of marriage without this level of trust is completely unimaginable to me.

There are, however, some drawbacks to all of this caring and sharing. Sometimes, just sometimes, I like to know, without a flicker of doubt, that a particular item in my house is MINE. All *mine*! I don't care if it *is* an old, dusty wooden box picked up from a car-boot sale in which I store plasters and antibacterial cream:

it's mine – I saw it, I bought it, and you can't have it, so give it here, mister.

The sorts of things I like to feel are mine are the things he would never, ever want anyway, should it come to a marital split and that clichéd scene involving large cardboard boxes and family photographs, so there's absolutely no competitive element to my wanting to own them at all. Why would he *want* the eclectic jewellery collection I have spent fifteen years amassing, or my shoes, my photography and design books, my Woody Allen DVDs (actually, he might want those – I'd better put my stamp on them somehow . . .), the ridiculous works of art I have created over the years, all my vintage finds and reconditioned furniture? He wouldn't. He lives with it all, even likes most of it, but knows it is basically 'Her Shit'.

Similarly, he is safe in the knowledge that, should I ever be stupid enough to walk out of the door, never to return, with a handsome millionaire who is hung like a stallion and has a degree in Being a Top Bloke, all the Dick Francis and Stephen King books will remain, along with the *Star Wars* videos, all the computer games and a Lynyrd Skynyrd CD. Oh, and the dodgy nail clippers. That's 'His Shit'.

The importance of having stuff that you feel is just *yours* and nobody else's cannot be overstated in a marriage. Of course it's lovely to share most of your possesssions, but owning separate things as well is essential for you to feel that you are a person in your own right, as well as part of a couple. To have no individuality at all, to only exist as half of a pair, is to negate your *self* completely, and this is rarely healthy for you or for your relationship.

Money Matters: In for a penny, in for the lot?

Whether you have a shared bank account or not depends entirely on how you *both* feel about it. Not on how much you *trust* each other – if you don't trust somebody enough to share all your money with him, then you don't trust him enough, in my opinion – but it just depends on how each of you feels about having a shared kitty, where all of your combined income goes in, and both of you are free to take money out any time you like. For a few years I had no problem with having only a joint account – my other half has always earned considerably more than me, partly because I spent eight years either being pregnant, having a baby or getting pregnant again, and partly because he chose a sensible job with a desk, a swivel chair and a salary while I opted for freelance 'I'll take whatever is going' work, so being forced to share all of his hard-earned cash was something I was prepared to endure.

But there came a time when I longed to be self-sufficient, not because I wanted to cut myself loose from him at all, but because I got no sense of satisfaction or reward just using somebody else's money all the time. I have always loved earning my own money and treating myself to things as a reward – I used to sell crappy handmade pictures or objects to kind or insane passers-by as a child and then buy sweets and stickers on the way home – and never knowing whether my cappuccino was being paid for by some small job *I* had done or by my husband's last paycheque always left me feeling unsatisfied, guilty, and with a bitter taste in my mouth. (Although that could have been the coffee.)

So I opened my own account, and started paying the tiny sums I earned from occasional bits of work into it. The mood-lifting effect was immediate: I didn't feel any guilt when I treated myself, I knew exactly how much I was earning, and I could finally treat *him* to the occasional drink or night at the cinema, knowing that it really was my treat this time.

We still have our joint account, where most of our combined dosh sits earning almost no interest at all, but having my own separate one is something I would never want to give up, for my own self-esteem.

If you do share your money, then it's best to agree on how accessible all of this dough is, and whether what you do with it needs to be agreed on first. In some marriages, no questions are ever asked about what comes out and where it goes. The money is there, so you use it. In others, the woman is still treated like a child, and given a weekly 'allowance', or pocket money. This feels just a tad dated to me. Still, if it works for some people then let them do it their way.

We have a touchy-feely type of arrangement, where we just *sense* if something is a bit of a splash-out (usually over £30 at the moment). Anything under this figure is in No Questions Asked territory (unless it's in a lap-dancing club, but I don't imagine you get much for less than £30, do you? Maybe just a bit of thigh . . .). Over this benchmark and I have the gut feeling that I should tell my husband what I am about to buy, and see if he is cool with that. If it's a pair of shoes he knows he will have absolutely no say whatsoever, but it was nice of me to ask. But if it's something for the house that we really don't need, or something equally lust-killing like getting some new plants for the garden, then I just feel I should at least *mention* it before I buy. It's not so much asking, because I know I could go ahead and buy whatever I like if push came to shove, but more checking that it's something he's OK with me spending *our* money on. It's a very deep, ingrained sensation, born of having to ask my parents if I might have 20p or be allowed to make one phone call, but it's one I am glad I have, as it makes us more of a partnership than cohabiting, secretive shopaholics.

The Golden Ticket is honesty and communication. Hang on, isn't that two Golden Tickets? Well, I'll give you honesty and throw in communication for free, just because I'm being kind today. If you tell each other what you are spending and what it is going on (yes, even the staggeringly expensive boob-firming cream – say you're only using it for his benefit) you should avoid many, many rows about the length of your credit-card bills or the size of his CD collection. It's very simple, and it works.

The Secret Stash: Putting some aside for a rainy day . . .
I first heard about this a few years ago, and have since met several women who have secret bank accounts. The theory seems to be that 'You never know what might happen' and if your Mr Wonderful runs off with an Estonian model after twenty years of

marriage to lovely old you, you might stand to lose rather a lot of the money you have become accustomed to. Hence the Secret Stash – just a small amount each month, over the course of your marriage, should add up to enough to keep you in fresh highlights and sexy lingerie, which you will need to catch your next Mr Wonderful.

Hmm. I have to say that I am in two minds about this one. On the one hand it makes a lot of sense: accidents do happen, Estonian models are generally quite stunning, and all humans, especially those who have been in unexciting marriages for years and who have had a few too many after-work Caipirinhas, are fallible. But there's something distrustful about this kind of 'Preparation for Disasters to Come' that I find a bit distasteful. It's the same with prenuptials. To begin a marriage saying, 'If you start fucking around with our nanny, I want sixty-five per cent of your money, our holiday home in the Algarve and alimony for the kids we don't have yet' is pretty miserable.

The reverse side of this pot of money stored for a rainy, adulterous afternoon is that it's for Her fling. I am always suspicious of women who plan for the day their husband leaves them: anyone who is so obsessed with adultery must have it on their mind a lot, and it's a small step from having something on a woman's mind to putting it in her lap. That said, if your man is away eighteen hours a day, on business trips four months a year, and you haven't had a good seeing-to since the Christmas before last, then expecting it all to go tits up and planning for that is probably wise.

A Secret Stash could be seen as a sensible precaution, or it could be interpreted as a strong sign of problems in a relationship. You be the judge, and see what works for you.

Let's Talk About Sex, Baby

Oooh, yes! Let's talk about it. Hell, everybody else seems to talk about it, think about it, watch it or be exposed to it in some way most of the time, so what's to stop us having a little tête-à-tête about the wonderful, confusing, sticky subject of S-E-X.

Sex can be many things. It can be GCSE Biology sex (his bit goes in her bit, things jiggle about for a while and then a baby is made), lustful sex (clothes are ripped, ear lobes are bitten, tables are knocked over and inhibitions are abandoned), non-penetrative sex (his bit goes everywhere apart from her GCSE Biology bit, and there is quite a lot of mess to clear up afterwards) and even non-climactic sex (which men will claim is an oxymoron, but women know can be the most erotic of all).

There are hundreds of other types of activity that I would put under the heading Sex, and whichever is your favourite or most likely tipple, there is one thing for certain: Sex causes lots of pleasure, and lots and lots of trouble.

According to some very necessary scientific study or other, men think about sex on average every three seconds. I would love to know how they worked that one out, and I simply don't believe it. The males I know appear to have a lot more in their brains than T and A, but I am aware that this may be because whenever I see them they are talking to me: a stretched, exhausted mother of three. Hardly the stuff of sexual fantasy. Ah well . . .

Assuming, though, that many men do have a voracious appetite for sex – what about their female counterparts? (I am only ignoring same-sex relationships here because I know absolutely nothing about the ins and outs, so to speak, of gay marriage and sex.) So much has been written about women and their attitude to, need for and enjoyment of sex that to dedicate a mere page or two to the subject might seem lax. Perhaps it is, but for the purposes of this book I merely want to point out one glaringly obvious fact, and then suggest ways to overcome the problems it raises.

Here goes:

For two people to remain together for many, many years, both of them need to get the quality and quantity of sex they require. These amounts are very often not the same for each partner in the couple.

This pretty much sums up the reason why a colossal number of otherwise perfect relationships fall apart: their requirements simply don't match.

Which brings us back to women. I have talked to hundreds of women over the past eight years, over coffee, wine, gym machines and shopping baskets, and I have yet to find a single one – a *single woman* – who has a greater appetite for sex than her partner. It could well be that I am surrounded by middle-class, frigid, academic Cambridge mothers whose primary concerns are getting their offspring into a private school and then Oxbridge, who are sleep-walking through achingly dull marriages to men they haven't fancied since they were twenty and whom they suspect of having an affair in London anyway, whose feet are as dry and cracked as their relationship and for whom sex is a necessary chore required of a Good Woman to keep her husband. It could be that.

But I suspect not. The women I generally talk to are outgoing, intelligent, kind, interested, busy, passionate people. They are probably just as good in bed as the nubile young blonde in any semi-erotic film you care to mention. Many even *like* having sex – no, they love it! But there is a major difference between these real women and those of sexual fantasy: for ninety-nine per cent of the time, these tireless creatures simply have *so* much going on in their lives, what with looking after their kids, keeping the fridge stocked, paying the bills, watering the plants, cooking for their family, sewing on name tapes, sending birthday cards to all the relatives, collecting the kids from friends' houses, arranging babysitters, remembering to take the DVDs back to Blockbuster *and* often having a paid job on top of all of this work, that there is no room for sex in their brain more than every three *days*, let alone three seconds.

If any of this sounds familiar then stop crying into your new dress and listen: you are in good company. You are one of millions and millions of women who, unlike the characters in *Desperate Housewives* (it's fiction, remember!), don't want to fuck everything that moves and would honestly rather watch a film than go to bed and have sex with their long-term partner. Not because you don't fancy him; not because you have no libido left, are the world's most useless lover or are a selfish, dried-up old prune who should be grateful for any sexual advances made by anyone. No – it's because you are totally washed out from dealing with everybody else's wants and needs, and would just like to be left alone for an hour or two. Sex would be lovely, but it's not on your mind right now, nor should it necessarily be. You just relax and wait for the moment to arise (usually about three minutes after Clive Owen appears on the screen, if you're me, but more on that shortly . . .)

Problem One: How much sex is enough?

I love reading quotes from people about the amount of sex they get: it's hilarious! You know the sort of thing: 'Me and the Missus, we do it twice before work, at least three times in the evening and all weekend. We're at it like rabbits, we are!' or 'I don't think we do it all that often – maybe ten or eleven times a week, usually?' Ten or eleven times a *week*? Jesus, what are you guys eating – Viagra-Bran?

Fear not. These people are either sex addicts or talking bollocks. I suspect the latter. I'm sorry, but for anyone other than people in the first flourishes of a romance, newlyweds or people who are having an affair but need to cover it up, this level of sexual activity is impossible. Sure, we used to be at it like student rabbits too in the early years – ah, such good times – but now that we actually have to get out of bed before midday and feel we should wait until our kids go to sleep before indulging in any activity that might result in shrieks of ecstasy, the level has dropped significantly to rest somewhere between just enough and not quite enough, the latter usually occurring during busy periods or unresolved arguments.

If you're Peter Stringfellow then four times a day is probably just about acceptable. Other men can exist on once a day or three times a week, but the most common, I suspect, from the information I have gathered by plying my friends with alcohol, is about twice a week on average. These moments of passion usually occur when both parties manage to go to bed early enough, stay awake long enough, don't have a book they want to finish and aren't in the middle of a passion-killing disagreement about who was supposed to send Uncle Tom's get-well-soon card. Given that this average includes that long week during your period when sex is O-U-T, the men walk around looking miserable the whole time and you feel like a saturated sponge, slowly leaking all energy, colour and enthusiasm, then I guess there must be times in between when it's more like three or four times a week, so it's not too bad really. Randy old you!

Whatever your optimum amount of shagging, fucking, humping, making love, doing it, or whatever you like to call it, the most important thing is that you talk about it if you sense one of you isn't happy with their lot. Maybe he is asking too much of you. Maybe you are neglecting his needs in favour of chatting to your friends on the phone or doing your evening Yoga whatchamacallits. Maybe he is too stressed at work to give you his all every night while you are in some hormone-related nymphomaniac phase. Maybe you just both need to talk it through and not assume the other is at fault. Keeping quiet about it always leads to the Dark Side, where there is either no sex at all, or sex with somebody other than your partner, and that's not what we're after here, if we're honest.

Problem Two: What *kind* of sex is good enough?

Woah there! We're getting into 'way too much information' territory here, aren't we? Yes, but it's a subject we have to address if we are to look around this room thoroughly, so here goes.

Many people like having good, old-fashioned, one-on-one, missionary-position sex, and I say 'Why not?' It works, everyone feels better for it, and there's not too much scope for broken ribs, groin injuries or dislocated hips. Some people like it so much that they are happy to stick to this chosen position forever, and I say, 'Hmmm, maybe that's just a *tad* dull?'

It's a very personal choice, but one thing is absolutely, *absolutely* essential in all sexual relationships, and applies as much to those first gropes in the bushes at school as it does to a long-term relationship with a partner or spouse: Don't do anything you feel unhappy about, and for heaven's sake talk about it if there is a clash of desires. If you are bored of The Usual and want to try something a little more adventurous then suggest it – he is very unlikely to say no! But if he wants you to engage in lesbian romps with some of the other mothers from the school playground, and seems irritated that you think he's stepped way out of line and have banned him from the school run forever, then perhaps you two have some serious talking to do. Unless you are up for it too, I guess, but that's way too weird for me.

Whoever is the more adventurous and experimental of the two, you both need to be aware of how the other person feels about things. Are the suggestions really so unreasonable? Might it keep things alive and fresh to have a go? Or is it something that he really should have kept to himself, or for drunken chats with his mates?

Problem Three: Why don't we have sex as often as we used to?

Seriously? That anybody can be surprised, worried or disappointed when sex becomes less frequent or mundane during various stages of a relationship is completely bewildering to me. What on earth did you expect? How could anybody possibly keep up *that* level of sexual activity and enthusiasm when there are newborn babies, work stresses, family bereavements, pregnancies, unaccountable bad moods and financial worries thrown into the mix?

It is completely normal to go through phases of inactivity or disinterest in the bedroom, for any of the above and also a million other reasons, which are all part of normal life. It does not mean your relationship is over, or that you have dried up or that one of you is getting down and dirty with a third – or fourth – party. Falling out of lust happens to everyone (even those celebrities who insist they have been hard at it for seventeen years without so much as a pause for breath) and it's not something to panic about. It's just a phase, which will probably sort itself out after a few weeks, or occasionally months if things are very bad, and you'll be back at it again. Maybe not as much as in those early years, but back to something you can both live on pretty well.

If things slow down and remain very infrequent or dull for longer than a few months, then you really should talk about it. Is he disinterested in your advances because he is tired, ill, or getting it somewhere else? (Tread carefully if you ask about that last possibility . . .) Does the thought of anyone touching you, or even *looking* at you, make you wince because you are unhappy with your weight, have recently had a baby or are stressing out about the fact that none of the kitchen cupboards close properly and three of the handles are falling off? Or is there really something wrong with your relationship now, which needs some serious attention? Only one thing is for sure: ignoring it or worrying about it will always make things worse.

Just say no

This isn't a suggestion, but more a reminder that it's perfectly OK to say, 'No thank you, I really don't want to tonight,' roll over and fall fast asleep. You shouldn't have to explain why – it's your right as a human being *not* to have sex with somebody – but maybe adding something by way of explanation might help him. 'I've got a headache' fell out of fashion years ago as men cottoned on to the fact that a good shag sorts out even the worst case of sore head (and absolutely everything else, they'll try to convince you) and women realised how pathetic it sounds, so the best plan is to tell it like it is. 'I'm just really not in the mood – I have no idea why but I just don't feel like it at all. I'm sorry,' should be completely acceptable. If it isn't, you need to ask yourself just how much this guy respects you and your emotions, relative to himself and his, er, more animal instincts. Letting him know you still love him and fancy him helps too, by the way.

That said, sometimes, in fact quite a lot of the time, if you can just have a go, and stop worrying about the fact that you will miss out on an hour's sleep, need to pop out for some milk before breakfast tomorrow and haven't written the cheque for your daughter's school trip, your brain can let go enough to transform you into Up For It mode fairly quickly.

Spice up your life

As much of the above should have convinced you, and maybe comforted you, sleeping with somebody on a regular basis for upwards of a year or two brings with it a certain amount of, shall we say, *routine*. I don't want to say boredom, because that's something you can sort out, but it's the routine, the habit, the roads already travelled and the been-there-done-that of sex with one person for years and years which is unavoidable.

Here are some points to remember that might help to keep your sex life, like the finest baked goods, fresh, hot and absolutely delicious:

☆ **Familiarity can make the sex better and better** as the years go on. No, really. When you know every mole, muscle and movement of a person's body, and when you have lived together long enough to almost be a *part* of one another, it can take as little as a look, a touch or a smell to send you over the edge. There's no fumbling around, wondering what works, what he likes, what that odd bump is, or whether he knows that you are ticklish in one small area beside your ribcage – the map has been charted, and now that you are deeply in love you can have some fun visiting all the favourite spots, relaxed and confident that you won't get lost.

☆ **Explore new territory.** Just as going to the same place on holiday year after year could get boring, so having sex in the same way, at the same time and in the same place week after week would try the staying power of even the most unadventurous explorer. You need some variation! I'm not going to list suggestions of positions you could try, sex aids you could use or games you could play – there are plenty of websites you can find for that kind of detailed information. Suffice to say that you will need to push the boat out just a tad occasionally, and see where it takes you. If you end up with groin strain and a sprained ankle, then maybe give it a miss next time. Butt (ha, ha) sometimes you stumble across a path to previously unknown ecstasy, and wonder how you could have missed it for all these years.

☆ **Pace yourself.** Just as with the sex-toys chapter below, so ticking every box in the Every Possible Sexual Encounter You Can Have list in the first six months is possibly not the best way to embark on a long-lasting relationship. When you've done everything there is to do and seen everything there is to see, it leaves very little left to look forward to, doesn't it? Instead of swinging from the chandelier, posting a homemade sex video of yourselves on the Internet and joining the local swingers group (Oh God, I feel a bit queasy now . . .), think about pacing yourselves a little and leave something to be discovered for next year, or for your tenth anniversary. You've got the rest of your lives, so there's really no rush.

☆ **Dress the part.** This has nothing to do with French maids, dominatrix boots or PVC catsuits with carefully placed parts cut out for, shall we say, easy access. For those who are into all of that, you go right ahead. Here I'm just talking about keeping up your own efforts at looking good and not 'letting yourself go' after you get married. It's very understandable why so many married folk do this: there's nobody to impress any more, so why bother? Why not walk around in fraying, greying underwear, leave a good two millimetres of visible leg hair and never use moisturiser? It doesn't matter, because he's all yours now, and you can just let it all hang out. Not so, my little hairy, smelly, scaly friend: making an effort at personal grooming, wearing beautiful underwear that makes you look and feel sexy, and continuing to feel like a desirable sexual being all play a vital role in keeping your sex life alive. Just so we're clear, you're not doing it just for him: it's for YOU. If you feel dowdy and unkempt then you are less likely to feel frisky and attractive. You're not trying to keep your man; you're trying to keep yourself sexually fulfilled: quite a different matter.

Taking your mood to bed

Here's a common thing my friends and I have all experienced, and which might therefore affect you at some point: getting into a moody rut and taking it to bed with you.

This is a very female trait, and is related to the 'And Another Thing' phenomenon where what starts as a small argument turns into a tirade of abuse and a catalogue of minute errors and oversights on His part, delivered at high speed and in a voice not dissimilar to Her mother's. It's all very silly, and the more we go on about it the more we hate ourselves for being so petty and unattractive . . . so the more we go on about it. (See page 203 for more on this terrible habit.)

With sex, the same can happen. Following a 'What do you *mean* you left his hat at nursery??' type of rant, you get in a bad mood and don't feel like having sex with somebody who is so useless, half-witted and *male* as to leave a small, navy blue hat hanging on his son's peg. So far, so understandable, normal and forgivable. But when you *still* don't feel like it the next night, because you are making a very drawn-out point about how much more childcare and general housework you do than him, then you will start to feel annoyed that you are being so immature, and feel like sex even less. Not because you are cross with him any more, but because you're cross with yourself. As the 'no sex' thing becomes a regular occurrence it can quickly escalate into a habit, causing many days, even weeks, of needless abstinence, followed inevitably by more Bad Mood due to lack of sex, and it's a cycle that can be very hard to break.

But break it you must. Admit to yourself that you are being an idiot, put on your best 'Come hither' look and see what an hour – or even a few minutes – between the sheets can do. It's more than likely to sort you out and put that smile back on your face. Hat? Which hat?

Toys for the boys – and the girls . . .

We humans just can't leave things alone, can we? Never satisfied with the status quo we feel the need to constantly embellish, improve, update and modify everything. Even if something works just perfectly as it is – a microwave with an ON/OFF switch and a timer for example – some clever sod decides that's just far too simple and adds hundreds of buttons and dials that promise to take all the strain away from poor old you who has to press ON and decide how long for, all by yourself. By some very clever, pre-programmed wizardry the new all-singing, all-dancing machine can now heat, defrost or cook your meat, veg, pizza or whatever to just the right temperature without you having to use your brain at all, except to choose the correct button in the first place. Magic! Of course, what *actually* happens is that your particular piece of food or drink isn't exactly the same as the one used when the machine was programmed, and you are left dashing for the pause button every thirty seconds as ominous popping and crackling sounds are heard from the interior. Some improvement.

And so it is with sex. Sex, in its simplest form, *works*. It makes everybody who tries it feel good, the component parts usually fit together fairly well from the start without much need for adjustment, and there is plenty of scope for variation using just the tools we were born with. But that's apparently not enough. Oh no. I mean, why only have sex with the person you love wearing nothing but, well, nothing, when you could jazz yourself up a bit with a cheap, tasteless piece of red and black lace and a whip? Why enjoy the pleasures of the flesh as they are, when you could enjoy them so much more dressed as a French maid and substituting a ten-inch piece of cold plastic for the real male deal?

I remember being invited to an Ann Summers party by one of my mother friends about six years ago, and spending the best part of three days absolutely terrified of going. Not to go would show that I was sexually inhibited and boring. To attend would mean spending an evening passing vibrators, whips, crotchless panties and edible massage oil around a group of women with whom I usually discussed the price of school dinners, after-school playdates and the prevalence of nits in Year Three.

I went, of course, and it was quite a lot of fun, though I suspect that was more because we had drunk enough wine between us to drown the most stubborn of inhibitions than because any of us actually *enjoyed* the event. I came away with nothing, except a strong desire that nobody would mention it the next day. Happily, this was fulfilled and there has been no mention of Rampant Rabbits or Orgasm Balls since. What I did learn was that everybody else was as hesitant and embarrassed as I was, and there didn't appear to be any suggestion that any of this paraphernalia was normal or desirable in any of my friends' bedrooms.

I had a much more enjoyable experience surveying the shelves at the boudoir-esque sex shop Coco de Mer in London (all in the name of research, you understand). Here was stuff I found not only attractive and sensual but even appealing, and I left with a small bag of booty and such a wicked smile on my face that I had to have a cold shower in the form of a long walk around the block and an unpleasant visit to the bank, before my next meeting with a disarmingly attractive man.

All of this is to say that you shouldn't feel under any pressure at all to use sex toys of any sort, and if you do, it should be because you really want to. Just because the Internet is crammed with women doing strange things to animals and each other does not mean you are letting the side down by passing on the dildo, thanks all the same.

Reading dirty, seeing dirty, writing dirty . . . talking dirty

I can't write dirty, as you have probably noticed, but many people can and there's a wealth of erotic literature out there to amuse, titillate or shock you. There is also pornography, of course, which can help you if you're really going through an Off phase, but most of it is so nasty and cheap that it either makes me laugh at the ridiculous set-ups and expressions or cry that women are still posing for such shots. There's also something unmistakably Spotty Teenager about top-shelf porn (which is now bottom and middle shelf, I notice, thanks to lads' mags getting raunchier by the month), which is enough to put the most determined reader off.

Thanks in part to the success of the now-defunct *Erotic Review*, and also to a resurgence in popularity of burlesque and more 'classy' eroticism, there is now more interesting erotic literature available than ever before, much of it beautifully written and thought-provoking as well as steamy as hell. And if it gets you in the mood then everyone's a winner.

Seeing dirty can be a great way to liven things up, but again, if you're not comfortable with it then there's no reason you should feel bad about that or be asked to sit through it. Everyone has their own limits of what they can and can't watch, and you are by no means alone if you find it more embarrassing than erotic to watch other people getting it on. Women have completely different triggers for what turns them on than men anyway, and it can be even the remotest *suggestion* of something sexual – a glimpse of torso, sensuous music or anything with Gael Garcia Bernal in it – that sets us off into a world of erotic fantasy and hasty removal of clothes. Or so I'm told . . . ahem.

Writing sonnets to your loved one is perhaps a little outdated, but quite a lot of people I know use suggestive (or downright blatant) text messages and emails to get their partners hot under the collar. Best to find out how public his email is before you try this, and never send lewd texts if you know he's in a meeting, especially if it's with a rather attractive colleague. This is one time you do *not* want him to get in the mood . . .

Talking dirty is for the professionals only. Despite what you may have seen in films or heard in radio plays (the ones that shocked Radio 4 listeners try to get banned from the sensitive airwaves) most adults in stable sexual partnerships do not breathe obscene, sexually explicit nothings into each other's ears every time they sleep together. Really, they don't. Ask any of your more honest friends and they will laugh at the thought. If you *want* to then that's a different thing, but you are not letting the side down one jot if the words, "Come here, you bad, *bad* boy!" sound just a little bit unnatural and peculiar. *Chaq'un à son gout!*

Playing Away: Affairs, flirting, and other naughty things

If the very idea of infidelity sends you into a panic, then perhaps you should spend a little time in this room trying to understand why this is the case. Nobody likes the idea of infidelity, but the statistics speak for themselves: a great many people are at it, and the more prepared you are for what *might* happen, the more likely your marriage is to weather any storms.

Here's hoping it never happens to any of us . . .

Affairs

Here's my ideal take on extramarital affairs: they are a very bad idea, fuck everybody up – especially any children involved – and shouldn't happen. Here's my slightly more realistic take on the matter: humans are only human, and we all make mistakes, do things we normally wouldn't do after five glasses of wine, and change as we grow older. What this means is that, despite my 'ideal' position above, I know that we are all fallible and don't know how we will feel about anything in the future, or what the future holds. Right *now* I don't want to have an affair, have no desire to flirt with people and am perfectly happy with my lot, and I hope my husband feels the same way.

But things could change. Maybe in fifteen years' time we won't feel like this any more, and the grass really will be greener on the other side. Perhaps. For now I am sticking to my ideal, hoping it lasts forever, and trying to remember the following things:

☆ **Keep your eyes open.** I don't only mean open for what he might be up to (unexpected entries on your credit-card bill, increasingly late nights in the office, lipstick on the collar – *surely* they've learned that one by now?) but also for how you may be acting and feeling, either consciously or without realising it, towards somebody other than your partner. If you start to make excuses to see somebody, or wander slightly down the sheet-ice slope of telling half-truths or even downright lies about where you have been, where you are going or what you have been doing all day, then it's time to STOP and think about what you are doing.

☆ **Is it worth it?** The answer in the majority of cases is surely No. How could a few afternoons in a hotel room or a fumble in a stationery cupboard ever, ever be worth screwing up a marriage, throwing all your money at lawyers, selling your home and half your possessions to pay those legal fees and watching your kids being eaten up with the hurt and incomprehension of what you have done? Even the Best Sex in the World Ever couldn't make up for that.

I do know of cases where an extramarital affair has saved a marriage – what had become stale and taken for granted gained a new lease of life as both parties realised what they were missing and totally changed the way they behaved towards each other – but this is by far the minority of cases, I should think. Only you know your situation, but it's always worth double-checking with yourself, just to be sure.

Sophie, married eleven years, mother of Jonny, eight, and Mia, four:
Any kind of affair, however short-lived, would signal the end of my marriage. It's an absolute no-go for me, and I would never, ever forgive him.

☆ **When is an affair not an affair?** If you meet somebody for lunch several times, have coffee together regularly and go to visit an art gallery one afternoon, are you having an affair? If you stay at work until the wee hours with a colleague, take the train in the mornings together and go shopping together in your lunch break, are you having an affair? It's a very fuzzy line. For many it's drawn at physical contact of any kind, but there is a good case to say that two people can have an 'emotional affair' without any physical shenanigans at all. Liking somebody that much is almost worse than just sleeping with them, because it is the beginning of falling in love, and the idea of a partner being in love with somebody else is the ultimate fear of most women. Whatever your own personal definitions, it's a very good idea to make sure you are speaking in the same terms. When his 'platonic friendship' turns out to be what you regard as a Class A affair, there will be fireworks.

Maria, married ten years, mother of Jessica, nine, and Claudia, five:

I can forgive innocent flirting over the dinner table, even among friends, but flirting to hurt would be unacceptable to me, and would mean there was a big problem.

☆ **Do unto others . . .** This is the rule I try to live by when it comes to such things: would I like it if he behaved towards another woman as I do towards other men? If I would find it hurtful or upsetting in any way, or if I think I would feel jealous or worried about it, then I don't do it. It's that simple. If you can honestly say that you would be comfortable with your partner having dinner three nights a week with the buxom beauty from Marketing then either you are being dishonest or you have a remarkably strong, healthy relationship and you shouldn't feel bad about going for a post-work drink with the six-foot hunk of muscle from Accounts.

☆ **Think how he will feel.** Having said this, the other rule I try to live by is to always bear in mind how he would feel about something, *regardless of how I would feel*. If one of you is very open-minded and trusting but the other is very possessive and jealous, then firstly you have a potential disaster on your hands that will need some serious work if it is to be avoided, and secondly you will need to consider the feelings of your partner much more than normal. Just because *you* would be OK with him spending hours a day with somebody, does not mean he feels the same way about it. Think!

☆ **The grass is rarely greener.** If, indeed, ever. It may *look* as though it smells sweeter, feels softer and tastes – well, let's not worry about that, we're not *eating* the grass just yet – but it doesn't. It's an illusion caused by the fresh, clear light reflecting off this drinks-buying, flirting, compliment-giving grassy area, and making it seem oh so much greener than the patch of worn moss you're standing on. Resist. You'll be kicking yourself when you find out it's actually just as barren as your original plot, but without the benefit of familiarity and love. Of course he seems more appealing – you haven't been picking his smelly socks off the floor and talking to him about nothing but kids and work for the last ten years, have you? Be reasonable, and try to see the wood for the very attractive trees.

☆ **Talk about it.** It really surprises me how many people I know who say any kind of affair would be the end of their marriage, but who never, ever talk about infidelity with their partner. This seems to me to be nothing less than complete denial and avoidance – both very unwise in a relationship. Just because you talk about it, doesn't mean it's either happening or going to happen, and *not* talking about it suggests a lack of openness and trust.

The eyes have it: why flirting isn't all bad

Flirting is another term that leaves the door wide open for misinterpretation and differing definitions. When, for example, does a 'look' become a 'flirtatious glance'? When does a humorous text message become suggestive, and therefore flirtatious? And when does harmless flirtation, such as that which often goes on between friends who know each other very well and would never even *think* of crossing the line into proper infidelity, become something more potentially problematic?

It's complicated, but I think part of the answer lies in the giver, not the receiver. If a man misinterprets my friendly smiles as being suggestive, that's his problem and he will be disappointed (or relieved if he thinks I'm – to use a *Heat* favourite – a minger). Either way, in that situation I am in the clear. But if I am quite intentionally giving off flirtatious vibes, however innocent or light-hearted, that's entirely different. Now *I'm* playing the game and I have to know what's acceptable, and when to stop, according to what I've agreed, or sensed, from my other half.

I have had a change of heart where flirting is concerned over recent years. After I met the man of my dreams (that's Mr Liz, by the way) I stopped flirting completely, because I was so completely wrapped up in him that I didn't even *see* anyone else. I also considered flirting, of any kind, to be completely out of the question and an unquestionable kind of infidelity. My flirting days were over.

But now I think I might have been wrong. I was introduced to a guy a few years ago who behaved very flirtatiously towards me, and I was shocked to realise that it made me feel really good about myself. After years and years of never being looked at in *that way* by anybody (husbands can look at you in many ways, but when the daily grind of kids, bills, home improvements and family diaries sets in, it is rarely in that unknown, dangerous, do-you-dare way) I suddenly felt as though a vital part of me that had died years before, probably when I had my first baby and started to feel very differently about my body and myself, had been given the kiss of life by one look from this stranger.

If some innocent flirtation can give you confidence and belief in yourself as an attractive, sexual being, then it can't be so bad, can it? I'll never see Mr Flirtatious again, but I am grateful for those looks – they were a real boost to the relationship I have with my husband, and I think he's grateful for that too, if you know what I mean . . .

☆ **Flirting is a vital part of every sexually active person's life**, and to dispense with it can make your sexual confidence die away. Of course you're not going to *sleep* with anyone else (we hope) but it's nice to know you could if you wanted to! And if an occasional seductive look across a room keeps you feeling hot and wanted, and if that can be used to good effect in your marriage, then that's got to be a good thing.

☆ **Flirt with each other.** When you are married, the exciting, erotic ritual of seducing each other can be somewhat dampened: it's a catch before you've started, so why bother? Because it's important to feel wanted, desired and lusted after, that's why. It makes you feel strong, sexy and more than just a wife and mother who picks up everybody's mess. Most marriages fall into an unexciting slump every so often, but if you can find ways of flirting with one another, whether over the phone, by email or across the sofa, then you should find things pick up where you left off fairly quickly.

☆ **Talk about it.** I'm big on talking about things, aren't I? Well, that's because it keeps things out in the open, guilt- and worry-free, and it avoids many an unpleasant misunderstanding along the way. If you feel uncomfortable about your partner's behaviour, then tell him, and explain why. If you wonder whether you may have overstepped the mark on Saturday night with his work colleague in the pub, then ask him if he thought so too, or if he minded. Some women are married to men who *love* to see them flirt – it's some kind of turn-on for them, I guess. Find out where the boundaries are, and remember to update every year or so – things change in a marriage, and what was OK in your early days together may no longer make the cut now, and vice versa.

If it happens

I know a few people who have either been on the receiving end of a partner's adultery, or who have been the adulterous party themselves. More have ended in a split than have managed to survive. If something like this does happen in your own relationship, you need to very carefully consider one thing: Do you want this relationship to continue, despite what has happened?

Infidelity need not be the end of a relationship. Of course, this depends on the type of infidelity: a drunken snog in a bar is not even on the same *scale* as a four-year affair, in my opinion, but I realise for others there is no difference between the two. Being unfaithful is just that, no matter in what form. If the unthinkable does happen it can be a wake-up call to the fact that you are not leading fulfilling lives together, a chance to redress some of the habits you have both slipped into, and to try to change things. Maybe you stopped going out so much after you had children and should find ways to reverse this. Maybe work dominates your lives, and you no longer have much time or energy left for each other. Maybe you have done that scary thing, and grown apart a bit. That's fine: everyone does at various stages in their marriage (see page 200) but it doesn't have to spell the end. Just as you grow apart, so you can also grow back together again, by finding things to do together, and ways of being in love again, rather than mindlessly cohabiting with somebody you hardly know any more.

Almost every woman I asked while researching this book said an infidelity or an affair on her husband's part would be the end of their marriage, without question. Most also said that they try never to think about it, because it is too upsetting. But when pushed, a few conceded that if it did happen, then giving it some time and talking it through together might be worth a shot, because there would be so much to lose by splitting up.

You don't know how you'll react until you get there, and I *really* hope it never happens to you, or to me. Of course there will be many instances when deciding to call it a day is the only workable option, because you have both gone way past the point of liking each other any more, and too much hurt has been caused. But keeping an open mind, and trying as hard as possible to make things work together again, is by far the most sensible option. Raising our children in a stable family set-up is one of the best things we can ever do for them.

The Art of Making Conversation

The very fact that you picked up this book shows you to be an intelligent, interested, humorous person, and therefore quite likely to know how to have a good natter. I am about to point out to you, in case you hadn't noticed already, that conversations between two people who live together for a long time and have kids together can quickly turn into little more than lists of child-related information and jobs still left to do. Worse, as though our brains came out with the placenta, we mothers have a terrible tendency to talk drivel for hours on end, to people who just want some peace and quiet – usually our spouses. A typical non-conversation like this goes as follows:

'Did I tell you about William's poo incident today?'

'No.'

'Oh, it was so funny! William did a huge poo in Boots this morning, which nearly cleared the shop, it stank so badly. I was so embarrassed I had to leave without my shopping and dash to find the nearest baby change. Then I realised I'd left my purse by the checkout, so we dashed back again, with William crying now because he still needed a change, and then I thought, well, since we're here again now I might as well get all the shopping I left behind, but you'll never guess what . . .'

'Hmm?'

'I said you'll never guess what.'

'What?'

'Well, some helpful person had only gone and put it all away already! So there we were, still smelling, with no shopping and now half an hour late for toddler group – which, by the way, has now moved from Wednesday to Thursday, which is a real pain in the neck because that's the day William has his nursery visits arranged, if you remember, but I don't want him to miss out on toddler group because it's such important social time for him, don't you think?'

'Oh yeah. Definitely.'

'Anyway, there we were, and I just thought . . .'

Nobody cares what you thought, least of all the thoroughly bored man sitting opposite you, who stopped listening somewhere between 'poo' and 'baby change' and is wondering whether that sexy woman he saw in Waterstone's at lunchtime has fake breasts or if she really is that well built, and if it would be acceptable husbandish behaviour to have coffee with her tomorrow, because she sure as hell wouldn't talk about bloody children all the time!

This kind of vacuous, uninteresting and passion-killing

conversation happens to us all without us realising it, and if it goes unchecked it will drive you both insane, apart or both.

☆ **Listen to yourself.** There is an art to listening to yourself as you talk, which seems to disappear the moment we give birth. Do try to imagine what your babbling sounds like to another person – especially one who has just got back from work and really can't handle any more information in one day, even if it is about his lovely family.

☆ **Just STOP!** If you think your account of how you've discovered that Chloe likes to eat her courgettes in sticks rather than cut into circles sounds just a little bit too homely and uninspiring, then try to bite your tongue and talk about something else instead. A certain amount of this is fine – important, even – but not in minute detail and not exclusively. Give him a round-up and move on.

☆ **How was _your_ day?** Better still, don't talk at all but ask him about his day instead. We are terrible at rabbiting on and on about every second of our (frankly very uninteresting) day, and never once stopping to ask how _he_ is, what _he_ did, what _he_ would like to do. This is a direct result of spending hours with small people who can't say more than 'Watch _Tweenies_!' and 'I dunna poo', but while it's very understandable, you do need to curb it occasionally.

☆ **Get out more.** A simple cure to having nothing to talk about is: find something! If you do absolutely nothing separately from each other you won't have anything to talk about that the other person doesn't already know. Go to the cinema with a friend, go out together for drinks with friends, go to an exhibition or take up a hobby. Couples who do nothing together and nothing separately, apart from looking after the kids and going to work, have nothing to talk about, and that's one step away from talking about splitting up.

Growing Together . . . Or growing apart

The man I married isn't the man I live with today. *What??! You said* . . . Hold on, tiger, and let me finish. That is, he *is* the same person, in name, but he has changed so much since the day he dressed up in a silly hat and said 'I do' that he is, in effect, quite a different man. This is fine, because I'm not the girl he married either: I was twenty-one (a baby!), fresh out of college, with no idea who I was or what I wanted to do in my life or how to dress properly or wear make-up. I'm still not sure about that last bit, come to think of it, but I've got another fifty years to work on it . . .

All of this change is, of course, only to be expected – indeed, to be encouraged. Who *wants* to stay the same throughout their twenties, thirties and beyond? Imagine if we were doomed to wearing the same ill-fitting clothes, liking the same naff music and decorating our walls with Athena prints for the rest of our lives – Jesus, it would be awful! It's the very process of changing, of discovering new interests, tastes and passions that shape who we are, which makes life worth living. That and Venice, dark chocolate and photography books, *bien sur*.

So far, so progressive and positive. But so just-you-on-your-own. The danger comes when two people live together for a very long time and they change and grow *apart* from one another. The emerging chasm between them is often cunningly papered over by a shared interest in their children, and by the pace of daily life and routine. But one day all efforts at concealing the inevitable prove futile: the ground gives way, and they are left staring at each other from a distance, wondering who the heck this stranger is they share a bed with. This usually coincides with the kids leaving home, but it can strike much sooner than that – even within a couple of years in some cases.

This 'growing apart' is as common as the muffin tops and bad haircuts to be found on every high street in the land. We all know couples who have grown apart over the years: perhaps it's some friends of yours, or your parents, or maybe even you and your partner. It's not a crime (unlike muffin tops, which should be – God, woman, wear a longer shirt or some bigger jeans!), but it can sometimes be avoided, given some careful introspection and effort.

☆ **Never take your relationship for granted.** This is almost guaranteed to make a relationship fail. When you're in that heavenly state which used to be known as 'courting' you have sex five times a night, every night, because you are desperately trying to impress. You talk at length – all day if possible – linger on every fascinating, witty, sexy word, and spend hours and hours hanging out, having fun and just *being* together. Fast forward ten years and you find that you barely exchange words any more – except to ask when the baby was last fed, if the bins are out or who's on school-run duty this week. You only have sex when you can't find a fresh excuse to get out of it and catch some decent sleep, and as for doing anything together – well, like what? What do you have in common any more? *Nada*, mate, that's what.

☆ **Relationships need to be constantly worked at, monitored and nurtured** if they are to survive longer than those first few heavenly months. To assume they'll survive despite total neglect and lack of interest on your part just because you were head-over-heels in love once upon a time is just asking for trouble.

☆ **Put it to the test.** If you want to know just how 'together' you two still are, then try this one: Get someone to have the kids for a day or two and go away together, somewhere with no distractions at all. You know you're in trouble when you can't think of a damned thing to say to one another after twenty minutes – an hour if you're lucky. We've all been there, and it's bloody scary. Realise what's happening and decide to do something about it.

☆ **Speak out.** If you think you're moving away from each other and you are worrying about what this is doing to your relationship then *please* tell your other half about it. He may not be aware of it and will be glad you aired your concerns, or he might say he has been thinking exactly the same thing but wasn't sure what to say (men are often like this – just not quite sure what to say.

Sigh.). One thing is for sure: waiting to see if things just sort themselves out is madness. In 99.9 per cent of cases, they won't.

☆ **Physical changes.** Just as you may change emotionally and mentally as the years roll by, so it's very likely that neither of you will cut quite the dashing figure you did when you first clapped eyes on each other. If you've had kids, ladies, this means it's very, very unlikely you will have the same figure as you did! Men tend to go bald or grey and develop a middle-aged spread and women just start to droop in all areas. If all of this leaves you just as attracted to each other as ever, then that's great. But if you find the new love-handles a bit of a turn-off, then talk about it, and see if you could both tone things up a bit, not just for each other but for your own self-confidence as well.

☆ **Come together.** If you feel that you're like two ships moving in different directions, then try to think of ways of steering back together again. This could be getting a babysitter more regularly and going out as a couple, going to more exhibitions, gigs, films or sporting events – anything to get you doing something together that you both can enjoy and share. It sounds really naff, but it works, so give it a go.

☆ **Keep it in context.** If you start to freak yourself out worrying that things have gone wrong between you, you no longer have anything to say to one another and you are destined for a split, remember one thing: since having kids your life as a couple is entirely different from the one you had together before this happy addition. Back then you used to go out with friends a lot, talk about what happened when you went out with those friends, about maybe getting married and all the planning that goes along with it, and ultimately discuss having kids. The difference now is that you have the kids, and you go out less, so the main thing you share now is the children. So in fact not all that much has changed, it just *feels* scary because you think you're turning into one of those clichéd, boring, parenty types. It's family life, and while it's different from what you had before, it's certainly not boring.

And another thing . . .! Common rows, and how to survive them

If you never argue with a person you have been together with for a year or more, then you are in a teeny, weeny minority of people who either have no emotion or show no emotion. Or you are lying. Arguing, however slightly, is something which comes hand-in-hand with long-term relationships, and just knowing that it's quite normal to have disagreements and petty rows can help if you are worried that your relationship is doomed.

There is a huge variety in the scale of arguments between lovers, from the moody brush-off to the physically violent, but one thing has been shown by Busy Researchers to be true: couples only ever fight about a very small number of things, and they can go over and over the same ground for years. You probably know some of them already – you do too much housework, he leaves his shoes in the middle of the floor, you leave your pots of cream all over the bathroom, he doesn't help enough with the childcare, he tries to help with the childcare and messes it up, one of you wants more sex than the other, he doesn't respect your work enough, he works too much, you never leave the tea bag in long enough and so on and on and on *and on* until you are both blue in the face, fifty years older and still bickering over the hoovering. It's absolutely bonkers, and a huge waste of time and energy which would be better spent shagging each other on the lounge carpet, thus sorting out one of the problems and making you both feel better.

However stupid it may be, the point is that we *all* do it, but there are ways to reduce the amount, and the type of arguing you do.

Here is a typical argument, which my husband and I, and most husbands and their wives, have had many times over, or something very similar, and will have again before the month is out:

He comes into the kitchen, just home from work, looking a bit deflated. I am cooking, quite happily, and the children are playing outside.
Me: *(chopping vegetables)* Hiya. Are you OK?

Him: Yeah. Why?

Me: I don't know, you just look a bit grumpy.

Him: I'm not grumpy. I've just had a hard day at work. *He sits down heavily.*

Me: Oh, OK.

I start to make a bit of a fuss over the chopping and stirring. He looks at some paperwork on the sideboard.

Me: Do you mind tidying some of that up please? It's been there for a week.

Him: I will. There's no rush – it doesn't have to be dealt with for another few days.

Me: (*draining the potatoes vigorously*) Yes, but if it stays there it's in my way, and I don't *want* it there any more. *Brushing past him to the fridge in a deliberately annoyed fashion.* Excuse me.

Him: I will deal with it all - I just don't want to do it now because I'm tired. *He puts the envelopes down again.*

Me: Wow, can't imagine what *that* must feel like.

Him: Oh don't be like that. *He gets up and moves to the cutlery drawer.*

Me: Like what? *I dollop half a pound of butter on the potatoes in a huff.*

Him: Like –

Me: I'm just saying it would be nice if I got a little help around here, that's all. I'm tired too. Do you want to look after the kids all day? And shop, and cook and tidy up after everyone? And try to have a job as well? God I'd do anything to go to work for a day and come home to a cooked dinner. *Trying to get to the serving dishes cupboard.* Sorry – you're in the way.

Him: *slamming the cutlery drawer.* Oh I just can't win can I? I'm trying to help, and I'm in the way.

Me: I asked if you could sort out the paperwork, not set the table. I can do that myself . . .

And so on. It then usually dissolves into me talking to myself for a little while, about how hard my life is and why I am suffering more than anyone else on the planet and he is just living the life of Riley and should be kissing my feet and offering me a gin and tonic, until one of our kids comes in and makes us laugh for some reason or another, and the whole thing is forgotten until the next time.

If you are in an even semi-normal relationship with a person who shares your dental floss and knows what you look like naked from every possible angle, then you will recognise at least some of the above displays of irritability, attention–seeking, need for appreciation and love and general silliness of most domestic arguments. The even sillier thing is that during almost every row we have, I hate myself for the petty, hurtful and arse-clenchingly juvenile things I say, and this only serves to push me even deeper into the role of Nagging Wife, which in turn makes me say more stupid things. Part of me is able to float above the scene of domestic disharmony and hear every word I utter from afar, and such is the revulsion of everything I say, and the way I say it, that I am sure I end up being much more angry with *myself*, rather than with my nagged-to-death husband.

This is very, very common, as are 90% of traits of rows between long-term lovers. You are not alone! Here are some Top Tips which might make you feel less inclined to file for divorce or eat the entire contents of your biscuit cupboard:

☆ **Stop Talking:** If 'Going On And On And *On* About Something' were a competitive sport then women would win hands down at every level. We *rock* when it comes to finding yet another thing to say on a subject which has just been argued to death and should be left to rest in peace. Men find this deeply unattractive, so try to put a sock in it once you've made your point.

☆ **Quit while you're ahead:** Again, many women are hopeless at this, compared with their male counterparts. Men can make two or three succinct points in an argument, feel they have won, and leave it at that. Women see the faintest whiff of being victorious as an excuse to throw the doors open and invite every other petty quibble about the most unrelated issues into the argument, and thus talk themselves out of poll position and back into the pits. Realising when you have overstepped the 'making a good point' mark and are now striding down the rocky road to sounding like an idiot is crucial to surviving argument. And another thing . . .!

☆ **Match your arguing style:** Research has shown that to survive in a relationship it doesn't seem to matter how often you argue, or even over what, so long as you both argue *in the same way*: if you're both explosive, then venting your mutual frustrations through a shouting match can be cathartic and helpful. If you would both rather ignore things for a fortnight and then gently bring the subject up over a civilised glass of wine before bed, then fine. Problems tend to arise when a firecracker marries a shrinking violet – he scares the shit out of her, and she just frustrates his need for a good shouting session.

☆ **Listen to Yourself:** If you think you sound like a repetitive, sexually frustrated, shouting old hag, then he probably does too. Sometimes it's worth just taking a step back, listening you how awful you sound and changing your tune. This can often help the situation.

☆ **Admit when you're wrong:** *You know* when you are in the wrong (yes you do!) and holding your hands up and admitting 'OK, I'm being a prat and I did say that *I* would take the DVDs back, not you, but I *was* annoyed about the dirty socks on the floor and I stand by that' will win you more points than any harping on about sexual inequality and who said who was doing what, when.

☆ **Define your terms:** People's perception of arguments differs widely, and what you might consider to be a minor disagreement, he might describe as a full-blown row. If you talk about this, and understand how the other person feels about confrontations, it could avoid a lot of misunderstandings and overreactions later on, eg 'I wasn't *shouting*, I was just saying . . .' Well he didn't think so.

☆ **The Last Word:** Having the last word does not mean winning an argument. OK? Sometimes it's better to just leave it . . . I said *leave* it!

☆ **Do A Post Mortem:** This can be ten minutes after you've finished slagging each other off, a day or even a week later, but having talked to a great many couples about their arguing survival strategies there seems to be agreement amongst those who still have a strong, solid relationship with their partner that always making sure a row is properly resolved helps a lot. Talk about what happened during an argument, and whether you both understand what it was about, and what was concluded, and you should be able to repeat going over the same ground before the day is out.

If you think you are the only couple to have the same arguments every few days, over a period of more than ten years, then think again. Your parents probably did it, and your grandparents and great grandparents before them. So, probably, does everyone else you know, even though they smile and seem to be living in perfect harmony every time you see them. You are not alone, but luckily for you, you have all the wonderful tips above to follow, which should make things more harmonious in your own house too. Who's cross now?

Nine Lives . . . And all of them important

There's common misconception in newly married couples that they have to live in each other's pockets. Unless you have enormous pockets and a remarkable tolerance for being in very close physical or mental proximity to someone else twenty-four hours a day, this situation cannot do anything but drive you both insane, or apart, within a few years.

For the first few years of our marriage I did my very best limpet impression: everywhere he went, I went too. When he went to the pub, I came along for a pint; when he played football, I was on the sidelines; if he wanted to go for a run at the weekend, I'd tag along. I'm quite embarrassed to even think about it now, but there it was, and I now know I wasn't the only one doing this:

I'm not sure when the penny dropped, but I'm very glad it did: we couldn't have sustained this 'Siamese twins' thing for very much longer than we did, as it meant we never had anything new or revelatory to say to one another:

'I was in the pub on Tuesday and John said . . .'

'I know – I was there.'

'Oh yes, so you were.' Silence. 'Oh, there's this amazing bit in *Gladiator*, when Russell Cro—'

'I know, we saw it together last week.'

And so on.

The solution is to make sure you both lead several different but interconnected and compatible lives. There are a great many, but the four main ones you need to give attention to are:

- ☆ **yours on your own** or with your friends
- ☆ **his on his own** or with his friends
- ☆ **yours together** as a couple, and
- ☆ **yours altogether** as a family.

If any of these get neglected or overdone, it can lead to unrest in the home: not spending enough time together is as bad as spending too much time together. Everyone has their own balance which works for them, and the main challenge is to figure out what works for your family. What *doesn't* work is when your wants and needs are incompatible with his, and you'll have to solve this imbalance quickly if you are to get any balloons at all on your ruby wedding anniversary.

When Two Become One . . .

There is a very strong desire in some women – strong enough that it almost looks like an instinct – to slowly but surely *change* their men into their perceived 'ideal man'. It starts with a few new shirts and maybe a new tie for Christmas, and progresses rapidly through dictating his haircuts, shoes, choice of music and friends. This kind of Man Makeover is about as insulting to anyone as you can get, and basically means 'I love you very much, but I would love you quite a lot more if you wore the right clothes and were, oh, I don't know, just more like *me*!'

Try not to be like this. Sure, he might have a really rubbish sense of style and you might find his choice of footwear almost too embarrassing to bear, but you knew this when you married him, and you should have the decency and sensitivity to butt out and let him be. A new suit or shirt, yes. A new wardrobe, CD collection and social life, no siree.

Taking the Rough with the Smooth: Long-term
relationships are a bumpy ride

If you've been poking around in this room for a while you'll already have learned all about falling in and out of love, the most common rows you will probably have and how to stop them, and you might be getting a sense that this marriage lark isn't quite the bed of roses you hoped it would be.

This is very good news, because it means you have been doing your research properly and you've already picked up on the most essential point of the whole room: long-term relationships are a bumpy ride, and anyone who imagines they will coast along without a flat tyre, a burst radiator or even a complete breakdown is heading for a nasty shock.

What I really hope to get across in this book, though, is that none of this should be surprising or spell the end of a relationship. We should *expect* all of the hitches above, and worse – we've had to replace our carburettor and change the oil twice, but we're cruising in the fast lane for a while again now.

I remember going to my grandparents' fiftieth wedding anniversary, and being very affected by the strong, close, supportive relationship these two old, wrinkly, quite different but absolutely inseparable people had. They had lived through a war, raised four children, watched those kids leave home to start their own families, and all that before another thirty years of just being together, day in, day out. And there they were – still in love, despite all the things they disliked or found intensely irritating about one another, and, crucially, still being the glue that held the assembled motley crew of grandchildren, great-grandchildren, dogs and cats together.

It wasn't always the happiest, most exciting or most enviable marriage in the world (those were the unenviable times when most women had to put up with their lot and get on with cooking dinner and making the beds), but it lasted and it worked, and I had never respected or admired any two people more than at that family gathering. Of course they could have gone their separate ways many years ago to discover new people, lives and experiences – and I rather think they would have liked to at times! But by working at it, sticking it out and staying together for over fifty years, through thick and thin, in sickness and in health, in grumpy times as well as happier days, they gained a relationship, a friendship and a love most of us could only ever dream of.

I realise the windows in this room have all just misted over a little, and that some of you may have fallen asleep, so I'll stop being so sentimental and preachy. Before you move on, though, let me just hammer the point home. Old people have the annoying habit of saying things that have more than a grain of truth: 'Oh, the young folk these days – they want it all handed to them on a silver platter. They've no sticking power, respect or sense of commitment at all. In my day . . .' Yeah, yeah, we get the drift, Mavis. Just the first line will do, thank you.

If I may, just for once, I'd like to side with the Zimmer frames. Of course things go badly wrong in some marriages, and separation may be more sensible than staying together. But for the rest of us (so far) an expected bump or two should never be enough to call the whole trip off.

Sit back, strap in, try not to be sick and enjoy the journey.

The Show's Over: What happens when things go wrong

Despite some of my more saccharine-coated descriptions of marriage and family life, I am not living in Cloud-cuckoo-land when it comes to relationships, and I do realise that they aren't always happy or sustainable. Much as we'd all rather they didn't, and that everyone could remain in wedded, loved-up bliss for ever and ever, amen, many marriages come to an end as a result of 'irreconcilable differences'. What exactly these differences are varies from couple to couple and can be as serious or trivial as you like: you may fall permanently out of love because you have just grown apart, there may be infertility issues, infidelity, disagreements about work–life balance, whether you should work at all, how many kids to have or what to name the dog; you may find his snoring unbearable, he may find your nagging unbearable, or he may simply turn out to be a complete arsehole which you somehow hadn't realised until now. Ooops.

Whatever the cause – and there are usually many, which overlap and interfere with one another – you may have to come to the decision that things cannot go on as they are, and the two of you need to move apart.As you know, I have no personal experience of divorce, though some unluckier members of my extended family and some of my friends sadly do. Here is some advice from them, and from me, having watched their marriages break apart, which might help you should the awful day arrive:

☆ **Are you sure?** Being frustrated, angry, bored or resentful is not enough at all. You have to be absolutely certain that staying together is impossible. To help you decide, answer the following two questions:

1. **What are you leaving?** A husband, your life with your children as you know it, shared memories, familiarity, a stable home and family, and much, much more.

2. **What are you going towards?** Another man? Sex? A new life? These can seem very appealing before you live with them for a long time and the initial excitement and interest wanes. Let's be honest: who wouldn't like to have a lover occasionally; to run away from it all; to start afresh, to live again and to relish all the excitement such a change would bring? I would, at least once a year! But a lover would soon become boring, the sex would become routine, the new life would soon be another old life and everything I have now would be lost. The grass always looks greener but, unless you are in an abusive or dangerous relationship, it rarely is.

☆ **Try it out first.** Before burning all your bridges and separating permanently, why not have a trial separation? For some couples it can confirm their suspicions that life really *is* better apart, but for others it can be a much-needed break that makes them realise that they miss each other, they are happier and stronger together and they are determined to have another go.

☆ **Think of the kids.** Every counsellor, psychologist, teacher and relationship adviser will tell you that children whose parents go through a divorce while they are still at school have more problems in life than those from stable family backgrounds. Of course, staying with a man you hate for the sake of the kids might not be the right thing to do: if there are terrible vibes in the house then this will affect the children negatively anyway. But if there is any chance – any chance at all – that you can put your differences behind you and find a way to move forward together then grab it and see what happens.

☆ **A clean break.** There is also much evidence that, when parents do split up, the ones who do so amicably and sensitively have a much less negative impact on their kids. Arguing in front of your children is a complete no-no, as is saying bad things about your partner in front of them or trying to turn them against him. Furthermore, if you can try to get along enough to meet for family gatherings, share the school run, both turn up for school events and both participate as parents, this will help your children a lot. Never forget that you are splitting up with their father, not from them, and you are both still, and forever, their parents *together*. Make sure your kids know this.

☆ **Talk to them. A lot!** How are they feeling, what do they want, how can you help them to cope better? Let them talk openly and freely, and make sure they feel their opinions and thoughts are being considered in this process too. You can really help by giving them a voice and keeping the communication very open.

Divorce is a really shitty thing, and I hope it never happens to you, me or anyone we know. But it's real, it happens, and it's best to be prepared and to handle it as best you can if the time comes. Here's to happy marriages . . .

Ten Years Down the Road . . . and still struggling with the map

For anyone who thinks that marriage gets much simpler, clearer or easier to negotiate as the merry years roll by, may I just say that no married people I know have found this to be the case, and nor have we.

We may well be patting ourselves on the back for managing a whopping ten years together (thirteen, if you count the years before we tied the knot and lived very happily in sin), but that doesn't mean we can switch to automatic and let the marriage steer itself. There are bound to be cliffs, sharp bends and potholes ahead, and I have no idea when they will come or what form they will take: A new job involving a change of location? Financial troubles? An unexpected pregnancy (no, not that one, please! I've just got over the last three)?

I have no idea what lies ahead, and I certainly don't feel that I know where I'm going at times. What I do know is that I am prepared to go to great lengths to succeed at and enjoy my marriage for as long as I can, and my Ingenious Master Plan is to keep my eyes firmly on the road ahead and try to avoid any nasty crashes.

This may not be the reassurance you were after, but at least it's honest: you'd rather I told you how it most often is than spun you some yarn about marriage being one long trip to the chocolate factory, surely?

If you wonder whether yours is the only marriage that still seems to be hitting bumpy ground regularly, or whether you are alone in feeling that you are stuck in the join between two pages and can't see whether you should turn left or right, then please don't worry: you are just like every other normal, long-term couple. Unless your lives become indescribably dull and predictable then you'll probably be struggling with the map from time to time forever. Don't give up, and don't worry: you'll find your way.

Yes, marriage is a tricky business, and it takes some work to keep it going. But if you are prepared for the potential pitfalls and know how to get over most of them, you are more than halfway to making it work. However, before you get too complacent, just across the landing is the room that is guaranteed to shake things up a little and keep you on your toes . . .

PART THIRTEEN

The Children's Bedroom

STOP! There's a sign on the door, in case you missed it, which says, 'KNOCK BEFORE YOU ENTER! Girls only, except Charlie.' Guess we'd better knock, then . . .

OK, there's no reply. What now? Oh, they're at school – duh! I think this means we can go on in, but let's try not to move too much around – it may *look* like a bomb has just exploded, but this God-awful mess has been carefully crafted by my little ones and they always know when I've been meddling.

Kids, eh? Who'd 'ave 'em?

August 2005

I've just had a lovely sleep-watching session. I went to tuck each of the kids in and spent about five minutes with each one, just lying next to them, hearing them breathe, smelling them, feeling their warmth, their soft, squishy arms and cheeks and just staring, inches away from their relaxed, flawless, indescribably beautiful faces. Huge closed eyes, long eyelashes, perfect mouths and button noses. I love putting my nose on their foreheads and breathing in their warm, sweet smell – they are simply the most perfect things

I have ever seen. I don't care how tired I am – I could stare at them all night.

Children are given such bad press these days that it's a small wonder so many of the little rotters are still produced. If you believe what you hear and read (elsewhere) you will be in no doubt that kids are obese, loud, rude, spoilt, irritating and expensive. They destroy your marriage, screw up your career and cause your body to resemble a deflated balloon.

This shamefully negative attitude towards kids is doing immeasurable harm to the little darlings, and it's a load of old cobblers too: children are fantastic! They are imaginative, thoughtful, energetic, enthusiastic, helpful, kind, quick to learn and sensitive. Sure, they can also be stubborn, loud, dirty, jealous, annoying, thoughtless and ungrateful. But then so can we all. Only this morning I managed to be annoying, thoughtless *and* loud. And probably dirty too, but let's not go into that . . .

If we focus on the bad and lose sight of the good then we not only do all children a huge disservice but we also create sad, unloved children who will grow into *very* sad, *very* difficult adults. Here are some things we should all bear in mind the next time our kids drive us up the wall (as they will do at least once a day):

☆ **There are no Problem Kids, only Problem Parents.** Every baby I have ever seen (and I've seen a heck of a lot) is as gentle, faultless and good-natured as a human can ever be. It's our job to keep them that way as they grow up. If we are aggressive, controlling, impatient and rude, so will they be. It's then a little bit hypocritical to turn around and say 'Oi! Behave!' as so many charming people seem to do.

☆ **Shut up and listen.** Children have the most incredible minds and ideas, but they rarely get a word in edgeways in between all our telling them what to do, correcting and brainwashing. Be quiet, and listen to what they have to say – it's probably a lot more inventive and sensible than anything most adults could come up with.

☆ **A child is for life, not just for a season.** Pretty obvious, I know, but still a huge number of people have a baby, think it's quite cute for six months or so, and then get bored of it. If you're gonna have a child, then make sure you're in for the LONG haul and make her life as enjoyable as possible. She's not getting in the way of your life: she's *part* of your life, so treat her that way.

☆ **Watch your mouth.** Kids pick up on everything. No matter how quietly or subtly you say something critical about a child, he will hear it, misinterpret it and process it. This is because kids have small radar in their inner ears that are specifically tuned to pick up negative comments. No, that's bullshit – actually it's because kids, like all of us paranoid adults, sense when someone is saying something nasty about them. Be careful what you say about your children if you think you might be within hypersensitive earshot. If it's good, then fine, but if it's something critical then wait until they are asleep.

☆ **Let it be.** There is a very strong instinct in many parents to interfere, correct, adjust or finish what their kids say and do. Without listening, waiting, taking a step back or just letting go, they have to take control of every aspect of their child's life. 'No, put your hat on like this; no that's not how to draw a boat; no, kick the ball like this; no, brush your hair like that' and so on and on and on. It's actually quite hard not to do, sometimes, because often your way is the most effective, efficient or generally accepted as normal. But if you can butt out and let your kids figure out their own, sometimes better, ways of doing things, they will learn to be much more independent and self-confident.

☆ **Give them responsibility.** Research has shown that one of the most detrimental things about the way many children from affluent backgrounds are raised today is that they are given no responsibility at all – their 'helicopter' parents hover nearby constantly, taking them to classes, helping them with everything, and not requiring the kids to do anything for themselves. Don't. Ask them to tidy their own rooms, clear their plates from the table, put their dirty clothes in the laundry basket, and so on.

Even young children can perform these simple tasks and it's a good way to start the responsibility curve.

☆ **Who are you?** That's the question we should be trying to answer when raising our children. Not 'Who do I want you to be?', but 'Who are *you*?' The only way to find the answer is to sit back and watch. Spend lots of time with your child, not dashing from school or nursery to ballet or recorder class, but just being with them, playing, chatting, daydreaming – taking the time to let their own personality shine and develop. It's the simplest form of parenting (and one of the easiest: doing nothing, hoorah!) but it's one of the most important and far too few of us do it.

☆ **Who am I?** For his part, this is the most important question a child needs to answer as he grows up. Who is he? What does he like? What makes him tick? A child who grows up with no sense of self is a child heading for big problems in his teenage and adult years. The way to let a child figure this out is not by continuously taking him to after-school clubs and throwing presents at him when you feel guilty about spending too much time at work or when he has done well in an exam. It's by letting him be alone sometimes, without any pressure to do, achieve or learn anything in particular, and to have some free time to do whatever it is he wants to do. Again, very simple, but very, very important.

☆ **Let them get hurt.** *Whaat?* you say. You foolish, irresponsible woman! No, I don't mean sit back and watch as your toddler saws his arm off, but stop wrapping them up in cotton wool. Kids are given so few chances to take small risks, have a few knocks and scrapes and learn about life by experiencing it that's it's a wonder they manage at all after they fly the soft, fluffy nest. Let them learn their limits and capabilities themselves and they'll survive much better in the Real World. Is that a tree I see ahead? Go, climb it!

☆ **Love them.** In all the chaos of getting kids ready for school, picking them up, taking them to lessons, worrying about what they eat, wear, drink and say, fussing about homework and telling them off for swearing at the dinner table, it's very easy to forget to show them any love at all. This is a big mistake and correcting it is just a matter of being aware of it, and putting it right. Cuddle your child every day, even if she seems a bit old for that, tell her you love her *soooooooooo* much, that she's wonderful, and give her a kiss. Never make this love conditional on anything – even if she's been a pain in the neck all day, show her you love her anyway. Maybe suggest she tries to be a bit nicer tomorrow, though . . .

☆ **It's the little things.** Yes, some kids are quite little, but here I'm talking about little gestures or surprises. If children expect presents they are rarely as grateful or moved as if something comes out of the blue. I leave short notes and sketches for my kids Sellotaped to their beds at night, so they can read them in the morning. Sometimes I send them postcards for no reason except to say, 'Hello, I love you. Hope you've had a lovely day at school.' I also pop silly messages or pictures into their lunchboxes sometimes. These sorts of unexpected surprises let them know I think of them when they are away from me, and I don't only say nice things to them for a reason – I can do it any time because I love them all the time. I did ask if they minded all of this, fearing I might be embarrassing them, but they all said they love it.

These points are a drop in the ocean compared with all the essential things we have to do for our children. But they are so important, and simple, that even if you rip the rest of this book up to use as papier mâché I won't mind so long as you keep these few pages. If more of us tried even half of what's suggested half of the time, I think we would have a lot more confident, happy, well-adjusted children running around our parks and streets. Kids, eh – who'd 'ave 'em? Me, please.

How Many Times Have I Told You? Common rows and how to reduce them

March 2005

I feel really bad about something I did today. It started as a normal 'Can you PLEASE put your shoes on' type of thing, like every morning, but for some reason I just snapped. I'd asked about fifty times, and still not a single one of them had shoes, or coats. P hadn't even brushed her hair even though I asked her two hours before and again an hour, half an hour and twenty minutes before, and C was lying on the hall floor throwing plastic cannon balls into the shoe rack. I went nuts. I started shouting and listing all the things nobody ever does around here. I went on and on about all of them, and my work, and the house, and how nobody ever helps me to do anything and I have just had enough of it. It was really bad, and the kids looked a bit stunned. I did feel crap though and shouldn't have lost my temper. Told Becky later, and she said she had done exactly the same thing yesterday, and that cheered me up a lot – I'm not the only one who is driven over the edge sometimes!

Kids affect their parents' mood and behaviour enormously, both for good and bad. My kids have made me more patient, loving, considerate, gentle, open-minded, fulfilled, positive and happy than I've ever been in my life. But they also turn me into a five-headed, red-faced screeching monster from time to time. Ah well, you have to take the rough with the smooth, I guess.

There are many reasons why kids drive their parents insane, but the main one seems to be a low-level but almost constant amount of dispute or disagreement. It can be as minor as wanting to go outside at different times (you have to go out now to get to school on time, but he is refusing and wants to sit on the carpet and not budge), or as major as a two-week stormy silence because you refuse to let her have her ears pierced at the age of eight. (You're right, I think.)

*I find that the constant badgering I have to do wears me down,
physically and emotionally, until I feel I want to cry, and sometimes do. All the things we argue over are so silly and small, but
they add up to a huge amount of resentment on my part, and
when I get cross or down, it pulls the whole family's mood down
with it.*

What Eva says above is common to the majority of mothers I
asked: most of the tiffs we have with our kids are tiny and petty,
but it's the constancy and relentlessness of them that ultimately
wears us down. Nobody minds asking someone to put their shoes
on, but even the most patient woman in the world would get a bit
narked if she had to ask the same question ten times, *every* time,
before she got either a reply or a result.

The most common rows we have with our kids are about
everyday things like table manners, getting ready for school or
going out somewhere, tidying their room, how much telly they can
watch, brushing teeth, taking shoes off and putting them neatly
away where they live instead of leaving them in the middle of the
floor, not flushing the loo, chocolates and sweets, whether they can
have a friend to play or what they choose to wear, and many, many
others. All very minor when compared with the bigger issues in
life, but on a day-to-day scale they are very significant, and it's
completely understandable if you lose the ability to see the funny
side every so often.

When you feel this happening, try some of the following:

☆ **How many times have you asked?** You could ask your kids a
hundred times and sometimes still get nothing more than a sore
throat and a headache. If you feel your persistent requests are
falling on deaf ears, then it might be worth having a little chat

with them and asking if they've heard you, and why they are ignoring you. If you keep on and on, repeating the same 'Can you hang your coats up please?' with no effect, you need to change tack.

☆ **Keep it quiet.** I've said it before but I'll say it again as it applies here as well: raising your voice can get the result you want sometimes, but if you do it often it will lose its effect and make for a very negative, aggressive household. *Try* to keep calm if possible and remember that it's not how loudly you say something, but how well you communicate what you're after that makes the difference.

☆ **Say it to my face.** We got into a habit last year of shouting instructions and requests from neighbouring rooms, or from upstairs to downstairs, and even from the house to the bottom of the garden. It meant we were constantly yelling around the place, and still getting poor results. I put an end to that by insisting that all communication took place face to face, and more quietly. Success! The neighbours no longer hate us, and more is getting done when we ask, because we have asked nicely and directly rather than hollering it from the next room. Use your legs, not just your voice, and see what happens.

☆ **You're not going out dressed like that!** A common complaint from parents, which can kick in with kids as young as two or three who have a very clear idea of what they want to wear. Two of mine were like this, insisting on going out in Arctic conditions in a T-shirt and sandals, or wearing the most revolting outfits imaginable, as chosen by their dear selves every morning. I used to be very unhappy about it, but now I realise it's just another example of adults trying to control what kids do. Why not let children experiment with their clothing and wear what they want from time to time? It usually settles down after a while, and if not you might have the next Vivienne Westwood or Alexander McQueen in your house – who knows? Oh, and as to the T-shirts in the Arctic situation – let him try it and see how far he gets. He'll come round soon enough and beg for some sensible clothes without you having to raise your voice once. 'Told you so . . .'

☆ **Does it really matter?** Often it doesn't. It's very easy to get into the habit of insisting on things, giving orders, making requests and so on, when, really, the thing we're giving ourselves frown lines over doesn't matter that much at all. Stop, and think about how important it honestly is. Maybe it *is*, but maybe, just this once, you could let it pass.

☆ **Give up.** Sometimes defeat is less stressful than sticking to your guns. It's not a very good example to set, but then neither is being a miserable, bossy old cow. Maybe it's going to be one of those days (or weeks). Accept it, don't fight it, and let them go to school with unkempt hair and a messy room. There's always tomorrow to try again.

☆ **Be polite.** I'm always surprised at how many parents insist their kids say 'please' and 'thank you' when they themselves never bother. If you ask your child to tidy his room, then ask nicely. When (if) he does it, let him know you've noticed and say thank you. It's not much to ask, and it's just rude not to.

Without a doubt, frequently arguing with our children over irritatingly minor issues is common to almost all of us, and it can be the cause of a lot of foul moods and general malaise in the family home. This can take a real hold and be very hard to shift. If you can gain strength from the fact that you are *not* the only one going through the same thing, and try to reduce the amount of bickering, cajoling and badgering that you do using some of the tips above, you should find the mood improves and everyone reaps the benefits.

Where did you Learn *that*?

Exposing your kids to inhabitants of the Outside World after you've been carefully nurturing them within the home can be a little like watching the sandcastle you spent all afternoon making get decimated by a gang of ice-cream-waving, pot-bellied, sunburned thugs. It's a wreck whichever way you look at it, and most of your hard work is destroyed.

It's not always quite so destructive, of course, and sometimes there's a parapet or a piece of the moat still standing, as evidence of the fine structure that once stood. But mostly, the day you wave goodbye at the nursery or school gates is the day all your hard effort at child-rearing will slowly start to sink into a heap of wet sand, and you start running about trying to fortify the ramparts and stop dogs and small children weeing on it.

This is just a part of life, and trying to protect your children from the wicked ways of the Outside World would be pointless, and damaging. All you can do is to prepare them as best you can, and hope that when the first pot-bellied, sunburned yob bashes them over the head, they handle it well.

For the first few years, the outside influences are fairly tame: we have had to deal with spitting, biting, pinching and throwing food across the table learned from children at nursery, and pushing, screeching and biscuit-stealing from various mini-thugs at toddler groups. I remember being quite shocked when my angelic daughter came home from nursery one day and said I was a 'smelly fart-head'. Where did she learn *that*? I couldn't recall ever calling her, her father or my father-in-law a smelly fart-head – at least not within her earshot – and I wondered if I was the owner of a Bad Child who thought of Bad Things and would be tattooed and drugged up to the hilt by the age of seven. As it turned out, neither she nor the Bad Influence (aka Thomas) is heading towards the tattoo parlour imminently: 'smelly fart-head' turned out to originate from Thomas's older brother, Naughty Nicholas, who is clearly off the rails already, poor chap.

All of this spitting, hitting and saying rude things might worry you at first, as you see your angel turning nasty before your eyes. But if you consider that this is all part of growing up, of learning that not everyone behaves in the same way, that some people are not quite as nice as others and some can be downright Bad, then you soon realise you have nothing to worry about – it's all healthy learning, and your careful handling (see below) will remove the worst new habits.

As your children get older it gets more complicated. Outside Influences quickly stop being as heart-stoppingly awful as saying 'fart' or pinching people who snatch a toy away. Before you can say 'Who has drunk all my gin?' your lovely children will be coming home with all kinds of ideas in their pretty little heads which you sure as hell didn't put there. Recent examples in my household include:

Being vegetarian. *We're not. New Best Friend is.*
Having their own computer. *Nice try.*
Saying 'what-*ever*' as a final word. *Hate it! Hate it!*
Getting ears pierced. *Still working out our policy here.*
Wearing pants on the head. *Assume this came from nursery.*

There are many more, but this gives you an idea of the kinds of intrusions from the Outside World we are currently trying to wipe out. None of them are terribly Bad, but all of them are things that other kids do, or so I'm told, and which we're not so keen on our own children doing just yet. Or ever, in the case of the pants. If you think I'm being an overprotective control freak, then do bear in mind that my eldest is only eight: when she's a teenager I know I will have lost the battle, so I'm clinging on to my last few years of having any influence over her life whatsoever.

We have found a number of ways that work when trying to cleanse your kids of some unwanted outside influence or other:

☆ **Blank it.** We did this when one of our kids started saying 'shit!' at the age of two. Not sure where it came from, but within a few days it had vanished, as it never got a response.

☆ **Ask where that came from.** Instead of getting cross when your child starts spitting or asking for sweets before breakfast, just ask where they got that idea, or who else does that. If you're lucky enough to get a name, then say that what that person does isn't something you want your children to do, as it's not very nice/bad for their teeth, etc. Try not to say, 'Yes, well, have you seen his mother's hair? With roots like that, what chance have her kids got.' That's your itchy bikini stubble talking.

☆ **Press repeat.** When children are asked to repeat something they know you disapprove of, they usually go quiet. This works even on two-year-olds, who suddenly sense that 'bloody shitty hell' is actually quite bad, and keep schtum.

☆ **Keep calm.** Getting a reaction is half the reason why children provoke their parents. Silly, but true. If they know that asking for a Bratz doll sent you into an impressive rage the last seven hundred times, then having one more go seems like a fun experiment – will she explode? Will she turn all red and blotchy like before? Will we have to scrape the dinner off the ceiling again? Such fun. Keeping calm shows there will be no fun here, just a very definite 'No.'

I should mention that not all outside influences are bad: some of the things my kids have picked up outside the home have been really useful and positive. Charlie clears his plate at the end of every meal and goes to wash his hands without being asked – something he picked up at nursery; Emily knows more about using a computer than I have ever taught her, and can create a PowerPoint presentation in a matter of minutes thanks to tips from her friend Jack; Phoebe has learned 'Chopsticks' on the piano from one of her friends. There are many, many other things I could list, which I certainly didn't teach, and which are really useful, helpful or to be welcomed. It's just a shame the good bits have to be watered down with so much rubbish.

All of this leads us neatly on to a new character in this little play of family life:

Introducing '*Everyone*': Your new worst friend

Amanda, mother of Sophie, eleven, and Georgia, eight:

I am so sick of the girls saying 'Everyone' has this or that. I find peer pressure really hard to handle, because there are just so many things kids can have nowadays and I have to say 'no' to almost all of it. Then I feel guilty. But we have our principles and beliefs about what's best for our children and we want to stick to them.

I know an '*Everyone*'. You do too, and so do, or will, all of your children. *Everyone* (whose name can only be spoken in italics, at high volume and preferably accompanied by dropping the arms and shoulders and adopting an imploring, desperate facial expression) lurks about at the back of the classroom, doing all the things you never want your children to do, or can't afford to do, or just don't have the time to let your children do, and spreading the unchallengeable word that not to do exactly the same as him or her is to cast yourself out from anything resembling 'cool' and to become a social reject, a lonely nerd, a square, a geek – *forever*.

Everyone can be just one person, or sometimes a small group of four or five people, but almost never *everyone*. When I was a little girl, *Everyone* wore Dash sweatshirts, shopped at Tesco's and watched *Neighbours*. I wore hand-me-downs, had to make do with Sainsbury's carrier-bags – *so* un-cool back then – and watched *Horizon* and *Tomorrow's World*.

My daughters have an *Everyone* at their school too, who does the following:

Watches telly before school.
Phones friends without asking parents.
Stays up until 9 p.m.
Has crisps in her packed lunch every day.

Has a TV in her bedroom.
Has a computer in her bedroom.
Wears shoes with small heels and no backs.

As you can imagine, *Everyone* is not flavour of the month in my household at the moment, as every day brings a new something-or-other that *Everyone* does, and my girls implore me to let them do too. I am often stuck for an answer for the following reason:

☆ I want to say Yes, so that they can fit in with their peers and not be as embarrassingly un-cool as me.
☆ I want to say No, because they are all things that I just don't want my kids to do/wear/eat/watch, etc.

This is a very common parental dilemma, and I can only suggest the following if you are being pushed into an uncomfortable corner by this irritating intruder:

☆ **Define '*Everyone*'.** I always ask who *Everyone* is, and also always suggest names: Does Georgia have a guinea pig? No. Does Isabel? Or Millie? Or Aidan? There – so in fact *Everyone* doesn't, but Millie does. I think you will survive without one for the foreseeable future then, just like all the others.
☆ **Set a time limit.** This is similar to the Tantric Shopping theory on page 50. Instead of just saying 'No', suggest that you wait a few weeks and if *Everyone* still has a denim crotch-length mini-skirt then you might review the situation. By this time the latest thing will be floor-length gypsy skirts and you can oblige. Magic.
☆ **Turn the tables.** Ask your child what he would do in your position: give his own children bags of salt, fat and flavouring five days a week or try to keep them as a weekend treat? Even if he insists he would hand out the Lard Bags without question, at some level he knows you are right, and it can work.
☆ **Make them pay.** Not in a *Fame Academy* 'Right here's where you start paying – in sweat!' kind of way, but in a real, pocket-

money kind of way. Suggest they save a certain amount towards whatever it is they so desperately want, and you will make up the rest. If you pick a suitably impossible figure then they might rethink the idea. It can also make them realise just how much money they are asking you to spend on them and they might understand your refusal.

☆ **Give it a go.** We tried this with the late bed proposition, and it lasted a week before my daughter waved her white flag and went back to her normal bedtime. She became so exhausted and irritable that we did nothing but argue, she looked rough as hell and developed four cold sores from lack of sleep, and she over-slept and missed breakfast twice. We tried hard not to say 'I told you so' too loudly . . .

Claire, mother of Jake, six, and Emily, three:
We don't have as much money as other parents seem to, and I have little choice but to say 'no' to buying lots of things. It embarrasses me, and I know it upsets my kids. They have lots of things and seem happy, but I know there are lots of other things they'd love to have, like their friends do.

This last point is a very good one, and it's felt by more parents than will often admit it: there is such huge pressure on us to buy hundreds of toys, clothes, games and DVDs for our children, but, frankly, we can't all afford it. This was a big problem for my parents when I was growing up, as we had far less expendable cash than most of my peers did. Hence not buying me a Walkman, some of the clothes I so desperately wanted or taking me on posh holidays wasn't so much a matter principle for them as of circumstance: they had no choice.

We do tell our kids about this, and have a very open line of communication about money and the cost of things. It seems to work, as they understand why we have to say 'no' sometimes. It doesn't explain why we're not vegetarian or why they can't stay up late, but it deals with some of the issues.

If you are plagued by peer pressure and by the unwanted habits of *Everyone*, just remember that you knew one too, and sometimes giving in to just one small demand can make a child deliriously happy for a while. Flashing toothbrush it is, then.

Money Munchers: Cutting the cost of kids

One of the reasons I often hear people giving for not wanting to start a family is that it will cost too much. Children, otherwise known as cash-guzzlers, pension-pinchers, money-munchers and much worse, do indeed use up a lot of your hard-earned dosh, and the older they get the worse this money draining becomes. Lego and nappies are replaced by trampolines and scooters, and eventually by university fees and houses. Start saving now.

When you realise that almost every penny you earn, and sometimes more, goes on paying the mortgage, nursery fees, football lessons and new school shoes, then, as well as wanting to jump in a deep hole because your life has become so boring, you know you have to start watching those pennies, and the first things to go are any treats for yourself. This is a cruel fact of family life, but it's also one of the benefits in human terms: being forced to put the needs of others before your own makes you a much kinder, more generous person, in my opinion. Yes, I know those shoes would look gorgeous with your new summer dress, and that candelabra would be the *pièce de résistance* in the hallway, but if it's that or replacing your five-year-old's raincoat, which was already a tad tight last year, then what you want will need to wait until next month.

There are ways to ease the strain on the family kitty, and to keep family finances in the black. Most are quite boring, but then nobody said money matters were exciting, did they?

☆ **Join a toy library.** See p. 131.
☆ **Just say NO.** One of the most important reasons for saving

and being careful with money is for what it teaches your kids. Oh, and because it means you don't go bankrupt. There's almost nothing quite as ugly as a child who expects, and gets, it all. Teaching my kids the value of waiting for things, and saying 'no' when they ask for something they don't need is something I feel nauseatingly Good and Worthy for, and also rather mean, but I am prepared to go through this self-hatred because I'm sure it will ultimately do them good. They still think 50p is quite a lot of money, which I'm pleased about: it is, if you're six years old. It's enough for some sweets and, if you save for a few weeks, just enough to buy a crappy pink fluffy pencil that you don't need. If I had bought them the crappy pink fluffy pencil after the first ask, it would have been left on the floor with all the other junk they don't use, within an hour. Spending their own money makes them really value what they have, and it will be a good three or four days before the pencil is committed to the bedroom-floor grave.

☆ **See, buy, store.** If I see a special item of clothing for my children in the 'seventy per cent off' sale, I usually buy it, even if it's about three years too big for them. It goes in my 'Too Big' box, and then, when the time is right, I can whip out a Jigsaw or Monsoon treat, and not feel that I've broken the bank – because I haven't.

☆ **Bring your own.** I am terrible for this: I bring pastries to cafés, popcorn to cinemas and drinks to restaurants. I save a small fortune, but it embarrasses my kids no end. You have to be subtle, of course, but at nearly a fiver for some tiny, exploded corn kernels, I think we are justified in bringing our own. You can always claim your child has special dietary requirements and your bring-along snack is organic/wheat-free/gluten-free or whatever you choose. Naughty!

☆ **Packed lunch.** School dinners came under the spotlight thanks to the marvellous Mr Oliver a few years ago and they improved dramatically in many schools. Thank you, Jamie. But in most cases they still cost much more than a very healthy packed lunch. The argument against, which claims it's too much hassle to make a packed lunch, holds absolutely no sway with me. It takes about three minutes once you've had enough practice, and if you do it the night before while you're clearing up the after-dinner mess it hardly eats into your day at all.

Packed Lunch Tips

☆ **Variety is the spice of packed lunch.** Don't give them ham sandwiches and an apple every single day – it's so boring! Vary the fillings and extras at least twice a week and they'll be much happier eating it.

☆ **Pitta bread** is a great alternative to normal bread, and if you supply fillings like cheese and cucumber slices, ham or a small tub of tuna and mayo, they can fill it themselves. Beware that this takes time, though, and if they aren't managing to eat enough because they're spending time stuffing the pitta bread, then go back to sandwiches for a while.

☆ **Small is beautiful.** Kids like small things, so chop up sandwiches into smaller shapes, add lots of cucumber sticks, carrot sticks, cherry tomatoes and mini cheeses such as a Babybel, and it not only looks lovely but goes down a treat as well.

☆ **Check what's left.** The good thing about packed lunches is that you know what's being eaten. If the tomatoes are still there every evening then suggest an alternative. Similarly, if there is always a sandwich left over ask why (it's probably because they are chatting instead of eating) and see if you can get them to try and eat it all up for a few days. You can always threaten to take away the pudding if not . . .

☆ **Hot or cold?** Ninety-nine per cent of packed lunches I've seen are cold and come in Tupperware boxes. But you can now get all kinds of funky containers to keep food hot or cold as required. One of my kids loves having a hot packed lunch every so often, and it takes only a few minutes to pop in some hot pasta and add the cheese, chorizo or whatever in a separate box for her to mix in at lunchtime.

☆ **Pudding?** I think kids always need something sweet in their lunch – they burn so much energy running about, learning and beating each other up that this needs replacing. Chocolate is banned in many schools, but yoghurt drinks, a flapjack or a favourite biscuit are all good alternatives. If the rest is consistently not eaten then omit the pudding for a while.

☆ **Treats**. Friday is treat day for my kids (if Mummy remembers, which I cunningly don't at least two Fridays per month – oops) and I stick a small packet of crisps in their packed lunch. If you don't include any surprises or treats the lunch becomes boring and they don't enjoy it or eat it.

☆ **Add a napkin.** Eating is a very messy business when you're also talking, kicking somebody under the table and trying to show off your new 'Gorilla with a pea in his nose' impression. A napkin can make things a little better, but not much. Worth a try.

Pocket Money

Aha, a subject of much debate and negotiation in many households: should they or shouldn't they? If yes, then how much, and from what age? What are they allowed to spend it on? Anything they like? Or anything they like and we approve of? And so on.

We started our eldest on pocket money when she was five, and she got a very uninventive 50p every week. This has gone up by 10p every year and she now gets a whopping 80p, aged eight. This is very mean, as 80p can't buy you anything at all these days, except for some sweets (which I'd rather she didn't have) or . . . actually, I think that's about it. She does save up well, and after a few weeks she would be able to treat herself to a packet of stickers or a pencil or something, were it not for the embarrassing fact that we forget to give her any pocket money half the time. Horribly mean!

We have been much less principled with our other children (that's the way with most things, I'm afraid – sorry firstborns!) and they both started out with 30p or whatever coppers I had rattling around in my purse from the age of three or so. I still forget to give them anything, but there's nothing malicious in that – I honestly just forget.

Whatever you decide to do about pocket money, here are some things you might want to think about:

☆ **Learning about the value of money** is a very important lesson in our hideously money-driven, consumerist society. If a child has her own savings and wants to buy something, she will have to feel what it's like to part with her much-loved, shiny pennies. Now she's not so sure she really *needs* that *Charlotte's Web* pencil case after all.

☆ **Fitting in.** Sorry, chaps, but if everyone else in the class gets pocket money, you really should give yours some too, or he'll feel like the odd one out. It doesn't have to be the same amount, but *something* would be kind.

☆ **What's yours is yours.** We disagree on this one: my husband says that our children should be free to do whatever they like with their pocket money – it's theirs and it's their choice. In theory I completely agree with this, but when it comes to it I can't help feeling that they should spend it on something 'good' – something useful, or that they need, or really, *really* want. Not some cheap tat that will lie about on the floor for two weeks and then get broken. It *was* my money, and I don't like to see it wasted, but I know that I have to learn to let go and realise it's theirs.

☆ **Keep it safe.** Our kids have lost lots of money by leaving it lying around, dropping it down the back of beds or hiding it and never finding it again. Get a nice money box/piggy bank/treasure chest and make sure all the money goes in straight away!

☆ **Bank accounts.** For tiny sums this isn't very practical – withdrawing 50p isn't worth queuing for half an hour for – and it's the holding and admiring of the money that is most of the fun for young children. But as they get older, and they get larger sums for Christmas from Granny or something, then opening a child's bank account is a good idea. 'Out of sight; out of mind' comes into play here too, and they are less likely to spend money they don't physically have. If only it could work like that for adults!

Growing Pains: It starts very early!

May 2006, 10 p.m.

I have just finished applying a third coat of thick, white emulsion to Emily's bedroom ceiling. As if my aching shoulder, back and neck weren't enough, there is added pain in the fact that I have just painted over the perfect clouds, sun and rainbow I so lovingly created for her to gaze up at when she was a baby, in this same room eight years ago. I'm not sure which I feel sadder about – that I've just undone all the hard work I did while teetering, giddy and pregnant, up a ladder, or what this covering up symbolises: that time has whizzed by without my realising it, leaving Emily no longer my baby, but a lanky, gorgeous young lady who wants a room of her own and a door that locks. I know things have to move on as our family grows up, but there's something so in-your-face about physically removing the baby evidence, and it hurts. Not as much as my shoulder, mind you.

Everyone says it, and it just gets truer and truer: kids grow up *so* fast these days! When I was eight, I spent all of my free time building tree houses, dens and secret paths at the bottom of my garden, setting up secret clubs with my friends and collecting odd specimens of aquatic life from the local stream. Oh, and getting my older brother into trouble. I was a *child* – a rather geeky, awkward child, I admit, but not entirely dissimilar from my friends at school.

These days the eight-year-old girls I see (and I see a lot) act like thirteen-year-olds of twenty years ago: they are often moody and difficult, they want to dress in sexy, 'cool' clothes, their interests include applying make-up, doing their hair, watching television and sulking, they are shy around boys and they spend large amounts of time staring in the mirror saying they are ugly or fat. It's horrible.

I don't see quite so many eight-year-old boys, but from what I have seen they don't appear to be suffering too badly from the 'growing up at an alarming, unnatural rate' problem as their female peers. They run about a lot, pretend to kill each other, play football and swap cards with strange creatures drawn on them, the names of which I can never remember. Much like boys have always done, in other words.

If you think your child is developing earlier than you did, then the following should put your mind at ease a little, and possibly slow the transition into full-blown teenagehood somewhat:

☆ **Exposure.** I am quite, quite convinced that what is making young children want to be teenagers not long after they've come out of nappies are the images and relentless commercialism they see all around them. Every time they walk around town they are exposed to something else they want, want, *want* and images of children looking cool and grown-up. If you can reduce the amount of exposure they have to such things, by banning music videos, reducing the number of times they go shopping, not buying magazines you feel are inappropriate and trying not to let them watch any adverts, you can go some way to prolonging their innocent childhood. Almost impossible, in other words, but certainly worth trying.

☆ **Present alternatives.** Just as it's possible to influence a child into wanting to dress older and cooler, so it's also possible to sway them the other way. If you read them exciting books about children who, despite not dressing in boob tubes and being covered in glitter, still seem to have a great time and are very likeable, restrict the TV they watch to programmes that are age-appropriate, buy them beautiful clothes more suitable for young children than mini-adults, and encourage simple, imaginative play, then you can reduce the 'Mum, I want to be grown-up now!' problem.

☆ **Slow things down.** It's a fact that modern life is much faster and more hectic than times gone by, and kids are often dragged about from pillar to post in adult surroundings such as cafés, restaurants or shopping centres. This is almost certainly contributing to children's desire to grow up, because they are given so little time or opportunity to be children! Try to create chances for them to really *play* – to dig about in the garden, make models out of egg boxes or put on puppet shows. *Blue Peter* here I come!

☆ **Go back to your childhood.** Suggest some of the games you used to play, activities you loved doing, films or programmes you loved watching (my kids love *The Railway Children*, *My Family and Other Animals*, and so on, and there's hardly anything too grown up about them) and toys you used to have. A lot of the old stuff is having a revival these days, with pogo sticks, space hoppers and skipping ropes all making a comeback.

☆ **Don't beat yourself up.** Whatever you do to protect your children from the Evils of modern consumerism and marketing, they will be exposed to it at some point. You don't want your child to live in a bubble, so accept that things will never be as they used to, and just do your best.

☆ **Emotional changes.** Just as children's wants and desires are a lot 'older' than you might expect, so their emotional development can seem several years ahead of schedule. Many of my friends are finding, just as we are, that their very young children are far more moody, emotional, and difficult to manage than they were at that age. It comes as a real shock, but I think the only way to deal with it is to accept that they are living in a very different world from the one we were lucky enough to grow up in, with far less opportunity to be carefree and childlike. The argument 'When I was your age . . .' really doesn't hold because nothing is as it was when you were their age. Just look at your haircut in those old photos for starters! Much better is to try and understand why they are acting as they are, talk to them and find ways of getting them to enjoy being themselves again. They are confused too – getting angry about it will only make it worse.

✫ **Do some research.** If you ask some of your friends who have kids the same age, a good number will almost certainly tell you that they are finding their child is growing up much faster than they expected, if not physically then emotionally or in terms of how they think they ought to be. It's a struggle for all of us, and sharing your concerns will almost always make you feel better, and less worried that you are an old fuddy-duddy, or that your children are abnormally troublesome.

✫ **Change with the times.** Nobody wants their child to feel like the odd one out (or I hope they don't). Even if you really, really, *really* don't want to them to visit the Groovy Glitter Fashion Superstar Girls! website or watch *Killer Robot Machines* on telly, if everyone else is talking about them at school you might be wiser to concede this one time. Go on, Mum, get with the times.

✫ **Get to know each other.** Once you've come to accept that you now have a fire-breathing Tweenager in the house, the best thing to do is to be properly introduced: talk to her more, find out what's going on in her head, and get to know her better. You might not *like* everything you hear, but at least you know what you're dealing with and then you can slowly try to put some of the hottest flames out. If you keep on-side with this new moody, unpredictable inhabitant you will be in a much better position to help him through this tricky stage. Having arguments, trying to lay down the law and forbidding everything you disapprove of will only push him further and further away, and you'll lose him very fast . . . which is the opposite of what you're trying to achieve!

It's really sad that kids grow up faster now than ever, and there's nothing we can do to stop it completely. It's good to be prepared, though, and to know how much to relish every moment you have with them before the change sets in. It should help to known that if you think you are dealing with a particularly difficult seven-year-old, there's someone down the road thinking exactly the same thing. You haven't made a mess of it – but you might if you don't learn to deal with it fast.

Behind Closed Doors: When they want their own space

At some point around your child's eighth or ninth birthday (or earlier if you are very unlucky) he will announce that he is now far too grown up to share with his sibling, and requires a room all of his own. If he is lucky enough to already have a room of his own, then the move will be to attempt to shut the door at all times, and to lock it if possible.

'Hey!' you will exclaim. 'Where did my child go? Why does he hate me so much that he wants to be as far away and out of sight, sound and smell of me as possible? What did I do? What did I say?'

Nothing. You did nothing wrong and said nothing wrong, but you are now verging on the point of being embarrassing, annoying and painfully un-cool, and the sooner you get used to the idea the better for you all. I was really shocked at how young my children were when they started to drift away from me occasionally and want some more independence. I expected it to be at the age of twelve or so, not six! I actually think it's a good sign, and shows they are able to be by themselves, entertain themselves and operate without me holding their hand all the time, but it still hurts like hell. I want my babies back, and I don't care who knows!

☆ **Let them have their own space.** It's absolutely vital that you let your children have some space where they can be alone and that they call their own, even from a young age. It might not be a room all to themselves if, like us, you don't have enough rooms in the house, but it can be an area in the room, or some time every day when nobody else is allowed in. Kids need time to think, be secretive and feel independent, so find a way of letting that happen.

☆ **Keep some closeness.** A child who disappears into her room every day after school and only comes out to eat is somewhat worrying. We have a rule where doors can be closed for a while every day, but never as soon as the children come home (some kind of 'Hi, how are you? Nice to see you' type of chat is compulsory) and never for more than an hour at the most. I'm sure this will increase as they get older, but for now it's a compromise: they get some time alone and also some time with the door open, allowing them to be more a part of the family.

☆ **Make an effort.** Time-consuming and costly though it was, we spent an entire two weekends redecorating our daughter's bedroom recently. Since its completion she has been visibly and audibly happier. It's not my choice of colour scheme or decoration, but that's fine: it's her room, so she should be able to put her stamp on it.

Discipline

I *hate* the word 'discipline' when it's used as a verb, with reference to children. It's reminiscent of gothic novels where warty, mean-looking schoolmasters dole out cold gruel before beating all the bad, disobedient children – who look like they'd really rather have some pizza and chips instead – into submission with a large, knobbly stick. I only called this chapter 'Discipline' to get your attention – it worked! – but now I'm going to rename it 'Establishing and explaining the rules', which is much more what we're after.

Getting children to behave well is very difficult, and to behave 'properly' is even harder. Why? Well, firstly, what exactly *is* 'properly'? Not talking at the table? Not telling Mummy she's a f***ing slag? Not standing up straight when being spoken to? Only one thing is certain: your 'properly' is not the same as mine, and that's fine. We all expect different standards of politeness and manners both from ourselves and from our children. What doesn't work is if these two are different – you can't expect your kids to be little angels if you are a pig. Pigs breed pigs, see, not angels. It's basic biology.

Secondly, how can we raise well-behaved children, and ask that they have any respect for us or our rules at all, if we are rarely there, and spend what little time we do have with our kids either shouting at them or trying to tidy up the bloody mess they've made? With great difficulty, that's how. And so we either need to think of much nicer ways to treat our kids or we should have our ovaries removed at puberty.

The reason there are so many programmes on the box called *Help – My Kids are Beating Me to Pulp!* or *Little Bastards – How to Punish Your Kids into Submission the Kind Way*, is because somewhere between about 1950 and today, kids have gone from being eerily quiet, scared and obedient, to resembling wild animals on speed with an attitude problem. *How* this happened is a question worthy of a further five thousand pages, and it still wouldn't cover it, but I'm convinced of two things: neither situation is desirable, and the kids aren't to blame. Let's leave it there, and see what we can do to reduce the level of disruptive, violent, rude and generally horrible children we have trashing the walls of our own homes, replacing them with thoughtful, happy and socially well-adjusted individuals.

Giving advice on how to 'discipline' your children is not new, but here's my take on it: I'm not going to tell you how to do it, or to recommend a 'naughty corner' or a carefully calculated scale of punishment from 'no sweets today' to 'up the chimney with you, and don't come down till I call you!' or whatever. Instead, I shall tell you how we have (so far) managed to raise three reasonably well-behaved, self-confident, independent-minded, happy individuals, whom we can usually bring along to restaurants without fear of them destroying the place or disturbing the other diners:

☆ **Start on day one.** This is absolutely crucial. Establishing clear rules and acceptable behaviour at a very early age should avoid you trying to reintegrate your unruly ten-year-old back into polite society one day. Once habits such as sitting down to eat, saying 'please' and 'thank you' and not shouting at Mummy or Daddy are learned, they are relatively easy to keep on going. Even babies can understand and learn simple rules such as: 'No, the biscuit does not go in Mummy's hairdryer, it goes in your mouth, see?'

☆ **Be consistent.** Children find inconsistencies in the application of rules and in the reaction given when rules are broken to be very upsetting and disturbing. If a child knows when he's being naughty and what the reaction from Daddy is likely to be, he doesn't get the shit scared out of him when said parent bawls 'What are you *doing*?' rather loudly. He knew it was coming, and half-expected it. But if he is minding his own business, doing something that was perfectly acceptable yesterday and suddenly the wrath of a sleep-deprived parent descends in a torrent of rage, he is likely to get a nasty shock. This breeds fear and insecurity, and we don't want that *at all*. Be consistent with what's allowed and how you react when little people do naughty things.

☆ **Don't shout.** Three things happen when you shout at children: they learn that shouting is what we do when we're cross (which it shouldn't be), you get a hoarse voice and you feel like shit. Don't shout at a child if you can help it. Shouting leads to more shouting and more shouting, and nobody can hear a thing or remember what all the shouting is about. Keep the level down, and things can be sorted out much more effectively.

☆ **Lead by example.** If you behave well, your kids probably will. It's that simple, as far as I can tell. If you eat food with your fingers, so will your kids; if you hit people, so will your kids, and you have absolutely no grounds for saying they shouldn't. You do, so why shouldn't they?

☆ **Explain yourself.** If a child is told off, or told either to do or not to do something but doesn't understand *why*, she learns nothing and just feels confused and powerless. Kids are smart, and if you just explain why they aren't allowed to touch the CD player (because they broke the last two) or why you want them to go to bed at 7 p.m. (because they were up late last night and you would like to talk to Daddy before you fall asleep) then they can usually see your point and oblige. It can take four or five gos at getting your point across, but keeping calm and trying to get them to see what you're saying is well worth the effort.

☆ **Something MISunderstood.** Sometimes it's plain obvious when a child is being naughty, stubborn or moody, but quite often there is a genuine miscommunication or misunderstanding. Children don't often hear what you say properly, as they are too busy humming 'Supercalifragilisticexpialidocious' or trying to stuff a piece of tissue into a small hole in the wall they've just made, and so their refusal to do as you've just asked is quite simply because they didn't hear you properly. Misunderstandings are also very common, because kids can misinterpret what we adults take as obvious: one classic example is when we say 'Right, let's go to the playground.' Kids understand this as, 'Let's go right *this very second*,' which is silly because what you *obviously* meant was 'Let's go after twenty minutes of faffing, finding shoes, putting on coats, answering the phone and so on.' When they pester you every thirty seconds with a 'Mum, can we go now!' it's easy to snap 'Oh, will you be patient!' Try to see things from their perspective, and understand that they have no idea what's going on.

☆ **Three strikes and you're out.** Crashing straight in with a 'Right, that's it, I've had enough – go to your room now!' will make your kids jump out of their skin. We operate a 'three strikes and you're out' policy, where I give them warning of what will occur if whatever it is they're doing/not doing doesn't change, and they get updates on how many strikes they have left as things go along. It's also important to say what will happen if they're 'out', e.g. go to your room for ten minutes, can't go to so-and-so's house, won't go swimming this week, etc. 'Three strikes and something bad will happen' isn't incentive enough.

☆ **Never, ever hit.** Don't need to say much here. Even if they are about to get themselves killed by running into a road, sticking their fingers in a socket or something similar, it is still no reason to hit children. Pulling them away strongly and quickly, holding them very firmly, raising your voice and gesticulating wildly is usually enough to scare the crap out of them, which, *in this one particular circumstance*, is no bad thing. Next time they might just remember to be more sensible. **Note:** I have to confess that I have, on several occasions, smacked all of my children. Not hard, but a smack is a smack and it's horrible. These occasions were always when I was at the end of my tether, had tried every method known to Mother for *days* to stop my child behaving appallingly and deliberately annoying me and his or her siblings, and I just flipped out and thought a smack might do the trick. Sometimes it has, but it's not a method I encourage at all. I have almost no friends who haven't done the same thing, so if you have found yourself in a similar situation, don't worry: you are not a monster or an irresponsible, child-beating parent, and so long as this kind of thing is very rare, you shouldn't feel too worried about it. Do *always* apologise, though, and explain what happened. It's important that kids understand you are sorry and regret it.

☆ **Laugh it off.** It's surprising how many times a situation that has the potential to end in a big row can be turned into something funny and enjoyable. Before you have a go at your kids for dropping *another* fifty peas on the floor, see if you can diffuse the anger you feel by making a joke about it, clowning about a bit and making them laugh. If you can get a serious message across at the same time, about eating properly and not wasting food and making your life a misery, then you've just scored double points!

☆ **Am I bovvered?** Some children respond well to this, others don't. Often, a child is being naughty to get a reaction out of you, even if it's a cross one. (They're weird, I know.) If you show that you've noticed the bad behaviour, but make a kind of 'What a silly thing to do – ah well, if you want to be so silly that's your choice – I don't care' kind of face, you might take the enjoyment out of it for him. **Note:** This face requires a good deal of practice, so don't worry if you fail for a few attempts and just look a bit pained. Stick with it.

☆ **Change the record.** Sometimes we all get into a rut of telling our kids off far more than is necessary. This is usually when we are unusually tired, worried about some aspect of our marriage, job or haircut and just feeling crap. Try, *try* to get out of this rut by playing a different, more humorous, likeable tune. You *know* you're being a rubbish Mum, and only you can stop it.

☆ **Show your feelings.** If my kids are driving me to the point where I want to either scream at them or throw a rather nice coffee cup at the wall (both Bad Things – even the not-so-very-nice coffee cups cost a lot), I sometimes sit down and cry. I keep this for very rare occasions, because I don't want to lessen the effect, but it is quite amazing to see how lovely children become when they realise how much they can affect *your* life. 'Oh, you mean you *really* don't like it when we ignore everything you say and treat you like our slave? Oh, we're so sorry.' Sniff. Big cuddle.

☆ **Use threats wisely.** We all use threats as ways to get our children to do as they're being asked, but you have to be prepared to carry them out, and to keep them as infrequent as possible, or they lose their impact. It is very effective, though, and seems to work well as they get older too. Try to avoid really rubbish threats, like my favourite one ever, which was: 'Charlie, if you don't put that down *now* you won't have any . . . good . . . times . . . Ever!' It worked in a way, because it had us all laughing until we nearly wet ourselves.

☆ **Bribery.** Kind of the reverse of threats, but just as overused and potentially disastrous. Bribery can work well, but it always feels quite cheap somehow. Saying, 'If you come downstairs and get ready quickly you can have ten minutes' more telly' just doesn't sit easily with me. Promising sweets and chocolates is a bad plan, because they shouldn't be seen as rewards for good behaviour, but as something to enjoy now and again. But hell, it works, and we all resort to it sometimes.

☆ **Revise the Rules if necessary.** As children grow up and your lives all change, the Rules need to be revised and updated occasionally. Perhaps you no longer mind if your kids eat on the sofa sometimes, because they manage not to spill stuff. Maybe you want them to help out more with the housework, or don't mind if they stay up until much later. Keep things flexible and make changes according to what feels right at the time.

☆ **Listen to yourself.** When you are telling one of your children off, take two seconds to listen to what you're saying and how you're saying it, and ask yourself if it's *really* worth making a fuss about, or if you couldn't handle it in a different way. If parents did this every time they yelled at their kids, the world would be a happier place.

Other People's kids

Geeta, mother of India, four, and Misha, one:
I was really shocked the other day when India had two friends to play, and they threw her new alarm clock around until it broke. I felt well within my rights to tell them that was really not OK at all and that they should apologise. I hope other people would feel able to step in if my kids behaved badly. Don't we all have a responsibility to teach kids right and wrong?

It's a good question, and yes, I think we do. But telling other people's children off? Criticising someone else's little darling? Surely that's way off the socially acceptable scale of child-rearing?

Well, no, I don't think it is. Obviously there's a very big difference between asking other people's kids firmly to stop drawing on your wall in crayon and actually telling them off as you would your own ('If you do that again there'll be no pocket money for a month!'), and you have to work out what feels right for you. I've seen several mums in toddler groups having very strong words with kids who have hurt their own child, and there is always a very uneasy moment where everyone else wonders if there is about to be a huge cat fight between the respective mothers. Usually it's fine: both realise that something had to be said, and there are no hard feelings – except for the poor blighter who got whacked on the head with a toy digger.

What has made the whole issue so tricky is that we are all afraid of interfering in other people's lives lest we get sued for any emotional damage that may have been caused by a curt 'Don't do that, please.' People are also far more ready to become aggressive or intimidating if they feel you are sticking your nose in where it's not wanted, and we all walk on by if we see a child spitting at old ladies or kicking bus shelters as though nothing had happened – *It's not my business, so I'll ignore it.*

Well, I think this is a shame, because it means kids have no respect for others at all. Oh, I'm sounding like a grumpy old biddy now, but I think it's an important point, so I'm going to make it: if a child comes to your house and walks upstairs in muddy shoes you should jolly well be able to tell her you aren't best pleased. Of course she'll tell her mum you're a horrible lady, but if you get in there first and say what happened all should be well and social order will be restored!

Don't F***ing Swear, Kids

I have changed my mind about this in recent years. I was brought up in a swear-word-free zone, and remember the looks of shock and disgust whenever I would venture into unchartered territory with an occasional 'bum' or 'fart'. (The latter never made the cut, I'm sad to say – it's still one of my favourites.) I didn't mind much – I got plenty of chances to swear at will at school, but I did find it odd that people who knew each other as well as we did couldn't say 'fuck', 'shit' or 'bollocks' (oooh, another favourite) in front of each other. I know there was sound logic behind the idea – we should learn to speak properly and politely at home, so that we spoke properly and politely in public, but I still feel it was a terrible waste of expletives, and one I am still trying to bloody well make up for.

So now we do swear at home, in front of our kids (the F-word is still considered Very Bad, but I use it if I hurt myself badly or if I burn the dinner to a crisp *again*), but we never swear outside the home. In a very unfair piece of legislation we have ruled that our kids can't swear, except for the occasional 'Oh damn!' and any amount of toilet-related words, but we don't mind if they hear us doing it. There will come an awkward time when we phase in the junior swearing, but we're some way off that yet. In the real world, people swear, and if you can do it with style I think that's to your credit, rather than something to be ashamed of.

You have to make up your own mind on this one – I'm just telling you what we do, and so far there has been not a single 'shit', 'fuck' or 'bloody hell' uttered by any of my kids in public. Three-year-old Charlie thinks his sister is a 'bloody stupid pig', but he has no idea what this means and we are choosing to ignore it until he stops saying it, which he seems to be already. Making a fuss about it would only make it stick.

Manners

I remember spending time with friends recently whose daughters never once said 'please' or 'thank you'. The children didn't seem remotely aware of it, and neither did the parents. In an uncharacteristic display of undermining somebody else's authority, I began adding the missing words, and waiting for them to be said back to me. Yes, it was probably quite rude and irritating, but by the end of the week these two little girls were saying all of their pleases and thank yous as though it was second nature.

To what level you take this instilling of manners is up to you, but here are some simple ones in my Manners Revival Plan:

☆ Saying please, thank you and sorry, where appropriate.
☆ Holding doors open for others to go through first.
☆ Asking to get down from the table.
☆ Not interrupting when somebody is speaking.
☆ Not speaking with mouths full.
☆ Not wiping their mouths with their sleeves.

☆ Not talking to somebody who is on the phone, except in emergencies.

☆ Offering things to others before helping themselves.

I could go on, but this is a simple, good start. Together we can do it! The Manners Revival Plan must work!

Birthday Parties

You've no doubt heard all about CPS (Competitive Parent Syndrome): pushy mums, designer-clad babies and gym-honed abs are common symptoms exhibited in playgrounds up and down the country. But nowhere – *nowhere* – is this battle for the top spot in the Fabulous Parent Chart enacted with more blood, sweat and credit-card damage than at children's birthday parties.

I have been to birthday parties for three-year-olds that make anything Elton could lay on look Spartan. Where I had a few cold sausages on sticks, some dry sandwiches and a game of musical chairs, kids these days can expect bouncy castles, professional face-painters, discos, melon balls, matching tableware, helium balloons, magicians and a visit from Charlie and Lola. Anything less than outrageously over-the-top and costing the equivalent of a loft extension is seen as a sure sign that this household is struggling to keep it together.

Well, I hope to change all of that. In fact, I have already made some progress among my own small gathering of nervous CPS sufferers, by putting an end to the unnecessary custom of giving out party bags. When I first did this, at my daughter's sixth birthday party, I was fairly apprehensive about the reaction I would get: Tears? Tantrums? A telling off? And that was just from the other mums – what about the poor wee children, doe-eyed and expectant, sent home without so much as a useless plastic toy, bottle of bubble mixture or a ticket to Disneyland?

What actually happened was that the kids didn't notice and were just as glad to take only a slice of birthday cake home to tease their siblings with, and the mothers were delighted. 'Thank you *so* much, Liz,' said one, clutching my forearm as though the weight lifted off her shoulders had caused her to lose her balance. 'I *hate* party bags, but I've never dared not give them out. You've saved me a fortune and lots of hassle, because Alex won't be having any at her party now either!'

So there you have it. Mission One, 'No party bags', successfully completed. Mission Two was less precise, but has been met with similar success and appreciation. It is: Keep it real. By this, I don't mean get some local rap artists in to teach your kids a thing or two about life outside the cocoon, but just that maybe we need to keep a sense of perspective about the whole thing, innit? What, and who, is a birthday party for? The answer is not 'to show what a wonderful mum I am by spending a month's salary on some baby sushi'. Instead, a birthday party should be for your child to have a nice time doing something special and fun. If that involves chartering a helicopter to fly to Alton Towers for the day, then perhaps you need to have a chat.

What children wish for as a birthday party depends, of course, on their age, and often those over seven or so can already consider themselves *way* beyond party games, and parties *at all* for that matter, as they enter the realm of sleepovers and discos. Oh help.

But up until that point, and even after that if you're clever, parties can be great fun without all the lavish entertainment and Michelin-starred food. Here are some Top Traditional Party Tips to put things back to rights:

☆ **Don't feel pressured by other parties.** If you go back to basics, other parents will be grateful, not horrified.
☆ **Always make the cake.** Bought cakes are outrageously expensive, and tend to be much less good to eat than they are to look at. Baking a birthday cake is not nearly as homely and challenging as it might sound to some. If it looks awful, as it will because you will be making it at 11 p.m. the night before, using out-of-date flour because you haven't baked since last year at the same time, then fear not: icing hides a multitude of kitchen sins. Nobody will know that under the concealing layer of

Smarties, silver balls and candles lies a crumbling wreck that should have a conservation order on it. Once the singing is over, you can cut the cake in the kitchen, wrap it up in a paper napkin and offer it to people as they leave. They will all assume that it got bashed about a bit on the way home, and that it was once a work of culinary perfection. Genius.

☆ **Provide half the amount of food you think you'll need.** We used to make mountains of sandwiches, allow at least four sausages per child, provide seven types of crisps and party biscuits, four varieties of 'healthy food' and more juice than you could consume in a year. The result: we were still living on Iced Gems and dry triangle sandwiches a week later. Kids spend most of their time at party teas chatting, stacking piles of food on their plates, and then dropping half of it on the floor. Now we make far less, they polish almost everything off, and there is no wastage and a great sense of satisfaction.

☆ **Go easy on the additives.** This is less out of any sense of preventing childhood obesity and more because of Liz's famous Partycle Theory: x (excited children) + y (chocolate + fizzy drinks) = $x - 1$ (hyperactive, uncontrollable kids).

It's fairly simple and you can replace x and y by the numbers appropriate to the gathering in question. If either exceeds twenty you should adjust the outcome to include vomiting on the dining-room rug as well, and the minus one indicates somebody who has been sent home in an additive-induced coma. Nothing wrong with breadsticks, water and some cherry tomatoes to dilute the sweet stuff.

☆ **Prepare some activities in advance.** Again, this can make you feel horribly worthy, but planning things to make, do or play can mean the difference between a happy hub of quiet creativity and a frenzied zoo. If the party is themed, this is a lot easier (for a fairy party try making fairy gardens out of old cardboard boxes, green felt and screwed-up tissue paper flowers; for a dinosaur party construct some Tyrannosaurus Rexes out of egg boxes, empty toilet rolls and paint). It looks rubbish, but it keeps them calm for fifteen minutes.

☆ **Plan twice the number of activities you think you'll need to keep them amused.** This applies mainly to parties for the under-eights, who are still prepared to tolerate activities and games. After that they are fairly able to think of ways to amuse themselves, most of which involve showing off or breaking the stereo. The traditional, simple ones are still the best, and here are the pick of the bunch in my house:

a. **Musical bumps.** Play some music while they dance. Switch it off and the last one to sit down (with a bump) is out. Loud, but successfully tires them out.

b. **Pin the tail on the donkey/body part of the Pixar character.** I've even seen pin the trident on the Poseidon at a Roman party, so see if you can beat that!

c. **Heads or tails.** Everyone stands up and guesses heads or tails. You toss a coin and those who guessed wrong sit down. Last child standing gets a sickly packet of sweets. Mmmm.

d. **Sleeping lions.** Children lie on the floor with their eyes closed, and you have to walk about and try to make them move or giggle without touching them. My favourite . . . all is quiet. Try to resist leaving them there for half an hour while you have a nice cup of tea!

e. **No-hands party-ring eating.** Hang the party rings by some string from a washing line and see if they can eat the rings without touching them. Great photo opportunities here!

These days pass the parcel seems to have died a cotton-wool-related death, and children expect a present in every layer. But the whole point is the anticipation that you *might* get something, you over-protected ninnies!! Sorry. I feel rather passionately about pass the parcel, and have difficulty accepting the New Age 'everyone's a winner' version. It also takes hours to prepare, and leaves your house looking like a landfill site. If you must do a pass the parcel then use different coloured paper for every layer to see who's ripping up two at once, and use small stickers or cheap bouncy balls if the sweet count has gone off the scale. Keeping the tissue paper that china or glassware is so often wrapped in comes into its own here.

☆ **Shared parties.** If your child has a birthday very close to her best friend's then combining the work and having a joint party can be a great idea. It can also halve the cost, which is great if you are renting a hall, a bouncy castle or some other hideously expensive form of entertainment. It can also be a problem, with disagreements over location, theme, who brings what and who organises most of it. I have seen tears, believe me, and that's just the parents. Know your friend very well, and be ready to back out gently if you feel it's running away from you.

☆ **Keep it simple.** Kids don't need half the stuff we provide them with at parties. They want to see their friends, scream about for a while, play some games and eat tons of shit.

☆ **Keep it short.** Two hours is plenty, believe me. We have even managed a record-breaking hour and a half, and nobody seemed to feel short-changed. Games were played, cake was eaten, fun was had and the birthday girl was delighted. Bye-bye!

☆ **Have a theme.** There's no end to what you can have as a party theme – I've seen Romans, Fairies, Robots, Underwater, Jungle and many others – and it gets the kids more involved because they have to actually make an effort at dressing up. If you can splash out a little for a themed party then try a company like Party Pieces (www.partypieces.co.uk) who do a huge range of themed plates, cups, napkins and so on at reasonable prices.

☆ **Hire somewhere.** If you can't face the mess, any damage to your house and the huge job of clearing up, then have a party in a church hall, a swimming pool or even a park in the summer. Yes, it costs, but then so do all the cleaning products and replacing the smashed vase in the living room.

☆ **Siblings.** Lastly, when one of your children has a birthday, any siblings can feel left out. I know: it's Life, and they should toughen up, but if you want to make their day a little bit more special, then have a small present for them at the ready. It's the little things . . .

Birthday parties can be exhausting, expensive and daunting, but most importantly they are for your children, not for you, and with a little planning they can even be a lot of fun. They also make you realise why you should always plan to have a baby in the summer months . . . we goofed twice but scored a June baby the third time. Everyone outside!

The Big Sleep: Getting enough, nightmares, bed-wetting and other nocturnal trials

Sleep is good. Sleep makes us look beautiful, process all the things that have occurred during the day, manage to get through the following day without wanting to jump into a deep pit with a pillow and some ear-plugs if possible. Like every parent I know, I crave sleep more than anything else in the world much of the time. I lust after it, desire it with all my being and, if I should be so damned lucky, I'd dream about it. Forget sex – sex is for wimps. I want hardcore, uncensored sleep and I want it *now*!

Children are just like us in that they need a lot of sleep too.

Without it they become unable to concentrate, have trouble remembering things and learning at school, and can be moody as hell. They are, however, quite *un*like us, in that they do almost anything to avoid visiting the Land of Nod. Getting children to go to sleep is often the biggest challenge in a parent's day: the little darlings need their sleep, have ample opportunity for getting some, but point-blank refuse to either go to bed or nod off once they're tucked in. Meanwhile, you are gagging for it but can't get within a clean sheet's breadth of any, because you're trying to get your kids to fall asleep. Oh, it's enough to drive any normal person to the bottle (which helps, but isn't advised as a long-term method of sleep-induction) or scream, 'Look, I'd give my left arm to be able to crash out now, and here you are jumping up and down as excited as a March hare on speed. Tell you what, let's swap – you go and tidy up downstairs, make packed lunches, phone your grandmother for an earful about why you haven't rung for the past three weeks, put away the washing and read the Ofsted report from your school, and I'll just bloody well go to sleep! *OK*?'

Ah, it is a trial, but one which needn't be too difficult . . .

Getting enough

23 June

I bought some blackout curtain lining for E's bedroom today. It stays light until well after 9 p.m. and we are having terrible trouble getting any of the kids to go to sleep at their usual bedtime. This is a nightmare for us, as we get no evenings together at all, and it's becoming a real problem for them as they are just shattered the whole time! E has a cold sore, C has massive bags under his eyes, and everyone is grouchy because they're so tired. Hopefully making the room darker will help. They need some sleep!

How much sleep a child needs varies enormously with age, amount of activity during the day and just individual character. Trying to be prescriptive about sleep is ridiculous, I think, as every child's needs are so different, and they vary from day to day as well. Newborn babies can spend more time asleep than awake for a few weeks, and this gradually changes and falls into a pattern of some periods of sleep and longer periods of wakefulness as the months roll on. One day can be quite different from the next, if, say, you stay out unusually late, your child is unwell, or she was woken at 5 a.m. by a magpie making a racket outside her window. Trying to stick to a 'recommended' amount or pattern of sleep is as sensible as trying to keep yourself to a fixed quantity or time of eating or sleeping – it's not always that practical or desirable because life isn't that boring!

You know how much kip your child needs better than anyone, but there are some signs to look out for that might indicate they need a little more than they are getting:

☆ **Being hyperactive.** Oddly, the more tired a child is, the more overexcited and hyperactive he can become. If you think your child is more excitable than usual, try putting him to bed an hour earlier and see what happens over a week or two. He won't like it, of course, but it may be a necessary step. Children can be misdiagnosed as suffering from Attention Deficit Hyperactivity Disorder when really all they need is a good night's sleep, or possibly three.

☆ **Irritability.** Similarly, kids can get very grouchy, touchy and irritable when they are tired. Just like adults, then.

☆ **Sleepiness.** This is more obvious: if your child has bags under her eyes the size of a large tote and is dropping off and yawning every five minutes, she needs to go to bed much earlier for a good few days to catch up on rest.

☆ **Slurred speech and nausea.** Once you've checked the booze cupboard is untouched, make sure your child gets more sleep. By this stage the sleep deprivation is quite pronounced, and something needs to be done, pronto.

The only way I have found to get my kids to sleep well, whether they are babies or older children, is to **stick to a bedtime routine**. This involves having a warm, relaxing bath after dinner, dimming the lights and closing the blackout curtains (essential in the summer), *always* reading them some stories, or letting older kids read to themselves if they prefer, speaking more quietly, and then finally lights out and cuddles. We have done this for eight years, and it works ninety per cent of the time. The other ten per cent is usually our own fault because we've let the kids play outside and get excited until later than usual or we are in a rush to get them to bed because we have visitors coming, and they sense that something is different and get all perky again. Drat.

If you have trouble getting your kids to sleep, here are some suggestions that might help:

☆ **Use a night-light or similar.** My younger kids have a string of butterfly lights going up their wall, which seem to calm them down and help them to feel safe.

☆ **Keep calm.** Getting all worked up makes a bad situation much worse. Tears before bed are a guaranteed way of ensuring a bad night ahead, and it's upsetting for everyone too. It's very hard to keep calm at this trying hour of the day, but it will always pay off if you can stick to your (quiet) guns.

☆ **Play a story tape.** During the hot summer months, if our kids can't get to sleep we leave a gentle story tape playing at low volume in their room. They don't usually last more than fifteen minutes before they drop off and I switch it off.

☆ **Tickle.** Our kids can't sleep without a tickle, however short. It calms them down, relaxes their muscles and it's a good way of keeping physical contact as they get older and you don't get as many cuddles and kisses as you used to. Boo.

☆ **Get them out more during the day.** I sleep much better when I've had a very physically active day, and kids are no different. Make sure they've had at least an hour running about, outside if you can, or take them swimming. If they're tired enough, they'll sleep!

Nightmares and night terrors
Just when you thought you'd got the sleeping thing cracked and you were beginning to enjoy some uninterrupted nights for the first

time in years, along come the nightmares and night terrors. The latter is not just an annoying child who won't sleep, but a condition similar to nightmares, the main difference being that the child doesn't wake up. Each condition occurs in both children and adults, usually starting from the age of about two to six.

Nightmares: A child wakes during the night, in the middle of a bad, frightening dream. They can often tell you what it was about, and are awake and aware of their surroundings. They can usually remember the event in the morning.

Night terrors: Similar to nightmares, but the child often kicks and thrashes about, screams or shouts, and is actually still fast asleep and unable to hear or see you. The pupils are dilated, it is very hard to get through to the child to comfort her, and she can't remember any of it the next morning. Episodes tend to settle down after a few months, and can run in families.

My eldest child suffered night terrors when she was about four years old, and they were certainly more disturbing for us than for her – she was completely unaware at the time and couldn't recollect anything about it when she woke up. We were bleary-eyed and freaked out.

The best way to deal with both types of night incident is to stay with your child and try to comfort him until he falls asleep again. Stroke him, sing quietly, talk softly, or whatever seems to help. If you are exhausted then crawling into bed beside him can gain you an extra half-hour or so of sleep, but it's best to go back to your own bed if possible to avoid starting bad habits. Talking it through rarely helps, as he will be so tired and confused that it often makes it worse, whether at the time or on the next day. Night terrors are not an illness, and neither are nightmares, but if the incidents are very frequent then you might like to talk to your GP about it, and she might suggest a remedy or plan of attack.

Bed-wetting

Bed-wetting is a very common problem in families, but nobody ever talks about it. I can kind of see why this is: nobody wants to embarrass their child, or embarrass themselves by admitting they have a bed-wetter. It's ridiculous that it's still considered by many to be a failure of some kind, because this is nonsense. Bed-wetting isn't a sign of any bad parenting or an abnormal child. It often runs in families, so try to remember (or ask your mum) whether you wet the bed when you were a child.

The reason most kids wet the bed is simply because, when they are asleep, they don't feel when their bladder is full and wake up to empty it. They sleep right through, and often wake up after they've done it. It's for this reason that bed-wetting can be reduced when kids are at a friend's house or excited about something – they don't sleep quite so deeply and so have less trouble waking themselves and going to the loo.

Most bed-wetting stops at the age of about five, but if your child is still having accidents then don't fret – it really is quite common, and it's not a sign of any abnormality. It's worth getting diabetes or urinary tract infections ruled out, though, and also checking that your child doesn't have thread worms, as this can disturb them just enough to make them wee, but not enough to wake them properly so they go to the loo.

Here are some methods of 'treatment' you might like to try:

☆ **Praise for dry nights.** It's a simple trick, but it can work. Give lots of praise and cuddles, and offer small rewards like stickers or other small things your child likes. Yes, like chocolate, but it's better to avoid too much of that for obvious reasons.
☆ **Don't scold.** A child who is scared of wetting her bed for fear of being told off is far more likely to have another accident. Scolding is a very negative way of dealing with the problem. It's not your child's fault at all, and you should make sure she knows this. It's worth letting her know that it runs in families too, so she knows it really isn't anything to do with her, but her family background.
☆ **Go to the loo before bed.** If the bladder is completely empty, you might just make it till morning without any leakage.
☆ **Get a bed-wetting alarm.** This is worn in the pyjamas or pants, senses when the child is wetting the bed and activates a small

alarm or vibration. This wakes the child, who, theoretically, stops weeing and gets up to go to the loo. The results are very encouraging, so it's definitely worth a try if your kids are having frequent little accidents.

☆ **Wake them up and take them to the loo every night.** We have been doing this and so far no wet beds for months. But I know that if we forget there's still a chance of a wet bed because there's no conditioning to wake up *before* the weeing starts. But as a natural method I give it the thumbs up and we will persist.

☆ **Practise holding it in during the day.** Many kids drink too little during the day at school, and then gulp gallons down in the evening. Cue a wet bed ... Encourage lots of drinking during the day and get your child to practise holding a full bladder longer than they normally would. Don't do this for too long, as you don't want urinary tract infections either! Then cut down on drinks in the evening and especially after dinner. It may not work, but it's worth a shot.

Bed-wetting is a problem for many, and it can cause embarrassment, guilt and a huge amount of laundry. Don't worry about it too much, and keep encouraging your child – he'll get there eventually, though for some it can last until well into their teens and for a few very unlucky ones into adulthood as well. Sweet dreams!

Sleepovers

We are still fairly new to sleepovers, but I want to mention it as it seems to become an issue very early on, and it's good to be prepared.

I don't think I had my first sleepover at a friend's house until I was ten or so, but it now seems fairly common to be packing the pyjamas and cuddly toys for children as young as six. This is causing quite a lot of uncertainty and confusion among all of us chattering mothers: Is this too young? Can they cope with it? What if they scream all night? What if they – horror of horrors – wet the bed at someone else's house? Will I have to go and pick her up at

2 a.m.? If I say 'no' am I being a meany and embarrassing my child, or should I stick to what I feel is right? And so on.

I don't think there is a 'right' age to start sleepovers, but here are some pointers that might help:

☆ **Know your child and be sensible.** If you know your child has a very sensitive nature, often has nightmares or wets the bed, then holding off on the sleepovers is a good idea. Just because Tough-as-nails Toby has been doing it for months doesn't mean your little one is ready as well. Trying too early and having a bad experience would put the whole thing back for a long time.

☆ **Pep talks.** Without building it up too much, it is a good idea to go through with your child exactly what 'sleeping over' entails. Some are under the impression that it means watching telly all night, eating chocolate biscuits and having the Best Time *Ever*. They don't seem to consider the whole 'waking up in the night to find they are in a strange house, with strange shadows, noises and adults' side of it. And no Mummy or Daddy. Go through it, and see if they still think it's a good idea.

☆ **Establish the rules beforehand.** On school nights we always say 'no' to sleepovers, as kids never get enough rest. When the happy event does occur, we have strict-ish policies about lights out, TV time, amount of chocolate to be consumed and 'wake-up and make loads of noise the next morning' time. If you have clear rules and spell them out beforehand then the kids know what to expect, and have a better chance of being allowed to do it all again another time.

☆ **Don't phone to check up.** It's embarrassing for you and your kids, and there is never anything to report anyway: if there were, you would know straight away.

Sleepovers are quite an event to begin with, so keep them to a minimum until everyone knows the drill and be prepared for some very grumpy, sleep-deprived children (and adults) in the morning. It's all meant to be fun, though, so don't be a killjoy and let them enjoy themselves. You can all catch up on some rest tomorrow.

Letting Go: When school starts

One day, your beautiful, annoying, slightly grubby, cheeky, funny, maddening child will go to school. And that's it: those early years you enjoyed together – and cursed from time to time – are over in the ring of a school bell, and your lives together will never be the same again.

Of course, the real 'letting go' happens twelve years later, at the far end of the school years when they actually flee the nest, but we're not concerned with that here. It's enough just losing them for six hours a day without crying at the thought of buying them their own kettle and toaster.

I cried uncontrollable tears of loss when both of my elder children started school. Sniff! This took my friends by surprise, because I am usually the one who is outwardly cheerful, coping and strong, thanks to my well-practised, foolproof disguise. Everyone else managed to keep their feelings hidden until they got home, but I lasted less than two minutes from the time the door closed before I was blubbing and sobbing my way across the playground, shaking and weeping like an old lady who has been pipped to the post at a cake-baking competition by horrid Mrs Grumble from number twenty-five.

It's a weird thing when your kids start school, because you've been expecting it (and occasionally secretly wishing for it) for years, but when it happens you have no way of predicting how you will react. You might be relieved to have a free morning for the first time in four years and skip all the way to Costa for an uninterrupted cappuccino. You might fuss and panic all the way from the front door to the school gates, tucking hair, straightening collars, double-checking lunchboxes and retying shoelaces. You might laugh, you might cry – who knows?

Whatever reaction you have at the time, the end result is the same: your relationship with your child will change faster over the next few months than you can believe, and you will need something stronger than Madonna's biceps to see you through the first year in one piece. Here are some Starting School tips:

☆ **Your days together are numbered in the last year before school**, so try to relish every day with your pre-schooler. OK, not *every* day, but as many as you can would be good. Nobody ever does, and then they regret it. It's over before you can say 'Why haven't you done your homework?', so savour the time you have together.

☆ **Prepare for exhaustion.** Not just on your part, but on your child's. Children start school cruelly young in the UK, and a six-hour day of learning, talking, playing, arguing, painting, PE and so on just knocks 'em dead. My kids went to bed at 6 p.m. for the first few weeks, because they were so tired. They do adjust, but it takes time.

☆ **Snatched moments.** Having spent every waking hour with your little darling, here's what you are left with: an hour before school, when all you do is chivvy them every three minutes into getting dressed, eating something, making themselves look reasonably presentable and locating everything they need like school bag, lunchbox, violin, PE kit and so on. Then you get an hour or two after school when they are so tired they can't speak, and it's all you can do to cook them tea, bath them and get them in bed before they pass out. As the years go by this time gets much longer, as they stay up later, but there are also more after-school activities, so in fact you still see your kids very little. What's left is the weekend, minus any activities they have on. All in all it's very little time, and I still find that hard to come to terms with: however much they may annoy me from time to time, I do love my kids more than anything, and really *want* to spend time with them.

☆ **Preparation the night before** is key to your survival in your child's first year of school. Packed lunch, clothes (easier if they have a uniform, of course), school bag, any cheques/letters that have to go in, party invitation replies, shoes laid out, coats at the ready. This may sound idiotic, but just you wait for the morning rush, when you have five minutes to get out of the door and you have one shoe, no jumpers and an empty lunchbox to hand.

Sure, you'll be a dab hand at it all after a term or so, but just at the beginning, help yourself by planning ahead.

☆ **Blend in.** Much as we like to encourage our children's individuality, the first term in a new class is not the time for wacky socks or experimental hairstyles. Whatever 'everyone else' has or wears or is allowed to do, is all that matters now. This I where school uniforms come up trumps. Our kids don't have one and it's a nightmare getting them dressed every day.

☆ **Set your alarm clock.** Having spent the last five years getting up two hours too early, your child will suddenly develop the need to sleep until well after the school bell. Allow at least an extra hour for getting out of the door for the whole first term, by which time you will be a pro and you'll have whittled it down to fifty minutes.

☆ **Set it again.** While you should congratulate yourself on successfully dropping your child off at school, it's important to remember that they do need collecting again. In most cases this is at 3.15 p.m., and, unlike parties, it's not OK to be the last one to go home. Be early.

☆ **Buy lots of bread.** Obviously this only applies to those whose children are having packed lunch, and those who really like eating bread. Many a frenzied trip to Tesco's in the middle of the night can be avoided if you stock up.

☆ **Be prepared to be wrong.** From now on you are not the centre of your child's universe – their peers are. They are right and you are wrong. About everything. Forever.

☆ **Friends for tea.** Not content with being together for six hours every day, your child will want to bring friends round for a play after school. This usually entails disappearing upstairs as soon as they get home, only to emerge when food is offered. Best to stock up on fishfingers while you're getting the bread.

☆ **Cancel all social engagements.** You should probably do this until at least 2015, because from now on your child's social diary will dictate what the rest of the family does. Week nights will involve playing at someone's house or having a friend over, and every weekend will contain at least one birthday party.

☆ **Re-mortgage the house.** Or find some other way of having more cash around. The education may be free, but now you're tied to school holidays, which means paying through the nose for air fares, accommodation and visiting attractions. Not forgetting pester power, which really kicks in now – '*Everyone* has a *Little Mermaid* lunchbox!' – and will eventually make a hole in your pocket however hard you try to resist.

☆ **Debrief.** Among all of this egocentric worrying on your part is a child who has started school. Without coming on too heavy and asking a thousand questions he doesn't want to answer, remember to ask how things are going at school every day. Note that kids will lie if things are going badly, so your 'what's behind the smile' radar will need to be on full beam. Try to sense if something is up, and handle it with kid gloves: even five-year-olds can be very sensitive about goings-on at school, and you have to do some clever detective work sometimes.

☆ **Keep a low profile.** Nothing will screw up a child's status in a class like his mother dashing up to the teacher every other day, complaining about the state of the toilets, the brat in Class Two who pulled her daughter's hair or the fact that her little honeykins can't sit next to her best friend at lunch. Let children handle their own playground issues as much as possible and try to butt out. Sometimes there's a good case for making delicate enquiries, but never in front of the whole class as they line up. I've seen it done many times, and it's so painful to watch.

☆ **Take turns.** In our children's school there are a large number of dads who drop kids off or pick them up. This is very good for the children, who don't learn from day one that 'school' is Mummy's job, while Daddy is too busy, or too disinterested, to come. It also means you can all talk about the playground, teachers and friends together, which is very useful. If you are about to use the 'yes, but he can't take the time off work' line on me then I'm going to throw back a 'well, he should'. Not every day, perhaps, but *some* days. It's for your kids, so find a way.

I hope some of this is useful. Don't worry if you find the start of school very hard to deal with – you are among friends who understand and it's a huge emotional jolt for all of us, however 'together' others may appear to be. See if you can hang around weeping disasters like me, and you might feel you're actually handling it very well.

Education, Education, Education

This is not a party-political lecture on behalf of the Education Party, but a chapter dealing with potential clashes of opinion when it comes to educating your kids.

We are a nation obsessed with schooling and education, with many parents resorting to the most mind-boggling and elaborate schemes to ensure entry for their child into their chosen school. Moving house, using false postcodes, bribing the local minister and arranging private tutoring all come into play. It's quite sick, really, when you think of what it's doing to the child, but that's for later . . .

England is a particularly difficult country to sort out the 'Which school?' dilemma: there are so many options offering very different educational experiences and most people have very strong feelings about what is 'best' for their child prodigy. Local school on the corner? Posh private school? Steiner education? International school? None are better or worse than the others, but the fact is you will have to choose very soon after your child stops possetting unless you want to take whatever is left at the bottom of the pile. This can be very fraught if you and your partner don't have the same choices in mind, and the sooner you start thinking about it, the better:

☆ **Be completely honest.** Even if you know your partner will disapprove, or his mother will think you are a moron, speak your mind on this issue and damn what anyone else thinks. This is your child's education here, not the colour of your bed linen.

You will regret it forever if you keep quiet and go along with something you are very unhappy about.

☆ **Research, research, research.** If, like me, you haven't got much of a clue which way to go and could plump for any of a number of different options, then the key to finding an answer is in discovering as much as you can, as early as you can, about all of them. Don't just read the brochures: go there, look at the school, the playground, the other kids and the teachers. If this is somewhere you think your child would be happy and thrive, then put it down as a possible 'yes'.

☆ **Eavesdrop and talk.** I have got lots of insider information about schools in my area from overhearing conversation in café queues and playgrounds and by talking to parents about their children's schools. People are usually pretty honest and will tell you about the good and the bad. Learning about Mr Hargreaves's brandy habit might just swing it . . .

☆ **Family background** can be another killer when trying to choose a school for your child. If your parents are staunch left-wingers and disapprove of the very notion of private education, while your in-laws went to Eton and Roedean, then you are in for a tough time. Remember: they've had their chance with you, and now it's your turn with your own kids. It is a decision only for you and your partner to make, not for your parents. If they are unhappy with it, that's tough luck.

☆ **Get moving.** It's now commonplace for people to move house to live within the catchment area of their chosen school. Yes, this is just private education through the back door, but if you can afford it, and it's something you are prepared to do, then keep an eye out for properties even if it's years before your child is due to start. They tend to go like hot cakes, so you'll have to be quick.

☆ **Plan well ahead.** Like nurseries, good schools can fill up very quickly, and it's best to get your child's name down on a waiting list as early as you can if it's a private school, and at least to make contact with the school so you don't miss registration day if it's a state school. Calling from the maternity ward is perhaps being a little hasty, but if it puts your mind at rest . . .

☆ **Whose education is it anyway?** I think far too many parents choose an education for their children without considering what would suit each individual child best. I have no doubt that what's best for one child isn't appropriate for another, and it is always worth asking: is the education system I'm choosing for him one which he will learn and benefit from and enjoy? Where some kids thrive in the high-pressure environment of a very academic school, others are far more suited to something more creative with an accent on languages, drama or art. Similarly, with single-sex or co-ed schools it's important to think about how this will affect *your* child and whether you think they'll enjoy it. Siblings are often happier if they are in the same school – and it's easier for you! – but I do know families where the children attend different schools because what suited one didn't work at all for the other. Of course you're going to do what you think is right, but make sure it's what's right for your *child*, not for you.

Teaching at Home: Doing your bit

While we're on the subject of learning, I really want to get something off my chest: We need to stop passing the buck and relying on schools to teach our kids everything, and do some of it ourselves. There. We have a massive role to play in educating our own children and this is especially true in the pre-school years. Nobody is saying you should be sitting down to three hours of algebra before changing a nappy, but there is so much you can do to give your kids a great start in life, by doing the basics before they get to school.

☆ **Reading.** My favourite. You should read to your child every single day, at least once. Go to the library, a bookshop or swap books with a friend to keep your child's library new and exciting. Read, read, read to them from the day they are born and continue after they start school. Just because they can read it doesn't mean you can't read to them any more – you should, as it continues to improve their reading skills a lot.

☆ **The three Rs.** With a little help from their parents almost all kids would be able to recognise all their letters, numbers, colours and shapes before they went to school, and be able to read and write simple words and do very simple sums. There are letters and numbers everywhere, so point them out, write them down, make it fun and entertaining and just see how fast they learn. You're not trying to get them into Oxbridge; you are playing games with them, and learning as you go. They really enjoy it and the freedom this knowledge gives them can relieve a lot of frustration.

☆ **Music.** Again, you don't have to sit them down in front of a music stand and beat scales out of them: just sing together, bash a drum to time, listen to children's songs together and let them *enjoy* the music. Kids who are exposed to lots of music from a young age are much more likely to be musical when they are older, and music is a fantastic form of therapy that could be useful during the difficult teenage years! As to the theory that listening to Mozart makes kids cleverer, well, if you believe it then why not try it?

This isn't 'home education' on a grand scale at all, and I implore every parent to do more of it. If it's fun, it doesn't feel like learning at all, and your child will have great fun reading signs, adding up the shopping and pointing out all the circles on the playground.

The Things They Say: We do love them really . . .

Just as every day with children brings some kind of squabble, annoyance or new grey hair, so it also brings moments of such joy, hilarity, love and immeasurable pleasure that everything else pales into complete insignificance. It's moments like these that can turn a bad day into something wonderful, and you should treasure every one of them. Here is just a tiny selection of the hundreds of times my kids have lightened my spirits and reduced me to tears from laughing so hard:

Emily, aged two, on seeing a dog lifting its leg to do the necessary against a tree: That dog's doing an arabesque!

Phoebe, aged two, on a plane: I'm *not* going to eat my lunch until Stuart Little [*the steward*] has taken me to see the pirate [*pilot*]!

Charlie, aged three, brandishing a plastic screwdriver and looking very pleased with himself: Phoebe "Raaaaar"ed at Emily, so I'm going to drill a hole in her eye!

Emily, aged seven, sad that we couldn't afford to buy a house we had been hoping to: Why do people sell their houses for so much money, when they don't even want them any more?

Phoebe telling a joke, aged six: What did the cat say when it lost all its money?
Charlie, aged two: Oh bloody hell! [*Answer, for those who care, is, 'I'm paw'. Boom, boom.*]

Emily, aged two, after spotting a naturist walking butt naked down the main street in town: He's not really naked, is he? I mean, he did put his willy on.

Phoebe, aged five, watching my husband give me a rather longer-than-usual kiss goodbye: Are you two sexing?

Charlie, aged three, in a Narnia phase, waving a sword wildly: I am the King of Banarnia!

Phoebe, aged four, trying to remember what Chessington World of Adventures was:
Me: Don't you remember? You know, the one with the huge water

slide. And the Berry Bouncers. No? And the train ride, the flying elephants and the sea lions . . .

Phoebe: Oooh, is that where I did my bright green poo? [*It was – something to do with excess pea consumption, I think . . .*]

Emily, aged eight, combining two new words learned at school that day to accidental comic effect: So, you know Hitler? [*Long, thoughtful pause.*] Was he a bitch?

I think that just about covers it for now. There is much, much, *much* more I could write about children, of course, but there's a lot more of this house still to see and it'll be dark before we're done if we don't push on. I really hope this little visit to the children's bedroom has left you feeling that children are not all bad, and are in fact mostly very, very good, and they will bring more happiness and fun to your life than just about anything else, if you play your cards right.

For those who are really keen, and want to have another one, make your way down the corridor, past the bathroom, to the next extension at the back.

PART FOURTEEN

The Extension

Here we Go again: Having another baby

Just after giving birth, it's very common for women to say two things: '*She's/he's the most beautiful thing I've ever seen . . .*', and '*. . . but I'm never going through that again!*' Happily for the human race, Nature makes us forget the pain and the sleepless nights, and most people end up having another child within a few years.

Finding yourself pregnant again is a clear indication that you have crossed two major hurdles, for which you are to be congratulated:

1. You like your child enough to have another one.
2. You are having sex again.

Champagne all round! Oh, not you, though. Just Daddy for the next eight months. Remember that? Ah, it feels like only yesterday.

If you are just wondering what having more than one child might be like, then plough on, and consider these points:

Mind the gap: What is a good age gap to leave between children?

Well, the answer to this depends on whether you mean biologically, emotionally or financially, so let's deal with these separately.

Biologically. Most doctors recommend an age gap of not less than eighteen months, because this is apparently how long it takes for your body to truly return to normal, and for your reserves of minerals, vitamins and so on to recover after the baby drained them all away. And you were annoyed about the residual wobble above your hips after six weeks. *EIGHTEEN MONTHS*!

Emotionally. There is no best age gap here, but if you think about it too much you'll never go for it. Some women are so happy with their first that they cannot wait to have another; others hate being pregnant enough to need some serious encouragement and bribery; and still others need a couple of years to enjoy Number One before throwing Number Two into the equation.

Financially. In the near future the biggest financial effects another baby will have on your family is making you lose income as you stop work for a while again (if you have gone back), and then have to spend more on some new baby clothes, nappies, any extra childcare you might need and some new baby clobber. The good news is that you have most of the basics already, and you have probably got used to spending less on yourselves by now, but it's worth taking a look at your financial state before you embark on another pregnancy, to see if another six months might help.

My two experiences were quite different, and each has its own advantages and disadvantages. Between my first and my second there is a gap of two years and two months, and I found that very hard: both were in nappies, my eldest child wasn't old enough to do a lot of things for herself, she wasn't emotionally mature enough to handle the transition easily, and I was so tired from handling a two-year-old while being pregnant that going back to endless nights of breastfeeding and emotional turmoil took their toll on my mood (which is a delicate way of saying I was a grouchy old hag for a year, and didn't enjoy it as much as I'd have liked).

Between my second and third children there is a gap of three years and four months, and this was much easier: my three-year-old was very able to understand what had just happened to our lives, she was out of nappies, she could help me a lot with the new baby (running to fetch clean water, bringing me the phone if it rang when I was feeding, etc.), and I didn't feel like it was only yesterday when I last gave birth. I was much less tired and I enjoyed the whole process enormously.

BUT, having kids further apart means they are less 'close', and this is certainly true for my youngest: both his sisters are at school, and he is effectively an only child between 9 a.m. and 3.30 p.m. every weekday. Having them closer together may be really hard work, but there is a sense of bonding between similar-aged siblings that is wonderful to watch. I know they will fight like cats as they get older, but for now they love each other enormously, support each other beautifully, and fight like cats only occasionally.

Pregnancy: No, it won't be at all like last time

Now that you are a well-seasoned parent, you don't need to be told the basics of tiredness, sickness, tender boobs and ill-fitting clothes. All of these unpleasantries remain almost the same, except slightly worse, the second time around, and your familiarity is a great start because it means we can skip all the definitions, terms and dreary facts, and jump right ahead to throwing up with your toddler standing behind you saying 'Mummy sick! Mummy sick!' It really is *so* much more fun being pregnant with company. NOT.

In addition, good old Mother Nature is still keeping us on our toes, and your second pregnancy will not be at *all* the same as last time. Sorry.

The early days

Remember these days? Remember the energy-sapping exhaustion, the taste of metal in your mouth and the nipples that feel like they have been dragged over a cheese-grater and then plugged into the mains? Good, because then you will also remember that they don't usually last for more than a few months, and that you are still lucky enough to be able to wear jeans and belted waists. Enjoy.

The main difference this time around is that you are not alone. There is a little somebody with you almost all of the time, who still expects Mummy to be as full of fun as she always was. You cannot have a quick nap when you so desperately need to, your dwindling energy levels are no excuse for not running around the park playing hide and seek (although this can be a great game if you manage to find a quiet spot under a bush somewhere for some shut-eye), and if you are being sick every morning then prepare to be handed the tissue by a toddler, who wants some kind of explanation as to why Mummy performs this peculiar ritual each day before breakfast. Prepare also for this toddler to start trying to copy you. Yuck.

These early days are a killer if you have an active child, because it's too early to tell her why you are feeling so low, you can't expect much understanding of your predicament from her, and anyway she won't care a bit after a couple of minutes, and will get straight back to dragging you upstairs for a game of Twister, as though she somehow senses that you won't be able to play it for much longer.

However, there are some cunning strategies you can adopt, which might make these days more manageable:

☆ Do as many activities which involve *you* **sitting down** as possible. Lego, sticking, reading, and so on. Save the trips to the adventure playground for later, when your energy comes back.

☆ Use your baby's sleep time to have a rest. I am a total hypocrite for saying that, because I usually spent every child-free moment trying, in vain, to make my house look pretty again, preparing the evening meal or writing, but just occasionally, when the nausea and tiredness got too bad, I would have a much-needed rest, and congratulate myself on my wisdom. Ahhhhhh. Much better.

☆ If you are really finding it a struggle to stay upright and awake, try to sort out some **temporary childcare**. Even an hour a day with a friend (that's your baby, not you) can make the difference between getting through a day or collapsing on the sofa at lunchtime and spending the rest of the afternoon watching DIY shows with your frustrated toddler. She may well become very knowledgeable about the many uses of MDF, but I think she'd probably rather be making dinosaurs out of egg boxes.

☆ Get **Daddy** to do a lot of childcare on the weekends if he can. Catching up on sleep and rest before the next week at boot camp will determine whether you sink or swim.

The middle bit

This is the time you should try to enjoy every minute with your child. You (hopefully) don't feel so rough any more, you are not yet too enormous to be able to run about or pick her up, and you suddenly start to become very aware that these days of 'Just the two of us' are numbered, and life will never be the same for either of you again.

I give you this snippet of advice because I wasn't at all aware of it the first time, when I was pregnant with my second, and I wish I had been. I was so consumed with my pregnancy, and worried about the prospect of having to go through the birth and the first year all over again, that I didn't spend as much time enjoying my toddler as I should have. It was just linea nigra this and double buggy that, and I'm sad to say that I think I wasted a lot of prime time with Number One. When it came to pregnancy number three I relished (almost) every moment with my older kids, knowing that once the baby arrived my exhausted, baby-centric brain would struggle to remember their names, let alone keep up with elaborate games of doctors and nurses.

Mummy's having a baby

Bet you never thought of this one when you were pregnant last time. There you were, fretting about your boobs, your non-existent pelvic floor muscles and the end of all promotions in the coming year, and thinking you were having a tough time. And you were. But at least you didn't have this worry to furrow your pretty brow:

How do you tell your firstborn that there's another baby on the way?

This is a delicate one, because any screw-up and you could be in for a very rocky ride. What if he doesn't care? What if he *does* care, and starts behaving like a premenstrual woman who has just missed all the best stuff in the January sales because her boyfriend wanted her opinion on a second-hand car he'd spotted in the free ads, and she is left choosing between a size six pair of jeans she quite obviously cannot fit into and several white shirts with foundation smeared around the collars? What if your toddler gets all excited, starts rearranging the furniture in his room, and then gets annoyed an hour later when the baby *still* hasn't arrived yet?

Oh, the emotional minefield!

Fear not. Most older children go straight for option one. They don't give a damn. (Just you wait, mister. You will.) This is always hugely disappointing, because you have chosen the moment perfectly, bought him a new police car and delivered the news over a plate of his favourite dinner. 'OK' is not the reaction you had anticipated or wished for, but it's what you are more than likely to get. We were left blushing when both of our children said, 'Oh, we've known that for *ages*' last time around. That showed *you*, you unexciting parents. Moving swiftly on, then . . .

It *is* advisable to wait until your bump is showing quite clearly before breaking the news. Young children are as observant of their mother's body changes as husbands are of our hairstyles, so they probably won't notice the change until you're beyond 'bloated', and cruising towards 'huge'. Also, time goes by very slowly for young children, and nine toddler months is more like three adult years. Telling a two-year-old that Mummy will have a baby next year may sound exciting now, but when, *eons* later, there is still nothing to put in the washed-down Moses basket, he will go off and find something better to think about. Like being as annoying as possible.

More baby clobber

Oh dear. Yet again, I feel so bad about breaking this news to you, but I'm afraid you will need to get your credit card ready again, and prepare to buy yet more space-devouring baby bits. WHAAAT? Well, you can't expect your two-year-old to suddenly start walking everywhere at your speed now that she has been evicted from her buggy, can you? And your baby boy might not look so great in all your baby-girl clothes. And what about all the bottles and teats you swore you'd sterilise and store carefully in the attic, but which have now perished and smell irreversibly of rancid yoghurt?

Credit card it is, then.

There is some great news, though: you already have the basics, and this is more of a top-up than a full-blown buy-out. If you held on to your Moses basket, a few baby clothes, high chair, pram that lies down flat, baby gym and so on, then this time will be much cheaper. Here are some items you may want to invest in, now that you are about to become a mother, yet again:

Double buggy. If your elder child is too young to walk around with you, or you still like to take her out for a sleep in the buggy during the day, then a double buggy will be what you need. There used to be two main varieties of these wheeled monsters: two seats side by side, or two seats one in front of the other. Both will break your back, and both are a lot more tricky to manoeuvre than a simple one-child get-up. The best piece of advice I can offer is 'Try them out'. Some people just haven't got the strength for the long ones (I had to jump up and use the whole of my body weight on the handle to get mine up a kerb) and others can't bear the 'getting through doorways' restrictions or the 'annoying the person sitting next to you' potential of the side-by-side variety.

Recently I have noticed a few new buggies on the baby block, which look a bit like double-deckers, with one child almost underneath the other. This is probably the easiest type to push, but I do wonder whether the child below can see anything at all. It can't be much fun having your brother's bum two inches above your face every time you go out. You might not use this form of transport for very long, as your older one outgrows being trundled about, so getting a nice second-hand one is a good idea.

Buggy board. If your elder child is able to walk along a bit, but his pace is still enough to drive you mad and he is prone to the occasional 'Mum, my legs are tired!' then this piece of funky baby gear is a must. I *loved* my buggy board. It is basically a piece of plastic with two wheels that clips onto the back of your pram or buggy at the bottom and forms a ride-on platform for your toddler to hitch a lift on, while holding on to the main handle. The first time you use one you will wonder why you let yourself be talked into buying such a cumbersome piece of kit: the pram suddenly weighs a ton, you can't reach the handle because there's a child in the way, and this passenger has the infuriating and back-breaking habit of jumping on and off the buggy board with no notice at all. This either causes the pram to flip up wildly and throw your baby onto the pavement or you to slip a disc.

Persevere. Once you have cracked the technique of pushing *from the side*, using one hand only and walking next to your toddler, you will soon be cruising along at a terrific pace, chatting happily to Number One, and developing one very strong shoulder.

Note: Check the width of your pram or buggy before you buy. Some require wider fittings, and it can take a while to order spare bits. Also, if you do tie the buggy board up when you are not using it, tie it very, very tightly. I nearly broke my shins several times, as this heavy, hard piece of plastic suddenly crashed down onto my legs as I was walking along. Ouch!

Bed. If your baby is going to sleep in the cot within a month or two, where is Number One going to sleep? The idea of putting your child into a bed without sides is unpleasant at any stage, but having a new baby is a good excuse to take the next step. Yes, you will be disturbed almost every night by screaming as he falls out of bed yet again, or by the arrival of an unwelcome, two-foot-high bedfellow, but after a few weeks you might all be able to get some rest again as he gets used to the new arrangement.

You can buy 'mini-beds', which will do a child until she is about ten or so, but why bother when you can just go the whole hog and get a full-sized bed that will last until she finally goes off to earn her own keep? We just fill the bottom half of our daughters' beds with cuddly toys and pillows (and they top these up with school reading books, dirty socks and china ornaments I am not supposed to know about) and I know I don't have to fork out for more beds in five years' time.

TOP TIP: *Start the transition from cot to bed well before your baby is due, because it really can take a few attempts and a few months to get settled. If your child is aware of the imminent arrival, then try to make him feel special rather then evicted, by telling him he is the clever big brother who doesn't want to be in a baby's cot any more, does he? Actually, he does, but with enough brainwashing he might come round.*

Car seat. You've still got the old baby one, but your eldest will have to move into the next size up now that Baby has nicked it. These bigger car seats are enormous, they weigh a ton, and if you think it was hard strapping a baby car seat in, then just you wait until you take all the skin off the back of both hands while trying to thread the seatbelt through the back of this monster without letting it go at the crucial moment, thereby watching it ping back again so that you have to start all over again. Grrrr.

They are much more comfortable, though, because most of these ones can be made to lie back, allowing your toddler to sleep on long journeys without snapping his neck in half. They are also very expensive, so have a look on eBay, or in the local ads, and see if you can get a (clean, safe) cheaper one if you'd rather keep the cash for the new car you've just realised you need to cram four people's junk into.

Hey! What *is* my body playing at?

Now here's an annoying thing. The human body is amazingly clever, and can adapt, mend, learn and cope impressively most of the time. (That's not the annoying thing.) When a new, nasty bacterium comes along, our immune system quickly learns how to combat it, remembers it, and is ready to pounce the next time this cocky little bug dares to show its dirty head. Remarkable. It would seem reasonable, then, that this 'remarkable' body of yours would remember what happens when it becomes pregnant, and sorts out some strategies to deal with it better the second time around. It should know how not to feel so sick, how to hang on to those boobs a bit better, and how to fight against pigmentation marks now that it knows how horrid they are. Reasonable: yes. In reality: alas, no. *That's* the annoying thing.

The second time you are pregnant, you will fall apart much faster than you did the first time, and almost certainly even more dramatically. (And thus the trend continues until you learn to stop procreating.) Morning sickness, or whatever kind of nausea you get, may be worse, and your tummy will lose any flatness much earlier than last time, making you look six months pregnant at only three or four. There are other, more intense, differences too: if you had a dark line on your abdomen the last time, which may well never have disappeared, it will probably appear very quickly and be even darker. Skin pigmentation, my pet hate, may also be more pronounced, and any varicose veins or general pregnancy fall-out that *just* eluded you last time might jump at a second chance of leaving its mark. And so on. Thank you, body, for helping out so very much.

Before I start a trend for one-child families, let me swiftly move in with some good news. Having done it all before, you are *mentally* much better equipped to get through the nine months without too much distress. You know the morning sickness will end, you know the initial exhaustion should pass within a couple of months, leaving you hopping about like a pregnant rabbit, and you even know how to dress yourself through the various stages of 'bulge', which is a major advantage over those women doing it for the first time. (Sadly, this means you also know how bad it can feel to have no waistline, breasts the size of medicine balls and feet that don't fit any of your best shoes, but we are *trying* to focus on the positives here, so think of it as 'forewarned is forearmed', rather than 'forewarned is fore-freaked out'.)

It feels different – it's definitely a girl

Now just hang on one second, missy. Old wives' tales are based on old wives having too little to do after sundown in the days before DVD players, and *not* on medical research. Just because you had a low bump, no morning sickness and glossy hair last time, and produced a boy, does NOT mean that the bump sticking into your ribcage, the constant vomiting and the straggly mane indicate the presence of a girl. You are just as likely to have another boy, because, as we know, all pregnancies are different, and life just ain't that simple. My bumps *were* different for my daughters than for my son, but I know plenty of women who have had three girls and three wildly differing pregnancies. Beware the Brain Drain, and stick to what you know.

Preparative Pep Talks

Preparing your toddler for the changes to come shouldn't commence too early, unless you want a bored, disinterested older child who couldn't give two hoots any more about this phantom baby Mummy keeps banging on about.

The biggest challenge is how to interest your toddler in an as-yet unseen baby, and to make the arrival sound exciting, without her feeling that she is no longer exciting and has been downgraded to 'last year's news'. It's a tricky one, but here are some strategies that worked for us:

☆ **Talk about the baby in short bursts.** Twenty minutes of baby talk bores most adults, so pity the three-year-old who has to sit through an hour-long nappy-changing demonstration. A couple of minutes here and there is much less like baby overkill, and keeps the subject alive and interesting.

☆ **Read books about new babies.** There are lots of these, but check them through first – many of them appear to portray babies as screaming, puking, boring, Mummy-stealing creatures of Evil, which is exactly how your toddler thinks of them already, so try to stick to the ones that lie through their paper teeth, and make babies look permanently lovely and older children seem helpful and even more loved by their parents.

☆ **Big-up his role.** It works for screen divas, so it should work for your needy toddler too: tell him he's the most important thing in the world, and that this baby will dote on his every move, and his ego will receive a welcome boost. It also means he might try to set a good example, but that should never be more than an outside hope. 'The baby will *love* you to show her how to build Lego towers!' and 'I hope you will help me to feed her – you're so great at eating your food nicely' are both blatantly not true, but who cares if it makes Mr Paranoid over there feel more secure.

☆ **Try not to over-egg the pudding.** There's a point at which playing up the baby's plus-points becomes raising wildly un-realistic expectations, and this can only result in a huge disapp-ointment for your toddler when baby Mia doesn't want to play with his car-transporter after all, and just throws up on it instead. Best to alert him to some of the unexciting aspects of a new baby as well as the groovy ones.

☆ **Get something special for your older child** as the big day approaches. This doesn't need to be the entire first floor of Hamley's, but something which makes him feel that his new role is one he'll be eager to adopt. We usually went for the 'first desk' or 'first grown-up bike' options, and there are many variables here to try. Any earlier than a month or so before the birth is going to cost you – kids have very short memory spans, and the 'new' bike will be old news by the time the baby comes.

☆ **Remember he is still your baby too.** With all the preparation for becoming the Older Sibling, it's easy to forget that this child still wants to be your baby on some primal level, and banging on about what a big boy he is now, and how grown up he will have to be when the baby comes, will terrify his 'Mummy's baby' side. He's confused, and wants to be both the Big Guy and the baby that Mummy and Daddy cuddle and dote on, so try to continue telling him he's still your little one sometimes. I didn't with my eldest, partly because she was always very precocious and just *seemed* very grown up, but I think perhaps she missed being my baby for a little while longer.

The final months

This is where it can start to get tough, both mentally and physically: you are probably bigger now than you were last time at this stage, you know how painful the birth is likely to be (unless you had an easy time before, in which case try not to get too complacent – labour is never the same twice) and you have a needy toddler who is trying to get as much of your soon-to-be-limited attention as she can while it's there.

It's usually when you are pushing a heavy trolley down the nappy aisle, carrying a wriggly two-year-old on your big, uncomfortable bump because she refuses to go in the trolley seat, bursting for the loo *again*, even though you only went ten minutes ago, that the following thought will hit you:

God it was easy last time!

Think back to your first pregnancy, when you only had yourself to work around (and probably a partner too, but he can look after himself if he needs to, I hope): bedtime was whenever you chose it to be; if you felt sick or tired you could take a five-minute break or have a lie down; and when the baby's weight became too much to hold any more you could sit down and give your legs, back and feet a rest. Last time you didn't have to get to playgroups, change pooey nappies when you were ready to throw up anyway, or endure bad nights caused by a child who wants to 'come into Mummy and Daddy's bed' from 3 a.m. until you give in and carry her through. Last time there was you, your body and your life, and that was it. What was the big deal??!

Well, before we start to feel too sorry for ourselves, let's remember that last time was the first time, and that makes it hard for very different reasons. The 'Oh, I remember how easy it was when I only had [x – 1] children' trap, where x is the number you currently have, is an easy one to fall into, because what you are saying is a little bit true, but it will win you no friends, and is very harsh on the lady struggling to manage her x − 1 children.

Activities to avoid

All the don'ts from last time still apply of course, but there are a couple of new ones that probably didn't apply before, because life in the office didn't generally involve hurling yourself down small slides into a ball pit full of writhing, tough toddlers – except if you were sent on a 'bonding weekend' at Center Parcs.

Here are some activities you might like to put on hold until . . . well, until you feel the urge to do them again after the birth:

☆ **Contact with animals.** The onus on you to traipse around farms and wildlife parks was far less first time around and the main concern was household pets. Now your life is completely different, and there is nothing to say that you won't find yourself being cajoled into spending a cold, muddy afternoon gawping at cows and sheep, feeding the horses and stroking the farm cats. Resist. She may get upset and stamp her little feet for a while, but there are some seriously nasty bugs and germs waiting for your gestating baby to come along, and you should give the bovine-watching a rest until after the birth.

☆ **Vigorous sliding/running/jumping.** This may sound very obvious, but last time you were pregnant you weren't keeping a toddler amused at the same time. Now you are as likely to spend an afternoon drowning in a ball pit in your local Sweat and Junk Food Den (aka a soft play area) as you are to be found sliding down a pole in the playground and giving your unborn baby a squashed head. However much you wish you could carry on these hilarious and enjoyable activities, you must look after your bump and suggest gentler ways of having fun together instead. Cue another box of Lego . . .

Taking Care of Number One

Unlike the unfathomably grim Olden Days, when fathers tended to peer round the hospital curtains after a day or so to take a derogatory sniff at the baby (unless it dared to be a girl, in which case he would largely ignore her until somebody showed signs of taking her away and marrying her), these days it is expected that we have a birthing partner, other than the midwife, to share in the joy of seven hours of screaming. And the choice of who gets this somewhat dubious honour is getting wider: no longer is it only the father who's in the running. No, it's now just as normal to ask your mother, sisters, bridesmaids, nanny, neighbour's nanny or dermatologist to hold your hand as you draw blood from theirs. Whom you choose should be entirely up you, but there is one member of your family whose presence I would advise against at all costs, from the very first 'Ouch!'s in the kitchen to the final 'Oh Holy Fuck!' in the delivery room.

No, it's not your father-in-law, although this would give you a great excuse never to speak to him again. It's your older child.

Children are obsessed with bottoms, willies, nipples, you name it, from the earliest age, and there really is no need to complicate matters by showing a head emerging from your vagina. It is very impressive, but that's exactly the problem – such impressions are impossible to erase, and will cause unimaginable damage to future relationships. Luckily most hospitals won't allow children anywhere near the delivery rooms (they'd be balancing on birthing stools and inhaling laughing gas before you could say 'Darling, Mummy is about to say some very rude words, so could you possibly go and watch *Fimbles* with Auntie Becky?').

All of this is very sensible, but it means you now have one more thing to sort out for the birth: **Who is going to look after Number One?** Whoever it is had better be very flexible – the 'I can have her until 6 p.m., but then I've got a Pilates class and we're going for drinks afterwards – you'll be done by then I should think' attitude is not going to work. You might well be done by 6 p.m., but then again you could still be huffing and puffing until your child-sitter is well into her second bottle of wine. Best to find someone with no commitments for the next thirty-six hours, just to be safe. Oh, and somebody who knows your child very, very well. This is a terribly confusing time for him, and he will be much more settled with somebody who knows exactly how he takes his milk, and whether he likes his pyjamas on *before* brushing his teeth or afterwards. It's the little things, you know.

☆ **Ask your child whom he would most like to stay with** for the day (and possibly night). Obviously you will have to veto ninety per cent of these candidates – 'I like Jake's Mummy best! I want to stay with Jake's Mummy!' might sound imploring, but bearing in mind that you've only met her once should sway you towards grandparents or friends you know very well instead – but it is important that he should feel he has been asked at least.

☆ **Spend some time with the people on your hit-list in the last few months,** so that he is familiar with the surroundings and the people who might end up child-sitting.

☆ **Have at least ten people on your 'Who will look after whatshername when labour starts?' list.** The first four (all the grandparents) will be visiting elderly relatives or wasting your inheritance on last-minute trips to the Galapagos Islands ('Yes, but we didn't think you were due for another two weeks!'), at least three will go straight to answerphone, one will be in labour herself (why was *she* on your list?), and it's not until you get near the bottom of the list that someone will come up trumps and be available. I know you hadn't *planned* for him to stay with your sister's boyfriend's best mate's girlfriend, even though she is 'good with kids', but it's that or watching *Postman Pat* videos in the delivery room.

The Birth

Just because your last baby popped out in six hours leaving no scars does not mean *this* little angel will follow suit: no two births are ever exactly the same, and you should be prepared for this. Maybe it'll be a Caesarean delivery. Or an induction, or a ventouse, or a 'Bloody hell, it's come out in the back of the car!' This also applies in the reverse: a hellish labour and complicated Caesarean last time does not mean you can't squeeze this next one out in the traditional way, and still have time to touch up your foundation before the paediatrician comes to check things over.

Nobody knows, but I think there are some very encouraging things to remember when going in for your second birth:

☆ **You *know* the pain will go away very quickly after the birth.** Of course, this also means you know how unbelievably painful the contractions and actual delivery will be, but this time you know it will **stop**, and this is a hugely uplifting thing to concentrate on when you think you are about to die.

☆ **You know how gorgeous a newborn baby is**, and how fantastic it is to be a mother. This point won't help you at all if your eldest has been a little shit for the last two months, in which case you might wonder why you're bothering, but in all other cases the thought of having another child should be enough to make the pain seem not quite so bad.

☆ **Subsequent births are often quicker.** Could anyone who has had the opposite experience please stop saying 'Huh! I don't bloody think so, Liz' and spitting at this page in deep-seated rage, and try to remember that I said 'often', not 'always'. It's something unpleasant to do with all the stretching last time, which your partner still doesn't want to talk about, but which might come in handy as the next eight pounds of Baby tries to make its way towards the light.

☆ **You have packed all the things you wished you'd had last time**, thus avoiding any 'Oh God, why didn't I bring any antacid!' moments. We'll treat Birth Number One as a practice run.

Meet the Sibling: Fingers crossed ...

There's not quite as much scope for humour and slapstick in this movie as there was in previous *Meet the* ... instalments, but with a little effort I'm sure Ben Stiller could squeeze out some terrific 'poking new baby in the eye', 'tantrums in the hospital corridor', and 'pressing buttons on the vital medical instruments' scenes.

Meeting a new sibling is something most of us forget, and it's probably just as well or we would never speak to each other again. It's not that most toddlers *dislike* their new friend from the start (that kicks in about twenty-four hours later) but most of them are only mildly interested at best, and disappointed at worst. And who wouldn't be, to be fair? This arrival has been talked about and long-awaited to the extent that anything short of a visit from *Bob the Builder* is bound to be a let-down. No squashed, blotchy, half-blind, bald creature could ever be expected to appeal much to a two-year-old who wanted to stay outside smashing Mummy's tomato plants with a football. To make matters worse, this poor excuse for a sibling has viciously sharp fingernails, dribbles foul-smelling fluid from the corners of its mouth, and only seems interested in one thing: Mummy's breasts. Great. Can we go now?

This is not the rosiest picture of sibling meets sibling and, as ever, things are rarely as gloomy as this. We have had two reasonably successful introductions to new babies in our family, but I think the elaborate planning and comprehensive worrying helped a lot. I would have been as happy with an 'Oh' as a full-blown declaration of everlasting toddler-love, but a definite dislike would have been upsetting, I think.

Here are some strategies both we, and our friends, have adopted to make the event pass without trauma for anyone:

☆ **Try to get the new baby in a good mood for the first visit.** There is usually a phone beside your hospital bed (assuming you made it that far, and didn't give birth in a lay-by between an articulated lorry and a roadside café), so try to tell your husband when you think is a good time for both of you, and then see if you can get baby fed, burped, changed and generally spruced-up in time for the presentation.

☆ **Have a present ready for your older child**, and say it's from the baby and not from you. I'm never totally sure whether they buy this ridiculous story at all, but we've done it both times and it seemed to go down very well and give the general impression that this baby is not only generous but also has great taste in helium balloons and small plastic toys.

☆ **Keep it short and sweet.** This is for everyone's benefit: your older child will get bored within ten minutes, the baby's nice mood won't last much longer than that, your partner will be itching to get away from all the lactating ladies, and some medical person or other will probably come along and start poking around the areas best kept hidden from inquisitive children – far too many questions there! Much better to let everyone leave with a good impression.

☆ **Spend some time alone with your older child while Daddy holds the baby.** I think this is very important because it will show your child that the baby isn't just Mummy's domain, and that the two of you can still have special times together without the dribbling accessory. A trip to the hospital shop for some chocolate and a wildly overpriced cuddly toy is usually a winner.

☆ **Plan a treat for later that day.** Unless the first visit is in the evening (which, by the way, it probably shouldn't be – everyone is tired, kids get overexcited and will never go to sleep, and you are grouchy because you realise you are missing *Corrie* yet again) then it's a good idea to have something special lined up for Number One after the obligatory baby-adoration is over. The zoo, swimming, visiting Granny – whatever will make it a special day for her.

And Then There Were Three: New challenges with two kids …

If Mother Nature had got herself sorted out properly when she was writing the Reproduction chapter, and had stopped popping downstairs for more tea and copying rude emails to her friends, she would have been able to concentrate much better, and wouldn't have made so many glaring slip-ups. We've come to accept the fact that babies don't fit well through vaginas and that breasts should have been left to the enjoyment of adults only, but there is one piece of carelessness that I find hard to excuse. The lack of limbs.

Babies have plenty – any more and we'd have no chance, what with six arms throwing baby food at the walls and five legs kicking the blankets off at night. No, babies are doing just fine. But what about their mothers? Why oh *why* can't we get an extra arm for every baby we deliver? Two would be even better, but I'd settle for one. While one arm held the baby's legs in place and the other got the nappy into position, the extra arm would be able to lift the two-year-old down from the window-ledge, from where he was throwing tiny polystyrene balls from the packaging of his latest 'Mummy and Daddy still love you' toy. Meanwhile, a couple of extra legs to hold the bedroom door open, which the polystyrene devil is now trying to slam, and to keep the lid on the toy box would also come in handy. It makes perfect sense, but sadly we will have to manage with just the two arms and two legs. Cheers.

Relative to last time you are as dexterous as the *Cat in the Hat*, but with two you will need to improve on this. Two kids does not mean twice the number of potential disasters requiring immediate attention. They mean about ten times that number, and I'm not just talking about knocking a cup of tea off the coffee table onto the carpet, but full-on toddler disasters involving marker pens and white walls, DVD players and marbles, and fake tan and toddler legs. Messy, exhausting, often dangerous and constantly surprising, the trouble your kids will try to get into is too frightening to tell, and the sooner you improve your reaction speed and limb agility the better.

TOP TIP: *If you ever find yourself in the position of watching a seasoned mother of many perform seventeen physical tasks simultaneously while making your perfect cup of tea and telling you about her latest business venture, try not to sink into deep, pregnancy-fuelled 'I am never going to manage this' depression: she has had tons of practice, and within six months or so you will be a skilled octopus too. Not sure about the business ventures, though – maybe she's just showing off. Or lying. Or both.*

But I thought I already had no free time!

I know. You did. 'Before' (when you only had one baby to look after) you really did feel like you had almost no spare time in which to get anything done for yourself, be that to rest, sort out your wayward eyebrows, do some work or fold eighteen pairs of baby socks.

But now that there are two kids to look after you finally realise that 'almost no time' was a luxury, because now you have none. You suddenly notice how many windows of opportunity you had, but never appreciated, and how many of those have now disappeared.

This is one *huge* hurdle to struggle over (not surprisingly really, given the double buggy, foot-dragging toddler and emotional baggage you now heave about with you everywhere), but once crossed you can get on with your life as though nothing had ever been any different, and it doesn't feel too bad at all.

The emotional minefield worsens

You've had a few years to get used to the emotional issues surrounding motherhood: guilt, worry, intense love, anxiety, jealousy, addiction to buying baby clothes, frustration, mood swings, and so on. But having more than one child adds a new dimension of Time, which has a knock-on effect on all the rest. Guilt is trebled ('Do I love them both equally? Am I neglecting the older one?), the amount of love you have to give doubles at least, making you concerned that your heart might reach bursting point and explode, while the amount of attention and pampering you receive doesn't change at all – in fact, it almost certainly lessens with the reduced amount of free time you have now. So, here is a run-down of some of the main NEW emotional minefields you will encounter, and some mildly helpful tips on how not to step straight onto them.

Favouritism

Here's one I bet you hadn't thought of before. It sounds nasty, and you'll think I'm way out of order for suggesting this might happen to you, but I speak from experience, so here goes: When you have more than one child, you can, if only for a short time, have a favourite. You can *like* one of them more than the other, and when you do it feels wrong, unfaithful and dirty.

Fear not. There's nothing bad or unusual about this – it's highly unlikely that all of your kids will be adorable all of the time, and far more likely that one will be a pain in the arse for a week while the other one becomes angelic (just to emphasise the other's arsey-ness). I've found my favouritism swinging from one to another regularly as they have each gone through awkward, difficult phases for some unfathomable reason.

Some of these stages have lasted for a worryingly long time. When my second child was born I adored her – she was a real living doll: blonde hair, huge blue eyes, the cutest mannerisms and a happy countenance. Her sister was a stubborn toddler with a perma-scowl, a grumpy, negative disposition and wonky teeth (not helped by the fact that I accidentally knocked one of them out when she was eighteen months old, but we'll skim over that detail). I am wildly exaggerating, but what is true is that I *preferred* my baby for about six months, and it worried me. Was this right? What did it say about me as a mother? Could my eldest sense that I liked the baby a bit more?

Yes, I think she could, and it wasn't until I came out of the post-birth fog that I saw how biased I had been towards the smiling, gurgling blob, and how I had neglected my confused, needy toddler. Within a year the 'living doll' had turned into a living nightmare, as she started testing her powers (and my patience) well before she was supposed to. At almost exactly this stage, which I don't believe was a coincidence, her older sister became adorable: she came to me for cuddles, laughed and smiled more, lost her 'Oh, life is *soooo* hard' expression and turned into a wonderful, sensitive, perceptive girl. A new favourite was born.

Since then the invisible Mummy's Favourite crown has moved heads many, many times and I don't feel guilty about it any more. We all like some people more than others, and just because they are both your kids doesn't mean you should like them equally all the time. You *love* them the same, and, so long as you show it, that's what counts.

Comparison

This isn't quite the same as favouritism, but it's just as common and unsettling. Comparison means just that: you compare what your baby does, relative to her older sibling, and makes judgements accordingly. She can't talk yet – she's not as clever; he can hold a crayon already – he's more artistic; she doesn't walk as well – she'll be less sporty; and so on. This is the curse of the second (and subsequent – just you wait) children: the first grows up on a blank slate, but after that you parents have certain expectations, whether realised or not, and something to compare the others with. It's not that a level has been set for others to match, or exceed, but there is a level present, and comparison is inevitable.

I think it's futile to try to resist comparison – and anyway, it doesn't have to be a negative thing. It's lovely to see the differences between your kids, and that has been one of the joys of having more. But when harmless comparing turns into a *Strictly Come Dancing* judging round, complete with scorecards, then it's time to take a look at how you're handling things.

Changes to your Daily Routine

My what? My routine? Are you having a laugh?

Oh, come on now, don't be modest – by the time your second baby comes along you will have been through about ten different 'routines', as sleep patterns, work requirements, feeding times and so on have changed, and, whether you think it or not, you have a well-established sense of routine and expectation for what can be achieved in a day.

Put another way, when you become a mother of more than one, you will look back on those heady days of single-childhood, and yearn for the (relative) simplicity to return. The days when there was only one person to put to sleep at lunchtime, one bottom to change and one child to put to bed. What you are now faced with is three people to work around, and this brings a multitude of new difficulties and changes:

☆ **Trying to keep three people happy (your kids and their father) is much harder than two.** It's like living in a warped mathematical world, where levels of difficulty go from one (just you) to fifty (you plus one child) to ten thousand (all four of you), and your success does the reciprocal, because you all want different things out of the day. Baby wants to eat, sleep and shit on demand, or because she can't help it. You want to play with your kids for the morning, then have an hour off to read a book, order some more printer cartridges and have a quick surf through Zara's new collection, followed by some more child-entertaining and then a relaxing evening with your partner, some wine and some friends. Your toddler wants to do exactly what he wants at all times, however impractical, impossible or infuriating that may be. The result: you either all have a miserable time, or you learn to compromise. That's *you* learn to compromise, not your toddler. Even a baby can be made to work around others a bit, but a three-year-old is less considerate.

☆ **Your toddler has to learn to wait.** What each of you wants is mutually exclusive for the most part, and this means that somebody has to compromise. In quite the reverse to traditional set-ups, where the oldest, biggest or richest gets his way, for the next six months or so it will be the reverse: Little Miss Newborn over there will call the shots, and this means that Mr Jealous will need to learn how to wait. Sometimes this waiting can last for a long time (when a feed is followed by a poo and then a huge vomit and clothes change, and then another feed to replace all the lost milk, and then another unexpected poo) and he is quite right in feeling put out. Try to get him set up with an activity he likes while you do the baby-fussing, and try as hard as you can to keep some of his routines going: Tuesday toddler group, after-lunch stories, afternoon tea – whatever it is you normally do together. This will help *a lot* in keeping his sense of normality alive and will help you to keep it hanging together!

☆ **Your toddler stops having a lunchtime sleep.** This is a huge change, for both of you, but it isn't *compulsory*: I have witnessed friends successfully putting both of their children down in their cots for a lunchtime nap, and it is something to behold. I, however, have never managed this, partly because my babies have only ever had daytime sleeps in their prams after being trundled about for a while, and partly because I have never tried, which is probably the bigger factor! But as your older child passes the magic 'two' mark she will gradually stop needing these sleeps (see page 314 for more on this) and they will eventually peter out.

Your Relationship with your Partner: Who?

If you still have a good one of these with the father of your children, then you are doing better than average, and this bodes pretty well for the future – getting through the first few years with a baby is the toughest time in any relationship, which is why so many fall apart before Junior can say 'I want shared custody please, Daddy.'

But having more than one child brings fresh challenges to the way you two get on and live together, and being prepared for these might help you:

☆ **All hands on deck.** One of the biggest changes in your relationship heralded by the arrival of Number Two, is that the number of children needing attention doubles. Obviously. What this means for you guys, mainly on weekends and in the evenings when Mummy's Big Helper isn't at work, is that while one person is bathing, changing or feeding the baby, the other person no longer has their hands free for a short while. If you are living with an example of Modern Man then this was the time he used to do the washing up, cook your dinner or write you a sonnet describing how absolutely wonderful you are. This time has now vanished. Having one child happily occupied still leaves another who wants something – usually something you can't or don't want to give at that precise moment – and when both children are soundly tucked up in bed you each spend the next hour doing all the jobs you used to do while your partner was looking after the only baby, and you both become (more) exhausted. It also leads to problem number two:

☆ **Child swap.** Not the title for Channel 4's new reality TV series as far as I know (although by the time this book goes to print it may well be) but rather what you and your partner will find yourselves doing within days of the birth. In order to keep up with the doubled demand from the Little People, you start child-swapping: 'You have him, I'll take her.' SWAP! 'Pass her to me and you can sort him out.' SWAP! And so on. The net result of all this Junior Juggling is two people who never get a break, who spend no time alone together any more, and before you can say 'Falling out of love' you will have forgotten who you used to be and what you used to do together. Being aware of this is half the battle won. The other half requires doing something about it by finding some time to be together *sans* kids.

☆ **Cumulative exhaustion.** Whaat? Cu-mu-la-tive ex-haus-tion. It's what you get after three years of relentless bad nights, followed by having another baby. I know you were tired last time, but back then you only had a few years of clubbing and late-night showings at the Odeon to take the edge off your mood and skin tone. This time you have all of that, plus nine months of pregnancy, plus a year of no sleep, plus another year of random sleep patterns, plus another pregnancy, plus another birth and back to no sleep again. Who's tired now? You. And your partner. And we all know what happens to you and your partner when you both get tired: you have less sex, you row, you become grouchy, you have even less sex, he becomes more grouchy, you feel inadequate, guilty and worried that he may be having sex elsewhere, you have reluctant sex, he says you're just doing it to make him happy, you say 'Oh, well done, Sherlock – and I thought you'd be grateful', he says, 'Well, if it's such an imposition then don't bother', you say 'Fine, I won't', and you both try to go to sleep before the baby wakes up, which, to your enormous irritation, your partner manages immediately, while you lie there thinking self-loathing thoughts until you give up and go and make a cup of Horlicks. Two minutes later the baby starts to cry and you have to feed her. Marital bliss, I'm sure you agree.

The solution to this age-old problem is to remember that this nightmarish phase should only last another six months or so, and to **get more sleep!** Stop sorting out the baby photos and writing thank-you cards until midnight, don't answer the phone after 8 p.m., don't even *think* about watching any telly after 9 p.m. (that's all the decent stuff out then) and GO TO BED. If he can come to bed at this time too then you'll have the chance for some quick nookie and that almost always makes everyone feel happier.

Regression, Regression, Regression

What the hell is going on? What has happened to your toddler? Last week your two-year-old could walk, talk and behave in a reasonably civilised manner most of the time. Last week, you sat down together at the table for lunch, he was doing quite well at potty training, and you felt that you knew each other well. You were buddies. You were in love.

This week he has become selectively deaf and only hears 'Would you like some chocolate?', never 'Please can you stop doing that, honey?' This week he pours his milk on the floor while looking you straight in the eye, takes his own nappy off and poos on the living-room carpet, and refuses to eat anything. What is happening? Where has last week's baby gone?

Ah, well this is *this* week, and that was *last* week, you see, and the two are quite, *quite* different. Last week you didn't have a new baby in the house. Last week your toddler was the darling of the house. The King. The Champ. The undisputed apple of your eye. But this week there is some major competition in the way, and this apple of yours is about to become very sour indeed.

This is a period where your toddler's true intelligence and cunning show themselves most clearly. You may have been impressed by the garbled sentences and impressive ball-skills this young lad has already developed, but just you wait and see how sophisticated his ability to wind someone up the wrong way is. Beneath that cherub-like, sweet-as-honey exterior lies a fearsome creature of deep Evil and unforeseeable mischief who is about to revel in his newfound powers of irritation.

Fear not. This is completely normal, almost expected, and it is a good sign that your firstborn loves you, and doesn't want to share you with anybody else. Especially somebody who makes Mummy too tired to play any more and confines her to bed much of the time, who requires a vast amount of her time and energy, and who can't even play with Lego properly. A mewling, puking baby, who will only be shown the door if the King demonstrates just how bad things will get around here otherwise.

Things your elder child may do for a few months after your baby is born:

- ☆ **Stop eating properly, or at all.** What were fun mealtimes now turn into a battle of wills, as you both try to out-piss-off your opponent using fishfingers and peas.
- ☆ **Want her dummy back**, when she has been happily without it for months.
- ☆ **Speak like a baby again.**
- ☆ **Go back to weeing on the carpet**, when she was already potty trained, especially if she knows you can't get to her quickly enough because you are changing the baby. Clever.
- ☆ **Become aggressive**, and start hitting and kicking you or other children.
- ☆ **Stop sleeping at night** (oh joy!).
- ☆ **Say very hurtful things to you**, from the common 'I hate you. You're a horrid mummy!' to the almost unforgivable 'You have a big bottom.'

There are many more regressive changes you might notice, and all of them are very frustrating and tiring. They will go as she gets used to the new set-up, so bear with it if you can and take a deep breath.

Gently, Darling!

This is something all mothers of second and subsequent babies say frequently, mostly through gritted teeth and with their eyes half-closed, in order to block out the indelible image of their new baby's head being dented by a Tonka car transporter.

It's a very good idea, and also important, to involve your eldest with the new baby as much as possible, both for them to feel needed and helpful, and for them to bond a little with their new brother or sister. Unfortunately, toddlers are not best known for their delicacy and sensitivity of hand. Rather, they are like very powerful demolition machines, which can break, snap, smash, crack, destroy and hurt almost anything that comes their way. And Baby is no exception.

She doesn't *mean* to break his arm. She doesn't *mean* to poke his eyes out with her skipping-rope handle. Or does she? There's a look in her eye that makes you wonder exactly how accidental this latest injury was. Could it be that darling Phoebe was fully aware of how hard she was patting her brother's head, and was waiting to see how much pummelling it would take before Mummy reacted and gave her some attention? Yes. It could very well be, and almost certainly is. Bad attention, good attention, any sign that Mummy knows she is still there is what's demanded, and demand it she will.

So what are you supposed to do with your hooligan toddler? Tell her off? Try to gently explain what she's doing wrong? Bribe her away with chocolates and half an hour in front of *Angelina Ballerina*?

No. Or maybe. Or sometimes, depending on how the last few hours have gone. *You* know how your toddler responds to your attempts at calming her down better than I do, and the only thing you need to keep in mind the whole time, no matter how you decide to proceed once the damage has been done, is this:

> Your toddler wants you back, hates the new intruder
> much of the time, and is desperate for a taste of the
> Old Days again.

This can be hard to remember when you are mopping up the blood spilled from a recent metal-toy-car-hits-delicate-forehead episode, but if you can resist the temptation to scream 'Oh just LOOK what you've done NOW! You horrid, horrid girl. You've hurt the baby. How can you be so bad? Go and sit on your own while I make her better', before lavishing yet more kisses, cuddles and milky nipples on your baby, that should make things better between all three of you in the medium run.

☆ **Let your older child hold the baby as often as you can remember.** When he feels how delicate she is, he might think twice before trying to tie his policeman's hat on to her with rough string. Let him feel her wrists, hold her head up, and generally get a sense that this is a sensitive, living being. She may *look* exactly like the plastic baby in the bathroom cupboard, but she doesn't like having her face pushed under the water quite as much.

☆ **Try not to fall into 'See? You don't like it either' territory.** It's very tempting to want to bash him on the head just after he's done this to your baby, to give him a sense of what he's inflicting on her. Very occasionally this can work (in less brutal instances) but I've found that a brusque 'Hey, that's really not nice at all', followed by something *nice* for your older child is much more effective.

Age One to Two: Walking, talking and all that jazz …

It is dawn. Through the thick morning mist, a huge, red, life-giving sun slowly reveals herself. Gently rising, struggling to penetrate the murky, wet air but gaining in intensity, warmth and vibrancy with every minute, she finally emerges, resplendent, to light up another day.

This is what happens to your life with your baby in the second year (albeit in a less pretentious, figurative way), and it feels even better than watching the mother of all sunrises. In this next year, any gloom, fog and thankless drudgery should be lifted away by the miraculous (and long overdue, some would say) arrival of your child – not your baby, but your *child* – and all the hard work you have put in starts to show.

This is the year of talking, walking, properly interacting and communicating, understanding each other and finally getting some more satisfying feedback than the odd giggle and a burp. This is usually the stage at which I want to administer some magic potion that will halt any further development – it's like having the cutest, most playful, cuddly kitten that you just know will turn into a haughty, flea-ridden cat who only comes home for food and a good wash. PAUSE right there please! Don't change! Don't grow up and start having tantrums, acne, weight problems and unsuitable boyfriends! Just stay exactly as you are *forever*.

As the growth-stunting hormones have never materialised and my kids have indeed continued to move on into the next stage of childhood, I have been continually relieved and delighted: just when I am convinced that they couldn't get any lovelier and that *this* is actually the best stage of all, they go and get even nicer. This may be because none of my kids have hit puberty yet, and I'm sure my rose-tinted glasses will be shattered the day that first spot appears, but for the first eight years at least I have only found they get more and more fun to be around, and this fun really gets going around the first birthday. Perhaps it's the first taste of cake that does it.

What follows is a brief rundown of some of the main changes you and your child may go through in this second year, and some ways of coping with them. As ever, nothing is concrete, and every child does things at his or her own pace. Your little Paula Radcliffe may already be jogging around the living room, while others are still not that keen on moving from wherever they were plonked down, but all will level out in the end. The main thing is to enjoy the changes as they happen, when they happen.

Walking

At some point near your child's first birthday, you will have the following conversation, or one very similar:

'Come on! Come on, Charlie, you can do it! That's it – walk to Mummy! Good boy – keep going! That's *brilliant*! Careful now. Steady – oh shit! Watch out! Mind the coffee table! Charlie . . .!'

Crash.

'*Waaaaaaah*!'

'Oh my God! Charlie? Are you OK? Somebody get some plasters and antiseptic – quick!'

There is something so deeply rooted about our desire to see our offspring walk that I think it must be an evolutionary drive – 'Child must hunt woolly mammoth. Child must walk.' That kind of thing. And so, when they are no bigger than a large teddy bear, we begin to encourage our babies to stand up, shuffle their feet and walk.

There are several phases to learning to walk, some of which you may already have mastered during the first year:

1. **Air dancing.** This occurs almost from birth (it's one of the reflex reactions the paediatrician should check within a few hours) and it's very amusing. Hold a baby upright and let its feet gently touch the floor, and it will start bending its knees, tapping its feet and generally looking as though it would run off if you would only put it down for a moment. This continues right through the first year until they are ready for phase two.

2. **The drunk**. This starts around eight months or so, when your baby is strong enough to stand up for a while when leaning against a low chair, coffee table or your knees. After about thirty seconds, her legs forget what they are supposed to be doing and she collapses onto her big, padded bottom. Ta-da! Just like closing time on a Saturday night outside every pub in the land. You should be quite careful at this stage, because the temptation to do it as much as possible is strong, but babies still have very soft, delicate joints and ligaments, and too much weight-bearing can damage their legs, knees and hips. It usually goes on for a good few months, or until she has taken all the embarrassment she can stand.

3. **Hands free.** With almost as much glee as a woman who first gets

her hands on (or rather off) her first hands-free phone, so a toddler-to-be will one day let go of whatever it is that's keeping her upright – and remain upright! That first 'Look – no hands!' moment is thrilling, and the look of surprise, joy and immense pride on your child's face will almost match yours. Try to be close by for these feats of death-defying balance and co-ordination: they usually don't last longer than five seconds before she either topples over backwards or sideways, still as straight as a board.

4. **First steps.** What a wonderful moment! I will never forget watching our first child stagger towards me across the blue rug in our lounge, arms outstretched, teetering occasionally for dramatic effect, with a huge grin across her big baby face (tinged only by slight uncertainty about which foot should come next and whether she might trip over the small plastic elephant that lay in her path) and diving ecstatically into my arms – just. These first steps, and the many lunges like it, will bring joy to even the most stressed, tired and sexually frustrated of parents.

5. **Back-breaking.** Aha! Sting in the tail number one. As mince pies bring fat thighs and late nights bring under-eye frights, so teaching your child to walk brings backache. And no rhymes. As soon as your child has discovered that he can get from A to B using his legs and feet, rather than his bum or his knees, this will be his preferred mode of transport. Sadly, he can only get about fifty centimetres this way, before having to resort to those knees again, causing severe bruising to his pride, especially if there are pretty girl-toddlers present. He will make his displeasure known – by crying and wailing – until you do what you will do all day for the next four months: you stoop down, help him up, and hold both his hands as he walks slowly along, like the King of all Things once more. He feels very clever. You have a sore back. Why were you so keen to get him to walk again? This is awful! You can't talk to anyone any more because you are constantly bending down holding baby hands; if you do try you just crick your neck as well; and now your child is constantly unhappy if you don't help him to stagger about. Aaaargh! It will pass.

6. **The only way is up.** This is sting in the tail number two. Now that your child can stand up and walk about the place a little, she can also reach all the things you carefully moved up a shelf last year, so you have to do it all again. Up go the remote controls, jewellery boxes and gorgeous candle displays.

7. **CONGRATULATIONS!** You are now the proud owner of a toddler. This is a huge leap for all of you, and having a child who can move about unaided, and increasingly fast, will change the life you have together forever. It does, however, bring sting in the tail number three: your child will never sit still again. You can only appreciate the gravity of this once it happens, but when you have spent six months dedicating much of your time and energy into getting your child off her bottom and onto her own two feet, only to find yourself chasing after her and asking her to *sit DOWN* for the next four years, you do wonder why you were in such a rush!

When should my child start to walk?

As with most questions of this nature, there is no 'correct' answer: my kids all started walking between eight and ten months old, but from what I have observed, the average tends to be around one year old. Why this should be is anyone's guess. Maybe it's in their genes (I walked early and haven't stopped moving about since), maybe it's what you do with them (either encouraging them to stand and using a baby bouncer in the doorway or letting them sit at every opportunity), or maybe it's because some kids are more mischievous than others and want to start wreaking havoc as soon as possible. Who knows?

What I have found, though, is that children who are encouraged to walk earlier seem to progress more quickly in some other areas too, because they have access to so much more new stuff all of a sudden and their brains are used more as they develop their co-ordination. They also don't seem to get frustrated as often as those who sit and bum-shuffle for the first eighteen months. The freedom and sense of achievement that walking about brings is a huge relief for many babies, who no longer have to wait for mummy to pass that toy down off the shelf and who can suddenly use their legs more, which must feel fantastic and is almost certainly good for their heart, lungs and general physical health as well (unless they keep crashing into door surrounds and toppling onto toy baskets). Their new mobility and height allows toddlers to explore a whole world of things previously out of reach, and paths ne'er before travelled, and it can really improve their mood.

Warning: The hazardous, unstable, accident-prone nature of this stage can result in your first bouts of obvious physical injury. Be prepared for some tut-tutting in the supermarket as you wheel around a child with two black eyes and a split lip. *You* know he walked into the bathroom door – twice – but Nosy Nora doesn't, and will give you a look you'll never forget. This will continue for years, so best be prepared for it.

Talking

By the end of the first year it's very likely you will already have lots of 'Ma Ma!' and 'Da Da!' words already, and possibly even some sounds that could be understood as 'ball', 'duck', 'car' or 'straightening irons' to the trained ear – i.e. yours. Training your ears to hear things that your toddler says, but which don't sound anything like the way you or I say them, is a crucial part of helping your child to speak. If you can translate 'Gee-ba! Gee-ba!' as 'Please can you give it back', then not only is your child instantly satisfied because she gets her spoon/teddy/chewed wooden block back, but you can also reinforce in her brain that 'Give it back' was correct, and it means what she thought it did. Well done her! (This trained ear is responsible for a lot of inter-parental stress, as people try to convince us that their fourteen-month-old really did just say 'MP3 player', it's just that we couldn't understand her. Yeah right.)

The only way I've found to understand the mutterings is to try and blur your mind, and imagine how you would speak if you were really pissed. Thus 'Eyedooit' means 'I'd like to do it myself please'; 'I don't like that' becomes 'Don-lie-da' and, of course, 'Eyelaaaarvoo' is 'I love you'. Understanding, or at least trying your hardest to understand, what she is blurting out is absolutely fundamental to you being able to help your child to talk, and the speed of your progress together will impress even the most sceptical Yummy Mummy.

Here are some common stages for talking:

☆ **Single sounds.** This is the initial 'Ba', 'Da' stage, which can kick in as early as six months. Good news: you have already flown past this stage, so move swiftly along to stage two, and grab a congratulatory biscuit on the way.

☆ **Multiple sounds** (surprise, surprise). After 'Ba', it's a short leap to 'Ba-ba', 'Ba-ba-ba' and even, for the ambitious, 'Ba-ba-da!' Again, by the beginning of the first year you may well have cruised through this stage, and be into more interesting sounds including 'oo', 'ee' and 'sh', and possibly even the beginnings of some combination work, such as 'ooee' or 'shooee'. If you are now starting to wonder just how dull and pathetic your life has become, and how long it will be before it's acceptable to have your first gin and tonic of the afternoon, please try to remember that to compensate for your lack of brain activity your baby's is in overdrive, and the more effort you can put in now the faster you can get onto some decent chat. It really won't be long.

☆ **First words.** Rejoice! Cue peels of church bells, fireworks, champagne corks popping and much cheer! Your child can say something! And it's no longer a best guess at something vaguely similar to the actual word she's after, but the spot-on, absolutely intended, real McCoy – the word! I have pages full of words that my kids started to say from one year onwards (actually that's a small lie: I have lists of words my first child said, and a few notes of what my second child said, and no record of anything number three ever said or did. Sorry Charlie – something to do with running out of time and inclination). What these first words are depends on where you live and what you do with your child: for us it was always duck ('du!'), ball, bus, car, tree ('tee!'), pram ('pam!'), milk (muck!), banana ('nana') and spoon ('boon!'), which reflects our penchant for taking the pram along a busy road to feed the ducks in the park and then coming home for some mashed banana. For others it may be more a case of buggy, taxi, Harvey Nicks, cappuccino, posh bag and organic banana, but whatever your routine, your child will start to pick up words at a staggering rate, and you will suddenly reap the rewards of all your dedication last year, when you spent hours a day talking to a four-month-old baby, who only ever drooled back. If you didn't do this, you may start to wish you had. Still, you know for next time . . .

☆ **Gobbledegook.** Much as a child wants to run before it can walk and ends up taking the skin on their forehead off on the pavement, so he also wants to talk before he can utter more than a few new sounds. The result is what Italian sounds like to a non-speaker: an uninterrupted string of vowels and consonants spoken at high speed, accompanied by much arm movement, ending in a question mark and followed by expectant raised eyebrows. Shit. What did she say?

As you can see, these first semblances of speech are nothing more than a series of sounds, copied. You child has little or no concept of what each individual word means, or even that 'Eyelaaaarvoo' is made up of three words, but she knows that that sequence of sounds means whatever it is she means.

If you keep repeating them and congratulating her every time she says something roughly like what she was trying to say, she will make huge progress very quickly.

If your child makes no discernable sounds at all, then you must go and talk to your doctor about it. Nobody is expecting 'My milk is a little too hot' speeches just yet, but sounds like 'Ba', 'Da', 'Ga' and 'Ma' should be there after about ten months.

The Terrible Twos: Why tantrums happen and how to cope with them

Where? Which terrible twos? In my experience, two is a wonderful age, where your child stops being a baby, and really starts to become *somebody*. This somebody has his own thoughts, opinions, ideas, ways of doing things (which are usually crap, but we'll let that pass for now – he's learning), talents and skills that all need to be discovered and enjoyed. If learning how the world works and how he fits into it requires a certain amount of patience-testing and arguing then so be it, but I would never call this age Terrible. This label was invented by mothers who were annoyed at having their complete autonomy undermined by somebody no higher than their waxed thighs, and wanted to put the blame somewhere.

Tantrums

Just in case you think this is going to be an 'All Kids Are Wonderful All the Time' chapter, let's put that idea firmly to rest by dealing with one of their least wonderful traits: tantrums. This feels like a good day to write about tantrums, as my three-year-old had a minor version of one this morning, so I'm in sympathetic, understanding mode. I am tilting my head to one side, nodding slowly and saying, 'Yes, yes. Oh I know exactly what you mean.' This won't help, however, so I'll try to do better.

Many people falsely believe that tantrums are the Holy Grail of toddlers. According to them, just as women seek the perfect bum and cleavage, and men seek – well, the same actually, so all two-year-olds strive to perfect the mother-of-all screaming fits, because that is what they believe they are meant to do.

WRONG! So, so, so wrong. This theory is encouraged by the disturbing number of 'real life' TV programmes showing dysfunctional families who have no idea whatsoever how to look after a gerbil, or indeed themselves, let alone a developing, intelligent, needy child. Scenes of these 'Devil' children writhing on the floor, red-faced and screaming to the point of vomiting while lashing out with arms and legs, throwing heavy toys, ripping their hair out and shouting abuse at their parents, are common in such programmes, and if anything is going to put someone off children for life then this is it. They should make sixth-form students watch *Supernanny* in sex-education classes instead of banging on (so to speak) about penises, ovaries and suchlike. Penis, yes please. Howling banshee-child, hell no – pass me the contraception!

Here's the much happier truth: not all toddlers have tantrums. There. That feels better, doesn't it? Some are simply more placid or amenable, others are miracle children belonging to people who also have nice hair and a clean bathroom. Of course, every child will have his or her very trying moments, but hopefully, with a little preparation and effort, it won't have to get as far as a tantrum.

When do tantrums start?

This is a little bit like asking, 'When do people grow up?' I know grown men who have tantrums, and it's no less embarrassing or endearing. I also know children who had their most stubborn, difficult stage at about ten months and quickly got bored of it, moving on to become startlingly mature, calm two-year-olds. (I think I saved most of my own toddler rage until I was fifteen, but we won't go there!)

What is a tantrum?

The description I gave above is somewhat stereotypical, and there are a million variations on this theme, but I think they can all be summed up thus: a child is having a tantrum when she doesn't want to do whatever it is you are asking her to do, refuses to co-operate, won't listen to your pleas and bribes and makes a lot of noise and fuss about it. Especially in a public place, and almost always in a supermarket queue. This can last for two minutes or two hours, depending not on how difficult your child is, but on how you deal with it. More on this in a sec.

Why do kids have tantrums?

In contrast to what you may have heard ('All two-year-olds are bloody nightmares, and are just trying to see how much they can wind you up'), tantrums are not there just to piss you off and make you late for your 9 a.m. meeting. Instead, they are all about power and control, according to Liz's Armchair Theory of Tantrums.

Humans are very simple creatures: we like sex, food and glossy magazines. Most of all we like to have some control over what we do and to feel some sense of power. Even if it's only as feeble as

'I decide to put the washing on, and what colour the living-room cushions should be, not you', this small amount of power keeps us happy. Take all control and the right to an opinion away, and you are left with a very frustrated, angry human. Enter the Toddler. This poor creature is developing his mental and physical ability at a terrifying rate (just watching it makes you certain that you're on the fast road to dementia) and wants to try his new skills out at every opportunity.

Tantrums occur when this (as he sees it) able toddler feels suddenly powerless again, because you aren't letting him do what he wants. It really is as simple as that.

I am completely convinced that, on some level, toddlers can see that what you are saying makes sense, but such is their frustration at being ordered to stop making a fantastic fortress out of the clothes-horse and your best shoeboxes, or being dragged off to town because Daddy needs a 5 mm. drill-bit, or told to finish the last mouthful of cold, congealed boiled egg – which they never asked for in the first place – that throwing a wobbly is absolutely understandable. Any of these, and an uncountable multitude of other things, can trigger the beginnings of a tantrum, and this is where you come in. Because once Mr Terrible Two over there learns the effect that such a show can have on you (and however much you try to hide it, there will be a very clear effect, which he just loves to see), he will use it for his great amusement until he moves on to greater things (like being an annoying four-year-old. Ah yes, it just goes on).

What can I do to prevent tantrums?
I hope you know by now not to expect a 'How to' chapter in this book. I can tell you what I do, and what some of my friends do, and you can give it a bash and see what happens.

☆ **Nip it in the bud from day one.** This is about as 'How to' as I'm going to get, and I think it's crucial. If you have a strategy in place from the start, then things should never escalate into hair-pulling and spitting. As soon as you let your toddler have a full-blown tantrum, in the Textbook Cases from Hell sense, you have lost the battle, and it'll be twenty years before you come up for air again.

☆ **Try distraction.** This is the simplest method of tantrum control, if you can make it work. In the same way that you will distract your husband away from the bag your heart is set on with a 'Was that Cameron Diaz walking past?' while you quickly slip the cashier your credit card, so a casual 'Look! An aeroplane!' can work for the toddler whose mouth is turning square and is gearing up for a fight. This easy technique can avoid eighty per cent of tantrums, but you have to be quick, and, if possible, get in there before the penny has even dropped that you are not going swimming after all.

☆ **Completely ignore her.** I personally hate this technique, as I think it makes the ignorer very rude and is utterly infuriating for the ignor*ee*, but I know lots of people for whom if works, so I thought I should mention it. After a minute or two of shouting and fussing with no reaction coming from Mummy, your toddler may well shut up and put up. If it doesn't work, usually indicated by the presence of foam coming out of his mouth and all the expensive glasses shattering beneath the strain of the high-pitched screams, then keep working your way down this list after some cuddles and comfort.

☆ **Get down to her level.** By this, I don't mean throw yourself on the kitchen floor, turn scarlet and hit your head with a plastic fork. I *do* mean squat down until your eyes are at the same level (as your child's, not as each other. I hope they are level already), try to hold her gently by the shoulders, or at least make some soothing physical contact, and look her straight in the eyes. Toddlers often respond much better when you are at the same height as them – I know I wouldn't want to reason with anyone who was three times taller than me – and it's the first step to getting some agreement.

☆ **Speak softly.** Even if she is shrieking so loudly that she cannot hear a word you're saying, or can't even hear that you are making a noise, persevere with the quiet, gentle voice. Just as is the case for adults, so shouting at a child just makes them shout more, and it's escalating carnage from then on. Talking quietly usually makes them turn the volume down a little, especially if you can quickly squeeze out the words 'go to the park' while she is pausing for (large, powerful) breath.

☆ **Try to make him laugh.** Again, not the most subtle method, but if it works then who cares? One way I sometimes do this is to pretend to have a tantrum too: I cry and stamp my feet, and demand to be given all the chocolate and crisps in the world. I beg my kids to give me what I want, until they end up telling me to stop it because they're so embarrassed, and we all have a giggle. Sarcasm is also a winner in our house: 'Oh yes – of *course* you can go out dressed like that. Come on, let's all go into the snow in our pants and socks! Come on! It'll be fun!' Suddenly, when Mummy puts it like that, the suggestion seems a little stupid. And the thought of somebody seeing Mummy's pants is too much, even for one so young.

☆ **Give him the floor.** It's likely he already has the floor (or at least, has his back on it), but try to let him have his say, and explain what he wants. If the cause of tantrums is wanting to have some power then why not give him a teeny-*weeny* bit, by listening to him, and letting him have his way a little? This is where the next point comes in:

☆ **Make a deal.** This is the best kind of deal-striking in the world: you cunningly dictate the terms but make her think that she is. You come off much better than your opponent, but she still thinks she's won, feels good and is nice to you for an hour or so. It's perfect. In the non-coat-wearing example above, you could have the following conversation:

Child (*defiantly*): I don't want to wear my coat!

You (*in a mock-casual voice, with forced smile*): OK, that's fine. It's a good idea – let's go out like this. I'll carry your coat for you, and if you get cold I don't mind helping you to put it on – you stubborn little blighter. (*That last part is muttered under breath and through clenched teeth.*)

There. That should work. The most important part of these tantrum-averting deals is that you stick to them, or next time you will be powerless. If all else fails, try this next technique as a last resort:

☆ **Bribe him.** It's easy and it works, thus:

Child (*defiantly*): I don't want to wear my coat! (This boring repetition is important for you to get a sense of how boringly repetitive this kind of conversation gets.)

You (*imploringly*): Please?

Child (*defiantly*): NO!

You (*getting irritated now, because you know you're about to cave in*): Darling, it's cold outside, now will you please put on your coat, or I'll get cross.

Child (*defiant . . . oh, you get it*): No!

You: (*pause*) IfyoudoI'llgiveyouthreeSmarties!

Child puts on coat.

You: (*walking through to the chocolate cupboard*) Bugger, bugger, bugger! (*Check there's enough wine in the fridge for later – you're going to need it . . .*)

Bribery does work, but, as with new facepacks, its impact and effect lessens every time you use it. It's also not the most mature or subtle method, which leaves you somehow dissatisfied and feeling like a two-year-old yourself.

Joking aside, tantrums are very disturbing for all concerned: for the toddler, for you, and for anyone observing the scene from the restaurant table next to yours. Try to prevent them if at all possible, and give yourself a big pat on the back every time you do.

Losing the Lunchtime Sleep

Oh God, this is a catastrophic change, and it will signal the beginning of a new, less privileged phase of Mummyhood (unless you already use full-time childcare, in which case this will have little or no effect on your daily life. Carry on). Most children stop having a nap during the day at some point during their third year – *when* exactly depends mainly on the child, but also partly on how you want to play it. You can definitely influence your child's sleep habits according to your needs, but there will come a point when no amount of darkened rooms, long walks in a pram and soothing 'Baby Sleep Time' tapes will work. The eyes are open, and will stay that way.

Losing the lunchtime sleep can takes months to adjust to if, like me, you relied on this time to get some jobs done and read *OK!*. As each of my children has reached the point of going through a full day without any kip I have been filled with dread, and have tried to prolong the napping as long as possible. Inevitably there always came a day when the sleep just didn't happen any more, and we moved on to full days with no rest for mummy at all.

The good news is that this phase will only last for about two and half years, at which time your child will go to school, and you'll have a bit of time to yourself again. Unless you have another one, of course. Great. It can also be a very special time for you to be alone with your older child while your baby sleeps. I have fond memories of these days with both of my older kids, as I used to take them to a bookshop at lunchtime and spend a solid hour reading stories to them with the baby asleep in the pram next to us. This was special, private time for us to be alone together without the Drooling One, and they loved the secrecy of our story times: 'Don't tell the baby what we've been doing!'

That'll have to do for now – the kids will be home soon and we don't want them to find us poking around in their things. Time to spend a while with the rest of the family, and with some of your friends, by going back to the landing and taking a right turn, into the guest bedroom.

PART FIFTEEN

The Guest Bedroom

The bulk of this tour so far has dealt with issues concerning yourself, your partner and your kids. But families are much more than that, and in this room we will turn to the other people in your life: your wider family and your friends. Without them things would be very lonely and very difficult, so plough on and let's see who we've got . . .

Your Parents: Getting to know each other all over again . . .

> ### 18 August
> *I can't believe what I'm seeing. Dad is in the garden with C and E, showing them how to play golf, and he looks like he's loving it, and so are they! He is being really patient and helpful, and they are getting quite good already. Mum is sitting with P doing some sewing, and it's like a scene out of a 1950s Perfect Family programme. They were never like this with us, I'm sure, and it's really great to see. Grandparenthood definitely suits them!*

In all the excitement of becoming a new family, learning the ropes and setting out your new crockery, it's easy to forget about your

Old Family for a while. You know – the ones who raised you, paid for your piano lessons, took your to see Santa every year in the stuffy shopping precinct and went without any peace and quiet for the eighteen years you spent at home. In short, the people who went through everything you are going through now.

Whatever the relationship you had with your parents was like before you set up your own little family, it will never be the same afterwards. It might be better, it might be worse, but it will certainly be very different. Of course you are still their little girl, even though you hate to think of it that way, but you are also a mother and wife in your own right, which is where the biggest potential for conflict lies: **you are inhabiting the same space for the first time**, which can lead to all kinds of treading on toes, sticking noses in where they're not welcomed and making tut-tutting noises that make your blood pressure shoot through the roof.

Happily, this kind of interference and tension isn't always present, and many people find the relationship they have with their parents becomes much better and stronger once they have a family of their own, as it did for me. However it goes, there are some facts about your parents' new roles which you might benefit from being aware of, before you turn around and snap: 'Mum, I *know* how to peel potatoes, OK?!'

☆ **They are finding their feet too.** Unless you have five siblings who beat you to it and have been married with kids for years, you might find that your parents take a little time to adjust to their new roles as grandparents or just 'parents of children who are married'. They've never done it, and they have to learn how to handle it too: when to butt in, when to butt out, and what to say when you announce you are going to move to Australia to be nearer his parents . . . ouch. Give them time, and allow them some very undiplomatic, annoying teething problems.

☆ **They mean well.** I know this is a horribly patronising thing to say about someone, but in this case it's so true that it's not insulting. Yes, it may be infuriating when your dad insists on playing football with your son and giving your daughters flower presses instead, but that may just be the way he is, and he means no ill at all. Sexist, yes. Deliberately provocative, no.

☆ **Parents bring constancy.** With so many changes going on in your life in these first years of marriage and parenthood things can feel a little uncertain much of the time. This is where parents can help a lot: there they are, still griping about this and that, still reading the same paper, having tea at the same time and going on holiday to the same place year in, year out. This kind of constancy can be very reassuring when everything else seems to change every two days, so go and spend some time with them and get that 'grounded' feeling again.

☆ **They are often right.** Ooooh I hate it when my parents are right! I can handle my husband being right, my kids and my friends, but when my parents turn out to know better than me about anything to do with marriage or child-rearing I get a bit tetchy. 'Look, you've had your chance, now let me do it my way. Oh damn, your way *is* better after all. You win.'

Parents are often wrong as well, of course: locking a screaming child in a bedroom until she cries herself to sleep is not a method I'd employ to get some rest. But, much as we'd like to be all grown up and make up our own rules and systems, the fact is that parents have had a lot more experience of family life than we have, and it's quite likely they have some handy tips to pass on. Listen, take the good advice, and ignore the utter nonsense.

☆ **They might be missing you.** Even though you only live an hour's drive away or still come and visit in the holidays, it's not impossible that your parents feel you have finally left the nest for real this time, now that you have a nest of your own to feather. Consider this, and keep in touch a lot.

☆ **Time is ticking.** When you move on to set up your own place and start producing children it can be a rude reminder to your parents that they are getting on a little. Even if they are still in their youthful sixties and living life to the full, they might be suddenly aware of a new generation signalling the passing of the years.

☆ **You are their mirror.** Watching you raise your kids and settle into a new marriage can stir up long-buried memories of their own efforts at home-making. Seeing the way you do it might open their eyes to different or better ways *they* might have done it, and this can be unsettling and thought-provoking. Remind them what good parents they were (even if that's not entirely true!): they might benefit from a confidence boost right now.

☆ **They are grandparents!** One of the main reasons for making an effort to get on with your parents once you have children is for the wonderful relationship they can develop with your kids. Every parent I have spoken to says their parents are much better grandparents than they were parents, and this is fairly under-standable: they are older, calmer, less stressed and often more patient. Make every effort to let your parents know your kids and spend time with them: they have years of knowledge and skills to pass on, and it's vital for kids to understand where you come from, and why you are the way you are.

☆ **They are free babysitters.** Need I say more? Perhaps a box of chocolates wouldn't go amiss . . .

☆ **Get to know each other.** It might take years, but the more effort you can put into understanding and enjoying your new relationship, the happier you, and your family, will be.

I get on better with my parents now than ever, and I know that settling down, having my own separate life and my own kids has made this happen. It can be tricky at times, when their over-enthusiasm for certain activities or ways of doing things is misread as interference or criticism of your ways, but if you can learn to step back, let them do their thing and appreciate all the good they can do for you and your family, your relationship with your parents can have a new lease of life.

Your Grandparents

If you are lucky enough to still have grandparents alive, then taking your children to visit them as often as you can is something you'll never regret. My kids adore their great-granny, and see her as some kind of delicate, kind, generous, fun-loving relic from an age gone by who has an inexhaustible biscuit and toy supply and far too many bird tables. Here are some reasons to pile into the car and drive a hundred miles for a weak cup of tea and some out-of-date Hobnobs:

☆ **Where did those manners come from?** When they are with great-grandparents and other older members of the family they aren't very familiar with, children often become very well-behaved and mature, as if they can somehow sense that these people were brought up in an age of manners, respect and smacking. I've never told them to be on their best behaviour when we visit elderly relatives, but they seem to pull their angelic card out of the hat every time. As soon as we leave they are back to mischief as usual, but it's good for them to feel this sense of respect for and appreciation of older people.

☆ **Keeping the memory alive.** Those grandparents who have sadly died in the last few years are still alive in my children's memories, as well as mine, and this means they live on in our lives as we talk about them and remember their funny ways. I will always be glad that they knew my kids, even for a short while, and it was worth every visit.

☆ **New lease of life.** Your own (relative!) youth can revitalise older family members and give them another few years of life, and this is doubly true for your children: seeing those energetic, excited faces gets my granny into the garden to kick a ball around every time.

☆ **Story-telling.** I've never met anyone who could tell a story as well as my granddad. They were all wildly exaggerated, mostly untrue and not even all that exciting, but the way he told them had us all hooked for hours. If your children never hear stories of the Old Days, the War, rationing, sharing cold baths in the yard, walking seven miles to school each day in shoes with holes in or stealing boiled sweets from Mr Brown's corner shop, they will miss out on a whole life that went before them. Let them listen.

☆ **Know when to leave.** Old people get tired very quickly, even if they don't like to admit it. Don't wait until they have collapsed into a glass of sherry – stay for a few hours, try to keep the kids less rowdy than usual, and go before you outstay your welcome.

An astonishing generation is about to die out: if anyone in your family from those olden days is still alive then pack lots of fresh fruit, humbugs and love, and go and see them.

In-laws

I have to be very careful what I write in this chapter for rather obvious reasons. If I were, for example, to write something along the lines of 'In-laws are complete pains in the arse, they stick their noses in where they're not wanted, turn up uninvited, expect you to be pleased to see them and then don't know when to leave, spoil your kids rotten and never stick to any of the rules you work so hard to lay down and enforce', I would not only lose the friendship and company of two people I like very much, but I would also be telling lots of untruths for the sake of a chortle or two from you.

There are lots of wonderful things about in-laws (I'm talking about parents-in-law for now . . . brothers and sisters to follow, below) but also rather a lot of potential pitfalls, which have the habit of becoming *actual* pitfalls with the passing of the years and the weakening of the resolve to 'be nice' all the time.

On the positive side we have:

☆ **In-laws are not your parents**, so they don't bring any of the 'you fucked up my childhood' baggage so often accompanying the latter, whether true or not.
☆ **They are your children's grandparents**, and so come bearing wonderful gifts that you wouldn't normally buy because they are too expensive, extravagant or tasteless.
☆ **They are your husband's parents**, which makes you very grateful that they managed to produce somebody so utterly gorgeous.

☆ **You are their daughter-in-law and the mother of their grand-children**, which means they are eternally grateful to you for having saved their son from a life of take-away pizzas and computer games and for having provided them with adorable grandchildren.

There are many more good things about in-laws, but that's enough to be going on with for now. So far so good, until you look at the downsides:

☆ **In-laws are not your parents**, so you probably don't feel in a position to tell them to *butt out and leave you alone* if they are getting on your nerves by plying your children with chocolate and suggesting games of rounders at bedtime.
☆ **They are your children's grandparents**, and as such they feel it is their right to undo all of your good work by being all grand-parenty. This they do by bearing expensive, extravagant and tasteless gifts and far too much chocolate and sugary drinks, which they know you disapprove of, without prior notification or the slightest suggestion that it is disruptive, irritating or downright rude.
☆ **They are your husband's parents**, which means they will always side with him and are a constant reminder of what your partner will look like in thirty years' time, and that's enough to make any semi-rational person panic and run for the hills.
☆ **You are their daughter-in-law and the mother of their grand-children**. The first point can cause conflict with his mother – not only have you stolen the apple of her eye but you have also had your wicked way with him, the evidence for which lies in the second point. This makes you the target of much fear that you will try to raise his children the way *you* were raised and not the way he was. Cue constant battles over private school versus state education, strict bedtime over do-as-you-please, working parents over stay-at-home mums, and so on.

Yes, yes, I know – they are the same points. I didn't copy and paste by mistake – that *is* the point! Where there's Well-intentioned there is often Irritating as Hell lurking not too far away, and this all leads to one important point, which you must bear in mind the next time you are about to go off on one of your 'Ooooh, your mother drives me mad . . .' rants:

In-laws cannot win.

Whether it's interfering too much or not helping out enough, giving lovely treats or making your kids hyperactive, these poor people simply cannot please everyone, which is quite sad because most of them are just trying to do what they think their role requires as best they can. Sometimes they get it right, sometimes they don't, but isn't that the same for all of us? The vast majority are learning as they go, finding out who we are and what we believe in and trying to be our friends.

So here, for the struggling, is a list of some things that might help to keep – or make – the peace between you and those little extras your hubby came with:

☆ **Accentuate the positive.** If you focus on all the intrusive, potentially explosive aspects of the relationships, you are really not helping anyone in your family. Enjoy the good and leave as much of the bad as you can, and you might find yourself starting to really like – even love – the new family you gained without asking for it.

☆ **Reap the benefits.** One of the best things about in-laws is that they are a whole new family you can turn to if things go a bit sour with your own parents or siblings. It's a delicate balance, as you don't want to upset anyone by appearing to jump ship, but it can be very helpful and supportive to have fresh shoulders to cry on should you need them. They are also a fantastic source of new ideas and new ways of doing things, which you would never have got from your own family. Listen, learn, and adopt as you see fit.

☆ **Be respectful.** In-laws have become the butt of many a bad joke or rude remark. What often seems missing is anything to redress the balance and point out that they are a big part of your partner's life, your children's lives and, by default, your own life, and they can offer much useful advice, experience and help. Even though they are not your own *direct* family, you need to treat them with respect.

☆ **Don't become over-sensitive.** It's easy to fall into this trap with anybody, but in-laws are the worst because you see them only occasionally and so there is less opportunity for sorting it out the next day after a good sleep and a mull over. Looking for trouble that just isn't there is bound to lead to you finding *something* to moan about, but it's a terribly self-fulfilling prophecy and a very destructive one at that, so try not to be too sensitive about the little things that niggle you, and focus on something helpful they do or say instead.

☆ **Avoid big confrontations** if possible. Again, the issue of infrequency is a player here, and having an argument that cannot be resolved for three months because you live two hundred miles apart is a sure-fire way to cause a deep rift. If you know them well, then raising the issue is a good plan, but prepare to step back if you think it's getting too animated.

☆ **Bite your tongue** if necessary. What you were about to say was almost certainly not very constructive, or even true, so hold fire and count to ten.

☆ **Use the middle man.** Some ladies would find this insulting to their ability to fight their own ground. I call it sensible. If things get a bit fiery between you and any of your in-laws, and you don't seem to be able to make much progress on the reconciliation front through the usual channels of endless cups of tea and fine English biscuits, then try getting your husband to act as a go-between. He is in a perfect position to play the neutral third party because he likes both of you and is unlikely to take sides. If pushed he must take *your* side, of course, or it's all-out war. Subtlety is key, so make sure he knows how to approach the subject.

✩ **Wear their shoes.** Please don't *actually* wear their shoes unless you have bagged yourself a man whose mother owns a collection of Blahniks, Louboutins or anything from Office. Instead, put yourself figuratively in their footwear and try to imagine what it must be like to attempt to fit in with your requirements. Maybe they are trying as hard as they can to please you but your assumption that they dislike something about you makes you blind to their efforts. It must be very hard to be a *liked* in-law, so cut them some slack and think about how you would feel in their position.

All of these problems stem from the simple fact that y*ou didn't marry them, you married their son.* The 'I do' referred only to the person in the funny suit next to you, not to his doting parents crying in the front row. You did not agree to have and to hold his parents, to cherish, love or honour these two people, who barely know you but somehow feel they have a say in how you live your lives and bring up your kids.

Oh enough! My own in-laws are great, and we get along pretty well, despite our differences. But talk to any normal married person for more than an hour about their family 'issues' and in-laws are bound to come up somewhere, so you are by no means alone if you find the relationship peppered with booby traps and prickly bits and even the occasional volcano.

Brothers and sisters-in-law too – oh help!

If you are lucky, your sister in law (SIL) will become one of your best friends and confidantes. She has known your husband since he was a baby, and can relate to all of your complaints and exasperations about him. She also knows how bloody annoying her parents can be and can therefore side with you on almost any moan you have about any member of her family. This is very useful when you are feeling a little bit like an outsider. Finding a friend from the opposite camp who agrees with you is very reassuring and encouraging – you are not just a whinging old wife, but you have a good case in point *and* somebody to give evidence should it be required.

If you are unlucky you could end up with an SIL with whom you don't get on very well. The best way to proceed is to keep being friendly but not too in-her-face at family gatherings and see if time knocks the edge off any tensions. Brothers-in-law can also be very helpful when you need somebody even-sided to chat to, but some women I know have said they find the 'I can't get *that* friendly with you because you're . . . well, you're my husband's brother, and that would be weird' aspect to be an issue. I absolutely don't: I have two adorable BILs, and I am very grateful for that. They're like extra brothers without all the sibling rivalry attached. They and my SIL also happen to adore their little nieces and nephew and will gladly take them off my hands for an hour or two, which elevates them to almost God-like status in my mind.

All in all, in-laws are a very peculiar branch of your family because they are only related to you by law, and not for any other sensible reason, such as liking them, or choosing them, for example. Having so many extra family members to juggle and get along with can be overwhelming, but remember that this is your other half's family – he grew up with these people and loves them, and it's probably very important to him that you all muck in and get along.

Make friends, make friends; never, never break friends . . .

Friends are one of the most valuable things you can ever have. Yes, your straightening irons may come a close third, after your kids and partner, who are tied in first place, but friends get in at number two, no question.

Friends will stick by you through thick and thin; they will help you in a crisis, never expect anything in return and tell you when your outfit doesn't suit you. Friends don't worry about you cheating on them (you are allowed as many friends as you like, unlike lovers) and don't mind if you disappear for a few months and then pop up again for a night out. And, crucially, friends are happy to talk about all the things your partner finds too boring, awkward or girly.

In your new life as a mother your friends will probably divide into two categories: those you had before you got hitched and became all 'wifely', and those you met afterwards, through your kids. Let's deal with the latter first.

Playground friends

One of the genes that most mothers possess is the 'making friends with random strangers in the playground' gene. And thank goodness for that – if we weren't blessed with this piece of genetic genius we would have to stand around in awkward silence all morning while pushing our babies in swings, and that would be a bit weird.

Making friends for no other reason than the common feature of 'having a small child to look after' is what we mothers do. It can take a few years to really get the hang of it (I spent nearly a year with no 'mother friends' because in my mind I wasn't really a *mother* like them, but just a groovy young girl with a baby, and I was terrified of having to hang out with 'motherly types'), but once you're off there's no stopping you. Before your bum has had a chance to find its way back up to where it once was, your address book will be bulging with names you don't recognise and telephone numbers of people you only know as 'that cute little girl with the squint's mum'.

On the face of it this sounds idyllic: with almost no effort required you gain more friends than you can shake a rattle at. But there is one big problem with all of this friend-making – which very few women are prepared to admit they agree with until you either know them very well or have given them enough alcohol to break down the 'Everything in my life is fine' barrier – if you didn't have kids you wouldn't be friends with half of them. There it is. In just the same way as most people's work colleagues are probably not their ideal 'having a natter' companion of choice, so we end up with a lot of mother 'friends' by default, rather than by choice. They're quite nice, you can pass many hours with them waiting in the school playground or sharing weaning tips over a latte, but honestly, if they were to move away you wouldn't really miss them all that much after a few days.

This is just one of the by-products of being a mother. Dads don't have the same level of 'default friends' because they either don't spend as much time looking after kids as we do, and so enter 'Oooh, isn't your little girl good at the monkey bars? I'm Susan, by the way' conversations far less frequently, or they are largely ignored by mothers when they do the Dad thing.

[**Note to dads:** I am very sorry that so many women treat you like lepers when you turn up with your lovely little children at playgroups or playgrounds. It's not because we think you smell, or have hairier-than-normal arms or seem to be doing a terrible job of it. It's just that you are very often crap at small talk – due to getting much less practice than we do – and the conversation becomes somewhat laboured; and also because we want to talk about breasts, periods and the annoying men in our lives, or because you might think we are desperate housewives who are trying to hit on you if we offer you our phone number. In some cases we probably are trying to hit on you, but in general we are honestly glad to see you, impressed that you are looking after your kids more than Shit Dads of Yore, and would quite like to chat, but we're as unsure as you are. Don't give up!]

If you ever feel that you spend a huge amount of time making idle chat with people you neither particularly like nor want to see, then fear not:

☆ **You are not alone.** You needn't think that you are horrible and unfriendly just because you don't want to talk to somebody. Especially if that somebody is a very irritating, do-gooder mother whose child seems to attend every after-school club going and is only allowed to eat one hundred per cent organic health bars as treats. Everyone feels the same way much of the time, but they are better at pretending to be interested. My patience ran out years ago, and I'm very selective about my maternal chit-chat.

☆ **They don't all need to be best friends.** With so many acquaintances vying for your playground banter it can be exhausting trying to be super-friendly and happy with all of them. I tried this for years, and ended up tired, emotional and having almost no Best Friends, just fifty Quite Good ones. Much more sensible and practical is to dedicate time to the three or four friends you *really* like spending time with, whether with kids or without (the true test), and not feel you need to invite every mother you ever meet for a coffee and a stale flapjack. Knowing people on a low-maintenance but perfectly polite 'Hi, how are you?', 'Fine' level works for most of the people you know. Trying to be the perfect friend to all one hundred of them will half kill you and make you seem a bit desperate.

☆ **Move on.** Some friendships come to a natural end. This is not usually because her nanny makes a move on your husband, *she* makes a move on your husband (surely the worst thing a woman could ever do to her friend?) or your daughter lets slip that you think this woman has a big bum. What normally happens is that either one or both of you just moves on from where you were when you first met, and you realise you have nothing to say to one another. This is fine. Say 'Hi' when you pass each other in Sainsbury's but don't get hung up on it. Lots of friendships just peter out, and it doesn't mean there was ever any falling out.

☆ **Cherish your 'real' friends.** With time, from the assorted rabble of mums, nannies, au pairs and occasional dads you chat to every week will rise a very small number of very special 'real' friends. These rarely number more than three or four, but they are worth the weight in gold of every other passing acquaintance you will ever meet. Real friends are the ones you *trust*. They can help you through the dark times and join you in the good ones, will listen to your every word without judging you or comparing themselves with you, can break down in tears in front of you and admit all is actually *not* as hunky-dory on the home front as they make out in public, and will always, always be there to offer support and lend you all the magazines and DVDs you wish you owned. Take good care of these rare relationships and you will find the journey through family life a lot easier to handle.

☆ **Try never to have a bust-up with another mother.** The dense network of friendships between females is intricate, complicated and very unpredictable. Similar to the seven-step theory, which states that any two people in the world can be linked in just seven steps, there is a two-step rule for mothers. Every mother you know knows another mother you know. What this means is that you will never turn up to a party at one of your mother-friends' houses and not know anybody (great), but that falling out with one mother will have massive repercussions for your entire friendship network (catastrophic). It's like primary school all over again, except that you can't buy some Hello Kitty stickers and hope that mends things. If you sense some tension between yourself and a mother you know, the best thing to do is back off and give it time to work itself out. Often it's because she is having problems at home and not because her son thinks your son is a bully. Having a row won't help the situation at all.

☆ **Explain yourself.** Often, in the chaos of getting your kids to school or nursery, remembering to bring your phone, wallet and overdue library books, wondering if your husband will remember to call his parents and tell them Sunday lunch is not an option this week due to the cooker being broken, you may get a little grouchy. Pissed off, even. If this happens and you walk into the schoolyard, say hello to nobody and leave with a black cloud still hanging over your head, it is always worth explaining yourself when the skies clear. Just a quick, 'I'm sorry if I was rude this morning – I was having a really bad start to the day and I was in my own little world' can make the difference between people thinking you are a bitch and them being glad you are so honest about being stressed out, as they undoubtedly are too.

☆ **Confront the issue.** Having discouraged bust-ups with your mother friends, I do think it's sometimes important to come straight out and ask if everything is OK if you feel that somebody you know is being less than their usual sunny self towards you. I often do this, because I suffer from unhealthy levels of paranoia and a lack of self-confidence, with the result that anything less than a big, beaming 'Hello Liz, my loveliest, bestest, specialest, most gorgeousest friend in the world!' sends pulses of rejection and dislike through every cell in my body, and I go home wondering why everybody hates me so much. A simple 'Are we OK? You seemed a bit annoyed with me yesterday' usually reveals that she was trying to figure out how to get child number one to ballet on time and dash across town to collect child number two from football before they closed the car park, and she hadn't meant to be annoyed with you at all.

Occasionally there is something lurking that needs an airing, and I have had some good, open conversations with friends about why our kids seem to be fighting. Sometimes mine have been bossing theirs around; sometimes theirs have been teasing mine. Either way, there's no point in *us* bearing a grudge, and talking it through can bring about a peaceful resolution.

When Kids Fight . . . and so do you

Anybody who thinks becoming an adult means becoming rational, mature, sensible and polite has never been involved in a disagreement with another parent. In two shakes of a child's forelock parents can turn from charming, friendly and really rather nice into snorting, stamping, charging elephants. If this change is brought about by something nasty *you've* said about *them*, I can almost understand it: a direct attack by you on them, their way of life or their choice of footwear can expect some kind of a defensive reaction.

But the kind of inter-parent disagreement I really hate and have never understood is what I call the Row Once Removed. This is not a direct disagreement between the two of you, but one that began between your *kids*, and then filters up to you. One child calls the other 'a stupid willy head', the other retorts with a snappy 'well you're a bum brain' and it quickly escalates into 'my mum said your mum had a fat bottom!' Unsurprisingly, this is all recounted to you at the end of the day, and war is officially declared: all signs of good manners, decency and the ability to reason fly out of the window as news of the 'willy head and fat bottom' incident spreads through the Parent Camp, and maternal over-protection, pride and wrath take over.

It doesn't always get quite as bad as this, but many an adult friendship has been tempered or lost as a result of Rows Once Removed.

Rachel, mother of Isy, nine, and Harry, five:

I was good friends with one lady for about three years and our kids played together all the time. Then I suddenly noticed that she had stopped inviting us round, always declined my invitations and seemed to ignore me or be quite unfriendly. This went on for months and we slowly grew apart. One day after a few too many drinks at a party I asked why this was. She told me that my daughter had bullied hers at school three years before, and she thought we should go our separate ways. I couldn't believe it! How could anyone bear a grudge so long over something so silly, which I never even knew about? I decided I was better off without her, but it really upset me. With friends like that . . .

If you are ever involved in such an incident it can be very upsetting, and any buried childhood memories you may have of being picked on, left out or bullied can surface quickly. Some of this may help:

☆ **You're not the first.** From what I can gather from my good friends, this kind of inter-parent spat is by no means uncommon, whatever its origin. Friends can grow apart either naturally or due to some child–child disagreement. It may be your first time, but it has happened to many people before and it won't be the last. You are not a horrible person who has no friends; you've just cooled one friendship for a while – it's no big deal unless you make it one.

☆ **Don't take it personally.** The state of your children's friendship should never be confused with the state of yours with their parents. Just because two seven-year-olds think each other stinky, bossy and babyish does not mean their parents need to think that way about each other. Separate the two, and don't take it personally: if somebody becomes a little standoffish after a playground spat, just remember that it's your kids who have had the disagreement, not you.

☆ **Don't argue through your children.** This is such an easy tactic, but it's really low, nasty and definitely to be avoided at all costs. Do not let any disagreement you may have with another parent be played out through your child. Cancelling playdates, suggesting your child plays with other children, or even something as unsubtle as 'If he's anything like his mother you're best to keep away from him!' is a terrible example to set. Rise above this kind of behaviour, and remember that even if you have reason to dislike someone that shouldn't mean your respective children can't like each other.

☆ **Get it out.** From tiny acorn spats, large oak fights grow. Or something. Avoid this by stepping in very early on and talking to parents about any fighting that may have started between your kids. Rachel's story above might have ended very differently if she had confronted the mother in a friendly way early on and asked if there was anything going on she was unaware of.

☆ **Move on.** Don't hold on to friendships that fall apart through rows between children. If somebody is unable to see past a spat between kids, takes it to a whole new level between the two of you and doesn't seem to want to put it to rest, then she's not worth it. Let go, move on, and make new friends who are more sensible.

Until you've witnessed it, it's almost impossible to believe how juvenile, petty and bitchy grown men and women can be when it comes to issues concerning their kids. It seems you can say whatever you like to their face, but when it's between your offspring and theirs then prepare for some difficult negotiation. It's all rather silly really, but who said all adults had grown up, you stinky fart-head?

Playground Politics: Emotional breakdown, anyone?

If ever scientists need to do experiments in human social behaviour and want a set-up that is a little more realistic, cheaper and less cruel than locking their test subjects up in a cage or a *Big Brother* house, then they should make for the nearest playground and observe closely. Within the short space of one school drop-off our lab-coat-clad friends would observe any or all of the following: fear, happiness, panic, jealousy, camaraderie, paranoia, group formation, rivalry between groups, overdressed women, overstressed men and much, much more. It's a melting pot of the best and worst of human interaction and it's sensible to be prepared for it, lest you get severely burned. Or, indeed, melted.

Becky, mother of Hannah, eight, and Daisy, five:
I hate doing the school run, but most of all I hate that I feel that way. It's so stupid and I'm surprised that I'm so childish about it. The playground brings all my worst school memories back. I don't feel part of 'the gang' and I always worry that I don't look as good or together as the other mums. I know it's not true, but I feel so intimidated by all those people that I want to run away into a corner!

Standing in an enclosed space with a hundred other people, all feeling under pressure to look like they know what they are doing, aren't about to have a nervous breakdown because they are the only ones to have left their child's PE kit and lunchbox at home *again*, and have more than two friends, is something many people find very difficult. I have had too many pre-school-run panics to count, mostly related to feeling out of the social loop or a bad zit is popping up from nowhere.

But, contrary to the popular image of bitching, competitive mothers and general negativity found in all school playgrounds, the school run is usually pretty enjoyable for most parents. It can be the highlight of your day if you are after some human contact and friendly banter, and it's where you see your children's friends and get a glimpse of their life away from you. If you do feel daunted, though, and need a little Dutch courage before you go, then try these for starters:

☆ **Keep it short.** If you are having an 'off day' then hanging around for twenty minutes looking lost and overhearing conversations about the great time everyone else had together in the pub last night isn't going to improve your mood. On such occasions just go, give your lovely little ones a kiss, and leave. Job done. Damage to ego: zero.

☆ **Make the most of it.** Rather than seeing it as a challenge or an inconvenience, use this time to see your friends, maybe make some new ones, and have a natter and a laugh. You're all in it together, so you might as well get on with it and enjoy yourselves.

☆ **Play the game.** If you do find it a tad competitive out there and need a little confidence-boost, then upping your glam factor a bit can help. I'm not talking the full Notting Hill designer clothes and skyscraper heels here – I would be laughed out of the school if I turned up dressed like that! – but at least a quick make-up fix and an outfit that is clean and reasonably stylish can make the difference between Frumpy Sexless Heap and Playground Babe.

☆ **Don't overdo it!** Remember these are your friends, not your competitors, and trying to 'out-glam' them is really stupid. They *know* you can look nice if you try, but now is not the time.

☆ **Wear sunglasses.** Sunglasses are a key piece of playground survival equipment: not only do they make you look a teeny-*weeny* bit like somebody very famous and fashionable, but they also hide your tired eyes and any recent tears caused by a hellish morning. Don't leave home without them.

☆ **Find your niche.** If you find the sheer number of people daunting then just stick to your little group and seek safety in small numbers. I rarely talk to more than about ten mothers in total on a regular basis, and on an average day it can be as few as one or two. Somehow blanking out the hoards of babbling, laughing, chatting, gossiping, and constantly *moving* people and focusing on just one or two makes it much more bearable.

☆ **Go with somebody.** This is a very old trick you probably learned at primary school, but it still works. Entering the school playground with a friend can really help if you find it intimidating. You have already crossed the biggest hurdle – finding somebody to talk to – and now all you need to do is avoid tripping over or dropping your child's lunchbox in a puddle before you leave again, and you're home and dry.

☆ **Be rational.** Even the most confident, mature women can return to a childlike state at the school gates and be consumed with 'She doesn't like me any more', 'That's not fair! She's *my* friend', and 'She copied me – I had that skirt first!' types of nonsense. Everybody does it occasionally, and you shouldn't worry that you are alone in being so immature – these are normal human feelings, not just childish ones. Embrace your inner child, have a good whinge to yourself and then go back to being rational again.

☆ **Remember at all times: Much of what you see is fake.** A front, a show and an attempt to portray an air of competence and contentment. The ones who have it down to a T are the women every man wants and every woman wants to be friends with. I have it down to about a B or C at the most, but that's good enough for me. I wouldn't want any of the dads I know to want to sleep with me, and I have enough friends to keep me very happy. So remember, the playground is also a showground and you mustn't let the other acts scare you – most of the time they are thinking how nice you are and look, not what a horrible old cow you are. No, really.

Old Friends

I made the mistake of losing contact with quite a few of my school and university friends after I had kids, because my life just became swamped with family matters. I was constantly either pregnant, breastfeeding or looking after my kids. In between I felt that none of these beautiful, career-minded, free and single people would want to talk to me any more, being the overweight, lactating family girl I had become.

This was a big mistake, and one I have rectified in recent years. Your Old Friends are vital to your sanity when family life starts to get on top of you: they are not involved in school politics, they knew you before you became all maternal so they know what a laugh you can be, and spending some time with them almost always lifts you out of your family fug and back into that carefree existence you once had.

☆ **Send texts and emails**, or call each other if you can't find the time to meet up. Whatever you do, try to keep in touch – you'll need each other one day.
☆ **Don't talk about your kids and family life all the time.** It's quite interesting for about three minutes and then you become a Parent Bore.
☆ **Try to meet up away from your home**, so that you can get away from 'Family You' and spend some time with your old friends as you used to be. It's a lovely break for you and it's much more relaxed for them.
☆ **Take it easy.** Friends can find it very overbearing to come into your home with your kids, all their toys and the whole family 'spiel' if they are still unattached and child-free. Be sensitive; notice if they are looking a little overwhelmed, and try to go somewhere else.

Family life is great, but also very hard, and one sure way to make it easier is to get yourself some good, honest friends with a strong sense of humour, an inexhaustible coffee supply and shared interests. Of course your family is your main source of support, but sometimes nothing but a good friend will do.

So there they all are: some of the other vital members of the cast in this 'Family Life' production. And jolly nice they are too. Look after these relationships: they may be tricky, or even downright unbearable at times, but without them family life wouldn't be half as rich, enjoyable or fulfilling as it can be.

We'll be taking a trip into the bathroom and toilet soon, but before we do, let's have a quick peek in the study next door. If you've ever wondered how combining employment and family life is supposed to work, then this is where you need to look!

PART SIXTEEN

The Study

One of the drawbacks of the otherwise delightful activity of spending money is that you have to earn it first – unless you rob a bank, inherit it or win the lottery. For most of us, paying for family life means getting down to the serious business of working at some point. In the old days it was mainly the men who were allowed to escape for a day and come home with a cheque; now we are all allowed to join in the fun and use our brains, and many of us have to in order to pay the huge family bills.

But where work and family were once divided clearly in both time and space, for many of us it's now almost impossible to separate the two: home computers, the Internet, mobile phones, Blackberries, laptops, and 'working from home' all mean that we can work almost any time and anywhere – and this is having a huge impact on family life.

Welcome to the study – just don't stay here after hours and remember to clock off as you leave . . .

Work–Life Balance: Yeah, right!

If you work, and you also have a life outside of your work (which, because you have been sensible enough to read this book, I know you do) then in order to remain reasonably sane, sociable and human you will need to find a way to fit both the 'work' and the 'life' into the small amount of time you have on this Earth, and still leave some spare for watching telly.

The word 'balance' is quite misleading, I always think, because it seems to imply that the two parts of your life should be *evenly* balanced, which is not the case at all. Very few people spend the same amount of time working as they do being at home, seeing friends or doing whatever hobbies it is they do. Some people work part time, others full time, others full time plus a bit (naughty), and still others as little as possible. I fall into the latter category because I have rather a lot of 'life' to attend to, in the form of my kids, plumping the lounge cushions and wondering why I haven't won the Booker Prize yet. It's such a mystery . . .

When you are young and single, and you have nobody else to think of apart from yourself, getting the balance right is easy: *you* decide. If you are knackered, or haven't spoken to anyone for a month because you've been sleeping in the office and eating kebabs on the way home, then all you need to do is cut down your work hours and see your friends a bit more.

But when you have a family, your work–life balance becomes a huge issue, because all of a sudden you don't operate in isolation, and the way you live and work affects everyone else. You can't just work eighteen hours a day and every other weekend and expect to carry on playing Happy Families until the year is out. Nor can you sit at home twenty-four hours a day for five years playing peek-a-boo if you are yearning for something that allows you to use your brain, talk to somebody over the age of three and earn your own income, however tiny it may be. Something's gotta give, and the only solution is to find a balance that works for you *all*, financially, emotionally and practically.

Amy is typical of many mums I've spoken to, but at least she is
thinking of solutions. It's very tricky, but here are some points to
consider if you are feeling a tad out of balance:

☆ **Are you balanced?** Often, people get into a work–life habit and
just chug along never really stopping to think if it's working
for the family, or if something couldn't maybe change a bit. Talk
about it, and see if you are both happy with your respective and
communal use of time. Even if only one of you isn't happy,
something will have to change if the family is to remain strong.

☆ **Married to the job.** One of the most common complaints in the
marriages I know is that one person (in the majority of cases
it's still the man) works far too many hours, while the other is at
home looking after the kids. This generally makes everyone in
the family miserable: the kids miss Daddy; Daddy misses his kids
and his wife; the wife misses her husband; the marriage suffers.
Once you have a family, you have to realise that work isn't the
most important thing in your life any more – your family is.

☆ **Prioritise.** Working out what is most important for you, *and for
your family*, is critical to getting the work–life balance right. Yes,
you'd like to be at work, because you enjoy the change of scene
or need the extra cash now that you spend a fortune on plastic
toys and babysitters every month, but you'd also like to be at

home with your kids. You can't do both, so talk about it together and work out what is most important. It will almost certainly change within the year, but what's your priority as a family *now*?

☆ **Make some changes.** If you decide that your work–life balance is hopelessly out, then ask yourself some questions. Could you cope with a drop in salary if one of you worked a little less? Could he give up the commute two days a week and work from home? Do you really need to work at the weekend? Could you move to live nearer his work? Wouldn't it be better to invite some people over for dinner instead of doing yet more housework and admin? Maybe you feel you're not getting enough 'work' to balance the childcare you're doing, and could take up a part-time job? Changes can almost always be made, but you have to make them!

☆ **Jealousy.** We both suffered from this after our children were born, and so have many of our friends. I felt I ought to be grateful that my husband was working hard to earn some dough, but actually I was insanely jealous of him. Here I was stuck at home again, with ten hours of housework and childcare ahead of me, while he could walk out of the door into a clean office with adult conversation, lunch-breaks and paycheques. He, in turn, was jealous of me staying at home and playing while he was in boring meetings and under a lot of work pressure. Our solution? We talked about this problem, and realised that neither had it easier or better – just different. I started part-time work, he did more housework and spent more time with the kids in the evenings, and things were much better.

☆ **Guilt.** This is a nightmare for all working mums and dads: when you're at work you feel guilty about not being at home with the kids; when you're not working you feel guilty because you're not doing the work you are supposed to be doing. It's totally destructive on all fronts and the only way to avoid it is to work very hard at separating the two completely. When you work, work. When you're with your family, do that, and forget work. If the two are allowed to overlap and become mixed up you can't do either well, or enjoy any of it. It takes practice, but you need to crack this if you're to enjoy yourself at all.

☆ **Communication.** I'm amazed at how many people I know who complain bitterly about their poor work–life balance and yet rarely discuss it at any length with their partner. This is nuts. If you are very unhappy that you don't spend enough time seeing friends or being together as a family, then say so. When he doesn't listen, say so again. He might be unaware of how you feel, or he might share these concerns but be reluctant or unsure how to talk about it. This is the first step in solving the problem, so get talking as soon as you can.

☆ **Laying down the law.** Many happy families remain this way because there are some very clear and obeyed Family Work–Life Laws in place. These could be: no work in the evenings (or except after everyone else is asleep); no work at the weekend unless it is agreed that that's OK; one night out every week; seeing friends at least twice a month, letting children have a sleepover once a fortnight, and so on. Make up your own rules and see if you can all stick to them.

☆ **Keeping Work OUT.** As more and more people are able to work from home, getting away from work has become an increasing problem. Only you two can solve this: shut down, switch off, close your book, put down your paintbrush, or do whatever it takes to STOP WORKING. You must, if you are to have any family life at all.

Anna, married to Pete and mother of Rosie, eight, Rory, five, and Lily, three:

I felt so resentful of Pete going off to work every day and leaving me to slog away with the kids and all the housework that I went back to work part-time this year. I feel much more fulfilled now, and less jealous, and Pete has managed to get one half-day a week so he can spend time alone with the kids and cook a meal. It has revolutionised our lives for the better!

The reason the term 'work–life balance' has become so overused in recent years is because it's something that almost all of us struggle with every day. It's a symptom of modern times, as we all try to 'have it all' all of the time. As soon as you realise that you can't have it all, but you can have quite a lot of it most of the time, you will start to live a much more fulfilled, satisfied and family-friendly life together. Yes, you *all* have to agree to live this way, which can be tricky, but it's what being a family is all about: making compromises and sacrifices for each other because – big pause for effect, and adopt an American accent . . . *you all love each other*. Ahhhhhhhh.

Who deleted Mummy's files? The pitfalls of working from home

May 2004

This is hopeless: I am trying to work from home today but it's just a joke: so far I have hung out the washing, folded and put away the last load, checked if the goal posts I'm bidding for on eBay are still there, phoned two friends, ordered some scalp masks because I'm so stressed about my lack of work that my scalp is peeling off in sheets, made three cups of mint tea, picked at food about ten times, tidied the shoe rack and Phoebe's room and cleaned up my desktop. Now it's lunchtime, so back to the kitchen for more food I don't need, and more time-wasting. I need an office far away from here.

The reason so many parents work from home is obvious: you don't have to travel anywhere and you can work around your kids. That's about it, really. When your baby goes to sleep you can do an hour's work then. If a child is taken ill at school you can go and collect them without thirty colleagues glaring at you. You can even work in the wee hours before your other half leaves for his work, and save on childcare altogether. But two problems remain: getting anything done and making sure your kids don't mess it all up.

The first problem affects only those people who think it's possible to do any decent work at all in a building containing a television and all their children's mess, but who have a severe lack of self-discipline. That's most of us, then. Self-discipline means overriding any animal urges to eat chocolate, check the TV guide, masturbate or sort out the sock drawer. It means ignoring the fact that you could quite easily have a nap, Google some rude words or walk about from room to room for a while. In short, it requires a will of iron stronger than a child who was raised on nothing but Irn-Bru and raw steak, and few of us possess such a thing.

The second problem affects *everyone* who has kids and works at home, because children have an uncanny ability to press the one button you never even knew was there, and erase a year's work permanently from the face of the Earth. Luckily there are some golden rules and cunning techniques you can employ that should make working from the family home, if not a roaring success, then certainly more fruitful than alphabetising the children's toys was ever going to be:

☆ **Dress for work.** A full suit and tie is perhaps a little over the top, but slobbing about in a tracksuit never made anyone feel motivated to 'go out there and get 'em!' (Assuming this is your aim.) Even putting on something semi-smart and work-like can really help to get you in the frame of mind for doing something more intellectual than finger-painting.

☆ **Find a place that works for you.** This is essential. The nicest room in our house overlooks the garden, and is light, airy and a joy to be in, but I just cannot work there. I prefer to hide away in the airless, cramped, overflowing with washing and miles of electric cables 'spare room', which doubles as my office. Find the space that works for you, and the more you use it, the more your brain will switch into 'work' mode the minute you go in. Best not choose the bedroom then . . .

☆ **Pretend you have colleagues.** I realise this has the potential to evolve into mild insanity, as you exchange 'office' banter and discuss the romantic affiliations of phantom colleagues, but imagining there is somebody around who wants to see some results can help to overcome the mañana effect. I tend to email stuff I've written to my husband at work, as I go along. He never reads it, but just knowing that somebody out there has evidence I'm not shirking my way through another long day is enough to keep me hammering at the keyboard.

☆ **Make a timetable.** Anal as it sounds, making a rough timetable of your day, with tea, coffee and lunch breaks pencilled in, can provide a framework within which to work. If the breaks exceed the work time, you may need to be a little more realistic, but forcing yourself to have a defined break for lunch and then get back to it at two o'clock helps me enormously.

☆ **Get your family to help.** My kids can be quite strict these days if I emerge before lunchtime for anything other than two necessary toilet breaks. 'Get back in there, Mummy, and don't come out until you've written a chapter!' is what I get. Husbands can also help, by keeping your kids happy and reasonably quiet while you work. Some can even go so far as to do all the jobs you would normally do while he works, but that is very unusual. More normal is for you to emerge after a day at work, only to find a bomb has exploded in the playroom, there is no food in the house and one child has been left at school. Ah well, he tried.

☆ **Keep the kids out.** This is not because you don't want to see them while you are at work (actually, it is partly for that reason – it's hugely distracting and reminds you of what you are missing), but because it is better for everyone if there is no room for misunderstanding and hurt. If the study is permanently OUT OF BOUNDS while you are working, your kids won't be surprised or disappointed when they are met with stony looks or sharp words if they do sneak in. A clear, unbendable rule works wonders for kids.

☆ **Never rush.** If you notice that you have only ten minutes left before the children have to be collected from school, don't quickly send that email, post a document or sign anything. Your mind is on your kids now, and you will make mistakes – possibly big ones. Stop, and get back to it when you are more focused.

☆ **Never mix work and play.** If you work on a home computer, as I do, never, ever, *ever* let your kids near any of your work. Coming home to find 20,000 words have been deleted and replaced by Emily's Funky Hairstyle Tips would not be good. Have a password, never tell your kids, and go over the ground rules (e.g. do not ever delete anything unless you ask me first) frequently.

☆ **Make copies.** If you work on a computer, make sure you have backups outside the house: email them to your partner or friends or keep some copies on disc elsewhere. That way, when Johnny spills his milk on your hard drive, you won't want to kill him.

To Work or Not To Work? That is *your* question . . .

An awful lot of hard graft was done by our fore-mothers to fight for the rights of women to go to work, just as their big, burly men had done since they first picked up a piece of flint and went out hunting. Whether we choose to work or not, we should be eternally grateful that all of this campaigning, protesting and persisting gave us such options. We can show this gratitude by making the right choice and not complaining about our lot.

Of course, many women *have* to work for financial reasons, and this is a different issue altogether. But some have the choice: stay at home and do the mother/wife/homemaker thing, or put on some work clothes, leave your child with somebody else for a few hours, and go off and earn some money.

If you have such a choice then the most important thing is that *you* choose. Not your husband, mother, best friend or overriding sense of guilt, but you. What do you *want* to do?

I have tried both, and I know that I vastly prefer having some kind of work to being a full-time stay-at-home mum. I like earning money; I like being able to pay somebody else to clean my house; and from time to time I like to use my brain for tasks other than folding small items of clothing, peeling potatoes and walking at a snail's pace to the swings. It's what works for me, and I don't need to justify it to anyone, ask permission from anyone, or feel remotely guilty or grateful for doing what I do.

Despite all of this sounding very obvious, I am surprised at how many intelligent, rational women wrestle with the 'to work or not to work' choice. They seem unable to decide for themselves, and need to ask their other halves for their opinion. For anyone having trouble deciding what to do, here are some tips:

☆ **Are you happy and fulfilled?** If not, then something has to change. Perhaps you need to find some part-time work, or work out a way to cut down your hours if you're working too much. If you are miserable then this grouchiness will be passed on to your kids and partner, which can only lead to miserable kids and a husband who wants to live with someone a hell of a lot more fun than you!

☆ **Living in the twenty-first century.** We do, but there are a large number of men out there who don't seem to have cottoned on to this fact. Despite portraying themselves as forward-thinking Modern Men, they would still rather like a stay-at-home wife who cooks their tea, produces a dozen children and has sex with them 365 nights a year. Wake up, guys – we have brains and ambition too, and we're not afraid to show it. Now, where's that business plan?

☆ **Why doesn't he want me to work?** Apart from the above, it's also a fact that many men worry about their wives having a job because this means they are likely to come into contact with other men, who are quite possibly more attractive, considerate, un-Dad-like and exciting than they are. No, *really?* If you don't believe me then go down the pub with some dads you know well, buy them a few pints and get them talking. I did, and that's honestly what many of them said. They weren't proud of it, but I am glad of their honesty, as it confirmed what I suspected.

Also, as soon as you get a job you realise how piss-easy even the most stressful, exhausting job is compared with looking after kids, and that's something most men would rather we never found out, for obvious reasons.

☆ **Be glad of the choice.** A surprising number of people ask me if I find it hard to be a woman in today's world, because we have so many choices. I always look at them as though they are mad: Since when has having more choice been a bad thing? It's much, much tougher if there's no choice and you *have* to work and rarely see your kids or enjoy your job, or have to stay at home when you'd rather work. The thousands of other women who *can* choose what they do are unbelievably lucky to be able to – now they just need to make the right one for them . . .

Childcare: Possible solutions for your 'can't be in three places at once' dilemmas

Let's assume here that you have had the discussion, and have both agreed you are going back to work as it would be beneficial for the whole family. Now the problem is how to make that happen. Having a job if you have pre-school kids rather assumes that you have somewhere for them to be while you are at work. 'Under your desk' is not a good option, and nor is 'in the park with a bag of crisps and a mobile phone in case of emergencies'. Much better is to find somewhere registered, supervised and really rather nice.

If your children are at school you have no such worries between the hours of 9 a.m. and 3.30 p.m. They are at school; you are at work; all is well. For everyone else there is much more of a problem because you have to find some suitable childcare for your most treasured little darlings, and this can be very difficult. Not only are you probably convinced that all child-carers are six-headed monsters with halitosis and poor dress sense, but you will also soon realise that paying for these supposedly terrifying people to wipe your child's bottom will cost you every penny you earn, and probably more. It can be enough to make you give up work before you even start.

Fear not. There is some fantastic childcare available out there, and all you have to do is some research to find somewhere you and your children are happy with.

☆ **Start early.** All childcare places are booked up unbelievably early, whether state or private, and you might have to put your child's name on a waiting list at least a year before you think you'll need the place. I know it's crazy. Now go – hurry up!

☆ **Nurseries.** Advantages: There are always several members of staff on hand to wipe any stray bits of snot and play with your little lovelykins; there is never a problem about illness because there are always supply staff to cover; they are great if you want your child to toughen up before school, as he fights it out with Billy, Johnny and Jemima for who gets the tricycle first; they tend to be open 363 days a year from 8 a.m. to 6 p.m. (but you can use as much or as little of this time as you like), and you can meet other parents. Disadvantages: They are very expensive; your child cannot have somebody's full attention as there are always other kids whose noses need wiping (I have an obsession about runny noses, as you can tell); there can be high staff turnover, which can unsettle a child.

☆ **Nannies.** Advantages: Very personal childcare, as you choose the nanny yourself, and your child forms a strong bond with him or her and has a lot of attention and care. Disadvantages: Many nannies are slim, six-foot Polish models, which might be ever-so-slightly hard to deal with – for you – and you may also find it upsetting that your child likes him or her almost as much as you!

☆ **Childminders** (look after kids during the day, at their own house). Advantages: Often very experienced with kids and also tend to look after other kids too, so there is company for your child. Disadvantages: You may find it unsettling to have your child in someone else's house and you might not be happy about any other children who are being looked after with yours, as their routines and behaviour may be very different from your own child's.

☆ **Au pairs.** Like nannies, these are mostly very gorgeous women who speak with exotic – some men might say erotic – accents.

The main difference is that they live with you – double trouble! Most au pairs are wonderful with kids and a fantastic addition to the family, but think carefully about how you will feel to lose so much privacy.

☆ **After-school clubs.** These are on the increase and we have had both excellent and miserable experiences with them. If you feel terrible that your kids are having to go there after school because they clearly don't enjoy it, then find an alternative. If you find one your kids love, you are sorted until 6 p.m.!

What Do People Do All Day? Showing your kids what you do for a living

Fifty years ago I imagine it was much easier for kids to answer the question above than it is for today's little tykes. When their parents (or, most often their dads) left for 'work' in the morning they were generally off to do understandable things, like teach, build houses, write books or make people better.

These days there are a massive number of newly created occupations, many of which have complicated, meaningless titles, and children are, understandably, less sure about what we do all day, or what they might like to do when they grow up. Would they also like to be a software developer? Or a data analyst, perhaps? Or how about a hedge-fund manager, a systems designer, a call-centre operator or a non-executive director? In short, a *whaaat*?

Exactly. None of these titles or job descriptions mean anything to a child. They understand things like waitress, author, lawyer or scientist because they have either seen one in action or can easily understand what it is they do – and, just as importantly, what the point of that might be. Try explaining to most adults exactly what a software engineer *does*, and what the point is, and they stare at you blankly (I know, I've seen people give my husband this stare every time he's tried to explain what the hell it is he does at many a dinner-party table). Try the same on kids and they've left the room before you've really got started. It's all numbers, analysis, unfamiliar terms and hypotheses. They want something concrete –

something they can see, understand and relate to – and preferably something involving heavy machinery, groovy clothes and lots of money . . .

If children are to understand why we sometimes leave the house to go somewhere else for the day while they are at school or nursery, then we need to make an effort to explain it to them. If they are to have a dream job, or an ambition to become something, they need to see what's out there and get an understanding of what 'having a job' actually means.

Here are some suggestions:

☆ **Take them to the office.** Kids love coming to see where their parents work (unless it's in a coal mine or a nail parlour – both of which are hazardous and stink). It's important to invite your kids to your workplace from time to time: how else can they picture you there, know what your desk looks like, or understand what kind of stuff keeps you away from them for ten hours a day? If you work in an office, why not take them in for an hour one day? Show them the photocopier, the pile of crap on your desk and the biscuit tin. 'See how clever your dad is, son?' That kind if thing . . .

☆ **Don't hide your work.** I used to try and work very separately from my kids, so that they didn't feel it was something that could take me away from them, or which I even *preferred* to them. Now I am happy to let them see me scribbling away, and to let them read some of my more suitable ramblings sometimes. I now have not one but two budding authors in the house. I know it won't last, but it's nice that they know what it is I do when I'm not cooking, cleaning or reading them stories.

☆ **Other people's jobs.** However mind-blowingly exciting your own work might be, it's a good idea to make your kids aware of other jobs as well. Friends' parents, other family members, shopkeepers, gardeners, postmen – almost every adult they come across has some kind of occupation. Unless most of your friends are pimps or insurance salesmen then why not tell your kids all about their work and see if anything interests them?

It may seem a little premature to get your kids thinking about what they will do when they are older, and exposing them to as many types of work as possible is more an exercise in fun than career planning. But making them aware of what you do is really important for them to get a sense of who you are in your weird 'other life' as person rather than parent, and this can have a big influence – positive as well as negative!

Right, time to shut down, put away your computer, close your books and take all your empty coffee mugs back to the kitchen: work time is over. After all that hard toil you have earned yourself some relaxation time, so why not pop down the hallway and into the first door on the left: the Family Bathroom. You are only two wet towels, three plastic ducks and some bubble bath away from a heavenly hot soak . . .

PART SEVENTEEN

The Bathroom

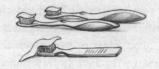

Can I come in? Getting some 'me' time in there

Unless you are very lucky, very rich, or both, you will probably have only one bathroom in your house. Like me. Being a 'Family Bathroom', it is already doomed to failure: like white trousers and black knickers, the two things really shouldn't go together – ever. A bathroom should be a place to relax, unwind and de-stress, while making yourself a little less smelly and hairy than you were when you crawled in. Attempting to do this in a room littered with plastic bath toys, five wet towels, fifty bottles of shampoo for every hair type and age group and several whingeing children is futile. In short, families and bathrooms don't mix well.

One of my favourite children's books illustrates the typical Family Bathroom scene wonderfully. In Jill Murphy's *Five Minutes' Peace*, poor, stressed-out Mrs Large hopes to sneak off for her thirty seconds of relaxation in the family bathroom, only to be joined by all of her noisy, insistent, toy-wielding kids before she's taken her first sip of tea. I defy any parent to read it without a sympathetic, knowing nod of the head. We've all been there.

Sharing a bathroom between four or five members of a family can feel like living in a Youth Hostel, with queues of half-naked, miserable people waiting on the landing, and no hot water left when you finally get your turn. It doesn't have to be this way. It is possible to have a lovely family bathroom for everyone to enjoy, but it takes some clever management:

☆ **Hide the mess.** This is the most important tip. Until three years ago we had no cupboards in our bathroom, and everything – I mean everything, from razors, to wind-up penguins to tubes of Vagisil – was on display. I would lie there, trying to imagine I was the Cadbury's Flake lady, enveloped in the deep, hot, bubbly water of a sensuous bath beneath a huge chandelier and with nothing but a six-inch stick of the crumbliest, flakiest milk chocolate in the world and a small lizard for company. This illusion was always shattered within minutes, when the slightest arm movement would cause an avalanche of plastic bottles and boats to tumble off the side into the tepid water, giving me a minor heart attack.

We are now the proud owners of a cupboard under the basin where most of this Family Bathroom crap is hidden, and several high cupboards to store the medicines and other nasties. I know it's a mess *inside*, but it looks fantastic, completely clutter-free and almost relaxing. Getting cupboards with doors is essential if you are after that 'look – no mess' effect. It all sounds a bit *House Doctor*, I know, but that Ann Maurice knows what she's talking about. Clutter is not relaxing.

☆ **Take turns.** There is no reason why you should have to have a bath, apply a face pack or wax your legs when your kids are wandering in and out every two minutes pointing out your worst features. I usually wait until they are not only in bed but also fast asleep before indulging in Me Time in the bathroom. If possible I also pick a time when my husband is also otherwise occupied – sometimes it's lovely to share a bath, of course (unless it's as small as ours!), but there's no reason at all why you should feel you can't shut that door and stick a huge (imaginary) KEEP OUT – LADY HAVING SOME ALONE TIME IN HERE sign on the door. Just because you live in a family does not mean you have to abandon any private time in the bathroom.

☆ **Burn, baby, burn.** Candles work. They are as cheap as chips (before chips became ludicrously expensive, that is) and are the quickest way to transform a bathroom from 'jumble sale' to 'heavenly retreat'. Do be careful where you put them – I have singed my toes and elbows several times, which was not the desired effect – and remove plastic objects nearby too. Charlie's purple plastic penguin lost a wing and turned my heavenly retreat into a toxic gas chamber recently when the flame got a bit too close.

☆ **Make it yours.** There is a common misconception that family bathrooms only need appeal to the youngest members of the household, which explains why so many people put brightly coloured storage boxes, tiles with pictures of ships and sea creatures and lurid towels sporting cartoon characters in their *salle de bains*. In fact, young children spend very little time in the bathroom compared with you – two minutes in the morning spreading toothpaste around their face, and about fifteen minutes in the evening splashing gallons of bathwater onto the floor. Compared with the hours you should be relaxing in there every week, this is a mere blink of an eye. They don't *care* how you decorate the room – so long as they have a toothbrush with a Disney character on it they are happy, so make it yours and enjoy every minute you spend in there. The grown-up man in your house should be consulted of course, as he might feel strange shaving and bathing in a room full of pink candles and girly chandeliers.

☆ **Keep things in their place.** My bathroom used to resemble a bombsite after every morning rush-hour. In our wake was a trail of destruction that almost always included three toothbrushes, two tubes of toothpaste – leaking from cracks in the side – two unused hairbrushes, several wet towels on the floor, ten hair-bands, a selection of discarded socks, and a wet school reading book. The solution? Apart from nagging them on a daily basis to be more considerate of other people and put things where they should live – grrrrrrr! – I realised that two of the offenders couldn't reach the toothbrush holder or towel hooks without performing some death-defying acrobatics from a slippery floor. They now have their own towel hooks, toothbrush holder and bathroom cabinet at a more accessible height, and things are looking up.

☆ **Family bath-times.** Having advised you to keep the kids away when you are trying to enjoy your time in the bathroom, it's really important that they can come in and see you in all your naked glory sometimes. We have a very strange, and I think quite unhealthy, relationship with nakedness, our bodies, our sexuality and physicality in this country, and children who never see their parents naked, and relaxed about being naked, are being given some worrying messages about how to feel about their own bodies and self-confidence. You don't need to adopt the full 'wandering around the house starkers' approach, but a degree of relaxed nakedness is a very good idea. It also means you can be put firmly in your place, as one child after another comments on your 'big, wobbly tummy', weird boobs, Daddy's hairy legs and other less than perfect parts. If they never see a naked adult body, they will be in for quite a shock one day!

☆ **There were three in the bath and the little one said . . .** Siblings should definitely bath together when they are young, not least because it saves on heating and using lots of water. It's hard to tell at what age kids should stop having a bath together, but I would say any time they start to be uncomfortable about being naked in front of others, or want some privacy, is the time to stop. Our eldest is eight and she is still quite happy to, and it's mainly the fact that there's just not enough room for them all which is putting an end to these three-in-a-bath occasions.

You Scratch my Head, I'll Scratch yours:
How to beat nits

Until my kids started school, I thought head lice were only found in the hair of dirty, nasty children. Not just slightly unwashed but properly *filthy* kids who also didn't eat organic vegetables, watched

ITV, wore ill-fitting shoes and didn't go to Junior Tai Chi classes. The shame of it!

Now, having had visits from the little critters regularly for four years, I have been forced to change my mind. Lice (those are the creatures; the nits are their eggs) can be found on the heads of the loveliest, cleanest, most well-behaved, vitamin-filled, well-heeled and precocious brats you could ever meet. And once you've got them, the little bastards are nearly impossible to eradicate. Weeks, even months of combing, conditioning, picking, scratching and hair-cutting can still leave eggs undetected, and just when you thought you were safe to go out in public again – holy cow! The lady behind you in the café queue spots one making a dash for glory along your daughter's parting. Social catastrophe.

We have learned a lot about nits and lice and are now pretty good at dealing with them, so here, for the uninitiated or plain desperate, are some handy hints:

☆ **What do they look like?** This isn't a stupid question, so don't worry if you're not sure what you are looking for. I had no idea, as I had never had them. Nits are tiny sacs attached to the hair follicle. Black sacs mean there's someone home; yellow sacs mean the egg has already hatched. Shit. The lice themselves can be anything from half a millimetre to a gigantic five milli-metres across (if your kids' lice are this big don't ever tell anyone – you are officially a Very Bad Parent and you'll get a visit from the Pest Control Agency within twenty-four hours), and are a thin oval shape, quite see-through, with six tiny legs and often a black head. They are hideous, and may cause you to shriek when you first see one.

☆ **Where do they hide?** Favourite spots include in the hair behind the ear, low down at the back of the head in the very thick hair there, and right on top where the parting often is.

☆ **How do I get rid of them?** Well, there's a question. There are actually two bits to remove: the lice and the nits. Lice can be combed out using a lice comb, and this can be done on wet or dry hair, but wet is far more effective. Dispose of the lice and nits carefully – down the plughole is a good plan. If you do it when the hair is wet and dripping with conditioner then you can get some eggs out too, as they slide off the hair more easily. The most time-consuming and labour-intensive method involves picking them out one by one, but this requires the patience of a saint from both of you, and also very sharp eyesight. If your kids love having their hair played with and there's something good on the radio it can almost be described as enjoyable.

Spring cleaning your house and washing all the bedding daily is said not to help, so save that effort for more combing: lice need to live on a human head, and die within a day if they don't get their blood fix.

☆ **What products should I buy?** Anti-lice shampoos and lotions are murderously expensive, especially when you consider that most don't kill the eggs, you will be using them several times a year at least, and chemical ones are also bad for the environment. Pharmacists stock several brands, and your guess is as good as mine as to which one works the best. In my experience they are just expensive, smelly and messy. One alternative is to buy an electronic lice comb, which costs even more, but you have it for life (or until your children drop it in the bath). It is by far the most fun for you, because you can hear the lice dying as you move the comb, with its small electric current, through the hair. If they could design one that emits a zapping noise that would be even better.

☆ **How long do I carry on treatment for?** Bloody ages! Nits take about a week to hatch, and as they are almost impossible to remove, you need to keep combing daily for at least this long to make sure you've caught the very last ones. Only then might you be in the clear, until Dirty Gertie from number thirty rubs her head all over your son again in assembly, and it's back to square one.

☆ **How do they spread?** This is where lice score points, as it shows they know how to have a good time: they don't jump or fly, as you might have thought, but swing from head to head on a hair shaft, like little six-legged blood-sucking Tarzans. Picture that the next time you're delousing and you might even raise a smile. Suggesting your kids try to stop rubbing heads together quite so much is a good plan.

☆ **Why are there so many nits about?** Another good question, my observant, curious friend. When I was a child, head lice were as rare as a family day out without any arguments. These days, if you get through a school year without at least one major outbreak in every class, you feel short-changed. What – no nits this year? That's what's wrong with this country! I tell you: nobody makes an effort any more.

One theory is that the increase is due to changes in hairstyles and social behaviour. Long, nit-infested tresses dangle and blow all over the place instead of being neatly tied back, making it much easier for the blighters to pass from head to head. There is also evidence that some really sharp-minded lice are becoming resistant to the chemical treatments available – another reason to keep going with that comb.

A Hairy Issue: Hairdresser or DIY for your kids?

When babies are born they have a huge price-tag attached, which the doctor kindly cuts off before you have a chance to see all the zeros and have a panic attack. There are, however, ways of reducing the monthly Little Cherub bills, and one of these is by cutting your children's hair. Before you laugh yourself into a coma, consider this: babies and young children don't know, or care, how they look. I know *you* know and care how they look, but unless you set about *trying* to make the biggest pig's ear of it, you should be able to get away with the occasional trim *chez vous* for the first five years at least. If you are very lucky you will have one of those babies who remains bald for a year, and doesn't have anything worth cutting until she hits three.

I learned the hard way – by making the aforementioned pig's ear of my first child's hair four or five times – but I have since developed some cunning techniques and strategies that should help you avoid such barnet disasters, as well as save you enough to pay for a decent trim for yourself:

☆ **Get sharp scissors.** Proper hairdressing scissors will take your index finger off just by looking at them, so tiny ears don't stand a chance. They also cost a fortune. One step down, much less dangerous, but effective enough for your purposes, are good hair-cutting scissors available from high street chemists. These will snip neatly through the toughest of locks. The scissors you have lying in your desk drawer will make the hair shafts bend and leave all the hair flying off to one side. I know because I tried.

☆ **Pick a GOOD time.** 'Good' is in capitals, because a *reasonably* good time isn't good enough. Neither is a not-too-bad time, a fairly good time, or an 'it'll do' time. It has to be a GOOD time, and that means you have *lots* of extra time available for minor adjustments (when you get round to the front and realise the left side is an inch shorter than the right, for example), your child isn't hungry, tired, ratty or desperate to watch *Dora the Explorer*, and you are not frying onions or expecting a call from the fish man at any minute.

☆ **The naked hairdresser.** Actually, more the naked client than the hairdresser. Any clothes your child wears will get covered in hairs, however careful you are, so strip them down to their underwear and remove this when you're done too. It's worth explaining that they don't do this in salons, to prevent any embarrassing misunderstandings in years to come . . .

☆ **Where to do it?** As far away from everything else as you can, is my suggestion. Outside works, unless it's windy, and the bath is another good option because kids are quite relaxed in there, they can amuse themselves a bit, and they can't run off. It also makes the hair stay a bit damp, which is useful for getting the level right.

☆ **Wash afterwards.** Whether you are cutting in the bath or not, make sure they have a shower when you have finished. Those teeny-weeny hairs that you can't see but are sure you've brushed off will stick like glue and cause no end of itching, scratching, screaming and general foul temper.

☆ **Little girls: beware the fringe!** Cutting a fringe looks so easy it's laughable: take scissors, pick a line, chop. *Voilá!* Ah no, DIY fringes have a habit of being either terribly thick and heavy, and resembling a bowl placed over the head, or being far too short and leaving the wearer looking like she's just come out of prison. If your child wants a fringe then get it done by a professional – they usually only charge a pound or two, or sometimes nothing as it's such a quick job, and it'll look good.

Before you embark on your child's first fringe remember these two things:

1. You have to have the right face shape to carry one off, and many children don't as their faces are still very small. Ask a professional's opinion if you're not sure.
2. You can't tie them back. Long hair may be a pain in the neck to maintain, but at least you can tie it all back and be rid of it. Fringes offer less variation in style, and within weeks of a cut they can start to obstruct vision, which can lead to poor eyesight and glasses.

☆ **Little boys.** Cutting boys' hair is a completely different ball game, because a manageable, shoulder-length bob is generally not what they're after. No, they want something far more complicated, involving short, neat hair, which is the hardest of all cuts. I took the very sensible step of going to my salon and asking them to show me how to cut short hair, and I advise you to do the same. It's all to do with lifting it up and cutting it *along* the head rather than across, but you have to see it to know what I mean. If it all seems too much then a number three all over with some clippers does the trick, and keeps the rougher boys at bay. Beware of their delicate ears and neck, though!

☆ **Salon treatment.** If you opt for paying for your children's haircuts then find a salon that is child-friendly (i.e. has toys, books, higher chairs and lollipops) and make sure they will charge you a child's rate before you start: paying £35 for a three-year-old's bob seems a little extravagant and unreasonable to me. It's also worth asking if they can cut it without washing your child's hair first, as some kids find this to be terribly uncomfortable. As do I – when *will* somebody come up with a comfortable washbasin neck?

☆ **Get the professionals in.** Some of my friends have a professional hairdresser who comes to their house and does the whole family in one go. This 'cutting in bulk' can be cheaper, and also means the kids are in their home environment, more relaxed and better entertained.

Where do Babies come from?

Just for the record, I know where babies come from (it took me three pregnancies to finally suss out the details, but I think I'm there now). But how about the offspring themselves? I mean, when to tell? *How* to tell? The old 'Mummy, where do babies come from?' question hangs above some parents' heads like a spending spree at Selfridges, ready to reveal itself on a credit-card bill. Any day now . . . any day now . . . Oh help, what shall I *say*?!

It's crazy, and I am now quite convinced that it's an English thing. I have many foreign friends and none of them seems to have had the slightest moment of uncertainty about how to explain the birds and the bees to their kids, or about when this should occur. My Irish friend told her daughter exactly how it is the first time she asked, aged five; my French friend sat hers down and went through the basic *oiseaux et abeilles* when they were six; my Italian friend left books lying about the place (which I would describe as semi-pornographic, but perhaps that's my North European roots showing), which showed in simple, easy-to-understand steps how a cute little sperm meets its cute little egg friend and they shack up together and turn into a cute little baby.

We are yet to broach the subject in much detail, and I have to admit that I think this is getting rather silly. My eldest daughter is almost eight, and I feel in danger of slipping into Prudish English Parent territory if I don't get out the map and show her what goes where soon, especially as I know some of her peers have received the full 'That goes in there' treatment. But, oh, I don't know, it just feels so *irreversible*. So final. Once she knows, she knows, and there will be no going back to the days of innocence she still enjoys, where boys are elastic (and a bit smelly) and girls are fantastic. It will be all penises and vaginas from here on in, and I'm in no hurry for her to get there.

When and how you spill the beans is a very personal decision, but here are some golden nuggets of helpful advice from my friends who have been there and done that:

☆ **Do what feels right for your child.** Some kids are so damned clever they figure it out in nursery and have no problems with it at all. Others get halfway through secondary school before the penny drops – quickly followed by their knickers. You just have to know your child very well and be sensitive to how you think they will take it. Just because your friends have told their kids does not mean you have to follow suit yet. Similarly, if you are asked and feel you should tell all (or almost all – the full *Karma Sutra* might be a tad inappropriate for a five-year-old), then go for it even if none of the other kids know. You understand your child best, and that's what matters.

☆ **Don't make a meal of it.** Those parents who had the easiest time of explaining where babies come from to their kids are the ones who made the least fuss over it: Here it is, take it or leave it, and ask me any other questions if you have them. More toast for anyone? Those who sat their confused children down at the head of the table and delivered a twenty-minute lecture about ovulation and erections may have over-egged the pudding a little and felt quite silly while they were doing it. Less is more in this case, so say what you've gotta say and move on.

☆ **Ask what they think it means.** I was quite shocked last week
when I told my six-year-old that she couldn't watch a film
because it had too much sex in it and she replied: 'But I love
sex!' Jesus, I thought. I knew she was going to be a handful but
this was happening just a little too fast. I decided to quiz her on
it. 'It means being, you know, really cool!' she explained. Panic
over for another few years, but still no film, young lady.

☆ **Don't tell lies.** This is true in general, but in this case it means
don't make up a load of old bollocks and hope you can get away
with it. You can't, and it's a really silly thing to do. If your child
hears the term 'gay' at school and wants to know what it means,
then for heaven's sake tell him it means when two people of
the same sex love each other, or lately it's become a horrible
playground put-down meaning a bit silly. You don't need to go
into buggery or lesbian sex aids. Just say it matter-of-factly and
he'll probably take it like a man – or say 'eeuugh!' Making up
some nonsense about being good at morris dancing is very
unhelpful and misleading, and will lead to your kid being beaten
up by the name-calling thugs he's been overhearing.

☆ **Try never to let your kids see you having sex.** If anything is
going to traumatise and put kids off sex for life it's seeing their
parents at it. Even overhearing this unthinkable activity is
enough for some to develop 'issues', and the more careful you
are about avoiding this the better. Of course they know you do it

(if not they really do see you as asexual, boring freaks, and that's bad too), but they don't need proof. This is where the 'sex only after the kids are in bed … and asleep' problem arises, which causes ninety per cent of married couples to be sexually frustrated. Ho hum, it's all a lot of fun!

☆ **Talk to other parents.** It's quite eye-opening to hear how other parents have dealt with the sex issue. Just knowing that others are either confused as to what to say or have taken the same approach as you, whatever that may be, can be enough to make you feel you've done the right thing, and aren't alone in wondering if you've paved the way to teenage pregnancies or a life of celibacy.

In Sickness and in Health: Family medical matters

12 March

We've just got back from A&E. Phoebe smashed her head open on a concrete step this evening as she was running around outside. It swelled up bigger than anything I've ever seen, and her nose might be broken. It was terrifying, mainly because none of us knew what to do: there she was, bleeding, going very pale and waiting for someone to make her better. They said she might have concussion so we have to keep an eye on her. I feel really shocked: she seemed so vulnerable and tiny all of a sudden, and I felt so useless. We take them for granted but they are everything we have – I hope she'll be all right in the morning. God I adore her.

One of the first things you notice when you have a baby, apart from the fact that you never have a full night's sleep again and the sound of a child crying now sends you into an uncontrollable sweat, is that you spend a truly ridiculous amount of time in doctors' surgeries and that your bathroom resembles a pharmacy. If it's not somebody checking your blood pressure or measuring your baby's head-circumference then it's a sudden unidentifiable 'condition' requiring a desperate rush to the surgery clutching a perfectly healthy baby, who just happens to be a little under the weather because it's too damned hot outside.

The good news is that the vast majority of the 'conditions' you will worry about turn out to be nothing worthy of such concern at all. The bad news is that these medical matters only get more frequent as your family grows and your kids get stronger, braver, and able to get themselves into more scrapes than you could believe possible.

I was terribly accident-prone (some kind people like to call this inquisitive and adventurous) as a child, and spent many a merry evening in A&E or being bandaged up by my poor mother. Alas, I seem to have passed this on to at least one of my kids, and as a result of their mishaps, scrapes and injuries I am now a dab hand at dressing wounds, treating burns, knowing when to reach for the frozen peas and performing minor surgery.

Here are some family medical tips to get you started. *This list is by no means comprehensive*, but it will hopefully get you thinking along the right lines:

☆ **Always call a doctor if you are unsure or worried** about somebody's health. Unless you are calling to find out how to get residue leg wax off, they almost never mind that you've called or popped into the surgery. 'Better safe than sorry' seems to be the sensible thinking.

☆ **Learn basic first aid.** Why they don't make this compulsory at GCSE level, and again the day you get hitched, is beyond me. 'I take this woman to be my lawful wedded wife, and I know how to perform CPR, remove splinters and identify concussion . . .' Every parent should know how to deal with head injuries, burns, cuts and high temperatures, among many, many other common family medical problems. Not to know any of it is to walk around waiting for something terrible to happen one day. If you are unsure then get a good family medical book, do some Internet searching and learn the basics.

☆ **Doctors are not magicians**, and scientists don't have all the right answers. If you go to your doctor the best he or she can do, in the five minutes allotted to each patient, is try to work out what the most likely problem is, and then offer the most likely solution. To waltz in there expecting miracles or a definite diagnosis and cure is madness. Give them a break, and realise they are only human.

☆ **Antibiotics are not the only answer!** We have become antibiotic addicts in recent decades, and, unsurprisingly, the clever little bugs have wised up and are becoming resistant. Don't go to the doctor expecting or demanding the stuff: it is only useful and effective in very specific circumstances, and you are not being short-changed if you don't get any – it just means you don't need them. Oh, and if anyone in your family gets antibiotics, you must, *must* finish the course or the bugs get even more resistant, and then we'll have more superbugs than ever.

☆ **Allergies.** Sadly, these are on the increase in this country, which I think is due to increased environmental pollution, central heating, over-use of chemical cleaning products and under-use of good old dirt to kick the immune system into gear in young children. If anyone has an allergy in your family, get some medical advice and make sure other children and their parents know about it.

☆ **Look out for signs that something isn't quite 'right'.** Because you all know each other better than anyone, it falls to you to sense if something is wrong: if a child is suddenly more withdrawn than usual or starts sleeping much more than normal, or if you don't feel at all as energetic as you usually do, and so on. Only you know what 'usual' is, and if you think things have become *un*usual, and it worries you, then go and talk to a doctor about it. They should listen to this kind of unclear but definite change, and help you to pinpoint what could be causing it.

☆ **School or no school?** It's very hard to tell sometimes whether a child is ill enough to have the day off school. I have found that if they are only a little bit under the weather, i.e. have a tiny temperature or a slight sore throat, sending them to school usually perks them up enough for them to feel much better, and it never develops into anything more serious. Staying at home can often make them descend into 'Oh me – I am so *ill*' mode, which usually means a week off school (and work, for you!). Think of others, though: sending an infectious child to school is very irresponsible, and rather mean.

☆ **Get a second opinion.** Never be scared to go back to the doctor and get a second examination. They can be wrong . . .

☆ **Men and doctors.** No, not a pay-as-you-come porn channel (though I'm sure it'll be along soon) but a serious point: most men I know hate going to the doctor and rarely, if ever, check themselves for lumps, bumps, odd-looking moles and other things that many women do routinely. If you think there could be something wrong then make the appointment for him and force him to go: it's just stupid not to.

☆ **And while we're at it . . .** When a woman is ill she still looks after the kids, goes shopping, cooks dinner and goes to work. When a man is ill he looks like he's dying, refuses to see a doctor and goes to bed for a week. There's no point fighting it, so remembering that it's the same in most families and realising that this makes us the tougher sex can reduce the resentment!

☆ **And eyes and ears and mouth and nose . . .** Well, eyes and ears at least. If your child doesn't reply much when you ask a question, it might not be insolence: there's a chance she could be hard of hearing so get it checked out. Similarly, if you notice he is holding his book two centimetres from his face, get an eye test. These early years are crucial for spotting any problems, so keep an eye on things. Ha ha.

☆ **First-aid kit.** Every house should have at least one: a main one in the bathroom and smaller ones downstairs and in your handbag. A quick Internet search will give you the basics you should always have in the house, but my personal recommended items to get you started are: electronic or strip thermometer, Calpol and Nurofen, nappy-rash cream (the best I've ever used is called Bepanthen, which also soothes lots of other skin irritations), antiseptic cream, e.g. Savlon, plasters (millions), chesty-cough mixture, Bonjela, verucca cream, Zovirax, tweezers and a head-lice comb. There are of course hundreds of other products you could, and possibly should, fill your bathroom with, and you will learn as you go along what works for your family and what is a waste of money.

TOP TIP: *For your handbag first-aid kit, always include plasters, sun cream and sachets of Calpol: the one time you go away without any of it you'll need it!*

Happily, most of us survive long enough to collect our pension, and the ones who generally chill out seem to outlive their more stressed-out neighbours. So get yourself some first-aid knowledge, stock up your bathroom, sit back and hope for the best.

Family Anxiety. When the pressure gets too much …

Keeping your family healthy and uninjured is something you will fret and stress about your entire life. I have found that the older they get the worse I worry: with every passing day we *must* be getting closer to a really big fall, illness or bad case of head lice, surely? I often can't bear the thought of what each day could bring: a near miss with a bus, being coughed all over by the library assistant who clearly has TB, leaving my kids in a room containing carrier-bags, glue, knives, scissors, electric sockets … oh God! Worrying about keeping my family healthy – or even alive – is enough to drive me to an early grave!

This kind of permanent, low-level concern is very tiring but entirely normal. If you don't worry about your family's health you should get yourself checked out for a severe case of Insensitivitis. But for some people it becomes very pronounced and can eventually lead to panic attacks, claustrophobia, agoraphobia and other psychological conditions.

Recognising and understanding this type of anxiety brought on by being a parent is only just beginning. In fact, increasing numbers of women are now being diagnosed with postnatal anxiety rather than what was previously misdiagnosed as postnatal depression. This is a very good thing, as it means they won't be prescribed anti-depressants when counselling or cognitive behavioural therapy (CBT) is more likely to be what they need.

I know all about this kind of anxiety as it was a problem for me for several years. What makes it hard to spot is that it can often take years to kick in, so it seems unlikely to be related to childbirth or motherhood. I spent a year being unable to go anywhere without a mobile phone, to go on a train, a plane or even a bus, unable to have work meetings and often unable just to go into a shop without having to run out empty-handed. In other words, unable to lead a normal life, and it affected the entire family.

Things are enormously better now, thanks to some CBT and lots of perseverance, though I still rarely drive. I now know about ten other mothers who have suffered similar things, and every one of us thought we might be cracking up. We weren't: we're just living under a phenomenal amount of stress, and worry too much about our own health and that of our families. If you have ever experienced anything similar, and find it frightening or hard to cope with, then please do talk to your GP about it and see if you can get some help. It's nothing to be ashamed of – if anything it just shows how much you adore your family – but it's much better for all of you if you face it and get over it than have to live with the anxiety.

Teeth. While we're at it . . .
While we're in here, a few notes about dental hygiene.

☆ **Look after them.** Most of us don't, and then we curse when we have to sit through all the drilling and filling. Even milk teeth need very careful attention, as it starts children off on habits and it protects the adult teeth from damage.
☆ **Don't use too much toothpaste!** I've seen people squirting mountains of the stuff onto children's toothbrushes. When it

says 'pea-sized' amount, I think they were thinking of frozen peas, not giant African Jumbo Peas (no – these don't exist). Too much means kids often swallow it, which is thought by some to be harmful, so use sparingly.

☆ **Don't stop brushing your kids' teeth** when they are old enough to do it themselves. They *can* do it themselves, but you'll find they actually do a ridiculously bad job. Step in once or twice a week and do it for them.

☆ **Replace toothbrushes every three months**, or sooner if the bristles show lots of wear – i.e. if your child bites them, like one of mine does. Grrr.

☆ **Go to the dentist every six months** and take your kids every year. I know, we all hate going, but Topsy and Tim got stickers and a ride on the funny up-and-down seat thing, so you never know – it could be fun. Also, getting kids into the habit when they are young means they won't be so nervous about it when they are older, and it's much better to keep teeth in good nick than to spend a fortune filling in all the holes.

☆ **Sweets.** Oooh, they're so very, very lovely and yummy, but they destroy your teeth, so keep them to a minimum and make your kids brush their teeth after they have had any. Same goes for all the evil, nasty, corrosive fizzy drinks out there. No, no, *no*!

☆ **Flossing.** Do it. Even children as young as six or so can floss their teeth if you help, and you will be horrified at the amount of food still left between them. Julia Roberts did it in *Pretty Woman*, and she's got the best teeth in Hollywood. It might not get you a millionaire boyfriend, but a beautiful smile isn't beyond reach.

With these indelicate matters out of the way, you'd think we could get back to something more civilised and 'homely'. Nearly . . . Before we leave our cleaning habits and private parts alone we need to stick our heads into one of the smallest and least glamorous rooms in the house: the toilet.

PART EIGHTEEN

The Toilet

Lifting the lid on personal hygiene

Welcome to the toilet. Not the most glamorous of rooms you could hope to enter, but one you will need to visit at some point during your tour, and given the level of usage it gets in an average family you're as well to get in there while you can, and while there's still paper. After the kitchen, the toilet is probably the most used room in a family home. So much so that I have had to wait long enough to cook an entire meal from scratch and felt my bladder almost burst on many occasions, as one child after the other goes in to kill ten minutes daydreaming, singing and goodness only knows what else in there.

You might think it extravagant to dedicate an entire section to the toilet, but in my opinion it deserves it. Not only does it supply more humour than any other room in a house (pants, bottom, poo ... see, there you go already), but it is also essential that the family bathroom and toilet be in separate rooms. Bathroom, then bricks and plaster, then toilet. If an estate agent ever tells you that having a toilet in a bathroom increases the value of your home, ignore him. He has either never lived in a house with three children, or is someone who doesn't mind having an aromatherapy bath in a room smelling like a French urinal.

There are many ways to tell a woman lives in a house, but two big giveaways in the toilet area are:

1. There are sanitary-towel wrappers sticking out of the bin.
2. Somebody has made an effort to make it look pretty in there.

Similarly, there are two ways you can tell that a man lives in a house:

1. There are magazines beside the toilet.
2. It smells ever-so-slightly of wee in there.

Yes, I'm sure there are New Men and more refined gay men out there whose sense of personal hygiene, standards of cleanliness and aim all outshine the other eighty per cent of the male population. But for the rest it's either a case of hit or miss (and it's often miss) or spending the best part of a morning in there with a copy of *FHM* and no sign of an open window or an extractor fan to cover their tracks. In order to prevent your family's smallest room from resembling a French public lavatory, there are some Golden Rules to drill into your family and ensure they follow:

☆ **MEN:** seat goes up for a wee, and down when you've finished. If you miss – even a tiny bit – wipe immediately. Thank you.
☆ **LADIES:** Stores of sanitary bits and bobs should be kept in a beautiful, closed container. Everybody knows we use it, but nobody likes to see it. And never try to flush the tiny plastic tampon-wrappers down the toilet – they just float about and look horrible.
☆ **CHILDREN:** Remember to lift the lid before you sit down, even if you are really, really, *really* bursting.
☆ **ALL:** Replace the toilet paper as soon as you have finished a roll, and throw the empty cardboard tube in the recycling bin or the activity box for future binoculars. Do not leave it lying on the floor for Mummy to pick up.
☆ **Concentrate on getting all of it *in***, and if you have a small

accident, tell somebody straight away. Do not wait until Mummy goes in two hours later to find it smells like a subway in there.

☆ **Always go before a meal.** I don't care if you don't need to – go anyway.

☆ **When you fit the last roll,** make a loud family announcement and ensure somebody is sent to buy emergency supplies as soon as possible. Preferably at the same time as you collect the curry . . .

☆ **Store the toilet rolls in a place accessible from the toilet** itself, and preferably in a pretty container, e.g. a basket.

☆ **Think of other people,** and get some ventilation going *before* you start if you think you'll need it.

☆ **Ask if anyone needs a quick one** before you settle in for a ten-page session. It's just courteous.

☆ **Put a scented candle in there.** Even if you never light it, it will keep things smelling better than they might, and looks a lot nicer than a can of anti-stink spray on the shelf. Yuk.

☆ **Get a small, stylish bin for those wrappers . . .**

☆ **Always wash hands afterwards.** Always, always, even if you were very careful.

☆ **Change the hand towel frequently.** If you have a small basin with a hand towel by the toilet, change this one more frequently than the normal bathroom towels. Some kids still interpret 'wash hands' as 'make them wet and then wipe all your germs on the towel'. Nice.

☆ **Share the cleaning.** Once a person has cleaned a family toilet – and I mean scrubbed every inch of the floor, toilet bowl and cistern with disinfectant – they will never be careless in there again. Even if you have a cleaner who washes it every week, make sure every reasonably grown-up member of your family has a go at least twice a year. I think you'll find the hits outweigh the misses very quickly.

☆ **Carpets.** I *hope* nobody in this country has a carpet in their toilet any more, but just in case there are some hangers-on, I need to say: GET RID OF IT!!!

There, now you can go in and enjoy yourself. Just make sure these rules are regularly refreshed in everyone's memory, or you'll be cruising towards public-lavatory territory before you can say: *Hurry up – I'm bursting!*

I did it! The joys of potty training

There comes a time in the first few years of its life when a human child learns to control its lower regions, and only goes to the loo when it is sitting on a hard circle with a hole in the middle, above a bowl of water. This is obviously not the case in all cultures, but it is generally accepted to be the social norm where I live, and probably where you live too. Squatting behind a lamppost outside the library, or weeing yourself at the cold meat counter, are both frowned upon.

Learning to go to the toilet on demand is a huge milestone for all children (and their parents) and should be something to celebrate and reward. Unfortunately it usually leads to a rather unpleasant amount of inter-parent competition, dishonesty and needless stress for all concerned.

If little Josephine from down the road was out of nappies before her first birthday, then good for her. She may be very clever, but more likely has a fantastically pushy or dishonest mother. My own mother claims I was out of nappies when I was eighteen months old, but having gone through this stage with three of my own children I am left wondering a) whether she is talking rubbish, and b) what on earth she threatened me with if I didn't get on with it. My kids were all well over the age of two before they seemed ready, and this seems to be the same for all of the other children I know.

Here are some top potty-training tips, as shared by my good self and my experienced parent friends, who have all come through the 'wee everywhere' stage:

☆ **Ignore what everyone else's children are doing.** You know your own child best and there is no 'correct age' at which to potty-train. It usually happens between the ages of two and three, but every child is different.

☆ **Take your cue from your child.** If he seems to be going for long periods of time with a clean, dry nappy, and is becoming interested in the toilet, then have a go at removing his nappy for a few hours.

☆ **Keep reminding.** Asking 'Do you need the loo?' every twenty minutes may seem a tad obsessive, but your toddler will be so busy squishing Playdough into your carpet that she will forget she needs to go until it's too late.

☆ **Buy lovely pants.** This was the clincher for all of mine. Pants with rockets on? Frilly pants with days of the week on? Take this nappy off *at once* – they're mine!

☆ **Don't push it.** If your child seems nervous or unhappy about it at all, then stop and wait a month or so. Making a fuss over it never works.

☆ **Toilet or potty?** The jury's out on this one, but for me it was straight onto the toilet for all of them. Potties need emptying ... enough said. It also means they don't need to jump over yet another hurdle from potty to toilet in a few months' time – one leap and you're there! Get a small step so the poor thing stands a chance, and make sure she can reach the paper.

☆ **Using a special toddler seat** means little children are less terrified of falling in, being flushed away or being eaten by the Toilet Troll. Damn those fertile imaginations. Do store this item away when visitors come: you might not mind your child's toilet seat, but everybody else thinks it's foul.

☆ **Do it in the summer.** Potty-training peaks in the summer months, as some parents try to get it over before nursery starts in September (most nurseries only take children who are out of nappies, though if you're only eighty per cent in the clear you can always *say* they are, and fake disbelief when Tommy comes home in a clean change of clothes *again*, but that's very naughty) and others use the warmer weather as a chance to let their kids run around *sans* underwear and see if that works. It also means all the extra washing you will have to do dries faster and doesn't fill every room in the house.

☆ **Give rewards.** First of all, heap on the praise for the slightest success or even an attempt at using the toilet. Secondly, using some kind of incentive (call it a bribe if you must) can also help: we used to give a Smartie for a wee and two for a poo. It's not the most highbrow approach, but it worked, and it's neither too evil nor expensive.

☆ **Always try before a bath.** Pooing in the bath was quite common among my friends' children and my own, and it is really, *really* horrible. Always have a long 'sit on the toilet' session before putting them in – read a book while they're waiting if necessary, but keep them there long enough to be sure there's nothing coming. Yuk, yuk, yuk!

Environmental Note: One theory for children being potty-trained later and later is that disposable nappies have removed some of the parental incentive. If you are washing every nappy by hand, then getting to the potty-training stage as soon as possible seems like a good idea. Disposables are also much more comfortable for the babies, as they don't feel so wet or bulky, so they are less likely to want to give them up for something smaller and softer either. This should be a big consideration for when you begin to encourage your child to use the toilet, as disposable nappies are generally accepted to be as environmentally awful as Chelsea Tractors and enormous washing machines.

Dingles, Wilvins, Wotsits and Doo-dahs: How to talk about those fiddly bits

Or rather, how to talk about those fiddly bits without sounding like a prat. If one thing is going to make a sexy, intelligent, grown man look like a buffoon, it's getting all embarrassed when talking to his child about their whatchamacallits. The truth is that for a language as rich and expressive as ours, English has few satisfactory words for our private parts. There are obviously the technical terms, but few people use these when talking to their young children. Much more common is to resort to some endearing, cute, silly term that is often unique to a particular family and very often a hybrid of things Mummy or Daddy said and their two-year-old's effort at repeating this. Hence all the wilvins, dingles, bitsies and frottoms I've heard. I could go on, but it's just too silly.

We need some new words. Some generally accepted, liked and not-embarrassing-at-all words to use when telling our daughters not to stick everything that comes into sight into their *thingamabobs* and our sons to stop pulling their *winky-doodles* as far as they will go. (Plenty of time for that in years to come, my darling.)

Because, much as you may rather not talk about private parts, you will. Kids love them – they are fascinated, obsessed, and just cannot get enough of them. Boys seem to get into this 'Hey – look what *mine* can do!' phase earlier than girls, but then, as my six-year-old pointed out recently, if she had one she would play with it all the time too. Good point! There it is, it's funny, it's wiggly, it makes everybody react when I play with it, so off I go, pulling, twisting, wrapping and generally fiddling about with it as much as I can. Hours of fun.

If you ever feel like you are on shaky ground and aren't sure how to talk about sex organs and bodily functions, then rest assured that nobody else has a clue either, and feels just as uncertain and silly as you do. The following will hopefully help:

☆ **Don't be shy about it.** Kids have no idea what sex really is until they are at least eight, and probably even older. Introducing any kind of shyness or embarrassment before then is unhelpful at best, and could be damaging at worst.

☆ **Talk about it with your partner**, and find words you can both use without cracking up in a fit of giggles. That won't help at all.

☆ **Using the correct biological terms can sound odd** coming from a very young child, but there is, of course, nothing wrong with it if you choose to use them. Younger siblings learn whatever their older brothers and sisters say anyway, and my three-year-old knows all about 'baginas' and his 'beeeniss'. It's quite cute, really.

☆ **Children are very curious** and you shouldn't worry if your young children touch themselves, or are interested in their friends' bits and pieces (there I go again). If it is more than a short-lived phase, then you might want to step in and gently explain that their private parts are not really for others to see, and that touching could also spread infections. So long as you never get angry, or make a big deal of it, they will probably go back to throwing sand at each other again fairly soon.

☆ **Dare to bare.** How comfortable you are with being naked in front of your kids, and how often they get to see you in your birthday suit, will have an enormous impact on how they feel about their own bodies and how body-confident, and, later, sexually confident they become. Hiding your body away is not a good idea, even if you haven't been to the gym for a year. Your kids don't know that, and to them you are just perfect, lovely, and their mummy. My daughter is never short of complimentary words to describe my body as she watches me dress or have a bath: my boobs are weird, my nipples look like bean sprouts (I assure you they do *not* – she is clearly mistaken), my tummy is squishy and I have lumpy bits on my bottom (Jesus – I know, I *know*, it's called cellulite!). Knowing that ladies' bodies look as peculiar as this should help when hers starts to change as she grows older. That's the theory . . .

A change of scene required now, I think, after all those personal hygiene and medical matters. If you grab the long pole in the airing cupboard (just to your left) you can reach the catch that opens the loft hatch. Careful, though: the ladder has a way of crashing down and decapitating visitors. Sorry about all the dead flies as well – we don't go into this space often, but there are some very important things stored up here, so, after you . . .

PART NINETEEN

The Attic

If you are like most of Middle England then your attic is in fact no longer a place for storing all your accumulated junk, but has long-since been converted into an extra bedroom, *en suite* bathroom and office space. We're not quite there yet, and the attic space you see before you is where we store all our suitcases, old clothes, school work and sentimental objects collected over the years, which we just might possibly need again one day. Let's have a poke around and see what we can find . . .

The Travelling Circus: Going away as a family

Scotland, 25 July 2006

I'm at the end of my tether. Really. We've been here for four days and so far it has been nothing – absolutely bloody nothing – but fight, fight, argue, bicker, snap, complain, moan, whinge and shout from all of us. The kids are being just awful and don't seem able to get on with having a nice time on the beach, in the house or anywhere, and this is making both of us really irritated and tired. What we really need right now is some time to get away from all the pressures at home, and instead we are getting even more stress from trying to keep three children from killing each other. We

*normally manage to have great family holidays, but this one is a
shocker. I know it will settle down soon, but right now all I want to
do is go home.*

You can always tell the people who have just come back from a
holiday with their family: they are the ones who look even more
than usually stressed out, who clearly haven't slept properly for a
week and who look like they are poised to kill the next person who
whinges, whines or complains about anything.

The most common thing I say when I get back from a holiday
with my family is 'Bloody hell, I'm knackered – I need a holiday.'
And it's the same for all of my friends. It's so common, in fact,
that if a mother so much as mentions that she is planning a trip
somewhere with her whole family she is met by pained looks of pity
and a slight fear than she might be insane. Going away? With your
family? For a *week*? Get this woman a drink!

It's sad really, because going on holiday should be the highlight
of your year: neither of you is working, you get to go somewhere
other than to the end of your road, the playground and the local
shops, and, crucially, *it's the only opportunity you get to spend a decent
amount of time with your kids once they've started school.*

Family holiday stress is really sad (and silly) because much of it
can be avoided, either by clever packing and organisation, or by a
drastic change in attitude. I have travelled a lot with my growing
brood, who all have their own strong opinions and very loud
voices, and I have picked up some very handy survival tips along
with all the foreign illnesses, an impressive rock and shell collection, and the ability to say ice-cream in seven languages. Try some
of these for starters:

☆ **Change your attitude.** If you approach a family holiday with
   dread and a certainty that it will be the most awful two weeks
   you've had since the last time you lugged a bag of cuddly toys
   and six bottles of Calpol to the south of France, then it almost
   certainly will be. If you set off with an attitude that is more like:
   'This is going to be *fun*! I am going to relax, get away from my

boring living room with its faded curtains, Lego everywhere and finger marks on the wall by the door, and feel some of that French *joie de vivre*. I might even begin to look like Juliette Binoche, if I try hard enough. Fun, here we come!', then you will probably enjoy yourself much, much more.

☆ **Be realistic.** In real life, of course, you will *not* look like Juliette Binoche or have endless fun and opportunities for relaxation. You will have *some* fun, relax a little and maybe get a slight tan and buy something chic, French, and Binoche-*like*. That, my friend, will have to be good enough. Being realistic about your holiday expectations is key to having a good time away. It won't be the best week of your life, but it hopefully won't be the worst either.

☆ **Doing it for the kids.** We have all become terribly self-centred about holidays. The attitude seems to be: we pay for it, we need the break, so you had better let us enjoy ourselves, kiddo, and keep out of our way. Once upon a time holidays meant kids could stay up late, play all day, get up to mischief and adventure and enjoy some freedom from the school routine for a change. Not so any more for many kids: now it's more often kids' clubs during the day, babysitters in the evening and lots of shouting in between if they should be so thoughtless as to get between you, your magazine and your suntan. It's awful, and what's needed is to try to remember that holidays are as much, if not more, for our children as for us, and to let them have a bit of FUN. I know you want to go shopping, read the paper or go out for a meal, but they want to dig a hole in the garden, fill it with water and then jump in it. Let them – they're on holiday.

☆ **Plan something for everyone.** It's generally accepted that as we get older we enjoy different things. I used to like going to theme parks and swimming in the sea for six hours a day on my holidays. Now I like visiting old buildings and reading for six hours a day. And drinking wine. It's probably the case that every member of your family has a different top-ten holiday wish list, and the solution to this potential disaster is to schedule in something to please everyone. Go to a theme park in the morning, check out the Renaissance church or art gallery on the way home, and buy your kids an ice-cream while you sample the local *vino* in the evening. Everybody is thus seventy per cent happy, and that's about as good as it's ever going to get, so enjoy it!

☆ **Prepare for the unexpected and be flexible.** Holidays have the habit of throwing more spanners in your carefully organised works than a pesky child with a bag full of spanners in a factory. Just when you thought you were about to escape for a weekend at the seaside . . . bang! – the car breaks down, two of your kids get chickenpox and your husband gets a call from work to say there has been a Friday-afternoon catastrophe. Weekend abandoned. This is where being able to leap gracefully to Plan B (stay at home and watch DVDs until the spots stop itching, the car is mended, the work panic is over and your mood improves) can save the day. When you are abroad things go wrong at a staggering rate, as museums close without warning, restaurants serve food your kids refuse to eat, and attractions turn out to be not quite as attractive as they looked on the web. Being able to adapt quickly and come up with something else amusing to do at the drop of a sombrero is key to surviving a holiday that looks set to turn into a nightmare. You don't have to go quite as far as we did recently, when we spent two hours in the launderette just for laughs because the weather was so bad that we couldn't play outdoors and we had no dry washing. It was rather clutching at straws, but the kids had a great time. Simple pleasures . . .

☆ **Beware the first and last weeks.** We have found, time and time again, that the first few days of a holiday are often the worst. Everyone is having to adjust to the new routine of being together twenty-four hours a day and there are arguments all the time. After a week or so everything settles down and we all get along beautifully. The last week is also often quite fraught, as everybody is tired after all the unusually late nights and the travelling, and maybe also nervous about going back to school. Two-week holidays are the worst, as you only get about three hours of everyone being lovely in the middle! Being aware of these potentially volatile weeks should stand you in good stead for when they arrive. You are not the Worst Family in the World: you are just doing what's very normal.

☆ **Get some time alone.** Now then, you know I just said it's important to let our kids have lots of fun during the holidays? Well, that still holds (it's only been about one minute!), but the importance of getting some time for *just the two of you* cannot be overstated. Find out if there are any babysitting facilities where you are staying, or a morning crèche, and grab some time to be a couple on holiday together.

☆ **Go with another family.** I am a lady who likes her privacy and peace so this doesn't appeal much to me, but I have heard many a very positive account of shared family holidays from my friends. There are always people on hand to look after the kids, allowing you some relaxation time or a free night out; there is plenty of adult company to enjoy; you can share the chores and cooking duties; and it can be a Godsend if your family is a bit on edge for some reason or another because you can get away from each other for a few hours each day. It's not for everyone, but as an alternative it is definitely worth a go. We are planning to go with friends for the first time this summer.

☆ **Who books the holiday?** A subject of considerable trauma in many families I know: who does all the research, decides where to go, and then actually *books* the damned thing? In our family it falls to me, for several reasons: one, I am not at work as much as my busy-bee husband so I have more time to think about it, and make enquiries; two, I know when the school holidays are and what playdates or birthday parties with friends have been arranged; three, he is chronically lazy and finds even the idea of thinking about where to go on holiday too much to bear; and four, I know that if I book it, I get to go where I want. Clever.

If you can give one person responsibility to book the holiday, and agree to go along with what they decide – if it falls within the bounds of what's sensible, affordable and available – then this can solve a lot of agonising and arguing.

☆ **Enjoy your time together.** Up onto my preachy high horse I clamber . . . and here goes: 'Your children are so *lovely*! You should enjoy the time you have to appreciate their utter *loveliness*. Don't be annoyed by their squabbling, moaning and bickering, and just look at how *lovely* they are!' And, if you haven't knocked me off yet . . . down I climb by myself.

Yes, our kids are a delight much of the time, but asking you to enjoy every moment with them would be like asking you to relish every moment with any other loved one – it's almost impossible, because sometimes they just get on your tits, to be frank. But even though this is the case, it is still vitally important during any family holiday to *try* – no, more than a bit: try *a lot* – to enjoy as much of it as possible, and to avoid the all-too-easy carping, arguing, snapping, sighing and any other childish but common behaviour brought on by spending too much time cooped up together. Try – if you can bite your tongue and say something positive even five times out of seven you will have a much more pleasant trip, and this happier mood will soon spread throughout the family. You set the tone, and others should follow.

✩ **Holidays *are* stressful.** Whether you have kids or not, holidays are always going to be fairly stressful, what with all the packing, travelling, missing connections and eating strange food that makes you throw up for three days. Don't put all of the blame for any anxiety and discomfort on the family. Yes, kids bring yet more patience-testing challenges and worries, but it wouldn't have been hassle-free without them either.

Scotland, 28 July 2006

Really sad to be leaving tomorrow. We have only just found our feet, un-knotted all the stress and got into beach life, and now we have to pack up and go. The kids are having a great time now, collecting shells, fishing, and they have made friends with some of the local kids. Next time we'll come for longer if we can – a week to adjust to the new pace and routines, and then more time to actually enjoy it!

Everything but the Kitchen Sink: Clever packing

Depending on how old your kids are, you will either travel with half of your house in the back of the car, or somehow manage to cut this down to only a quarter. Babies require a fiendishly large amount of clobber, from travel cots and jars of emergency food to buggies and half a ton of clothes. Older children are usually happy with a couple of games and toys, some books, some pens and paper and a few changes of clothes. Teenagers are a different ballgame altogether, and I'm not really dealing with them (thank God) in this book – save to say that *tons* of clothes and music come as numbers one and two in the Must Take with Us list, but whatever you pack they will be in a foul mood half the time anyway.

We used to travel with almost everything our kids ever used at home, until we realised all our suitcases were broken and we were leaving ourselves absolutely no room for any souvenirs or duty-free (or are these the same thing?). We are now far more sensible and have learned a thing or two about clever holiday packing.

☆ **Each to his/her own.** Buying small suitcases for kids may seem unnecessary and cumbersome, but we have actually found it to be very helpful. Segregating everybody's things into separate cases means you can immediately see what you have packed for each person, you don't end up with Little Mermaid pants jumbled up with your Agent Provocateur treats, and it makes unpacking when you arrive really quick too – in fact, if you are as lazy as me you don't even need to unpack, as everybody's clothes are already in separate places. Ta-da!

☆ **Compartmentalise.** Clothes are clothes and toys are toys and never the twain shall meet. Mr Kipling (he of *Jungle Book* fame, not exceedingly good cakes, by the way) knew that some things should just never come into contact with one another, and so it is with some of your holiday items. Pack a separate bag for *every* category: toys, craft stuff (e.g. paints, glue, scissors), books, chargers and electrical items, medical kit, wash-bag, shoes, underwear, and so on. These can, of course, be put together in one larger suitcase or travel bag, but the key thing is to have bags within bags and keep everything separate.

☆ **Accessibility.** When you have a major spillage on the back seat and need some wipes and a change of clothes quick-smart, you had better hope that everything you need isn't packed at the bottom of the biggest case, underneath all your shoes, cameras and hair products. Always keep one bag accessible with some basics such as a change of clothes for younger passengers, wipes, extra nappies if your child still uses them, small umbrellas in case the weather changes en route, and toothbrushes in case you all need a quick freshen-up. I find brushing my teeth relieves even the worst travel grime.

☆ **Travel bags at the ready!** Try to have a small shoulder bag for each child, which is emptied out and restocked after every holiday, so the next time you go away you know you can just grab them off the peg and have everything your kids need to keep them happy on a journey and while you're away. Some paper, pens, stickers, travel games and small paperback books usually do the trick.

☆ **Food and drink.** Travelling makes you want to eat. This is usually more to do with boredom than any actual need for sustenance, but either way a family can chomp through almost a week's worth of food in just a few hours while sitting in a car, on a plane or on the hard shoulder. Bored, munch! Bored, nibble! Bored, chomp! One way to avoid everyone either bouncing off the walls in a sugar and chemicals-induced fit or becoming clinically obese before you've arrived is to provide a constant stream of healthy snacks. **Carrot and cucumber sticks, grapes, raisins, bread rolls, bananas and cereal bars** can all keep bored jaws happy while avoiding a 'junk food and sweets' meltdown. The best thing to drink is **water** – get a bottle for each passenger and refill regularly. Fruit juices are full of sugar and anything containing caffeine means you'll need to stop for a toilet break every twenty minutes.

☆ **Decide who does the packing.** This miserable job seems to fall mainly to us ladies. We do all the packing, not only for ourselves, but also for all our kids and our husband. It takes ages, it requires the concentration of a celebrity on the red carpet, and we get little thanks. There are perks, though: you can be absolutely certain that everything you need is in, because relying on anyone else to bring exactly the right eye cream, knickers or shoes is just a ludicrous proposition, and you can also have a bit of fun at his expense. 'Oh, didn't I pack any underwear for you – I'm so sorry, I was sure I had.' Hee, hee. Once you've done it a hundred times it becomes second nature, and you'll be done in under an hour.

☆ **Make a checklist.** If you want to be hyper-organised, then print out a checklist of all the essential items you bring on every family holiday but are likely to forget, and refer to it every time you pack. You know the kind of thing: battery chargers, adaptors, camera, Calpol, address book for postcards, toothbrushes, buggy, driving licence, contraception, any foreign cash you have lying at the back of drawers, and so on. It will save hours writing out the same checklist every time the night before you go. Happy packing!

Home From Home: Bringing your habits with you

Part of the joy of travelling and going somewhere different is just that – it is *different*, and by its very nature it doesn't have any of the associations with your daily life, routines, bad habits or common arguments. You have a blank slate on which to sketch out an altogether more harmonious, peaceful picture of family life, until the kids start scribbling all over it on day two and you are back to a mess of arguments, squabbles and sighs.

Travelling as a family makes it very difficult to leave any bad habits behind, because all the main component parts – you, your partner, your kids and your essential toiletries – are all still there. Trying to carve out new lines of communication and leave the hard-wired reactions to common irritations behind for a few days is almost impossible when all the same interactions are taking place. What can result is the worst kind of home-from-home scenario, where things are just as fraught as at home, but now you don't have the support network of friends and the local toddler group or playground to take some of the strain off your shoulders.

Here are some ways of combating this all-too-common holiday problem:

☆ **Bring the good; leave the bad.** If you can try to leave all your quibbles and niggles in the departure lounge and just bring your sunny, happy, laissez-faire self with you then you are bound for a successful holiday. I know it's annoying when the kids argue over who has more juice than the other, but try a holiday 'Oh never mind we'll get another one later. Look, a boat!' rather than the more usual 'Oh will you just stop arguing! Right, no juice for anybody!', and things will be more relaxing for everybody.

☆ **Forget the time.** One of the best holidays I ever had was when my watch broke (actually I dropped it in a hot tub by mistake, but I didn't tell *them* that) and I had no idea what the time was for a week. When it was light I got up. When I was hungry, I ate. When I was tired I went to sleep. There was no routine, no sticking to timetables, bedtime, dinnertime and so on. It made catching trains a little tricky, but apart from that it was the most relaxing time ever. Holidays are the only time when you have nothing to rush for, and no need to make sure your kids are in bed early to get a good night's rest before school. Try losing track of time for a few days, and see where it takes you all.

Where to stay

I have done plenty of holidays with my family in all manner of accommodation from five-star hotels (a work trip, I hasten to add!) to camping (my silly idea), and my conclusion is that neither hotels nor self-catering are better – they are just completely *different* experiences and you have to decide which you feel like at a given time.

Hotels have the advantage of catering to your every need: there is a concierge on call twenty-four hours a day should you suddenly have the need at 3 a.m. to ask directions to the beach or the *en suite* bathroom, and there's a restaurant, babysitting facilities, a doctor, a lobby (where all the action takes place) and often a lift with lots of buttons to press in order to annoy the other guests. They also have the added luxuries of having the beds made up every night, bowls of apples or sweets on the front desk and writing paper and mini toiletries you can steal.

But for families with kids, all of this attention and organisation can be what makes hotels so hard to stay in. Kids often have routines that don't fit in with the opening hours of hotel restaurants and there are the other guests to consider, who might not appreciate having their romantic meal ruined by a two-year-old chipping pieces off the marble tabletop with a knife. Everything can feel just a little too precious and tidy, and then, of course, there is the fact that hotels have lots of other people in them who will almost certainly go out drinking late at night and return, pissed and noisy, only to wake your baby up and thus rub in the fact that you are not out having a wild time – like lucky, lucky them – but are tucked up in bed with your night cream on, reading last Sunday's *Style* supplement and dreaming of another life.

Self-catering solves many of these problems, but brings some of its own. You are free to do what you like, when you like, which for me is the most important factor in any holiday. There are no restaurants waiting to close, maids coming in to replace the shampoo and put a small triangle on the end of the toilet roll or other guests to disturb (assuming you are in a separate building, rather than a self-catering battery farm with four hundred minute apartments full of noisy families like your own). You can cook food you know your kids will eat, which is not only much cheaper but also more relaxing, and you can go out or come in at any time without feeling that the Spanish guy on the front desk is monitoring you and knows what a fun time you are not having.

But the downside is that staying somewhere self-catering is more of a busman's holiday for you: you end up shopping in rubbish local supermarkets, cooking, washing-up and generally behaving as you do at home, and many women in particular find self-catering to be less of a holiday and more of a boot camp because none of the utensils work as well as their own, there is often no dishwasher, and everyone buggers off to the beach as soon as dinner is finished, leaving her to tidy up. (If you are one of these creatures, by the way, then you really need to sort it out and make others share the workload with you. See page 58.)

Camping is in another ballpark altogether, and you really have to question just how much you are prepared to go through in the name of Having a Good Family Time. Yes, I do know that many people actually like camping, and as a seasoned camper myself I know it can be a lot of fun and very *Swallows and Amazons* – if you're into that kind of thing. But 'holiday', in the sense of relaxation, relieving stress and making it easy on yourself, it is not. Camping is tiring, physically demanding and rather uncomfortable, and gives you a satisfying 'we did it' sensation when it's all over. As such it should suit most English families perfectly – give it a go and see how you fare.

If you must do it, then find somewhere with **amenities** such as running water, hot showers and decent toilets, and preferably near a pub, shop and health spa if you can swing it. When nobody is looking you can make your escape and return four hours later, tipsy, glowing and stocked up with chocolate. If there are **activities** for children, such as a playground onsite, then so much the better. Young children often don't want to sleep without a brave, wine-filled adult to fend off all the wolves and four-headed monsters, so you will have to be prepared to sleep apart from your partner for the duration of the trip. No sex on this holiday, then.

On a more positive note, camping can be very beneficial for families, as it really brings you all together and forces you to co-operate with activities like putting the tent up and cooking, and there are none of the usual distractions such as televisions, CD players and biscuit cupboards to create any agro. It's just all of you and the great outdoors, and sometimes such simplicity can bring a family much closer together. For a while . . .!

Culture Vulture, Beach Babe or Adrenaline Junkie?
Finding a holiday for *all* the family

One person's holiday really can be another's week of hell. Some people like beach holidays. Stick me on a beach with nothing but the sun, sand and sea, and I will go mad within three hours. I need culture, mountains and shade. Oh, and somewhere to get a nice drink and maybe a massage or something. You know, as it's a holiday and all . . .

If you and your partner, and possibly also your kids, have widely differing opinions on what constitutes an enjoyable holiday, then I'm afraid the prospects really are quite grim, and you will *have* to work out a way that you can all have fun. If he is only interested in mountain biking around the Alps, your kids want to stay at home, see their friends and go to the cinema, and you had something along the 'Spa/cultural break in Italy' lines in mind, something will have to give.

Take turns. With the pathetic number of weeks per year most people are allowed or choose to take every year, it's a wonder we manage to get any time away as a family at all, and getting more than one holiday is a real luxury. But if you can manage it, and you are all very different holidayers, then try taking it in turns to do what each member wants. One year go to Paris and wander around the galleries; another go mountain-biking in the Alps, and during half-term stay at home and get a babysitter every night so you all get a break.

Cram it all in. If you are really clever you will find a way to go somewhere with something for everyone. Somewhere that has great sporting activities on offer, in a historical town, with a cinema nearby, for example. Spend the last few days at home, letting your kids catch up with friends while you have lunch with some of yours, and everybody is *almost* happy, which is pretty good by most family standards.

Home or abroad? There has been a bit of a comeback recently for the good old British holiday. I say this is fantastic: not only is travel hideously bad for the environment and if we carry on flying around the place there will be no world left for our grandchildren to see, but it is also great for the British economy if we spend our money here, rather than in the cafés and hotels abroad. Staying closer to home eliminates a lot of the airport/long journey/jetlag chaos, and lets you spend more time in your destination of choice.

BUT, taking your children abroad is, I believe, absolutely essential for their education, as it enables them to see some of the world they live in and learn about other countries and cultures. If children think the entire world centres around Tesco, the corner shop and Legoland, we are in big trouble. Every child should be able to say 'hello', 'thank you', 'yes', 'no', 'please', 'ice cream' and 'toilet' in at least six languages by the age of ten and understand '*Voulez-vous coucher avec moi?*' or its equivalent in other languages from about sixteen on, to avoid mishaps . . . If I were the education secretary I would make it the law. Take them abroad! *Vielen dank*.

Going it Alone: When you need a break

Being a member of a family is wonderful and everything, but it doesn't mean that *you* – just little old you, all by yourself, without all the appendages and sticky marks on your lapels – don't exist any more. *You* are still there, and, much as you do love them dearly, you still occasionally need time away from the noisy, cuddly rabble to be an independent being. To be the other you, the you who existed before you had children, before you were married for so long that you barely remember who you used to be, or the new you who has developed through having a family of her own.

I have only had one 'holiday' on my own, and I remember it as though it were yesterday, and very fondly. To be honest it was more of a weekend away, but it sure as hell felt like a holiday because the days were so long, so quiet and so peaceful. I ate alone, thought alone, read alone and walked about alone. It was absolutely bloody fantastic and I recommend it to everyone. By the end of the two days I was desperate to get back to my family, I had recharged all my batteries and I had made contact with Me for a while. It was very nice to see Me, and to tune into what I wanted, thought and felt for a few days.

Wanting to have a short break on your own or with a girlfriend should not be seen as a sign of problems in a relationship at all. In fact, if you are so united with your partner that you have ceased to be an individual in your own right, I would consider this to be far more worrying. After all, if you don't exist any more outside of the family unit, what on earth are you going to do when your kids all flee the nest and you are left rattling around with your hubby for another forty years? And who is he living with anyway by then – a copy of himself? A lost, empty figure pining the loss of her children and clueless as to who she is or what she wants to do? NO. Go away on your own you must, to keep in touch with yourself. The constant noise and demands of a family will make this almost impossible, so book yourself a couple of nights away and make a date – with yourself or with your friends. You might like what you find.

PS: It's worth being prepared for possible disappointment. Living in a family *is* awfully chaotic and noisy a lot of the time, but you get used to having all of that life and bustle around you. Suddenly being thrown into a world of orderly quiet can be very unsettling, and you might find yourself yearning for home life rather than enjoying your solitude. This is very common, and you're not weird, boring to the point of being unable to enjoy yourself without your family, or wasting your time. If you can just *try* to forget what you've come away from and make the most of the newfound calm, you'll be refreshed and ready to go back.

Travelling Rules

Families have a bad reputation when it comes to travel, and for good reason. Even as a seasoned family traveller myself, I still dread having to go anywhere near another family doing the same thing. There they are, carrying too much luggage, making too much noise, ignoring the fact that their kids are kicking the back of the seat in front of them on the aeroplane, filling these little monsters up with caffeinated drinks and then doing nothing when they become hyperactive and rude, leaving a table covered in spilled juice, a thousand bits of tissue, snapped straws and mountains of uneaten food in restaurants, and generally being incredibly antisocial.

Well, it needn't be like this, and we all have to club together and travel as neatly, quietly and considerately as possible, if we are to gain a new reputation as pleasant, even welcome travellers. Here are some rules we should probably all try to follow when travelling as a family:

☆ **Consider your fellow travellers.** Yes, even the really loud, smoking, inconsiderate ones. To be as rude as them is to sink to their level.

☆ **Stop your child** if you see him behaving in a disruptive way, or upsetting, disturbing or kicking anyone on your holiday. Then apologise.

☆ **Leave when you think you are about to outstay your welcome.** Art galleries are interesting for children for about ten minutes; after that they become glorified playgrounds. If you think your brood has had enough – you can tell this by the fact that they are lying on the floor, flicking bits of dry snot at each other or making faces behind other visitors – then do leave and try again another time. The same goes for restaurants, churches and anywhere else you might need to be well-behaved. Other people have paid to be there too, and it's not up to us to spoil it for them.

☆ **Safety.** Always have arrangements for what happens if somebody gets lost: arrange an obvious meeting place, like a church, fountain or huge tree, make sure your kids know your phone number and address and carry it on them somewhere, and, if you are going somewhere crowded, dress your kids in something very visible and identifiable. Matching hats are a good idea, or bright coats or umbrellas. Losing a child in your home country is terrifying enough; losing them abroad is unimaginably frightening for all concerned.

☆ **Explain before you go** that you are travelling, which means you are out there in the Wide World and exposed to Other People.

These people have feelings, and don't like being annoyed by rowdy children. Often kids just don't realise they are being disruptive, so if you give them plenty of notice, and explain what's required – i.e. be good, and don't cause too much trouble – you can get some very positive results.

☆ **Leave it as you found it.** Another awful habit I have witnessed from families who are holidaying is that they treat everywhere as though they own it and the staff who come with it. The mentality seems to be 'I tidy up all the time at home, so now that I'm away, somebody else can jolly well do it.' Er, no, sorry. When you are away you have even more of a duty to treat things with respect and try not to let your kids damage/break/draw on/spill things or to leave sweet wrappers and toys all over the place. Try to leave things as tidy as you found them, and this way whispers of 'What a lovely family – I hope they travel here more' will spread across the globe, and soon families will be regarded in a whole new, more welcome light. Maybe . . .

Top Family Hotels and Travel Companies

As more and more travel companies cotton on to the fact that families like to go on holiday somewhere where there are highchairs, kids' activities and soundproof walls, so your choice of such companies specialising in family holidays is growing.

☆ Our favourite to date has been Essential Italy, (www.essentialitaly.co.uk), who have always been ready to find the most family-friendly locations and accommodation, make sure there are cots and children's toys and generally make our stay as easy as possible while still retaining the 'independent travel' feel that we prefer.

☆ If you fancy something more organised and sporty then a Mark Warner holiday (www.markwarner.co.uk) might suit you: they have packages to suit every family, for kids of all ages.

☆ Less pricey but still offering plenty of choice is Take the Family (www.takethefamily.com).

☆ Many hotels now have special children's facilities and activities, and websites such as www.babyworld.co.uk or www.all4 kidsuk.com list lots – take your pick!

☆ Finally, don't forget Center Parcs, Disneyland and so on. Kids love that kind of thing, and just occasionally it's important to put your Culture Vulture hat aside and jump on a log flume . . .

Phew! After all of that travelling, packing and unpacking you'll be needing a nice sit down. Let's head outside for some fresh air, a cup of tea, and a wander around the garden . . .

PART TWENTY

The Garden

Garden or Playground? Keeping the kids happy outdoors

Not everyone reading this book will be lucky enough to have a garden. Most of us are grateful to own a house at all, and some green space outside is a real luxury. This is a terrible shame for families, because gardens and green spaces are invaluable for children, and for families as a whole.

We are very lucky to have 200 feet of garden at the back of our house – well, lucky in a way, but it takes much more time than I've got to maintain it, and I am absolutely terrible at looking after anything that photosynthesises, which is why it looks rather sad and unloved much of the time. When we moved in there were brightly coloured things, which I believe are called flowers, growing in the neatly edged borders, and a lawn that had grass on it as opposed to the moss-and-weeds combo we now boast.

If you have children *and* a garden, then lucky old you – now you have to work out how the two can live in harmony without your front room turning into a sandpit, or your garden resembling a Little Tykes catalogue. This is a lot trickier than it sounds because kids dash in and out all the time, and it's hard to resist the temptation to buy ride-on tractors, tricycles, swings, climbing frames and space hoppers. How far you go with all of this is up to you, but it's nice to keep a little child-free zone somewhere for you to have grown-up time outside.

A garden is not just a place for letting off some excess youthful energy and keeping your kids active and healthy: it is also really useful for children to learn about nature, growing things and lawn-mower maintenance(!). Below are some tips for getting the most out of your green space, for all of you.

☆ **Keep the garden outside.** Kids like to get messy in gardens, which is to be encouraged, but they do like to bring this mess in with them, which isn't. If you have a sandpit, try to keep it as far away from the door as possible, and keep a soft brush at the door for children to use to wipe any sand off themselves.

☆ **Bringing the inside out.** There has been a growing trend in the last few years to create an 'outdoor room', which is basically an area outdoors which is as cosy, comfortable and habitable as a living room. The idea is wonderful, because relaxing and 'living' outside is very restful and healthy, but it can be very impractical due to our somewhat predictably bad weather. Sofas outside are a no-no for me. Not all of us can afford the alternative, which is a fantastic glass extension making us feel as though we're living in the wild, so a good halfway house is to use big cushions and tablecloths, beautiful garden furniture and stylish accessories to create an 'indoor' feel, all of which can be whisked away or covered up when the heavens open.

☆ **The Hanging Gardens of Birmingham** (well, Cambridge actually). Lying in a hammock makes the most wriggly, fidgety child relax after a few minutes, and you don't even need two big trees to hang one up any more – they come with stands if you need one. The best thing we have ever bought for our garden is a huge, round swing-seat from Habitat, which all five of us can lie in together, propped up with cushions, swaying in the breeze and resting, reading or just having a cuddle, on the three days per year that it doesn't rain.

☆ **Create a playground.** When I was pregnant with my third child I realised I couldn't cope with a thirty-foot vegetable plot yielding five strawberries and five thousand weeds any more. I bought half a ton of bark, a wendy house and a big climbing frame and slide, and created a mini playground at the bottom of the garden. I haven't weeded since, and it still looks almost new. Putting it away from the house has its drawbacks – I have to run full-pelt down the garden to rescue dangling, stuck children every so often, but overall it's a good plan because they feel they can go off by themselves, have adventures and make lots of noise away from me!

☆ **Trampolines.** Once upon a time these were found in sport halls. Now they're in every back garden I know – except mine. Trampolines provide hours and hours of fun, give your kids a great workout and let you test how strong your pelvic-floor muscles are since giving birth (go to the loo immediately before you go on, is my advice . . .) but they are also insanely danger-ous. If you stick to the rules advised by the manufacturers (only one child at a time, no somersaults, no jumping off and so on) it's probably fine. But I am yet to see a single parent who is so rule-abiding. There are frequently four or five kids bouncing around all over the place, crashing into each other, getting whiplash and banged heads and being catapulted into next door's garden (almost). Supervising all of this is the least relax-ing thing I have ever done, apart from having my underarms waxed. If you are thinking about getting a trampoline, then think one more time . . .

☆ **Leave a wild patch.** Having a manicured garden may be something you aspire to, but leaving it until you retire might be a good plan. Kids should be able to run wild and free in gardens, not walk carefully around neat borders or sidestep delicate flowers. We have left one part of the garden to grow completely wild, and the kids can dig in it, plant in it and generally get their hands very dirty in it. This is not only a valuable lesson in horticulture and botany, but it's also very good for the natural environment: butterflies have come back, there are wildflowers blooming that I didn't know we had, and it looks like four square feet of English country idyll. And it takes no work – oh joy!

☆ **Vegetable patch.** The smallest vegetable patch can yield fantastic results, and even if it doesn't, kids love the planting and watering as much as the eating at the end. Top scorers include runner beans, tomatoes and sunflowers.

☆ **Tree-houses.** In my dreams, my kids have a huge tree-house, complete with 360-degree balcony, walkway to another tree and a rope ladder. In reality my kids have a small apple tree and a rather prickly bush to contend with. Ah well. Tree-houses are most children's fantasy – there is something magical and adventurous about having a secret hideout so high off the ground, and imaginations can really run wild up there. If you can possibly manage it, then it's worth consideration, but they are prohibitively expensive for most of us. If it's out of the question, a wendy house is a good alternative, and they can come in at under £100 so it's massively cheaper but still provides a lot of imaginative play potential.

☆ **Ponds.** Hmm. I personally don't think ponds are a good idea if you have children who still use hands and knees as their main mode of transport, and even when they've mastered the art of toddling there is still plenty of scope for toddling into a pond. We had one, but got it filled in after our daughter, and several worse-for-wear guests, had fallen in numerous times. Now I can relax and not worry whether the sudden quiet is peaceful or deathly. You choose.

☆ **Eating *al fresco*.** With the weather getting seemingly ever warmer each summer, the chances for a little outside eating are getting more numerous. There's something very 'on holiday' about eating outside, but it can be more trouble than it's worth if you have to spend hours carrying everything out only to bring it all in ten minutes later when it rains or the wasps descend. A large tray helps . . . Always eat in the shade, and do beware of wasps sitting on mouthfuls just before they go into small, unsuspecting mouths – I've seen it happen, and it's terrifying.

☆ **Shade.** I am a sun-phobe, and keep away from the evil rays as much as possible. But even for those who are less frightened of sun-damage to our skin, and our children's skin, having some shade in a garden is essential. It keeps children cool, calm and protected. If you don't have any natural shade then get a gazebo (you can get cheap ones from places like B&Q and garden centres) or a huge parasol, and stick the kids under there during the brightest hours between eleven and three. At all other times make sure they wear a sunhat and have lots of high-factor sun-cream on. It is a huge pain in the neck, I know, and they hate it being applied, but it's vital for protecting their skin from harmful rays.

The Green House: Planet-saving tips

Scientists are often wrong, and not just in the fashion stakes. It's the nature of their job – trying to extrapolate from weird-looking data or finding answers to Very Tricky questions – and we should forgive them their little glitches and errors. Maybe they were tired and didn't notice the decimal point lurking between the digits, or they spilled coffee on their graphs and had to take a guess. What-ever the reason, it happens and we have to be on our guard against 'you must eat seven hundred apples a day to remain healthy and sane' stories. That's that decimal-point problem again . . .

Where scientists are *not* wrong is when they say we are fucking up our planet BIG time, and if we don't stop being such selfish, wasteful, lazy pigs, there will be nothing left for future generations to mess up, and that's just not fair. They might want a slice of the destructive, self-indulgent cake too.

Nobody is sure when Planet Earth will bite the dust and either explode in a ball of fire or turn into a huge lake – in fact nobody can be certain that it really will come to something quite this bad – but it's certainly not going to look quite like it does today, or have quite so many cappuccino bars, and we need to do something about it NOW. If you have children this should be a real concern for you, because it might just be they who have to endure scorch-ing temperatures, floods, draughts, ice ages and an end to spa breaks – yikes.

So, putting on our greenest hats for a while, here are some things every family needs to start doing today. Most are so easy it will blow your mind that you didn't do them before, and almost all of them will save you money as well as the Earth you inhabit. Yes, it requires some thought, time and new habits, but it's not a lot to ask, is it?

☆ **Save energy.** This is the Number One thing we can all do, starting now. When you've finished this chapter, walk around your house and see how many electrical appliances are on standby, how many phone chargers are still plugged in, and how many lights are on. Switch the whole lot off! Unplug, switch off and save energy!

- **Washing machines and dishwashers** should only be put on when they are full.
- **Don't use a tumble dryer.** Bad, bad, bad!
- **Only fill a kettle with the amount of boiling water you need.** It's a bit stupid to waste a lot of energy heating water just to let it cool down again.
- **Use rechargeable batteries.** It costs a bit to get started, but after that it's almost free. With kids this can save a lot, as so many of their toys require batteries and they run them down all the time.
- **Switch lights off.** If there's no one in the room, it doesn't need a light on, does it? Kids are bad offenders, but threaten to take the cost of the electricity out of their small savings and you'll soon have lights off when they leave the room. If you tell them about the environment while you're at it, that helps – it's not really about the money, it's the cost to the Earth we're concerned about. TVs, computers and tons of other electrical appliances are also often left on standby: get into the habit of switching them off and you'll wonder why you never did it before.
- **Use energy-saving light bulbs.** They're often not quite as bright as normal ones, and there can be an irritating delay before they come on, but you get used to it and they save tons of energy – and money.

- **Go solar.** Solar panels are still only mostly affordable to those who are quite well off, but it's getting cheaper, and if you look at what you get back, it could be worth consideration.

☆ **Recycle.** Most city councils have cottoned on to this essential way of living and have a doorstep paper, glass and metal recycling service. Once you're into it, the idea of throwing away glass or cardboard is laughable.

☆ **Compost.** If you have even a small garden, try to start a compost heap, where all your vegetable, gardening, fruit and non-meat food scraps can go. That way you don't clog up landfill sites with tons of egg shells and apple cores, and you get free compost for your tiny flowerbed – perfect!

☆ **Re-use.** Rubber bands, envelopes, cardboard boxes, string, leftover food, wrapping paper, and so on and on and on. The amount of stuff we discard that could be used time and time again is shameful. Before you throw anything away, think whether you could use it again.

☆ **Turn the heating down**, or off if you don't think it's really necessary. Put a jumper on, and make sure the windows are closed if you have the heating on – it's just madness to watch all that heat float away. Radiators shouldn't be in front of windows, and keeping each one individually controlled means you don't waste energy heating empty rooms upstairs because you want to be warm down in the lounge. We are all used to living in ridiculously warm houses – which lots of bacteria love, by the way – so try to get used to having it a degree or two colder this year. Let's hope that chunky knits stay in vogue for a while . . .

☆ **Buy Green products.** The market for these has exploded in recent years, and most of them actually work, rather than just looking eco-friendly but not washing anything at all. Find your favourite and ditch anything with petrochemicals, enzymes or phosphates in it. Make sure the packaging is recyclable too. It'll take a while to get used to your new shopping list, but it's a simple, effective step in saving our water.

☆ **Save water.** Have a shower rather than a bath every other time; switch the tap off while you're brushing your teeth; don't use a garden hose or sprinkler and use any un-drunk water to water the house plants with. There are *lots* of other ways of cutting down on water wastage, and a good trick is to train yourself to see water going down a drain as horrible. The old 'flush for a poo, not for a wee' trick works too, but you'll have to put that to the family vote first.

☆ **Use the oven wisely.** Don't heat the oven up to max in the morning to cook some flapjacks, then let it cool right down again only to reheat the whole thing in the evening to roast a chicken. If it's on, use it for everything at once or you'll waste tons of energy.

☆ **Use less.** Of everything. Do you *need* eight pieces of Sellotape, or would three do? *Must* you use so much moisturiser on each leg? Did that piece of paper have to be so big, or would one half the size have kept your child just as happy (and did you recycle it afterwards)? These are the little questions you should be asking yourself all the time. Less is *so* much more.

☆ **Use Green nappies.** Some nappies are green because somebody has been eating rather a lot of peas. Others are Green because they don't clog up landfill sights for centuries. There are some fabulous reusable ranges on offer these days that don't make your child walk about with a wet mattress covered in scratchy plastic between her legs. The new-generation green nappies, are small, easy to use and look rather fetching if you buy a groovy outer covering. You can even get somebody to wash the whole lot for you and bring cleans ones back, for a middle-sized fee. Try www.cottonbottoms.co.uk or www.nicenappy.co.uk. Love the name, maybe love the nappies?

☆ **Fly less.** We've all had a lot of fun – more fun than any previous generation – travelling around the globe. Popping to Spain for a weekend doesn't even raise an eyebrow any more, and many people fly at least three or four times a year either for work or with their families. But something has to give, and at the moment it's the atmosphere, which is getting a touch unhappy about all the carbon being coughed out everywhere. The answer: stop flying so much. Believe it or not, this is a beautiful country, and holidaying in good old Blighty is becoming fashionable again at last. It's even better if you can take a train or get a fuel-efficient car, but just deciding not to fly is a very good start. There are great websites offering advice on eco-travelling. Search under 'Eco-friendly travel' and see what pops up.

☆ **On your bike.** It's free, it's very good for you (unless you get run over, but we'll assume you won't) and it has no negative impact on the environment at all, apart from any extra farting you may have to do. Sorry – it's just a fact. Firm thighs, glowing skin and no environmental damage – let's go!

☆ **Green clothes.** Usually best for those with slightly reddish hair I find . . . no, no, not green clothes, *Green* clothes, i.e. those made with little or no environmental impact. Thanks to uber-trendy designers like Stella McCartney, and hot labels like Edun (the brainchild of Bono's wife, Ali Hewson), hemp, organic cotton, and clothes free of chemical irritants or chlorine bleach are becoming highly desirable, and don't look half bad either. They cost a little more, but even that is changing fast. Even M&S has a Fair Trade Cotton range now, and there are lots of other places to get clothing for yourself and your kids online. Try www.naturalmatters.net or www.allthingsgreen.net.

☆ **Grow your own food.** Oooh, there's a thought. It does take quite a lot of time and dedication, but even some tomatoes and lettuce are better than nothing, because they won't need to be flown over from Spain or wherever it is the sun shines most. You don't need a big plot, just some enthusiasm and green fingers. That's me out then – I kill plants by looking at them.

☆ **Take carrier-bags with you.** Not all the time, you understand, but when you go shopping. Those old ladies with their hold-all, plastic gingham bags may not look the biz, but they know a thing or two about conservation: if you get into the habit of never going shopping without a bundle of carrier-bags you'll find helping yourself to as many as you like by the till quite obscene. Some chains used to charge for them – perhaps they should start that up again?

This is just a start, and there is so much more you can do. If this has inspired you, then there are websites and books available dedicated to making you the cleanest, greenest eco-warrior on your street. *The Little Book of Living Green* is a good start, as is *Save Cash and Save the Planet* (sounds good to me!) and www.naturally-home.com is a mine of eco-friendly information.

There really is no excuse at all not to do your bit for the environment these days. Yes, it's a bit of a shock not to be able to eat, drink and waste as much as we want any more, but you know what? It's now or never, and our children and grandchildren's future lies in our hands.

That's enough sunshine for you for one day – let's get out of the rays now and take a look inside a rather less fresh, more spider-webby place, known as the garden shed.

PART TWENTY-ONE

The Garden Shed

It is often joked that all husbands need a garden shed in order to have a place far away from their nagging wives where they can read weird magazines, have a smoke and fart at will. Our garden shed isn't quite big enough for the first two of these activities, and it is also chock-full of a lawnmower, hundreds of pots, seeds I don't know what to do with, loads of blunt secateurs, shears and garden forks and several unused kids' bicycles.

For our purposes the garden shed will house all the activities you and your family do. Whether it's flamenco dancing, dress-making or hill-walking, this is the place to look if you need to get away from the daily grind and get your hands a little bit dirty . . .

Hobbies and Hubbies: Keeping your own interests alive

When you stop living all by your little self and start living in your own, not-so-little family, you gain a lot: a husband, kids, love, security, plastic toys and numerous pairs of wellies. But life is mean, and dictates that if you are lucky enough to gain something, you have to forfeit something else. Harsh, I know, but then life has also dealt us multiple orgasms and millionaire shortbread, so we can't be too cross.

In family life the main losers are time and independence. Where once you had plenty of opportunities to sit around a bit, look out of the window, maybe fiddle with your hair and make a cup of tea, now such idle, solitary moments have vanished almost completely. Where there was peace there is noise, where there was space there is stuff, and where there was time there are a million and one jobs for you to be getting on with before slapping on your age-defying, glow-restoring night cream.

This loss of time means you have to prioritise and use what hours you have very wisely. Multi-tasking is essential if you are to get even half of it done, but however adept you are at this skill, some things will have to be abandoned, as there simply isn't the time for all of them any more.

One of the first things to go is often any hobbies or sporting activities you once enjoyed. When there are children to be fed, cuddles to be had and little teeth to be brushed, how can you go and play tennis for an hour, or indulge in some knitting (the coolest thing to be seen doing these days, in case you hadn't heard yet)? No, the hobbies will have to go.

This is a big mistake. What you do in your very limited spare time is a huge part of who you are. To kill off the hobbies is to kill off a vital part of you, and this can only lead to dissatisfaction on your part.

☆ **Hobbies are essential.** When you have nothing to take your mind off home life and nothing that you really enjoy doing outside the home, you can become very frustrated and even depressed. See your outside interests as integral to you and your life, and they'll stop being considered as an added luxury. You *need* some time to indulge in the 'other you' in order to remain happy, sane and fulfilled, so don't feel guilty about taking the time for it. In fact, you should feel guilty if you don't.

☆ **But I don't have the time!** Well, make it. Everyone has the time somewhere, they just have to find it.

☆ **Give him time too.** It may feel to you as though you need the time for hobbies more than him, because you are stuck at home with the kids more, while he lives it up in the office (irony here, please), cycles to work, goes to the gym at lunchtime, reads on the train or pops to the bookshop on the way home. He's had a great, varied day and *you're* the one who needs some free time. Not true, I'm afraid: unfair as it may feel, you may sometimes need to spend all day *and* all evening doing house and family stuff, so that he can get away from his work and family life and indulge in his hobbies too. A man who just goes to work, comes home, watches telly and goes to bed is not one you'll be happy to live with for long! So long as he makes the time for you too, everything should work out fine.

☆ **Don't give up.** Sometimes it can feel impossible to find the time in your lives to fit hobbies in. Keep trying different arrangements and schedules and you'll find something that works. Sometimes you have to give it a rest during very busy periods, but don't give up, and get back to it when the opportunity arises again.

☆ **Try something new.** People get bored easily. Going to the gym is fun once, or even twice if you're lucky, but after that it's an unpleasant, sweaty, expensive chore. The solution: try something new. Join a fitness class, a dance class, start an art course, learn to rock climb, enter a cycling race, get into origami – anything to inspire, amuse and cheer you.

☆ **Go with a friend.** Most of us are pretty hopeless at getting off our backsides and doing anything unless someone is there to whip us into action. This is where friends can be very helpful: just when you were about to sink into your comfy sofa and sigh at the tiring day you've just had, there's a knock at the door and you are whisked off to a salsa lesson. You'd never have gone on your own steam, and afterwards you feel much, much happier, upbeat and ready for a great day tomorrow.

☆ **Consider the kids.** Your outside interests and hobbies can have a big influence on those of your children. When I compete in a running race my whole family comes to watch, and my kids are now very interested in running, keeping fit and being active. It also means they see me being 'Liz' as opposed to 'Mummy', and

I think that's vital for them to understand what adults are: not just robots who dole out food and try to kiss their kids all the time, but real people with a variety of interests. Talk about your hobbies, show your kids what you do, and see if this sparks any interest in them. They might think Daddy's obsession with growing bonsai trees is the most boring, stupid thing they've ever heard of, but at least they've learned about it and had the chance to think that!

Anyone for Tennis? Getting active together

Keeping your own hobbies and interests alive is important, but it does mean taking time away from the rest of the family. If you are tied up twenty-four hours a day with young children this may be no bad thing at all – in fact, it's a life-saver. But if your time together is limited, you may feel that spending even more time away from the kids or your other half is the last thing you want to do, and you stop doing anything at all.

The solution in this latter case is to find a hobby or activity that you can all do together, and which most of you enjoy: nobody feels guilty or abandoned and everyone has a reasonably good time.

So far, so easy, but there's one problem: *what to do*? If your main interest is in medieval church music then your kids might not be so keen. If Daddy is mad about motorbikes and likes to go on death-defying rides of a Sunday morning, then again, this might not be a family affair.

Help is at hand, and often comes in the form of family-friendly clubs and groups, which will welcome you all in with open arms. It's a great chance to get your kids interested in something new, which could become a big part of their lives if they enjoy it. Doing it with the rest of the family can make it more enjoyable than being put in a class all by themselves.

Here are some ideas, as suggested by my rather family-orientated friends and my good self:

☆ **Walking.** It's free, it's very good for you and it requires no specialist training or equipment – just a pair of trainers will do and off you all go. Of course the kids will moan for half an hour and take ages to get ready, but once you're out in the fresh air, come rain or shine, you'll all start to feel much better – trust me!

☆ **The school run.** Unless the school is more than two miles away or there's a blizzard or an asbestos factory outside your house, then please, *please* get your kids to walk, cycle or scoot to school. Clogging up the roads with our horrible cars not only trashes the environment and pisses everybody off – thus giving families an even worse reputation – but it makes your kids unfit as well.

☆ **Cycling.** Again, it's free (once you've got the gear) and very good for you. Get some bike seats if your kids are too young to manage long distances, and off you go. You don't need to cycle halfway across Britain – just a few miles will do: find a nice pub, have some lunch and come back again. A great day out, lots of exercise and lots to talk about.

☆ **Gyms.** There are more and more gyms opening every year that cater for families. Don't expect to find five-year-olds pumping iron or pounding away on treadmills, though: these are far more child-friendly places where families can swim, play tennis, badminton and golf or take part in a variety of sport or dance classes. There is usually a bar or café where you can refuel afterwards, and lots of extra classes and coaching available, all taught by experienced staff. They can be expensive, though, so look out for special offers (usually in post-excess January) and reductions for young children. If you use it a lot it will be well worth it, as you'll all get fit and healthy and spend lots of time as a family.

☆ **Swimming.** Not very original, but very popular as it's very good for you, everyone can do as much or as little as they want if you take turns to watch the kids, and it wipes them out for the rest of the day so you can get some peace.

☆ **Sailing.** More hassle than I can take (I used to go sailing with my parents almost every weekend and it put me off for life!) but I have lots of friends who love it. This is team effort at its best, as you all have to work together to stay afloat.

☆ **Horse riding.** Don't knock it till you've tried it. There's bound to be a stable within half an hour's drive, and you are sure to meet some new friends when you get there. There should also be plenty of opportunity for laughs as various members of the family fall off and make fools of themselves, which is half the fun.

☆ **Art.** Keep an eye out for local courses offering a chance to do some painting, pottery, modelling or other craft activity. Local newspapers, the Internet and library posters are all good sources of information of this kind. Not everyone is into sport in such a big way, and this could be a perfect alternative. You never know – you might discover a Picasso you never knew you had living in your house.

☆ **Choir.** Bring on the next von Trapp family singers ... many local choirs are happy to have all levels and ages of warblers. Car journeys will never be boring again, as you all hum along in harmony. Tra la laa!

This is obviously a tiny selection of the things you could do with the rest of your rowdy brood. It doesn't matter what you find to do, but find something you really should, if you are to enjoy some time together, get out of the house and have plenty to laugh and talk about.

DIY: Divorce, anyone?

The British have an obsession with all things Italian – we love their language, culture, countryside and wine; we devour their food, buy up their dilapidated farmhouses and fill our homes with their antiques. We call them stylish and romantic and marvel at the way they spend entire weekends sitting around *al fresco*, talking, eating, drinking, laughing and being – well, so very *Italian*. We want to be like them, live like them, love like them.

... And then we spend an entire weekend in B&Q. So very *English*.

The more run-down a Tuscan villa, the better: it gives it character and intrigue. But if an Englishman's castle doesn't have Ikea shelving, a funky chandelier and a brand-new bespoke kitchen then he feels he is failing miserably somehow. Or his wife does, which is worse. To get our homes as close to that one we've seen in *Living etc* as we can manage, at a fraction of the cost and without the fresh flowers or original artworks, we have no choice but to get to work on it: sanding, sawing, painting, tiling, drilling, hanging and making a huge mess while we're at it.

We are a nation of DIY addicts, filling our sheds, garages and lofts with tools we can't use, bits of wood that don't fit anywhere, and paint we don't even like but that was reduced so we couldn't resist. Once we've started there's no stopping us: you can almost feel the bricks tremble of a Sunday morning: Who's going to get it this week? The bathroom? The bedroom? Oh *God* – is that a hammer drill she's holding? Everybody get down, it's going to be carnage!

Of course, not everybody loves brandishing a paint roller: for some, DIY is a form of torture, only undertaken when things have got so bad that their house has no running water or heating and there are no workmen left on the planet to do the work for them. Driven to up tools out of sheer desperation and more nagging than they could stand, they are terrified of the damage they might cause and would honestly rather eat their children's toenails than pick up a screwdriver.

Yes, when it comes to DIY, we all fall into one of two categories: those who love it, and those who absolutely hate it. Sadly, there is no correlation between how much somebody likes it and how gifted they are in the DIY department, as the many holes in our walls testify ...

But two things unify all those who live in a family home: one, it needs some DIY at some point; and two, this causes rows. Big mother-fucker rows that can bubble under for weeks leading up to the event ('Haven't you fixed that loose wire yet? Why not? I've asked you a hundred times and you keep saying you'll do it. I cook the dinner every day, you know, and you can't even look at one tiny loose wire. It's ridiculous ...') and which can rumble on for years afterwards ('Like that loose wire you said you'd fix last year, and it took you six months to even *look* at it, and then you blew all the fuses upstairs and nearly electrocuted yourself. And another thing . . .')

In our house I am the most DIY-happy. I grew up with either a blow-torch, a paintbrush or a hammer in my hand, and I love getting my hands dirty with some good old drilling, bashing or sanding. I'm not very good, but I do like to try. We've had our DIY moments like every other couple, and I've learned a thing or two about how to overcome – or avoid – some of the more explosive issues it raises:

☆ **Do as much as you can yourself.** This has several benefits. One: you do all women a favour by showing that we don't just sit around all day doing our nails and talking about dresses, and are quite willing to, and possibly even capable of, drilling a hole in a wall and sticking a wall plug in it. Lots of DIY requires nothing more than some kit, patience and care. Two: it'll get done much faster, because most men need asking for at least three months before they take up a hammer or paintbrush on your behalf, and by then you sound so much like a nagging wife that you both feel crap. Three: it gets done the way you want it. Ask some-body else to do a job for you, and it'll get done as quickly and simply as possible. You, on the other hand, can spend the time it takes to get it exactly as you want it, because you care that the skirting boards are a very slightly different shade of white than the walls.

☆ **Get the boys in.** Intelligent, sexy, strong and capable as we are, there are some jobs that need a little more muscle than most women, excluding Madonna, can provide. This is where we are allowed to get all 'Oooh, my, you're so strong! I am but a weak, feeble young lady who cannot lift half a ton of stone slabs for fear of breaking a nail' and call in somebody male to do the job. If we're sticking to DIY, this person has to be your husband/ stronger half.

☆ **Threaten to call in the professionals.** Nothing gets a man off his backside faster than telling him he can't do as good a job of something as the bloke down the road who'll charge £50 for the pleasure. (Except the prospect of some sex, but that's a very good instinct, I'd say, if you are the prospect ...) A quiet 'That's fine, if you don't think you can manage it I'll call "Put-Up-A-Light" tomorrow and get them round. Shouldn't cost more than £100 or so' is usually enough to have things fixed before the evening is out. Thanks, love.

☆ **Don't start any major DIY in the evening.** DIY is like plucking eyebrows – just when you think you've finished, another straggler pokes its head out. What can start as a simple 'sand it down; give it some undercoat' can turn into 'start sanding, run out of sandpaper, go to B&Q for more, get back to find it's the wrong kind, go back – they're now closed – try with what you've got anyway, make a complete balls-up of it because it's taken half the wood with it, have a row because you *said* you shouldn't start it tonight, go to bed in a huff and with bleeding fingertips, get no sex for three days'. The best time to do any DIY apart from replacing a light bulb is at the weekend, when you honestly have nothing else you'd rather be doing at all. Which is almost never, then.

☆ **Get the kids away.** Kids and drilling, plastering, wiring, painting, sawing or tiling don't mix. If you don't want to spend the whole night in A&E or in the pub after a stressful argument, then wait until they are in bed, or take them away for a few hours while your other half has a go with the heavy tools. Of course, as they get older this changes, and it's really good fun doing some odd jobs with your kids 'helping' a bit. They can hold stuff for you, have a go at hammering or sawing, and it's all really important if they are to learn how to mend, paint, decorate or improve their own home one day.

☆ **Have his 'n' hers tools.** This may sounds very extravagant, but it's rare to find two people who have equal regard for tools. There's always one who likes things labelled, neatly stored and alphabetically arranged, while the other leaves paintbrushes to solidify and puts odd screws, bolts and jigsaw blades anywhere they like. (Guilty!) It can lead to rows of epic proportions, so the best way is either to agree on the way everything will be stored and *both* stick to this, or to have your own tools. We meet halfway on this: we share everything, but divide ownership. His is the toolbox itself, while I get all the painting material and the drill. If the hammer is in the wrong place, it's his fault. If the paint roller isn't washed properly, or the drill bits aren't in the right order, it's mine. This is pathetic, I know, but it's the only way that works for us.

Being a family isn't as simple as living together day in, day out and putting up with each other's bad habits. If you really want to *enjoy* family life you'll have to find something to *do* – a project to work on, whether in the house or the garden, activities to do as a family, and things you all do on your own.

Close the door on your way out – the fox gets in and chews everything up otherwise – and let's go back to the house for that stiff drink I promised you right at the beginning, and you can be on your way again.

PART TWENTY-TWO

One For The Road

So here we are at the end of our short, but hopefully sweet, guided tour of family life. We've poked our curious heads into dusty corners, overflowing cupboards, messy corridors and private rooms and – among all the family clutter, baggage and general chaos – we've uncovered many of the main ingredients of everyday family life, and stumbled across some essential survival secrets. I don't know about you, but my feet are killing me.

As you reward yourself with a little light refreshment – or strong booze if that's what you need! – what I hope most of all is that you have thoroughly enjoyed the trip, and that you will leave the house with a sense that family life is not always the living hell many people would have you believe it is. Of course it's hard at times, when moods swing, tempers fray, children moan, bills arrive, holidays are exhausting and sex is . . . well, *isn't*.

But amid all of those trying, tiring, testing moments when you want to rip all of your hair out and run to the nearest train station for a one-way ticket to absolutely *anywhere else*, are glimmers of something beautiful. Something warm, protective, reassuring and important, which, through the happiness and stability it brings, makes up for a thousand times more hassle, stress and silly arguments than you can throw its way. Oh all right, maybe only a hundred times more, but it's still worth it!

Nobody is pretending it's easy, and I'm certainly not saying there are any 'right' answers. Everyone's situation is different, but hopefully some of what you've seen here will help you to enjoy *your* family, and give it your best shot. For you, for your partner, and for your kids.

Right, that's it. Time for me to get back to the boring chores and for you to make your way towards the door, I'm afraid. It was lovely to meet you, and please do come again. Just not on a Tuesday (gymnastics and swimming), Wednesday (violin), Thursday or Friday (I work), or at the weekend, when we'll be catching up on DIY and trying to spend some time as a family. Looks like a Monday then . . .

So, my friend, until the next time . . . Thank you for coming, and good luck!

Acknowledgements

Were it not for the following kind, helpful, patient people this book would never have made it beyond a jumble of badly filed, unfinished word documents and lots of scribbles on bits of tissue paper. Thanks, then, go to you Harry, for all the juggling you do to enable me to get to my desk, to Euan for being brave enough to want to go through it all again and for your moral support during times of (usually imaginary) crisis, and to Maxine for your marvellous editing skills and for putting up with my less-than-relaxed moments. Thanks also to all of my friends who shared such personal thoughts and anecdotes about their family life and to Becky for being a publicity whiz. Finally, to my children: thank you for your immense patience while Mummy disappeared for hours on end and hijacked the computer every time you wanted to use it, and for making every day one to enjoy and remember. This book couldn't have been written without you. Now put it down, and go and do whatever it is you're supposed to be doing instead!

Index